The Fred W. Morrison *Series in Southern Studies*

*William Lowndes
and the Transition
of Southern Politics,
1782–1822*

Carl J. Vipperman

William Lowndes

and the Transition of Southern Politics, 1782–1822

The University of North Carolina Press / Chapel Hill & London

© 1989 The University of North Carolina Press
All rights reserved

Library of Congress Cataloging-in-Publication Data

Vipperman, Carl J., 1928–
  William Lowndes and the transition of Southern politics,
1782–1822 / by Carl J. Vipperman.
    p. cm. — (The Fred W. Morrison series in Southern studies)
  Bibliography: p.
  Includes index.
  ISBN 0-8078-1826-7 (alk. paper)
  1. Lowndes, William, 1782–1822. 2. Legislators—United
States—Biography. 3. United States. Congress. House—
Biography. 4. United States—Politics and government—1801–
1815. 5. United States—Politics and government—1817–1825.
6. South Carolina—Politics and government—1775–1865.
I. Title. II. Series.
E340.L75V57   1989
328.73'092'4—dc19   88-17246
[B]   CIP

The paper in this book meets the guidelines for permanence
and durability of the Committee on Production Guidelines
for Book Longevity of the Council on Library Resources.

Printed in the United States of America

93 92 91 90 89   5 4 3 2 1

For Reggie
who has all the classical virtues

Contents

	Acknowledgments	ix
	Introduction	xi
I	Scion	1
II	Lawyer	17
III	Representative	33
IV	Federal Republican	52
V	War Hawk	73
VI	War in Common Form	99
VII	Federal Republican	119
VIII	Nationalist	145
IX	Constitutionalist	164
X	The Confrontation	181
XI	The Protectionist Crusade	201
XII	The Politics of Special Interest	217
XIII	The Politics of Geography	233
XIV	Ave atque Vale	252

Epilogue	265
Notes	271
Select Bibliography	307
Index	317

Acknowledgments

In pursuing this study I have accumulated scholarly debts in numbers far too great for more than a few to be acknowledged here. The late Bernard Mayo, my mentor and influential exponent of the biographical approach to history, introduced me to William Lowndes in a graduate seminar and lived to see his suggestion bear the unexpected fruit of a biography on Rawlins Lowndes, William's father. For whatever degree of clarity, thoroughness, and scholarly balance either that biography or this one may possess, the credit must go to Mr. Mayo. Colleagues whose scholarly insight and expertise have illuminated the chapters they read include Earl Hess, Lee Kennett, William McFeely, Barry Schwartz, and William Stueck. For the special interest he took in my project and the many ways he chose to remind me of the golden mean of moderation, I must say of my generous colleague Peter Hoffer that devil's advocate is by no means a thankless persuasion. I owe a special debt to Thomas L. Purvis, whose detailed and insightful analyses led to the restructuring of two pivotal chapters. My colleague and department head, Lester Stephens, in addition to reading portions of the manuscript, gave consistent support to this project through the arrangement of teaching schedules to allow periodic freedom from the classroom for sustained research and writing. I am particularly thankful for Louise Bailey, whose invaluable research on the South Carolina legislature has done so much to simplify the work of scholars in the field, and who generously made available before publication her findings on Lowndes and his legislative colleagues.

Historians who labor in the South Carolina vineyard with Robert M. Weir are among the most fortunate, especially when his rigorous and authoritative review of their work from its conceptual framework to its detailed execution permits prepublication correction of errors ranging from the more obvious to the least suspected. Orville Vernon Burton furnished an equally valuable perspective in his review and suggested similar revisions with that most persuasive combination of disarming tact and intellectual force. I am deeply indebted to both. Editor-in-Chief

Iris Tillman Hill and Executive Editor Lewis Bateman of the University of North Carolina Press, ever since they read a portion of the manuscript in its early stages, have been valuable allies in bringing this work to fruition. It need hardly be said, however, that the author accepts full responsibility for any and all errors in the book that bears his name.

I wish to thank the University of Georgia Research Foundation for their generous grant, which funded research on the tariff issue.

To archivists, librarians, and uniformly gracious staffs of repositories I visited in researching the life of Lowndes, I offer my profound gratitude for supplying the records that have made this book possible. These repositories include the Boston Public Library, the Massachusetts Historical Society, the Houghton Library of Harvard University, the New York Public Library, the New York Historical Society, the Historical Society of Pennsylvania, the Library of Congress, the National Archives, the Duke University Library, the Southern Historical Collection at the University of North Carolina, the South Caroliniana Library at the University of South Carolina, the South Carolina Department of Archives and History, the South Carolina Historical Society in Charleston, the Charleston Library Society, the College of Charleston Library, the University of Georgia Library, the Alabama State Archives in Montgomery, and the Henry E. Huntington Library in San Marino, California. My hope is that this book may approach the standard for my profession that the invaluable assistance, which these unnamed professionals gave me, has set for theirs. Graduate students whose assistance contributed to the accuracy of footnote and bibliographical support for this study include Alan Atkinson, LaFayette Hanson, and Richard Meixsel. Historians who write in longhand as I do will fully concur in my expression of thanks for typists Kathy Coley and Jennell Hutchins.

On a more personal level, I would be remiss in failing to express my appreciation to two Lowndes descendants, Charles Lowndes Mullally and Thomas Pinckney Lowndes, both of Charleston, South Carolina. Each contributed to this study by furnishing information on William Lowndes and the family history, and in the process, amply demonstrated that traditional lowcountry hospitality continues to rival that of their distinguished ancestors.

My wife, Reggie, deserves a special word of gratitude. Although to the reader she may remain unknown, she has contributed no less than Elizabeth Lowndes to her husband's endeavors, and far more than the mere dedication of this book could ever repay.

Introduction

If it is true that the meek shall inherit the earth, it does not follow that the modest shall enjoy posthumous fame. William Lowndes of South Carolina ranked among the most influential congressmen of his time, including such figures in the pantheon of American politics as John C. Calhoun, Henry Clay, and Daniel Webster. Although the public careers of his famous colleagues extended some thirty years beyond his, the fact that Lowndes descended into relative obscurity after his death and has remained there for more than a century and a half may be attributed perhaps as much to modesty as to misfortune, for he always preferred the anonymity of a selfless public servant.

In a characteristic gesture, Lowndes declined to sit for his congressional portrait when Samuel F. B. Morse was preparing his celebrated painting of the House of Representatives of the Sixteenth Congress, forcing the artist to sketch a caricature of the South Carolina congressman from the House gallery. A similar request to have his features immortalized in marble met a similar response, with the consequence that no correct likeness of Lowndes survives. Because his weak voice too often led the House reporter to summarize his speeches, his friends entreated him to engage in the common practice of writing out a speech after delivery for distribution in print, but he consistently declined, explaining that he did not want a reputation for making speeches. More seriously, he preserved virtually none of his correspondence, methodically committing it to the flames of his fireplace at the close of each legislative session. His wife, Elizabeth Pinckney Lowndes, saved the letters he wrote to her, which comprise the bulk of his extant papers, but even they display to the historian a disappointing aversion to the discussion of public issues. Fate seemed to indulge his quest for anonymity: he died in circumstances that left neither headstone nor common grave to mark his passing; one of the great Charleston fires destroyed most of his remaining papers; and the burning of Columbia in 1865 consumed the land and tax records of Colleton County where his plantation was situated. It should not be surprising, then, that the most prominent tribute to his memory, other than the name of an occasional county or crossroads village in the rural South, is a respectful record of his life compiled by his granddaughter largely from the letters her grandmother had saved.

As extant records impose limits on any work of historical scholarship, the loss of personal papers has dictated a more concentrated focus on Lowndes's public life than the author or his readers might wish. When Lowndes routinely burned his family correspondence, he condemned his wife and children to remain shadowy figures in his background; consulted, instructed, admonished, and loved to be sure, but never responding in voices of their own. If he was no different from Thomas Jefferson and many other public men in his desire to keep family matters private, it might nevertheless be said that he deprived posterity of a reasonable acquaintance with the woman who shared his life and who contributed more to his achievements than the extant record will ever show. On matters of family business, the record is more rewarding, primarily because of the generosity of a descendant of Lowndes, Marion Sass of Charleston, who made available the congressman's account book with his Charleston factor covering the decade of his congressional service from 1811 to 1821. The detailed accounting of crop production and sales, fluctuations in the price of rice, frequency of bank loans, and other financial transactions raises serious questions concerning the vaunted prosperity of lowcountry rice planters following the War of 1812.

Lowndes's career in state politics affords an opportunity to examine the background of South Carolina's shift from "qualified nationalism" following the War of 1812 to militant sectionalism after 1820. The most persuasive explanation for this historic reversal of public sentiment has stressed northern agitation of the slavery question during the Missouri Controversy and the alarm it aroused among South Carolinians living in the presence of a black majority. The sectional history of South Carolina since the Revolution, however, suggests that the "black majority" thesis, though valid, has received undue emphasis at the expense of other areas of contemporary concern. Sectional controversy within the state over unequal distribution of seats in the legislature, which gave the lowcountry minority control over the state government, dominated South Carolina politics from the Revolution to the compromise solution of 1808. The manner in which the lowcountry elite wielded power during this period, and the republican solution the legislature found to resolve this internal controversy, hold the key to a better understanding of South Carolina's radical reaction to sectional issues concerning slavery expansion and tariff protection from 1820 onward.

William Lowndes assumed an increasingly prominent role during his tenure in Congress, taking part in virtually every important public issue that came before the House between 1811 and 1821. I have devoted considerable attention to the tariff and slavery controversies—three chapters on the tariff and two on the Missouri question—because of the great importance of these interrelated controversies, the significance of Lowndes's efforts to resolve them, and certain aspects of previous scholarly studies on these subjects.

The history of the antebellum tariff, one of the more neglected areas of twentieth-century scholarship, has proven to be peculiarly susceptible to distortion. Edward Stanwood, whose pathbreaking scholarship on American tariff controversies of the nineteenth century has dominated discussion of the subject in the twentieth, was an avowed protectionist who did not hesitate to editorialize in favor of protection rather than adhere to conventional standards of objective analysis. Economic studies of more recent vintage have also argued that the cotton-producing South benefited from tariff protection. Economist Clayne Pope, for example, in a study of the impact of the tariff on income distribution, constructed a model of such complexity that dozens of facets would refract whatever light passed through that intellectual prism, and examining the southern economy through this complicated device, he found that cotton planters had reason to favor the protective system. When two colleagues in his discipline pointed out flaws in his model, however, Pope responded with as inspiring an example of intellectual integrity as may be seen anywhere in the literature. He publicly admitted his error, corrected the flaws, and pronounced the results of his study inconclusive. Pope also provided an excellent analysis of recent studies on the economics of tariff protection and explained that the central problem lies in the absence of an adequate data base for effective demonstration of his thesis.[1] Nevertheless, Stanley Lebergott in a more recent essay has argued that the cotton South employed the protective system to increase planter profits at the expense of northern textile manufacturers. In making his case, Lebergott converted the specific duty of three cents a pound on raw cotton, which never changed during the period discussed, into its ad valorem equivalent so that a fall in the price of cotton would appear as an increase in percentage of protection, and his argument appears to rest primarily on this ground.[2] William Freehling's prize-winning monograph on the nullification controversy in South Carolina typifies a more significant trend in historical scholarship on the tariff, the tendency to discount the protective system as a legitimate source of southern grievance and to attribute the surge of southern discontent after 1820 to concern over the future of slavery aroused in the Missouri Controversy. In developing his thesis, Freehling found it necessary to demonstrate the prosperity of lowcountry rice planters in the years immediately following the War of 1812 and made his statistical case on prices alone, omitting all reference to Lewis Gray's statistics on rice production that undermine his case.[3] We may grant to such examples of data management whatever merit they may be entitled to, but their effect is less to enlighten than to mislead.

Judging from the congressional record of William Lowndes, preoccupation with the slavery question and such specialized areas of investigation as the economic impact of tariff protection has led scholars to approach this era with questions that tend to mask an area of more fundamental concern to Lowndes and many of his contemporaries, North and South. This was the nature of the Union and the legitimate limits of governmental power. Because Lowndes addressed virtually all the major issues that came before the House of Representatives during this pivotal decade, his congressional career offers an opportunity to define specific areas of concern and to assess their significance within the context of his times.

The dominant political philosophy of this era was traditional republicanism. For the man in public life, the fundamental tenet of this value system was civic virtue. That commitment to civic virtue set a high standard of selfless service is well known. That it set an equally high standard for judging public measures is not always considered and very important to the thesis of this book. Succeeding generations of Americans from the Age of Jackson down to our own have tended to blur important distinctions between republicanism and democracy, so that the terms as commonly used today often appear to be interchangeable. For the sake of clarity in the argument of this book, a cursory examination into the classical origins of traditional republicanism, certain aspects of its evolution through the British political experience, and what it meant to South Carolinians of the revolutionary generation may be useful to the general reader. (Because republicanism from its classical origins through the nineteenth century relegated women to the status of dependent persons incapable of self-government, regardless of individual circumstances or ability, I have used the masculine gender in discussing matters relating to citizenship throughout this book.)

Aristotle erected the framework of classical republicanism on the durable foundation of Platonic virtues: courage, justice, wisdom, moderation, and the paramount rule of reason.⁴ In the republic he envisioned, the essential requirement for citizenship was independence, being one's own master, for a man not in a position to govern himself was not qualified to participate in the government of others. The selfless subordination of particular interests to the general interest represented the ideal of civic virtue, and deviation from that ideal defined corruption, for the good of the whole citizenry was the supreme law.

What determined the legitimacy of government was not its form but the interest it pursued. The fundamental purpose of all legitimate government was the distribution of justice to all citizens. Because democracy created the kind of system in which numerical majorities exercised power without taking into account differentiations between groups within the body politic and consequently judged the validity of one measure or another on the assumption that the interests of all citizens were basically the same, Aristotle rejected democracy in favor of a balanced distribution of power among constituent elements of society, traditionally categorized as the One, the Few, and the Many, so as to prevent the abuse of power by any one of the three. Hence, any government in which the dominant individual or group ruled as if its own interest were that of the whole was despotic, even if that group constituted a majority, for nothing in the classical republican tradition would authorize the majority interest to exercise an unshared power over the whole.⁵

Of the problems inherent in putting the Aristotelian ideal into practice, none proved more persistent over the centuries than that of maintaining the stability of republican government, for the dereliction of one citizen invariably compromised the ability of others to maintain civic virtue, tempting them to similar corruption and producing what historian J. G. A. Pocock has called the "Machiavellian moment," the confrontation of virtue with corruption.⁶ Niccolò Machiavelli, confronted with a general collapse of republican government in the Renaissance era amid such pervasive disregard of civic virtue as to suggest the need for a universal reform of human behavior, outlined in *The Prince* methods to meet the various contingencies a man might face when he found himself in power, thrust up by fortune in the aftermath of a general breakdown of civic virtue. The type of leadership he advocated for such circumstances was not civic virtue but *virtù*, that quality of skill and courage necessary to dominate events and impose form upon fortune.⁷ Machiavelli's despotic alternative to the Aristotelian ideal offered to all future advocates of order over liberty a rationale for consolidating power at the center, where the One alone might determine what constituted the good of the whole as well as the propriety of means to achieve it. Even so, Machiavelli's amoral appraisal of the harsh reality of Renaissance politics did not diminish his appreciation for the Aristotelian ideal nor prevent him from joining other Italian humanists in transmitting the republican system of values to the wider European world.

As civic humanist thought spread into England along with the Protestant Reformation in the sixteenth and seventeenth centuries, the accompanying infusion of ideas exerted a profound influence on the British political tradition, contributing to collisions between Crown and Parliament that resulted in civil war and the Glorious Revolution. Among Englishmen whose writings perpetuated the republican tradition even as they modified it, James Harrington, Jr., John Locke, and an influential group of eighteenth-century authors gave specific shape to the version Americans of the revolutionary generation eventually received.

When the limited constitutional monarchy of English tradition disappeared in the upheaval of civil war in the seventeenth century, James Harrington in his *Commonwealth of Oceana*, published in 1656, urged the creation of an English mixed republic grounded on Aristotelian principles. In Oceana, a senate and a popular assembly would share governmental power and authority, with an executive added for administrative purposes. The Few would consist not of a hereditary but a natural aristocracy chosen through election by a free, independent, and arms-bearing citizenry. The talent, wisdom, and leisure of the Few would qualify them for service in the senate, whose power would balance that of the popular assembly so that neither could pursue its interests at the expense of the common good. Harrington attributed the instability of republican government to faulty distribution of land: when all land belongs to One, the consequence will be monarchy; when land is in the possession of the Few, aristocracy will be the natural result; but when land is distributed among the Many, a stable commonwealth with potential for indefinite durability becomes possible. In the utopian commonwealth of Oceana, landed property would be the durable basis for the individual citizen's Aristotelian independence, guaranteeing his freedom to pursue the ideal of civic virtue and securing the historically elusive stability of republican government.[8]

Scarcely thirty years after *Oceana* appeared, John Locke formulated a theory of government that deviated from the Aristotelian ideal in the direction of democratic despotism. Locke presented his arguments in *Two Treatises of Government*, written in the crisis atmosphere surrounding the Glorious Revolution. In the first he argued against the unrepublican doctrine of divine right monarchy and in the second he advanced the unrepublican doctrine of unchecked majority rule. Similarities between Locke's democratic philosophy and the republican system of values tended to obscure their differences. Both stressed the paramount rule of reason in all practical affairs, both assumed a free and equal citizenry whose right to self-government rested on property, and both depended on a virtuous citizenry to achieve what both considered the primary goal of legitimate government, the good of the whole.[9]

But the Lockean principle of majority rule and his liberal definition of property were at least a century ahead of their time and fundamentally incompatible with republican tradition. In advocating majority rule, Locke failed to take into account differentiations between groups within the body politic and neglected to make provision for the protection of minority interests from potential tyranny of the majority.[10] Moreover, his definition of property went well beyond the time-honored meaning of real and personal estate, and included the individual's person, labor, and liberty.[11] With the right of self-government resting on so liberal a conception of property, virtually all men in society except slaves would qualify for citizenship, even those who lacked the essential republican prerequisite of personal independence. The Lockean doctrine that his contemporaries found more readily acceptable viewed government as a trust, deriving its authority from the consent of the governed and subject to overthrow when the exercise of its delegated powers extended beyond or attempted to subvert the legitimate ends of government. This idea, whose time had come, heralded an age of revolution in the next century and an American experiment in republican government on an unprecedented scale.

The primary focus of English constitutional debate in the early decades of the eighteenth century concerned the increasing influence of the Crown, which was threatening the traditional constitutional balance between king, lords, and commons. War and commercial expansion were transforming England from a medieval kingdom into a premodern commercial power, creating in the process interest groups of varying degrees of influence associated with the national debt, the standing army, banking, trade, credit, and other forms of enterprise. The king's ministers, most notably Robert Walpole, appealed to the particular interests of such groups, employing various forms of influence and bribery to fashion a "Court Party" in support of the ministerial program.[12]

These developments gave rise to a storm of protest and criticism from opposition members and their friends, who were styled the "Country Party." The writings of Joseph Addison, Thomas Gordon, John Trenchard, Henry St. John, and a number of others idealized the landed gentry of England in terms that have come to be called the country ideology. They pictured the independent country gentleman as the honest practitioner of all the classical virtues, standing incorruptible on his acres and voting his conscience. By contrast, elements of the Court Party with their more fluid, less durable forms of wealth were portrayed as mercurial and corrupt, willing abettors to tyranny and the destruction of English liberties.[13] The country ideology took firm root in the continental colonies south of Canada, becoming a plant of vigorous growth in their overwhelmingly agrarian societies and furnishing the main lines of argument leading to revolution and the War for Independence.

South Carolinians, like southerners generally, found this latest version of traditional republicanism especially appealing. Robert M. Weir in a seminal essay published in 1969 explained the basic assumptions of this value system from the perspective of South Carolinians of the revolutionary generation. According to Weir, these South Carolinians defined freedom in traditional republican terms as the ability to act according to the dictates of one's own conscience. But human nature, subject to passions, was not to be trusted, for the basic human motivation was self-interest. The central problem in society was to maintain freedom, which required that human beings curb their own passions through self-discipline and limit the exercise of power, for aggressiveness was a natural attribute of power that constantly endangered freedom. Personal independence, the bulwark of freedom that was indispensable to virtuous public service, could be achieved only through the possession of property in the form of real or personal estate. To lack property was to be dependent, and those without independence were servants incapable of self-government. Government was established to aid citizens in protecting their property, their freedom, and their lives from the aggressions of their fellow creatures. To governments discharging this responsibility the citizen owed obedience; but if government abused its power or exceeded its authority, the citizen had the right and the duty to resist. Constitutions defined authority, set limits on the legitimate exercise of power, and denoted principles for the guidance of government. The good of the whole was the supreme law; particular interests were never to be set in competition with the public good. The best constitutions maintained a republican balance between the One, the Few, and the Many. Because they were the natural guardians of liberty and property, representatives had to possess personal independence and be elected by a constituency of independent citizens. Factions and parties were combinations of men acting together to promote their particular interests; they allowed the particular to predominate over the general interest and were susceptible to corruption by the executive.[14]

William Lowndes and his generation of the South Carolina elite inherited this value system directly from their fathers. The degree to which the sons embraced it and the way in which it affected their response to the issues they faced is a major theme of this study, which the author hopes will provide some insight into the origins of intersectional controversy. In developing this line of thought, I have been influenced primarily by Daniel Walker Howe's important study of the American Whigs to assume a substantial degree of genuine conviction in contemporary rhetoric. Such an assumption requires that special care be taken to avoid overstatement; the pervasiveness of republican ideology in public rhetoric throughout the antebellum era might support a similar interpretation of any number of congressional careers chosen at random. The plan here has been to allow the narrative to present the evidence, limiting interpretive commentary to occasions that seem particularly appropriate.

But this is first and foremost the story of a man's life, dependent for the telling on the art of narrative biography. So that the general reader along with the specialist might be included in his audience, this biographer has tried to strike a balance between provisions to promote continuity, passages to clarify issues, and commentary to assess significance. I have endeavored throughout to stay as close to Lowndes as the sources permitted and to regard events from his vantage point. I have also made an effort to allow Lowndes to speak for himself and have tried to avoid speculative "must-have-beens" on subjects where he remained silent. On this last point I have made one exception. Although Lowndes owned more than two hundred slaves and showed consistent consideration for their welfare, nowhere in the records I have examined did he venture a defense of slavery or record his opinion on the relative merits of the peculiar institution. In this case I have presumed to speak for him in spite of his silence, rather than permit so compelling a subject to pass without comment from either Lowndes or his biographer.

*William Lowndes
and the Transition
of Southern Politics,
1782–1822*

I
Scion

Cold weather, "uncommonly cold and severe," settled over the broad coastal plain of the South Carolina lowcountry in the closing days of January 1782.[1] The freezing temperatures multiplied demands for fuel in Charleston, crowded with loyalists and virtually all British regular troops in South Carolina, who had withdrawn into the port city and provincial capital during the three months since Lord Cornwallis surrendered at Yorktown, Virginia. The British Barracks Office, having commandeered all manner of lodgings to house the troops, now advertised good prices for firewood hauled in from the country.[2] Frigid weather and high-priced fuel compounded the misery of hundreds of Tory refugees driven within the British lines by their victorious Whig neighbors. Unable to find housing in the city, the refugees huddled together in the squalid huts of "Rawdontown," their makeshift camp on the northern outskirts of Charleston.[3]

Thirty-six miles to the westward, the Continental regulars and militia under General Nathanael Greene, suffering a severe shortage of shoes, clothing, and blankets, shivered around their camp fires in the penetrating cold.[4] Camped at Jacksonborough, a small village situated on the west bank of the Edisto River, they offered protection to the Jacksonborough Legislature, the first session of the South Carolina General Assembly to meet since the fall of Charleston in 1780. Lookouts braved the cold to keep watch on the Edisto for British galleys, while the legislators warmed themselves at the roaring fireplaces of the Jacksonborough Masonic Hall and Tavern, the temporary capitol, or by the rising heat of discussion on the amercement of loyalists and the confiscation of their property.

Seven miles farther down the road that ran southwest from Jacksonborough through forest and swamp toward Beaufort, a secondary road branched off to the westward and, a mile beyond the turnoff, crossed

Price's Bridge over a meandering stream called Horseshoe Creek. Downstream or south of the bridge and visible from it, a wooden plantation house stood in a grove of ancient live oaks on the high ground above the west bank. This was the property and current residence of Rawlins Lowndes, former president of South Carolina and principal moderate among the state's revolutionary leaders, who was now in considerable disfavor for having accepted British "protection" after the fall of Charleston.[5] Lowndes had subsequently given up his mansion in the city to British occupation and removed to Crowfield, his country seat on Goose Creek some twenty-five miles north of town. When warfare returned to the Goose Creek area toward the end of 1781, he again removed his household, which included his pregnant wife Sarah, their seven children, and eleven slaves, to the Horseshoe plantation within the protection of American lines. Here in late January 1782 the Lowndes family discovered that their lowcountry plantation house was not built to offer much protection from severe cold.

As February came on without a break in the weather, the British Barracks Office in Charleston called repeatedly for fuel in subsequent issues of the *Charleston Royal Gazette*. At Jacksonborough the vengeful legislators wrangled over the fate of loyalist estates, finally dropping Rawlins Lowndes from the hundreds of names of Carolinians whose cooperation with the British in any fashion now marked them out for retribution. General Greene, with no British forthcoming, detached a portion of his troops southward down the Beaufort road toward Georgia. Down on Horseshoe Creek there was cause for celebration and additional reason to see that the house was kept comfortably warm. Here on February 11, 1782 Sarah Lowndes was safely delivered of a fine, healthy boy. He was named William, and in honor of his mother's distinguished Georgia family, was given the middle name of Jones.[6]

And then it snowed,[7] a sight wondrously rare and beautiful to residents of the tidewater parishes. For William's brothers and sisters, indeed for children all over the lowcountry, the snowfall offered an occasion for excited outdoor play. But children of the Carolina lowcountry witnessed falling snow too seldom to appreciate fully the danger inherent in the frozen loveliness of a winter storm.

The weather aside, the circumstances surrounding the birth of William Lowndes suggested the broad outlines of the course his life could be expected to take. As the son of Rawlins Lowndes, he entered at birth the planter class of South Carolina, inheriting thereby the privileges, expectations, and responsibilities of the lowcountry elite. These dictated that he would own slaves, plant rice, and study the classics, history, politics, and law to prepare himself for political leadership within the state and the new nation as well. Republican tradition and the revolutionary experience having taught the tidewater aristocracy to distrust popular majorities on the one hand and executive power on the other, they had no intention of exchanging British tyranny for democratic despotism. They drew up a state constitution that withheld power from the executive and, through an arbitrary distribution of seats, gave the lowcountry, containing a minority of the white population, the dominant voice in the exercise of political power concentrated in the legislature. The lowcountry minority found justification for this undemocratic arrangement in the republican principle of a mixed and balanced distribution of power to guard against its abuse.[8] Nothing in the republican tradition would recommend the submission of minority interests to the unchecked power of majority rule.[9] Convinced that such lowcountry interests as slavery could not be entrusted to majority rule, the lowcountry elite reasoned that the only secure protection of their minority interests was to retain power in their own hands until the upcountry majority proved responsible enough for political equality. Thus lowcountry planters of the revolutionary generation expected their sons in due course to enter public life and assume a dual responsibility: to protect lowcountry interests from the upcountry majority in state politics, and to protect southern interests from the northern majority in the national government. This dual burden of responsibility, imposed by expectations growing out of the circumstances surrounding his birth, promised to become a dominant theme in the life of William Lowndes.

In a society disposed to regard circumstances of birth, family fortune, and social connections as matters worthy of the most serious consideration, the Lowndes family enjoyed very definite advantages.[10] Initially their status had derived from the prominence of English relatives in the imperial government who influenced affairs in the colony during the early decades of the eighteenth century. More immediately significant was the distinction Rawlins Lowndes had earned in a long career of public service that extended into the Revolution. While Rawlins could not deny that he had benefited from important ties of kinship, it was equally clear that kinship ties alone could not guarantee his personal success, as his father's career too plainly proved.

Charles Lowndes, father of Rawlins and founder of the Carolina family, had within six years of his arrival in 1730 squandered a comfortable fortune and ended his life by committing suicide in the Charleston jail. His dubious legacy to fourteen-year-old Rawlins terminated the boy's formal education, made him a ward of the resident provost marshal (for Ruth Lowndes returned to her West Indian home following the death of her husband), and left him to make his way under a burden of family scandal not easily forgotten in the limited social world of the Carolina gentry.

Rawlins took a realistic view of his circumstances, developed the character traits they demanded, and, after reaching his majority, moved steadily up the ladder of success. From 1745 he served successively as provost marshal, representative, Speaker of the Commons House, chief judge of the provincial courts, member of various revolutionary committees, and finally, president of South Carolina during the Revolution.

Faithful public service restored honor to the name of Lowndes in South Carolina while diligent attention to his private affairs rebuilt the family fortune. Through timely purchases of real estate, an occasional land grant, and shrewd investments, his fortune grew until it produced an annual income of £3,500 sterling during the years immediately preceding the war. Because the bulk of his wealth lay in extensive tracts of rich lowcountry rice, indigo, corn, and timber lands, he emerged from the war in stable financial condition in spite of suffering heavy losses in depreciated currency and slaves carried off by the British.

Only a small fraction of his fortune was gained through wedding contracts, although Lowndes had married three times. His first marriage in 1749 established a valuable alliance with the influential Elliott family of South Carolina, but when his wife, Amarinthia, died a minor, her dowry reverted to the surviving Elliott heirs. The *South Carolina Gazette* described his second wife, Mary Cartwright, whom he married in 1751, as a young lady of "great beauty and blessed with the most valuable accomplishments." Readers understood that such compliments, though genuine, probably meant that her dowry was not her most valuable asset. Even so, the beautiful and talented Mary was of exceptional value to an "unfinished" man like Lowndes, who had achieved wealth and status without finding the opportunity to acquire the trappings of culture and taste appropriate to his improved station in provincial life. And while helping Rawlins to become more cultivated, Mary also presented him with three sons and four daughters, all of whom survived her death from the complications of childbirth in 1770.

Sarah Jones, the third wife of Rawlins Lowndes, was sixteen and he fifty-two at the time of their marriage in January 1773. The child bride brought to the match a dowry that included several slaves and some real estate inherited on the death of her brother in 1768. This "dark-eyed, rosy-cheeked girl" became to Rawlins a devoted and loving wife. Notwithstanding the great difference in their respective ages and the fact that she also became stepmother to a house full of children, some of whom were older than herself, the marriage appears to have been harmonious in every respect.

Sarah's ardent wish to enlarge the family by bearing children sounded the first clear note of sadness in her marriage. She made a good beginning, producing two sons within four years. But neither enjoyed robust health, and when both of them died in the summer of 1778, she sank into grief so deep that the whole family became alarmed. At length she recovered and endured with perseverance and genuine courage the dislocation and distress brought on by the war. Then in early 1782, with the bright prospect of peace and national independence looming on the horizon, the birth of William brought great joy to the Lowndes household.[11]

The Lowndes family returned to their town residence on West Tradd Street in Charleston following the British departure from South Carolina in December 1782. Here blond-haired and blue-eyed "Billy," as he was called, became the pet of the entire family. His father was from the first more indulgent with this child of his old age than he had been with his older children. The boy also received much attention from his sisters, who seem to have regarded him as something more than an ordinary child. One remembered years afterwards that she "saw in that baby a great man." Another recalled that "his looks and expression were his own, very different from all the other children of the time, that his eyes seemed to gaze at objects with intentness and understanding."[12] His mother, after having lost her first two children, showered affection on her bright and attractive son, and he, in turn, developed a strong attachment to her.

Surrounded by so much attention, affection, and parental indulgence, William was before long well on the way to becoming a spoiled child. This was clearly demonstrated on one memorable occasion when the four-year-old created a noisy scene during a formal ball at the Lowndes home, tearfully protesting his mother's being led away to the dance floor. When his tears failed to gain his object, he refused to be consoled, and ran off and hid away under a sofa in a remote part of the house where he was found later in the evening, having cried himself to sleep.[13] Episodes of this sort encouraged his parents to bring this indulgent phase of his young life to an abrupt end. A few months later Eliza Fullerton took over the responsibility of diverting the focus of his interests and directing his exceptional learning potential into more disciplined and fruitful channels.[14] At the age of five his formal education had begun.

After a year under the guidance of Eliza Fullerton, William would probably have followed the educational path of his older brothers and entered a Charleston school if the health of his mother had not taken an unfavorable turn during the winter of 1788. Her doctors, hampered by the narrow limits of current medical knowledge, found her in need of a change of air and climate. They recommended a residence of two years in England away from the "sickly seasons" of Carolina, the hot summer months when fevers ravaged the lowcountry. She would go, of course; and his father agreed that William might accompany his mother to England and be placed in a boarding school there. Mr. Lowndes had just been elected mayor of Charleston and planned to serve out his term of office before bringing his daughters over to join them the next year, but the press of business later aborted these plans.[15] Now he arranged for the firm of Bird, Savage, and Bird, his business agents in London, to handle affairs for his wife and son on their arrival there, and booked passage on the *Amelia*, Captain Hill. In the spring of 1789 with William and his ailing mother aboard, the *Amelia* rode a fair April wind across the bar and spread full sail for England.[16]

Arriving in the Downs early in June, Mrs. Lowndes and the boy enjoyed a warm reception from several Carolina friends, then traveled on to London. The accommodations arranged for them by Bird, Savage, and Bird were found to include a reputable physician to advise Mrs. Lowndes. His examination confirmed the findings of her provincial doctors, and he advised that she "leave all to change of air, and climate, and Nature."[17] She followed his advice and drew encouragement from the fact that advancing summer brought steady improvement. With the arrival of autumn she was judged well enough for travel, and placing William in a boarding school near London, she sought the healing balm of the waters of Bath.[18]

There are no letters to tell how William was received by his British classmates or how a seven-year-old might adjust to the loneliness imposed by distant separation from home and family. He took what consolation he could from the discovery that his circumstance was not unique, for such isolation was not unusual for a boy his age. Actually he seems to have done better than might have been expected. Reports of his progress were quite favorable during his first year, and he was permitted to rejoin his mother for the periods of vacation from the school.[19]

William's scholarly progress during his second year seemed equally promising until well into the winter term when a heavy snowfall spread over the English countryside. On their release from classes, William and his schoolmates rushed outside to frolic in the falling snow. In the midst of play, a fellow student wagered that he could climb up the steep slopes of a nearby hill and reach its distant summit before the American could. Unfamiliar with the potential hazards, William accepted the challenge and the two set out together, climbing side by side up through the deepening snow. Soon his companion began to fall behind, and as they climbed higher the distance between them lengthened until he disappeared from William's view. Toiling onward for some considerable time, William at last reached the summit and found himself triumphantly alone. Thoroughly exhausted from the climb and apparently never suspecting that he might have been tricked, "he lay down to rest and fell asleep upon the snow." But his companion had turned back, and when no one came to awaken him, William slept on for hours. He might have frozen to death had school authorities not learned of the wager in time. In the deep night he was roused by a search party "sent to look for him, and then on awakening he felt pain in every limb." Brought back to school, he was "scolded and threatened with flogging instead of being put in a warm bed."[20]

By morning a long and dangerous siege of illness had set in, pneumonia, from all appearances, compounded by rheumatic fever.[21] Eventually the fever broke and he began a gradual recovery, but never again would he know the joy of robust health. His heart and lungs had been permanently damaged, resulting in periodic feebleness of health that would plague him to his grave. It was probably the poor state of William's health rather than his mother's that kept them in England through the summer of 1791, avoiding the sickly seasons of Carolina while his condition improved.[22] When they returned home toward the close of the year, she was completely recovered, but the joy of family reunion was dampened by his thin, emaciated appearance and obvious weakness.

Shortly after his return home William was enrolled in the Charleston school of Henry Osborne, an Englishman and a classical scholar reputed to be "strict and severe" in his discipline. His schoolmates found in

William a cheerful companion, even though his unstable health would not permit him to join in their vigorous outdoor sports or the usual boyhood games.[23] But with a mind of exceptional capacity and great retentive power, he outstripped them all in scholarly performance, often amazing them with a display of his intellectual gifts. One of them never forgot the time when William recited verbatim after only one reading a poem several pages in length that he had never seen before.[24] Another recalled a similar performance, which incidentally revealed that Osborne's most gifted student was not always the most conscientious:

> Young Lowndes, then in the Latin Classics, was called upon for recitation and translation, without having paid the least attention or knowing a word of his lesson. His preceptor told him that he deserved and would receive the rod, unless he gave him a translation, without the book, and at his little table, and to attend to the only chance he should have of saving himself. [Osborne] read to him fifty lines of the "Satires" of Horace and closed the book. Such was his intellect at that early age that he furnished a correct translation, to the astonishment of all his schoolfellows. He was always regarded by them as possessing a wonderful intellect.[25]

The feebleness of his body threatened at times to check the flowering of his strong young brain. On some days he was so weak that family servants carried him to school in a chair, and he had to recite lying flat on his back on a school bench.[26] At other times his poor health prevented his attendance at school for weeks on end. Rather than while away the hours of forced confinement, he subjected his mind to rigorous exercises much as other boys sharpened their physical skills, amusing himself by translating the odes of Horace, for example, into English verse.[27] Indeed, receipts for funds paid for his instruction indicate that he probably spent most of the winter of 1793–94 at home under the guidance of a private tutor, Thomas Coram.[28] If this winter of his twelfth year was the most severely debilitating of his protracted recovery, by 1795 the worst was behind him. His early teens marked a return to stable health accompanied by a surge of such rapid growth that he soon towered head and shoulders above his peers.

In the fall of 1795 the thirteen-year-old entered the College of Charleston and came under the direction of the most influential teacher of his life, the Reverend Doctor Simon Felix Gallagher. Formerly professor of mathematics and philosophy at the University of Paris, Gallagher had come to Charleston to serve as priest of the Catholic church and head lecturer at the college.[29] The depth and range of erudition in this thorough classical scholar so fired William's intellectual curiosity that the boy easily became Gallagher's favorite pupil. Particularly impressed by William's exceptional capacity and his voracious appetite for learning, Gallagher commented that "his mind drank up knowledge as the dry earth did the rain from heaven."[30]

That William held his learned preceptor in equally high regard was demonstrated when Gallagher resigned from the college faculty in 1796 in a dispute over teaching methods and opened his own school, the "Athenian Academy," adjacent to the college.[31] William promptly left the college and enrolled in the academy where he remained for the duration of his formal education. Another highly respected school called the Charleston Seminary soon after consolidated with the Athenian Academy. This move brought together on the academy faculty the three most respected teachers in Charleston: Gallagher, generally acknowledged to be the most accomplished; the Reverend Doctor Henry Purcell, rector of St. Michael's Episcopal Church; and the Reverend Doctor Arthur Buist of the Scots Presbyterian Church.[32] In this large academy, the best school in the city including the college, "William Lowndes was decidedly the first scholar, the most distinguished for exemplary deportment, and for proficiency in his studies."[33]

The Athenian Academy celebrated the success of the recent consolidation by presenting an all-student production of Joseph Addison's enormously popular play, "The Tragedy of Cato." Of all the opposition literature that gave rise to the "country ideology" in eighteenth-century England, this play ranked among the most influential writings of the age, both in England and America. Playing to packed houses ever since its first performance in 1713, the tragedy was a celebration of republican principles in the struggle for liberty against tyranny and of the virtuous man in public and private life.[34] William performed the role of Juba, the courageous and high-principled king of Numidia, the purity of whose private life and public character personified the virtuous ideal.[35] Whatever impression this ungainly adolescent boy with a roman toga draped about his emaciated frame made on the audience, there is reason to believe the experience made a lasting impact on the character of the boy himself. In mastering the role of Juba at this acutely impressionable and idealistic period of his own life, William appears to have absorbed the ideal of public and private virtue from the fictional character so thoroughly as to fuse it inextricably with his own. His familiarity with the classics—especially with the writings of Horace, his favorite poet, who sang of the virtuous life in a pastoral setting; with the letters of Cicero instructing Roman youths on moral obligation; and with inspiring examples such as Cato himself in Plutarch's *Lives*—heightened his sensitivity to the role of the pure-hearted and tragic monarch.[36] The experience of mastering the role gave durable strength to his own ideals and, ultimately, a code of personal conduct to live by.

With Juba's noble thoughts sounding their iambic pentameter cadences through William's receptive brain, the tragic death of a schoolmate moved him to try his hand at poetry. The incident occurred late one Sunday afternoon in October 1797, when a group of his schoolfellows idling about the town in search of amusement wandered into Fort Mechanic on the Bay and began to toy with the rope on the flagpole. Peter Benoit, caretaker of the fort, ordered them to desist, whereupon the boys began to make raucous sport of the caretaker. This horseplay suddenly produced an altercation followed by a heated verbal exchange between student Peter Smith and Benoit that so enraged the caretaker that he shot Smith dead on the spot. Charged with wilful murder, Benoit was jailed to await trial by jury.[37]

Shocked by the senseless killing of his friend, William wrote the following poem which appeared in the *Charleston Gazette and Daily Advertiser* on October 24, 1797:

> He's fallen, alas! in youth and beauty's prime,
> Nor is he fallen beneath the scythe of time;
> Time would have spar'd his youthful worth and grace
> Time would have smil'd compassion on his face;
> But murd'rous man, more cruel than time or death,
> Pierc'd his soft breast and quenced the vital breath.
> So some fair flower, in fragrant charms array'd,
> Rears its sweet head amidst the verdant mead,
> Joys in its colors, basks in solar ray;
> But doom'd, alas! to live but for a day,
> The fatal scythe its tender stem invades,
> It bends, it falls, it faints away and fades.
> Curst be the hand that gave the fatal blow,
> And chang'd a parent's raptures into woe;

> Blasted and wither'd may the fell arm be,
> Which snatch'd a comfort and a friend from me.

Whatever youthful pride William might have taken in this effort, its most interesting effect was to suggest his intellectual limitations. The composition displayed more study than poetic inspiration, a correct understanding of the structure of an elegy and proper technical form, but an uninspired reliance on formula phrases so common to eighteenth-century newspaper elegies of no particular distinction. If he ever wrote another poem, no trace of it has been found. Apparently more mature and objective reflection persuaded him that, in truth, he was no poet. His intellectual talents did not extend far into flights of fancy or poetic imagination. Time would reveal that his greatest talent lay in the power of reasoned argument wrought by a mind clear, unrefracted, and luminous.

As for the fate of Peter Benoit, the "fell arm" was neither blasted nor withered, nor even branded according to law. Passions had cooled by the time of the trial; Benoit was found guilty of manslaughter and sentenced to six months' banishment from Charleston.[38]

At sixteen William completed his formal education. Dr. Gallagher told him that, having progressed beyond the abilities of his instructors, "he must thenceforth depend upon his own guidance for further progress."[39] During the next two years he studied in the comfortable surroundings of the Lowndes family home on Tradd Street, reading Latin and Greek under the suggestion of Dr. Gallagher. The most valuable instruction he received in these years, though, came from his father, whose strong legal mind retained the agility of youth tempered by nearly eighty years of experience. Rawlins Lowndes took pride in the precocity of his youngest son and demonstrated his respect for the boy's abilities by frequently engaging him in discussions of current issues.[40] Although neither father nor son left any record of these fireside debates or the impressions gained from them, it is clear that the experience was one of mutual enrichment. The clash of wits with a worthy opponent—for their debates were marked by a free exchange of ideas—enlivened the final years of the old patriarch and instilled in the son a deeper appreciation for the political point of view of a member of the lowcountry elite.

The difficulties Rawlins had overcome early in life and the self-made character of his success had given to his politics a more democratic tone than that of his more privileged peers, such as John and Edward Rutledge and Thomas and Charles Cotesworth Pinckney, who now presided over the dominant Federalist party in South Carolina. Having proved his individual worth, Rawlins preferred to be judged and to judge other men on the basis of personal merit rather than inherited status. Quite conscious of the shortcomings of his provincial education and his lack of aristocratic polish, he seems never to have been quite at ease among men born to wealth and established social position. These surely were factors in his decision to support greater popular participation in government through the direct election of state senators under the state constitution of 1778, a decision that opened a rift between himself and the aristocratic Rutledge-Pinckney faction that widened in 1780 when Lowndes accepted British "protection" after the fall of Charleston.

But he was no democrat. A moderate liberal in the eighteenth-century sense, he had developed the habitual caution of men whose fortunes represent years of patient industry and are not to be exposed to hazard without careful consideration.[41] Thus he became the leading advocate of moderation during the Revolution in South Carolina. He also supported lowcountry control over the state government during the postwar years, not out of any particular regard for lowcountry pretensions to aristocratic status but because of inbred caution, class interest, and a belief in the republican distribution of power to prevent tyranny of the majority. Almost alone among his lowcountry peers, he opposed a strong national government dominated by the northern majority when the United States Constitution came under consideration. He warned that the northern majority would exploit the minority South. It was their interest to do so, he said, "and no person could doubt but they would promote it with every means in their power."[42] It is one of the ironies of South Carolina Federalism that his lowcountry peers should have brushed aside such warnings of majority rule in the national government while taking utmost care to guard against majority rule within the state. Taken altogether, the political views of Rawlins Lowndes were those of a traditional republican. He was thoroughly Jeffersonian in his distrust of a remote and powerful national government as well as in his disposition to extend self-government to the common man within traditional republican limits. As for slavery, he was a considerate master, but he never questioned the wisdom of the institution itself.[43]

In the absence of contemporary evidence, it is difficult to judge the extent to which Rawlins Lowndes articulated his political views in these debates with William over a two-year period, or how much William's thought was influenced by them. Judging from the political moderation that would distinguish William's public career in future years, the influence was substantial. This was due not only to the boy's love and admiration for his father but also to the exceptional kindness and parental regard extended to him. As William explained it, "To my brothers he was imperious, but my youth and miserable health made him very tender of me, except when he thought I needed rousing, and then he would give me a rub with the rough of his tongue, which did me good."[44]

Old Mr. Lowndes was without question the master of his house, and his extreme notions of parental authority were generally observed in his home. But while William loved and admired his father, he did not fear him. In the intensity of fireside debate the boy would state his views with such youthful candor and support them with arguments of such force that the elder Lowndes would sometimes break in with a sharp rebuke for his son's "insolence." William is said to have replied on one such occasion, "Oh, Sir, I thought we were arguing with freedom of speech on both sides. If not there is no argument, and I have only to ask your pardon for my mistake."[45]

The recollection of these exchanges, filtered through the memory of an admiring relative, was decidedly favorable to William, with Rawlins serving as foil to set off the brilliance of his son. The account conveys the unmistakable impression that Rawlins became so frustrated at the superiority of William's argument that he arbitrarily invoked parental authority in violation of the rules of fair play. If this was true to fact—it was certainly consistent with the father's generally imperious behavior within his own household—one suspects that it does not tell the whole truth. This was the sort of "rub with the rough of his tongue" that taught his inexperienced offspring to avoid provoking an opponent to anger, at which point the most carefully reasoned argument becomes ineffective. Rawlins knew from long experience that the true object of argument was not merely to win but to persuade and that an unnecessary provocation was inconsistent with truly persuasive argument.

These debates with his father provide the most plausible explanation for the distinctive character of William's discussion of public issues in later years. He avoided references to authorities of the past and theoretical discussion of abstract principles to a degree that virtually precludes useful analysis of his language as an index to his beliefs. Moreover, although he became an accomplished classical scholar capable of learned discussion of Greek and Latin literature and language throughout his life, William Lowndes disdained the popular practice of employing classical allusions to make a point in public debate. His style of argument was unadorned even to plainness as he relied almost entirely on the power of reasoned argument based on detailed information, occasionally supported by historical examples. It is true that the references to the classics that were so abundant in the rhetoric of the revolutionary generation had begun to pass out of favor among William's peers, as if their fathers had so securely established their inherited status among the lowcountry elite that the sons no longer felt the need for such proofs of gentility.[46] For William, though, the cause lay closer to home in the limited education of his distinguished father and the public ridicule the elder Lowndes once suffered because of it.

During the Stamp Act controversy, the friends of young Peter Manigault adroitly maneuvered Rawlins Lowndes out of the Speaker's chair and put the England-educated Manigault in it. Convinced that his personal merit had been disregarded, Lowndes complained of such treatment in a newspaper essay over the pseudonym "Bobbedel." Manigault's answer sidestepped the removal issue and ridiculed Lowndes for "ignorance," particularly the way he revealed the limitations of his provincial education in his Bobbedel essay and elsewhere. In a spirited response, Lowndes criticized Manigault for abandoning the rule of reasoned argument by forcing into the dispute the irrelevant question of education. That the ridicule cut deep was evident in the vigor of Lowndes's rebuke:

> It is now certain, that although [Lowndes himself] has not sense enough to advertise a horse, yet without a LATIN Motto or even studying *Orthography*, he could write intelligibly in some other Cases, so as to be understood by, and provoke the resentment too, of one of the Literati.... It is not, Sir, whether a *fictitious* name is rightly spelled; it is not whether an advertisement is wrote "Orthographically;" it is not about "*Literary talents*" neither; if it had, I should have given up the point, or rather I would never have made a *point* of it at all: No, Sir, it is not the "propriety" of WRITING, but the "propriety" of ACTING, that is the primary and known cause of our difference; keep to that mark, Sir, and let us take the opinion of the public upon it.[47]

Having scored the only point he wished to make, Manigault remained silent and the incident closed with Lowndes left smouldering in impotent indignation.

This unforgettable wound to the sensitive pride of his self-educated father helps to explain William's life-long aversion to anything resembling a pretentious display of formal learning in public address. There can be little doubt that William learned to avoid such displays in debates with his father, either by painfully experiencing repeated parental rebukes or by being informed of the incident and responding with sympathy for his father's point of view. In either case, the invaluable lesson he learned from his father's example was that formal education was a privilege confined to those who possessed the means and the leisure to acquire it. As such, it was less a measure of an individual's personal merit or native ability than an indication of fortunate opportunity turned to good advantage. Rawlins Lowndes had reason enough to regard a learned as opposed to an informed argument as more offensive than persuasive. And regardless of the subject matter in their debates, we may be sure that he rigorously kept his son to the mark of reasoned argument based on pertinent factual information. This lesson learned at his father's fireside was one William Lowndes never forgot.

His close relationship with his father enabled William to intercede in behalf of his older brothers when they had incurred the old man's wrath, and sometimes his interference brought the parental anger down upon his own head. On one occasion William objected so strongly and insistently against an injustice he felt his father had done to his brother James that the elder Lowndes, "in a transport of indignation," ordered him to leave the house, "which accordingly he did and remained absent about two weeks until the old gentleman had time to cool, when he recalled his son, acknowledged the justice of his admonition, and . . . granted his petition."[48] William's fairmindedness and strict sense of justice toward Thomas and James led them in later years to submit their own personal disputes over business matters to their younger brother for arbitration.[49]

Old Mr. Lowndes died following a short illness at his home in Charleston on Sunday, August 24, 1800. William felt the loss deeply, for notwithstanding their disputes, the recent years of close association had strengthened the bonds of affection between the man of eighty and the boy of eighteen.[50] A few months later William was driving his widowed mother in from the country in a chair, a light and fast two-wheeled buggy with a high seat, drawn by a single horse. As the road passed over a narrow causeway flanked by tree stumps where heavy forest had overhung the road, the horse suddenly took fright and bolted for the woods. By exerting all his strength William could barely keep the wildly careening vehicle on the road, when it veered off the causeway and crashed into a stump, catapulting both passengers forward into the woods. His mother slammed against a tree trunk, killing her instantly, and William was taken up severely bruised and unconscious by a party who happened along the road shortly afterwards.[51]

The tragic accident that killed his mother scarcely eight months after his father's funeral brought to a sad end the youthful years of William Lowndes. The very nature of the accident that took his mother's life had a particularly sobering effect on him. He blamed himself for lack of strength and skill as the cause of her death, nor would he be consoled by accounts of similar accidents that killed and maimed other chair drivers much stronger than himself.[52] The heaviness of personal loss compounded by a profound sense of guilt brought to his life more seriousness of purpose than ever before. His youth was suddenly over, and his manhood had begun.

II
Lawyer

At the dawn of the nineteenth century young William Lowndes faced an uncertain future. An ungainly giant of a youth, he stood six-feet-six on his nineteenth birthday in February 1801, but the ravages of prolonged illness had left him slightly stooped and "terribly thin and narrow chested."[1] Hollow cheeks gave undue prominence to a rather long nose, but while his face was not handsome, it had a certain attractiveness in its naturally pleasant aspect. His fine blond hair, now darkening with maturity and except for a middle part indifferently brushed in the general direction of growth, fell lightly about his temples. Mildness of temper was evident in the expression of his kindly blue eyes and the faint trace of a smile when his face was in repose.[2] These qualities, combined with his upright character, consistently pleasant disposition, and unassuming modesty, conveyed an impression of personal serenity that inspired trust and confidence, so that the overall effect was appealing in spite of his physical defects. Even so, his emaciated appearance reflected a precarious state of health that held little promise for an active life. His father's will provided liberally for William, but several clauses in it revealed that Rawlins Lowndes had hardly expected his youngest son to live long enough to reach his majority and claim his inheritance.[3]

Fortunately the expectations of his father proved erroneous and the clauses unnecessary, for about this time William's elongated frame ceased its inordinate growth, and he entered perhaps the strongest period of his life. Through his middle twenties his health appears to have been almost completely normal.[4] This enabled him to enter fully into the life of the South Carolina plantation gentry and to begin laying the foundation of a career in public life.

Rawlins Lowndes had encouraged his sons to take up the duty of public service traditionally assumed by the southern planter elite, but neither by precept nor example could he persuade his older sons to adopt his Jeffersonian political perspective. Both Thomas and James entered the Federalist party in full and frank acceptance of its enthusiastic nationalism and with a consciousness of class thoroughly characteristic of lowcountry aristocracy. Indeed their political assumptions if not their class consciousness might very well have been a source of irritation to their father that provoked his imperious behavior toward them. Nor was his autocratic bearing toward his older sons productive of mutual understanding and political agreement within the Lowndes household. Even so, their commitment to Federalism probably resulted more from circumstance and timing than anything else. His own wealth having insulated them from the hard life he had known and brought them up in circumstances as privileged as their typically Federalist lowcountry friends, he should not have been surprised that they embraced the politics of their peers. The element of timing placed Thomas and James among the first generation of southern nationalists, who came of age when the Federalist party was in full national flower and South Carolina Federalism was a recognized power in national politics. How much their legal training at the Federalist-dominated Charleston bar influenced their politics would be difficult to determine, since their preceptors are not identified in the records.[5]

Thomas Lowndes, a full generation older than William, entered active politics when his youngest brother was a mere schoolboy. Thomas began his public career in 1792 when he was elected one of Charleston's fifteen representatives to the state legislature. By 1800 he had achieved stature enough within state party councils to be considered seriously for the office of governor. He was chosen instead to fill a seat in Congress recently vacated by Major Thomas Pinckney and, standing off a challenge by Republican Robert Marion, won a second term in 1803.[6]

The record Thomas Lowndes compiled in Congress was marked by consistent adherence to Federalist principles and is most interesting for his reaction to two measures worthy of note. He opposed the Twelfth Amendment to the Constitution, which separated the elections of president and vice president, on the ground that the amendment would "diminish the influence of the small states."[7] The other congressional measure condemned a recent South Carolina decision to reopen the foreign slave trade and proposed a duty of ten dollars for each slave imported, "the highest duty the Constitution permits."[8] Because the tax would fall only on South Carolina, Lowndes denounced it as "the height of injustice." The state legislature had legalized the trade, he said, because of widespread smuggling into South Carolina "in numbers little short of what they would have been had the trade been a legal one." The state law had proved unenforceable, and though he would willingly vote against the traffic, he was convinced the proposed tax would not prevent the importation of a single slave.[9] His stand helped to defeat this "partial and unequal tax," and he might have been reelected, but he declined to be considered for a third term and retired to the management of his planting interests.[10]

James Lowndes, fourteen years older than William, proved himself a reliable party man and joined his Federalist colleagues in the state House of Representatives in 1800. Thrice reelected, he continued his service in this body until 1808. Like Thomas, James also aspired to national office, but neither political talent nor personal inclination could raise him above the level of state politics.[11] The golden age of Federalism closed with the Jeffersonian "revolution" of 1800. The new era belonged to the rising generation of younger men, whose politics would reflect a more sensitive regard for the aspirations of the common man, manifest a greater appreciation for state rights in domestic affairs, and focus on neutral rights and national expansion in foreign policy.

The decline of Federalist strength and the corresponding rise of Republican power on the national scene had been fairly recent, given momentum by the highly partisan application of the Alien and Sedition Acts of 1798 and accelerated with the Republican victory of 1800. Contributing factors included patterns of federal patronage, the reflection of sectional and class interests in domestic and foreign policies under Federalist direction, the failure of the old Federalist leadership to understand the nature of a loyal opposition, and the southward and westward flow of population. Within this matrix, several developments clearly influenced Federalist decline in South Carolina.

In the beginning, lowcountry support for the new national government had been overwhelming, with Rawlins Lowndes being one of the few who joined the backcountry men in opposition to the Constitution. After the new government got underway, however, Federalist strength within South Carolina steadily diminished. The policies of Alexander Hamilton seemed to many lowcountry Federalists to favor the moneyed interests of the northern commercial community at the expense of southern agriculture. By the middle of the 1790s, Pierce Butler and Charles Pinckney, two Federalist delegates to the Constitutional Convention of 1787, had swung over to the Jeffersonian Republicans. Then in 1795 when John

Jay's Treaty of London threatened the collection of prewar debts owed to British merchants while making no provision for payment for thousands of slaves carried off by the British during the war, even the Rutledges came out to harangue a Charleston mob that took to the streets in protest over the treaty.[12]

The state's disillusionment with national policy was clearly revealed in the presidential election of 1796, when Federalist Edward Rutledge helped to deliver South Carolina's unanimous electoral vote to Thomas Jefferson for president and to Thomas Pinckney for vice president. Virginia was expected to reciprocate with support for Pinckney. But Virginians threw away most of their second choice votes on Samuel Adams of Massachusetts, arousing bitter disappointment in the Pinckney camp. This set the stage for the debacle committed by the Federalist-controlled South Carolina delegation when the House decided the presidential election in 1801. South Carolina electors had been unanimous for Jefferson and Aaron Burr in 1800, but when the famous tied vote in the electoral college sent the matter to the House for decision, the lame-duck delegation steadfastly voted for Burr in open defiance of the wishes of the voting majority in South Carolina.[13] Jefferson eventually won on the thirty-sixth ballot, but by then the doom of South Carolina Federalism was sealed. The next election reduced Federalist representation in the congressional delegation to two House seats, and even these disappeared in the sweeping Republican victory of 1804. This paralleled a similar revolution at the state level. Federalists had held almost half of the seats in the legislature in 1800, but by 1806 four out of every five members were Republicans.[14]

It was against this shifting background of transition politics that William Lowndes moved to establish his credentials for a role in public life. Encouraged by his father, he took a keen interest in public affairs and resolved to pursue the study of law as the most essential tool for effective political leadership. Since he lacked a flair for oratory, a deficiency compounded by his weak voice, he joined the Philomathean Society to improve his skills in public address shortly after completing his formal education. This society was a debating club formed by a group of young Charlestonians. Among its members were his former schoolmates Charles Fraser and Jacob Cardozo and a studious young lawyer from the upcountry, Langdon Cheves. Their Saturday meetings, held in Furman's schoolroom in Stoll's Alley, were announced in the local papers and frequently attracted prominent Charlestonians Dr. Gallagher and the historian David Ramsay to judge their debates. The Philomatheans appointed two speakers in succession to debate both sides of an issue of current interest, such as "Ought capital punishments to be inflicted for any other crimes than murder or treason?"; "Would it be politic to establish a standing army in the United States?"; "Ought the interest of money to be regulated by law?" On the last Saturday in September 1800, the society debated the most volatile sectional issue in South Carolina: "Ought representation to be apportioned to population, or to property?"[15]

William Lowndes soon became conspicuous for "readiness and fluency" in these debates. Diligent preparation of both pro and con arguments on the questions debated became a settled habit with him; so much so, in fact, that it eventually gave a particularly disarming character to his personal style of debate. He would usually begin with a detailed examination of the opposing point of view, acknowledge its reasonableness and readily concede point by point its areas of strength. This permitted him to direct full attention to the weakness of the opposition argument without allowing its strong points, already conceded, to confuse the issue. Then he would follow with a careful exposition of the strongest points in his favor, which left at its conclusion the strength of his argument standing against the weakness of his opponent's. Because his method was more effective in closing than opening argument, William preferred to close.[16] But even in opening debate his method was effective; every point that he conceded, when mentioned later by his opponent, would redirect attention to himself and suggest the fairness of his position.

The experience of participating regularly in the Philomathean debates could not have been anything but encouraging to William. Here success or failure turned more on content than on style, with flowery phrasing or bombast serving as no substitute for carefully reasoned argument, the area of William's greatest strength. Obviously he could never expect to match the power and eloquence of Langdon Cheves, the most promising public speaker in the group and soon to become the most successful lawyer in Charleston. But in a select assembly of informed citizens willing to listen to reason, few men could be more persuasive than William Lowndes.

On January 9, 1800 William was accepted as a student in the law offices of Henry William DeSaussure and Timothy Ford, probably the best legal firm in Charleston. Although an occasional deserving student like William's friend George W. Cross was admitted without charge, Rawlins Lowndes before his death in this year paid his son's fee of a hundred guineas, about five hundred dollars.[17] Notebooks in William's handwriting dating from June 1800 to May 1803 show that he studied Blackstone's *Commentaries,* the Magna Charta and related British law, and the civil law of South Carolina.[18] The emphasis given in his training to the rights of property and its institutions reflected the staunch Federalism of his preceptors, for both DeSaussure and Ford were high-ranking members of the party in South Carolina. Blackstone's defense of virtual representation, in which each representative legislated for the people as a whole in the republican tradition rather than act in behalf of a narrow constituency, strengthened the lowcountry view of representation within South Carolina and the nation as well.[19]

Other students of the firm in addition to Cross and Lowndes were Daniel E. Huger, Joel Poinsett, and Thomas Pinckney, Jr.[20] Huger and Lowndes became lifelong friends through the association, and William's contact with young Thomas Pinckney facilitated his developing interest in Pinckney's older sister, Elizabeth. The students commonly completed their studies with the firm in three years, the duration of apprenticeship required by Carolina law for admission to the bar. The last entries in William's notebooks indicate that he left the firm in the spring of 1803, but the records are not clear on this point.[21] At any event, he narrowly missed meeting a bright and earnest Yale graduate from the upcountry in the person of John C. Calhoun, who entered the firm as a student in December 1804 after Lowndes had been admitted to the bar.[22]

While study of the law was his primary occupation during these years, by no means did it mark the limit of his interests. He began to familiarize himself with the operations of the Horseshoe plantation, looking toward the day in 1803 when it would be his by inheritance. More importantly in terms of his political career, he joined the Twenty-eighth Regiment of the South Carolina militia and by 1802 had been elected captain of his company. After years of severely limited physical activity, he found military life exhilarating and thoroughly enjoyed the colorful musters and the pageantry of military parades. His militia service encouraged an interest in military affairs that he would maintain throughout his life, but its more immediate effect was to improve his political prospects. A social and political as well as a military organization, the state militia served to bridge the social gulf between the average citizen and the local elite who commonly made up the officer corps. It brought the sons of the Carolina rice planters out of their exclusive clubs and lowcountry retreats onto the tented field, where yeoman farmers, town craftsmen, and clerks of the King Street mercantile trade might judge their traditional leaders at close range in an atmosphere of informal cordiality. Politicking over a convivial drink at militia musters was as common as military drill if not more so, for the officer corps included the political hierarchy of the state from the governor downward. In fact, military titles in the state legislature became so profuse and their employment in addressing members was often so confused that the practice was soon abandoned.[23] For Captain Lowndes, militia service represented far more than a pleasant diversion. It was his first real introduction to the burgeoning democracy that his father had known so well, and it widened his acquaintance with the political leadership of the state.

Of all the distractions from his legal studies, William found Elizabeth Brewton Pinckney, "a quiet thoughtful girl about a year older than himself," by far the most engaging. The Pinckneys were among the oldest families in South Carolina, and since the death of John and Edward Rutledge in 1800, the Pinckneys stood alone in social as well as political preeminence. Elizabeth's father, Major Thomas Pinckney of Revolutionary War and "Pinckney Treaty" fame, had served as minister to Great Britain and envoy extraordinary to Spain during the presidency of George Washington. Elizabeth had accompanied her father on his European missions, utilizing the time there to broaden her education and her international circle of acquaintances while she also polished her social graces and fluency in the French language.[24] Her uncle, General Charles Cotesworth Pinckney, a veteran of the Revolution and an outstanding lawyer, presided over South Carolina's political and social affairs.[25] Having served the John Adams administration as one of the commissioners to France in the "XYZ Affair," his highest national honor lay in the immediate future: nomination by the Federalist party for the office of president of the United States. The Pinckney brothers dominated their party in South Carolina as thoroughly as Federalism dominated lowcountry politics; and her quiet and thoughtful nature notwithstanding, the political views of Elizabeth were as completely and as durably Federalist as those of her father and uncle.

Relations between the Pinckney and Lowndes families had been mutually respectful over the years but never close as long as Rawlins Lowndes was alive. Ever since the Revolution he had been a persistent opponent of the Rutledge-Pinckney faction, and his hostility to the federal Constitution had pitted him directly against Charles Cotesworth in their famous debate in 1788 over its ratification in South Carolina.[26] Following his death in 1800, the Federalist politics of his older sons, which brought them into close political alliance with the Pinckney brothers, served to promote better understanding and more cordial social relations between the two families, facilitating the match between William and Elizabeth. Moreover, the sons and daughters of Rawlins Lowndes might reasonably have considered themselves objects of matrimony hardly less desirable than members of the Pinckney clan. Their father had amassed a fortune in plantations, slaves, and other properties by the time of his death, including more than one hundred thousand dollars in securities alone, and left his heirs in financial circumstances fully commensurate with their exalted social position. Most of the stocks and bonds and several real estate holdings went to his daughters, while the bulk of the estate in lands and slaves was left to his three sons in shares substantially equal. William's inheritance included the Horseshoe plantation, more than two hundred slaves, certain town properties, and several thousand dollars in bonds and cash assets.[27]

The courtship of William and Elizabeth, initiated with all due propriety, progressed through the usual round of afternoon teas and drawing-room parties during the winter months when most of their friends were gone to the country. In late January the pace quickened with the arrival of the plantation gentry, who flocked into Charleston for all the festive gaiety surrounding race week in February. Nightly balls, dancing assemblies, plays at the Charleston Theatre, and exclusive St. Cecilia Society concerts entertained the select circle of the Carolina aristocracy and dazzled the common folk, who observed their magnificent diversions from a respectful distance. An active member of the St. Cecilia Society, the most prestigious social organization in South Carolina, William helped to arrange and took genuine pleasure in these annual celebrations of privileged status that marked the high point of the Carolina social season.[28] Although he cared little for dancing, he enjoyed the concerts and plays, and he loved the races.[29] How he managed to comply with the formal custom that required a private carriage for attendance on the races, to accommodate visiting with friends without having to move about on foot with the multitude, must be left to the imagination;[30] from the day his mother was killed he had steadfastly refused ever again to drive a horse-drawn vehicle with a female as his companion.[31]

At length William won the heart of Elizabeth, but the consent of her father was not readily gained. The Major objected on the grounds of William's unstable health and the fact that, at twenty, he was a year younger than Elizabeth. Eventually, however, the intercession of Thomas Lowndes and several friends in William's behalf persuaded Major Pinckney to grant his permission.[32]

The wedding took place on September 10, 1802 at Moultrieville on Sullivan's Island flanking the entrance to Charleston harbor.[33] In this booming resort village set back among the dunes that overlooked the broad sweep of ocean beach, the river barons were building summer houses grand enough to evoke comment on their extravagance.[34] An epidemic of yellow fever emptied their Charleston townhouses this summer, swelling the island population well beyond the large contingent of lowcountry society summoned there for the happy occasion. The wedding itself touched off a succession of balls, assemblies, and maroons (dinner parties arranged by the gentlemen) that extended into October and threatened to eclipse the splendor surrounding race week in February.[35] The crowning event, a grand ball hosted by the bride's parents, was underway when a storm hit the island with shrieking ferocity, ripping away shingles and shutters and trapping guests inside until its violence abated enough to permit their leaving in relative safety.[36] As the storm spent its fury during the next week, Alice Izard wrote from across the bay in Charleston: "Heigh ho! the wind and the rain, the Rice is drowning, and the Cotton seeds are sprouting, the one can not be reaped, and the other can not be picked, and what can we poor planters do!"[37] The poor planters did as usual: they returned to join their slaves in the country as soon as the onset of cool weather in the fall made the steaming swamps reasonably safe for human habitation. Their human chattel, of course, had no choice in the matter.

The newlywedded couple rode out to the Horseshoe for periodic visits there over the next two years. Lowndes kept accounts of business matters relating to his birthplace, but occasional forgetfulness, as when he rode out to the Horseshoe only to discover that he had left his keys in town, typified his lack of attention to mundane matters of business necessary for successful plantation management.[38] Having resolved on a legal career, he spent most of his time in town completing his studies and left the major portion of the Horseshoe's operation and supervision to his overseer.

During their first summer together the newlyweds retreated from the city and its sickness to stay with relatives on the island, but by the summer of 1804 they had a retreat of their own, "the Grove" on the Ashley River near the race course just north of town, long noted for the beauty of its grounds. The Grove had belonged to a John Gibbes who developed its grounds into one of the more beautiful gardens around Charleston before the advancing British wantonly destroyed them in 1779.[39] Since then the place had changed owners more than once. By the fall of 1803 it was in the possession of Mary C. Vesey. The widow Vesey died that year without making proper disposition of her estate, and when the heirs failed to agree on its division into shares, the Grove was sold at public vendue in front of the court house on Broad Street on March 5, 1804. For a high bid of 3000 guineas Lowndes purchased the property, "containing 35 acres, more or less."[40] After Lowndes bought it, the farm came to be called "Lowndes' Grove." Here he built the spacious house on the banks of the Ashley River that as long as he lived served as the Lowndes's summer home and a most convenient gathering place for their circle of friends attending the February races.

On his admittance to the bar in 1804, Lowndes called on attorney John Cogdell to offer a proposition that would have made Lowndes a junior partner serving without pay while he gained experience at the bar.[41] He never recorded his reasons for selecting Cogdell, whose background and circumstances were so different from his own. Of a poor but respectable Charleston family, Cogdell was the son of a meritorious officer in the Continental army who had proved unable in the postwar years to provide adequately for his wife and three sons. As a result, John had assumed a share of responsibility for the family's support while financing his education at the College of Charleston entirely through his own efforts.[42] Because he also studied under Dr. Gallagher, it is likely that Lowndes had known him for years, although their contrasting circumstances would have discouraged extensive social contact. Cogdell subsequently studied law under Judge William Johnson, in itself an indication of considerable promise at the bar,[43] and entered practice in 1799 at the age of twenty-one. When Lowndes made his proposal in 1804, Cogdell was not prospering in a partnership with a Mr. Moody, an arrangement that would be terminated on settlement of their last outstanding civil case in the spring of 1805.[44] In view of their contrasting circumstances, one suspects that Lowndes made the offer probably out of admiration for a man whose personal struggles and strength of character bore such similarity to the early years of Rawlins Lowndes.

Flattered by the proposal, Cogdell insisted on a shared partnership from the outset and began to place the name of his junior partner alongside his own in legal documents laid before the Court of Common Pleas.[45] Except for lending assistance on a debt case appealed from common pleas to the Court of Chancery in 1804, Lowndes spent his first professional year preparing civil cases for the spring sessions of common pleas in 1805. Whether the partners engaged in the practice of criminal law cannot be determined with certainty, as the criminal records for this period have been lost.

The procedure in a session of common pleas actually began toward the close of the previous term when 240 names were drawn from the list of persons eligible to serve as jurors for the following term of court. On the first day of the next sessions, jurors were called to hear cases listed on the docket. As had always been the rule, the bulk of the cases concerned suits for debt brought by Charleston merchants, and as often as not the delinquent debtor failed to appear either in person or through representation by counsel when his case was brought forward. Guilt was therefore presumed and judgment was entered against him by default. This permitted a rapid disposal of cases, with as many as sixty or seventy being determined in a single day of the five-week term. The court took a lenient view, however, of cases in which judgment was obtained by default if the defendant appeared to contest it at the next term of court. In that event, the court usually set aside judgment by default and heard opposing counsel on the matter before rendering final judgment and issuing the appropriate orders. When the case involved conflicting claims not clearly covered either by statute law or common law, the case might be appealed to the Court of Chancery, a panel of three to five judges empowered to overrule decisions made in common pleas. This court preserved a detailed record of each case heard on appeal; but with rare exceptions the brief entries in the Minutes of the Court of Common Pleas merely listed the parties at suit, opposing counsel, actions of postponement, and the final judgment. The principal exceptions took place when the usual common pleas routine was interrupted long enough to permit an occasional immigrant to lay his petition before the presiding judge and receive the formal rights of American citizenship.[46]

The common pleas sessions of May and June 1805 were long enough for Lowndes to discover who among his fellow lawyers were most active in the practice of civil law. Of thirty-seven attorneys participating in this term of court, twenty-nine-year-old Langdon Cheves was clearly the leader, almost in a class by himself. His partner, Joseph Peace, was approaching retirement and rarely appeared in court, leaving his industrious young colleague the task of managing the case load of the busiest law firm in Charleston.[47] It was not unusual for Cheves to present as many as twenty cases for each one represented by Lowndes and Cogdell and several other struggling young lawyers. And he rarely lost a case. On June 6, for example, a particularly busy day when nearly a hundred cases were recorded, Cheves won twenty-two, lost three, and had postponed nineteen others on which he served as cocounsel with William Drayton and Keating L. Simons. On the same day James Ward had seventeen cases; DeSaussure and Ford, twelve; the firm of John Gaillard and Edward Croft, eight; Henry Bailey, six; Robert Turnbull, five; and partners William Loughton Smith and Henry Bacot, four. The nineteen remaining cases heard on this day were scattered among thirteen other lawyers. Lowndes and Cogdell were two of a dozen more who were active in this term but did not have occasion to appear on this particular day.[48]

As to volume of cases handled, the court activity on June 6 represents a pattern that may be observed throughout this term of court. This should not, of course, be taken as a guide to relative rank among members of the Charleston bar. The larger cases and more prestigious clients usually went to well-established lawyers like DeSaussure and Ford, Smith and Bacot, and James Ward. Langdon Cheves was exceptional. With talents to match his prodigious energy and neither fortune nor family name to undergird his personal efforts, he was determined to gain admittance into a society dominated by inherited wealth by building a fortune on sheer volume while his reputation for success drew about him a steadily widening circle of prestigious clients. Between these extremes, the younger men like Cogdell and Lowndes might secure more clients than some of their more experienced colleagues, but the type of cases they handled usually produced smaller fees.

The record compiled by Lowndes and Cogdell in the spring term of 1805 was respectable considering their status in the profession but not distinguished. Of twenty-three cases handled they won fourteen and lost nine. They won their largest settlement against Lowndes's mentors, DeSaussure and Ford, in the amount of $4,467.83 plus interest and costs of suit. Only two other cases, one won and the other lost, involved sums above $500.00. Of the remaining twenty cases the average award was slightly above $100.00, with the lowest being a defeat that cost their client one cent in damages in addition to court costs.[49] Their clients in the main appear to have been individuals involved in lawsuits over relatively small claims.

If his legal practice added little to his income, it nevertheless made a favorable impression on his colleagues, many of whom were in a position to advance his political prospects. In addition to Henry DeSaussure and Timothy Ford, Lowndes attracted the notice of John Julius Pringle, attorney general of the state.[50] Many if not most of his colleagues were active in the public affairs of Charleston, and seven of them were members of the state legislature: John Dawson, Jr., Henry Deas, William Lee, Thomas Hinds, Francis Dickinson, William S. Smith, and Keating Simons.[51] Langdon Cheves had recently given up his seat in the state House of Representatives, but would reclaim it after the next election. All judges and most other judicial officers were elected by the legislature, commonly from its own membership, which gave a strong political character to the structure of the courts.[52] Hence his legal practice, like his militia service, broadened the political horizons of William Lowndes.

At the close of this term, Lowndes abruptly concluded one of the shortest legal careers in the history of the Charleston bar.[53] The explanation for his sudden withdrawal from the profession after several years of professional training and only one term of actual practice was suggested by Lowndes himself. When Charles Fraser commented on the brevity of his career, he replied, "Yes, very short; and in that time I have had but one case in which my conscience and my duty concurred."[54] It seems plain enough that Lowndes had found the study of law a source of personal satisfaction if not genuine pleasure, but its actual practice revealed aspects of court litigation too unsavory to encourage his continuance in this line of employment.

The record of Lowndes's only appearance before the Court of Chancery in October 1804 helps to explain his withdrawal from the practice of law. The case involved a misunderstanding between two friends over a debt. Edward Johnson had left $320 with his friend James Moles prior to going on a sea voyage in 1800. Moles gave Johnson a note for the amount payable in ninety days. Upon his return Johnson fell ill at Moles's home where he was nursed back to health over a period of five weeks. When the note fell due, a misunderstanding arose as to the amount Moles was to pay. At first Johnson said he considered the debt fully paid but later brought suit against his former friend. When the case came before common pleas in January 1803, the defendant claimed that he had already paid in cash without asking for receipts almost half of the debt and felt justified in asking for some compensation for the expense of sheltering and nursing Johnson back to health. But since he had no proof of payment, judgment went against him for the full amount plus interest and costs of suit, for a total of $433.83. Attorneys Lowndes and Cogdell entered the case after Moles filed a bill of injunction to halt the seizure and sale of his few possessions and Johnson hired the law partners to represent him before chancery. Lowndes served his client faithfully, marshaling depositions and witnesses in support of Johnson that enabled him to win the case.[55] After his appeal failed, Moles was stripped of everything he owned except the clothes on his back.[56]

The whole affair was sordid in detail, pathetic in consequence, and thoroughly distasteful to a high-principled young lawyer with the background and temperament of William Lowndes. Because beginning lawyers have always had to depend on trade of this sort until they gain stature enough in the profession to be more selective, Lowndes could see no reasonable prospect of relief from it short of terminating his career at the bar. Besides, the nature and magnitude of his inheritance dictated that his principal economic concern should be with his lands and slaves, confining his law practice to the status of an avocation.

Even as he prepared the case against Moles, Lowndes's concern for his planting interests soared in September 1804 when the most violent hurricane since the incredibly destructive storm of 1752 hit South Carolina. Sweeping up the coastal plain from Florida to Virginia, the hurricane unleashed its full power on the Carolina lowcountry, leaving in its wake a task of rebuilding that would take years to complete. The Edisto basin was a scene of heavy flooding, drowned livestock, homeless slaves, and general devastation.[57] Reconstruction of the Horseshoe, with its intricate system of sluice gates and canals, might have commanded his full attention had the Charleston electorate not determined to keep him in public life. Before the fields had drained enough for the reconstruction work to begin, he found himself elected to the South Carolina House of Representatives.

William Lowndes had reached the minimum age for a seat in the legislature on his twenty-first birthday in 1803. Claiming his inheritance on the same day, he met the property qualification as the owner of at least "a settled freehold estate of five hundred acres of land, and ten negroes; or of real estate of the value of one hundred and fifty pounds sterling, clear of debt."[58] The next election was set for the second Monday and Tuesday in October 1804. On October 2, six days prior to the election, the *Charleston City Gazette* published his name in the first "ticket" of candidates recommended to the Charleston electorate by an anonymous subscriber.[59] The three Charleston newspapers, the *Courier*, the *Times*, and the *City Gazette*, published over the next five days a total of forty-two such tickets, all anonymously submitted. Each nominated a candidate to represent the Charleston District in Congress, another to serve in the state Senate, and fifteen others to compose the Charleston delegation in the state House of Representatives.⁶⁰

In spite of their number, the various electoral tickets promoted only two candidates for the seat in Congress being vacated by Thomas Lowndes. These candidates were evidently brought forward by their rival parties: Robert Marion was touted as the "Democratic" or Republican candidate in opposition to the "Federal" contender, Thomas Rhett Smith. All but three of the twenty-five tickets headed by Marion recommended Republican John Drayton for the state Senate, while all but one of the seventeen tickets headed by Smith preferred Federalist James Lowndes for the post. As might have been expected, the Federalist *Courier* published only one of the Marion-led tickets, while the Republican *City Gazette* found space for twelve. Publication of the lists that supported Smith reversed this pattern, with the *Courier* printing eleven and the *City Gazette* one. The *Times* gave a less partisan appearance by publishing five tickets headed by Smith and twelve advocating Marion for Congress.⁶¹

Except for the congressional race, numerical results were not reported when the election took place, either in the newspapers or the official election returns. The congressional returns showed that fewer than 750 eligible voters cast ballots in Charleston. Marion defeated Smith, carrying the city parishes 414 to 306, with 27 votes scattered.⁶² A nephew of the "Swamp Fox," Marion had failed in a bid to unseat Thomas Lowndes in the previous election, and his victory over the nephew of John and Edward Rutledge in 1804 marked the rise of a more democratic element in Charleston politics. John Drayton's victory over James Lowndes was probably by a wider margin; Lowndes received enough votes for the state House of Representatives to retain his seat in the legislature, votes obviously cast at the expense of his Senate bid.

In the election of state legislators, the published list of winners customarily ranked winning candidates by the number of votes received though not reported. The list showed that William Lowndes led the field in his first bid for political office; as listed, the winners were William Lowndes, Thomas Somarsall, Charles B. Cochran, John Dawson, Jr., Henry Deas, Henry Middleton, William Lee, Keating L. Simons, Thomas Lehre, William S. Smith, Daniel D'Oyley, Thomas Hinds, Thomas Bennett, Jr., Francis Dickinson, and James Lowndes.⁶³ That William ranked first may seem surprising until one considers the consistency with which his name appeared in the electoral tickets. He was named on every list headed by Smith and on all but one led by Marion. Only John Dawson, Jr., a fellow attorney with a one-term incumbency in the legislature who finished fourth in the balloting, could match William Lowndes in the number of recommendations received. There was substantial correlation between support received in the published tickets and final position in the election returns. The two notable exceptions were Francis Dickinson, an attorney whose presence at the polls as an election manager could have influenced balloting in his favor;[64] and James Lowndes, who obviously benefited from publicity received in connection with his Senate candidacy. Factors contributing to the breadth of William's bipartisan support include the prominence of his brothers in the Federalist party, his exceptional maturity in spite of his youth, his popularity and leadership as a militia officer, and his established integrity. There seems little doubt, however, that the factors that contributed more than anything else to his first-place finish were family connections, the continuing clout of lowcountry cousinry, and the political power of the Pinckney clan.[65]

To assign national party labels to the political neophytes of 1804 would be premature at best, nor do the published tickets give a clear indication of political sentiments among the legislative candidates generally. While the pattern of support suggests the Republicanism of William S. Smith, Thomas Lehre, Henry Middleton, and William Lee, there is little here to indicate the strong Federalist sentiments of Keating Simons and Henry Deas. For the other candidates, ticket support was either too balanced or too thin to serve as a reliable index. The fact is that national party affiliation would become a major factor at the state level only when national issues began to displace local issues in South Carolina politics. Because local issues were largely sectional in nature, the average Carolina voter in 1804 concerned himself primarily with the sectional interests of a candidate for state office, regardless of party affiliation. Charlestonians expected every member of the delegation to protect lowcountry interests in the legislature, especially on the critical issue of representation reform. With a role better suited to his talents and facing an issue that would require their full employment, William Lowndes in the fall of 1804 entered upon a new career, exchanging the practice of law for the more appealing prospect of making law.

III

Representative

When William Lowndes entered the state legislature in 1804, a longstanding intersectional dispute over representation dominated South Carolina politics. In the early months of that year a surge in population growth began to work changes in economic and social institutions that would bring about a settlement of the representation controversy within four years. Every public man, indeed every informed citizen in South Carolina, was familiar with the controversy. Lowndes certainly was, having heard it discussed at large and debated in the Philomathean Society. Moreover, Lowndes was destined despite his youth to play a prominent part in its settlement. The manner in which the lowcountry elite exercised governmental power and the solution they found to this internal issue hold the key to a better understanding of the subsequent course of South Carolina politics, both within the state and within the Union.

Following the Revolution, the central issue in South Carolina as in the nation at large concerned the distribution of political power. The coastal lowcountry, dominated by wealthy, slaveholding descendants of the early settlers, held, by an arbitrary distribution of seats in the state legislature, 144 seats in the House and 19 in the Senate. The upcountry, containing two-thirds of the land area and, through recent immigration, a majority of the state's free white population, was assigned 58 House seats and 11 in the Senate. Property qualifications reserved the highest offices to rich lowcountry planters and limited the franchise to free white males who owned a fifty-acre freehold or a town lot or the equivalent in taxes paid.[1] The arrangement not only gave South Carolina the most aristocratic of the early state governments; by concentrating virtually all governmental authority in the legislature, it made the issue of representation a matter of the first importance. And in spite of revisions of the state constitution in 1790, the lowcountry retained control of both houses, 70 to 54 in the House and 20 to 17 in the Senate, although the upcountry then contained a four-to-one majority of the free white population. The only real concession to upcountry insurgents transferred the state capital from Charleston to Columbia on the Fall Line.[2]

The growing disparity between population and representation intensified intersectional debate over the issue. The principal justification for lowcountry hegemony was the claim, stated as early as 1749, that representation rested on the dual bases of population and taxable property, even though no such arrangement existed in law.[3] Because the tidewater parishes contained most of the state's taxable wealth, they claimed a corresponding share of political power. No southern state, so the argument ran, had been so reckless as to base representation on population alone; besides, they said, most of the upcountry majority were recent arrivals with so little stake in society and so much potential for radical action on such issues as slavery that adoption of simple majority rule would justify secession of the lowcountry from the rest of the state.[4]

Advocates of reform condemned the injustice of a system that contradicted the principle of equality proclaimed in the Declaration of Independence. They complained of the dangerous potential for tyranny under aristocratic lowcountry rule, but their list of grievances contained no specific example of tyranny to support the complaint.[5] The significance of this fact should not be underestimated. In an era when prevailing philosophy held that power was naturally aggressive, the lowcountry elite governed with notable restraint. Under lowcountry rule, the power to tax did not seem to involve the power to destroy. They laid the heaviest taxes on themselves and distributed the benefits and burdens of government with a degree of fairness consistent with republican ideals of civic virtue and the good of the whole. It is true that the upcountry population had always suffered from varying degrees of governmental neglect, but they had little cause for complaint on the score of too much government; and the legislature routinely filled upcountry offices with upcountry men. Whether out of fear of majority retribution or respect for principle, the lowcountry minority showed little inclination to exploit the political weakness of the numerical majority.[6]

The dispute between the upcountry majority and the lowcountry governing elite in this era demonstrated the antagonism between traditional republicanism and popular democracy. Even though the lowcountry planters had kept power in their own hands since the Revolution, they had governed after the fashion of an aristocracy, which by republican standards could claim legitimacy so long as they practiced civic virtue, pursued the good of the whole, and did not degenerate into an oligarchy, an aristocracy gone corrupt. They were prepared to accept a state government structured on the republican model with a mixed and balanced distribution of power, but further than that they would not willingly go, either then or thereafter. Their established record of republican restraint in this era served to justify the perpetuation of elitist government within the state and to prepare the upcountry majority to accept less than the democratic state government they called for. How William Lowndes and his colleagues in the legislature managed to establish a state republic in a nation drifting toward democracy forms an important chapter in his public life as well as the link often missing from attempts to explain South Carolina radicalism after 1820.[7]

Invention of the cotton gin in 1793 led to the rapid expansion of upland cotton culture and stimulated upcountry demand for slave labor. Neither immigration from the northward nor the interstate slave trade could meet this demand, and South Carolina law prohibited the foreign slave trade. The result was widespread smuggling of slaves into the state through numerous bays and inlets along the Carolina coast. Governor James Richardson reported in the fall of 1803 the impossibility of halting this illegal traffic and directed the legislature to take action either to enforce the law or legalize the trade.[8] With majorities from both sections voting for passage, the legislature reopened the foreign slave trade in January 1804.[9] The subsequent expansion of cotton culture, slave labor, and the plantation economy gradually transplanted lowcountry institutions into the upcountry, paving the way for representation reform.

With the slave trade legalized, an endless succession of ships bearing their unfortunate human cargo began to arrive in Charleston harbor in the early months of 1804. By fateful coincidence, in February another stream of immigrants began flowing into the port city, immigrants whose distressed circumstances raised grave doubts concerning the wisdom of having reopened the slave trade. These were hundreds of French refugees fleeing the West Indian island of Santo Domingo, where a great slave insurrection had overthrown the oppressive French regime and driven the French planters from the island. Because most of the refugees had abandoned their material possessions to their victorious slaves, the resources of the French consul in Charleston proved inadequate for their support, leaving the newcomers dependent on public charity.[10]

The Carolina gentry rallied around the dispossessed French planters, converting the social season of March and April into an extended fund-raising campaign for their benefit. Henry William DeSaussure, John Prioleau, and Thomas Bacot, wealthy Carolinians of French Huguenot descent, spearheaded the drive, while the tidewater aristocracy closed ranks behind them. Attorneys John Cogdell and William Lowndes were among the more active participants, managing charity balls, selling concert tickets, and otherwise lending support to the campaign.[11] The unique purpose of the festivities in 1804 infused them with an unusually somber tone and raised above the surface gaiety the specter of insurrection, for the refugees were living proof that it could succeed. Nor could social conversation have been long diverted from this topic during the months that followed. And on through the summer and fall the slave ships came, each cargo adding new strength to the lowcountry's black majority and further disrupting established patterns of commerce by diverting capital out of its customary channels into the slave trade. By the end of October, more than 4,000 new slaves had come in through the port, all but 105 of them from Africa and the West Indies.[12] Then in November a frightening report flashed up the coast from Beaufort, that only through the warning of a slave had a planned insurrection been aborted.[13]

Against this background of apprehension and fear, compounded by upcountry anger over the representation issue, William Lowndes took his seat in the legislature on November 26, 1804. This was his first opportunity to share in, and probably his first chance to witness, the magnitude of legislative authority in South Carolina. The House organized and elected William C. Pinckney of St. Bartholomews Speaker of the House, the most powerful officer in state government. The Speaker's canopied chair and ermine-trimmed robe were appropriate symbols of his power.[14] He appointed all House committees, standing and special, and through them determined to a great degree the extent and character of legislation. He also presided over the election of a multitude of state officials, from governor down to road commissioners. Bills became law on receiving his and the Senate president's signatures and the impress of the state seal, for the governor's office lacked the veto power.[15] Balloting jointly over the next several days, the House and Senate first chose ten presidential electors, who crushed the bid of favorite son Charles Cotesworth Pinckney by delivering South Carolina's unanimous electoral vote to Thomas Jefferson and George Clinton. Next the two houses elected Paul Hamilton of St. Bartholomews governor of the state, named Thomas Sumter his lieutenant governor, and proceeded to fill all but a handful of lesser state offices that had become vacant or were subject to periodic election by the legislature.[16] Aside from certain minor officials in local government and the legislators themselves, only members of Congress were elected by the people directly; but congressional elections depended on the legislature's power to realign boundaries of congressional districts. Even Charleston had to secure permission from the legislature to widen a street. Sharing in the routine exercise of such wide-ranging authority was enough to convince any new member of the significance of representation reform, perhaps even the justice of the upcountry cause, but not necessarily the wisdom of unqualified majority rule.

With the legislature functioning by the committee system, Speaker Pinckney named William Lowndes to the standing committees on privileges and elections, the judiciary, incorporations, and schools. The most significant legislation resulting from his committee work this session came out of the Committee on the Judiciary. Chaired by Keating Simons, the Judiciary Committee pushed through a bill which increased upcountry court districts from three to four, a measure that could be expected to reduce case loads in the courts and to ease the strain of sectional discontent over lowcountry rule. Of Lowndes's special committee assignments, the Committee on Dueling attracted the most public interest. Shocked by the untimely death of Alexander Hamilton in the July duel with Vice President Aaron Burr, citizens from all over the state petitioned the legislature for effective laws against the practice. The petitions generated considerable legislative activity, but these proceedings ultimately proved unproductive.[17]

An issue of greater significance for the future of South Carolina involved the cotton gin of Eli Whitney. After transferring to state control certain rights to his invention in South Carolina, Whitney had privately sold several of the machines to individual planters, whereupon the state brought legal action against him. Now Whitney petitioned the legislature, admitting his error and promising restitution, and William Lowndes joined the House majority in voting to drop the suit.[18] This was only one incident in years of litigation for the mechanical genius whose simple machine profoundly influenced the history of the antebellum South. The relative ease with which the device could be pirated was a factor in the steady conversion of upcountry farms from tobacco and grain to cotton production,[19] stimulating demand for slaves in the region along with improved prospects for political equality.

Other than as a voting participant, William Lowndes was not directly involved in the two major issues considered this session, the foreign slave trade and representation reform. The House took up the first on December 10 when Charlestonian Henry Deas offered a resolution declaring that it was "inexpedient to permit the importation and introduction of Slavery" into the state. Several petitions on the subject from citizen groups as widely separated as Charleston and Fairfield supported termination of the slave trade. Backsettlement petitions complaining about the trade one year and fornication the next suggest religious fundamentalism as a key factor in the region's opposition to slavery.[20] For the coastal parishes there can be little doubt that the recent influx of French refugees, the insurrection alarm, and the tightening of credit caused by the diversion of capital into the slave trade had aroused lowcountry concern.

On December 14 in Committee of the Whole, Deas's resolution was under consideration when Richard Johnson of Edgefield moved to "except [slaves] from any of the United States." A lowcountry vote of 58 to 1 stifled Johnson's motion despite a 29-to-18 vote of support from upcountry districts that formed the northwestern third of the state. Then balloting on Deas's resolution produced an even split that cancelled the upcountry vote 23 to 23, allowing 44 lowcountrymen to carry the measure with 14 opposed. Judging from this second vote, the slave trade was most favored in Abbeville, Clarendon, Edgefield, Greenville, Laurens, Lexington, Marlboro, Orangeburg, Pendleton, St. Mathews, and York in the upcountry and by St. Andrews and St. Bartholomews parishes in the lowcountry west of Charleston. Clarendon, St. Mathews, and Orangeburg formed the heart of the Middle District between the tidewater parishes and the Fall Line, an area whose interior location had insulated it from the illegal slave trade prior to 1804. Otherwise the strongest support for the trade lay in the northwestern districts.[21] With Deas's resolution approved, Speaker Pinckney named a committee to formulate an appropriate bill, but before the House could return to the subject the session closed. Even so, the legislators found time to show their gratitude to Abraham, the slave who had disclosed the planned insurrection near Beaufort, by voting $1,200 to purchase his freedom. William Lowndes voted with the majority on each of these measures, but otherwise appeared content to observe how these legislative matters were managed by his more experienced colleagues.[22]

Meanwhile, petitions sent down from Abbeville and Pendleton in the far northwestern corner of the state encouraged William Falconer, chief of the upcountry reformers, to introduce the following proposal on November 29: "Resolved that a Committee be raised to bring in a bill so as to amend the Constitution of this State as to secure a more just and equal representation of the People thereof in the Legislature."[23] Falconer's resolution passed and Speaker Pinckney named a balanced committee of four upcountrymen and four Charlestonians, with Falconer as their chairman, to draft a bill. Introduced on December 12, the bill was taken up in Committee of the Whole and amended, then passed on to the Senate where it unceremoniously died. When news of its fate reached the House, Colonel William Hill of York gave voice to upcountry frustration in a resolution which opened with an allusion familiar to all:

> When in the Course of events any part of the people of a Republican Government lose their due proportion in the Representation from whatever Causes it may happen, it is their Birth right to resume it, it is a Right which their Ancestors could not alienate, and which no Covenant or supposed Compromise ought to impair, and from the Great Accession of Wealth and population of the middle and upper Country of this State within the last ten years, their great disproportion in the Representation as heretofore established is manifest[;] therefore the better to preserve that mutual balance of Representation and to promote that Harmony which ought to subsist throughout the State
>
> Resolved that it be recommended to the good people of this state to hold a General Election to elect [an equal number of delegates from each election district] to represent them in the General convention, to revise the present Constitution.[24]

Hill was certainly not placated but probably not surprised when the House tabled his resolution, to die when the session closed.

As divided as they were over these internal issues, the legislators could still unite in response to northerners who threatened South Carolina's position among the states of the Union. On the last day of the session the House considered a Massachusetts proposal to amend the federal Constitution so as to apportion "the Representatives among the several states according to their number of free Inhabitants respectively."[25] In this proposal, Massachusetts gave concrete expression to northern resentment over the recent loss of power to the slaveholding South in the national government. To the surprise of no one, the legislature unanimously rejected the Massachusetts proposal and adjourned to November 1805.

The adjournment came early enough for William Lowndes to be back home in time for Christmas at the Grove, but afterwards he had to devote considerable attention to reconstruction of the Horseshoe, owing to the devastation wrought by the great equinoctial storm of 1804. During the festivities surrounding race week in February, he and Elizabeth entertained their friends as disposition and circumstances permitted and measured their personal involvement in the social affairs of March and April by the same standard. May and June required William's attendance at court to discharge his final obligations under the law partnership with John Cogdell. Because Charleston enjoyed a summer of unusually good health, he could spend much of the summer at the Grove rather than resort to Sullivan's Island to escape the usual "sickly season" in the city. The convenience of his situation permitted frequent visits to town for the conduct of business. There he could see for himself the general inactivity of commerce brought on by the slave trade.

If Lowndes took time to discuss public affairs with Henry DeSaussure, who was back in town by early September, he doubtless heard in person his old law teacher's pessimistic views on the damaging effects of the foreign slave trade:

> The State of our Market is dreadful. There is a perfect Stagnation of every thing, but the importation and Sale of new Negroes, which continues in full activity. It is said most of them are Sold to the upper country people. Many do certainly go that way. How long our commerce is to remain so Stagnant I cannot say. . . . Will the ports be Stopped up of the further importation of blacks? If not the numbers imported will be immensely increased. And new & enormous debts contracted.[26]

Charleston merchants keenly felt the credit squeeze. Ebenezer Thomas, for example, after acquiring 50,000 volumes for sale to his usual customers, found to his dismay that the slave trade had destroyed the market for nonessentials, leaving him with an immovable inventory of books.[27] And the slave traffic was steadily rising, with 6,790 slaves imported in 1805 compared to 5,386 for 1804, an increase of 26 percent.[28] The worsening state of the Charleston market aroused active lowcountry opposition to the trade when the legislature reconvened in November.

Scheduled to meet on November 18, the House finally secured a quorum on the twenty-third and heard a letter from William Pinckney resigning the Speakership. As soon as they had elected Joseph Alston from the coastal parish of Prince George Winyah to succeed Pinckney, the House learned that the upcountry's strongest advocate, William Falconer, was dead. The loss of Falconer seriously hampered the upcountry quest for political equality, for without his guiding hand the movement faltered. Grand jury presentments from Spartanburg and Laurens districts moved Speaker Alston to establish a new Committee on Representation Reform. With Falconer gone, Alston named the veteran John Taylor of Abbeville to chair a reform committee composed of four upcountry members, two from the Middle District, and three Charlestonians including William Lowndes. With this appointment, Lowndes became directly involved in the management of representation reform. To devote more attention to the reform effort, he immediately resigned his chairmanship of the Committee on Incorporations. A few days later Taylor resigned from the reform committee to accept election as solicitor of the western circuit, and Falconer's mantle passed to Colonel William Hill of York. Hill was not unwilling to accept leadership of the reform effort, but he was unable to bring a satisfactory bill out of committee. This failure prompted him to call again for a constitutional convention, a motion that met a fate similar to his resolution of 1804. It was postponed to January and died when the session closed.[29]

In the meantime William Lowndes was rapidly gaining stature in the House. In addition to the chairmanship of the Committee on Incorporations, he served on a variety of others dealing with military affairs, attachment laws, South Carolina College, special claims, and the slave trade. He also chaired the Committee on Schools and a special committee on the powers of the Charleston city council. The report he delivered for the last-named committee would hardly be worth notice here except that it displayed a talent for compromising opposing interests which would become a hallmark of Lowndes's legislative style. His report recommended that the city council be authorized to appropriate a portion of certain lots fronting on Market Street to give the street a uniform width between East Bay and King streets. The amount of compensation due the landowners would be determined by five commissioners, two named by the city council, two named by owners of the lots involved, and these four would choose the fifth.[30] As chairman of the Committee on Schools, Lowndes pushed through a bill calling for free schools throughout the state, but the legislature's failure to appropriate the necessary funds defeated his object. His committee work was less evident regarding the slave trade, the subject of greatest significance for this session.

On December 2 in Committee of the Whole, the House resolved, "That the importation of Slaves is repugnant to the true interests of this State, Dangerous to its tranquility and Safety, and that . . . a Committee be appointed to bring in a bill to prevent the said importation from beyond Seas or elsewhere." The next day Samuel Mays of Edgefield moved to amend the resolution to admit slaves from any of the United States. With the lowcountry voting 49 to 1 against it and the upcountry divided 22 in favor and 25 against, the Mays amendment lost. Joseph Gist of Union then proposed to admit slaves brought in by immigrants from other states only to see his amendment defeated 26 to 66, with all but 1 of the votes in its favor cast by upcountry members. Next Starling Tucker of Laurens offered a motion to allow South Carolinians to bring in for their own use but not for speculation slaves from other states. The five lowcountrymen who supported Tucker's motion were hardly enough, and it failed 37 to 48. Finally the House by a vote of 61 to 27 approved the appointment of a committee to write the bill against the wishes of 9 members from the tidewater and 18 from the backsettlements. Throughout these proceedings William Lowndes voted with the lowcountry majority against the slave trade.[31]

To frame the bill Speaker Alston named a lowcountry committee consisting of planter Henry Middleton and four Charleston lawyers, Henry Deas, William Lowndes, William S. Smith, and Keating Simons. On December 4, Chairman Deas reported the bill out of committee, but the House postponed its consideration to December 11. The delay worked to the upcountry's advantage because of heavy lowcountry absenteeism toward the close of the session. When the appointed day arrived, upcountry members in attendance actually outnumbered their lowcountry colleagues 49 to 45. Although advocates of the slave trade were still in the minority, they appeared determined to continue it in one form or another. One advanced a motion to postpone the bill's effective date to December 31, 1806; it lost 31 to 62, with majorities from both sections voting against it. Another proposed to set the effective date at October 1, 1806; upcountry members narrowly approved this motion 24 to 22, but the tidewater men voted it down 33 to 12. Starling Tucker of Laurens now revived his proposal, defeated a few days earlier but since then slightly modified, to allow each citizen of South Carolina to purchase out of other states not more than ten slaves for his own use. His upcountry colleagues supported this motion 33 to 17, while the lowcountrymen rejected it 34 to 4. Richard Johnson of Edgefield offered the final proviso, that the bill should not prevent the movement of slaves through South Carolina from one sister state to another. Representatives of piedmont districts where such traffic would be heaviest endorsed the proviso 30 to 13, but only three lowcountrymen considered Johnson's proposal worthy of passage. Having turned aside all exceptions and attempts to delay the bill's operation, the House finally voted to close the slave trade by concurrent majority, the respective lowcountry and upcountry votes being 31 to 9 and 25 to 19.[32]

Taken as a whole, the balloting on these various motions showed that the upcountry members stood approximately four to three in favor of the slave trade in some form, while the tidewater representatives opposed it in any form by a margin of at least three to one. William Lowndes voted consistently with the Charleston delegation against the trade and contrary to the prevailing sentiment in St. Bartholomews where his Horseshoe plantation was located.

After the bill passed on to the Senate, opponents of the slave trade hardly had time to celebrate their victory when word came back that the upper house had defeated the measure by a single vote. Among the senators, sectional sentiment regarding the trade appeared to be diametrically opposed, with two-thirds of the upcountry in its favor and two-thirds of the lowcountry against it. The evenness of this division made lowcountry absenteeism a significant factor when the vote was taken. With two upcountry senators absent and twice that number missing from the lowcountry roster, ten senators from the hinterlands joined six from the coastal parishes to defeat the bill 15 to 16.[33] Distribution of these sixteen votes suggests that every district above the Fall Line except Abbeville, Greenville, and Union wanted the slave trade to continue. If the House delegations from Abbeville and Greenville, who disagreed with their senators on this measure, were more representative of local sentiment, then Union District would stand as the only exception to northwestern unity in support of the slave trade. Tidewater districts favoring the trade lay next to the North Carolina and Georgia borders, where development had been limited and illegal traffic across state boundaries was likely to escape detection; and in parishes directly behind and immediately west of Charleston, where the illegal trade prior to 1804 had in all probability been effectively controlled.

Following their failure to halt slave importations in the session of 1805, opponents of the trade allowed it to run its course undisturbed until terminated by act of Congress on January 1, 1808. Over the two remaining years, the volume of slave imports increased dramatically, to 11,458 in 1806 and a record-breaking 15,676 in 1807, bringing the total number imported during the four years of legalized trade to 39,310.[34] Figures from the national census that closed this decade indicate that probably three out of every four slaves legally imported were sold into the upcountry; during the decade the lowcountry slave population grew by 13,541, while 36,673 were added to the upcountry total.[35] These combined totals exceeded the number legally imported by more than 10,000, an excess that may be accounted for through immigration from the northward and natural increase. The phenomenal growth of slavery in the upcountry districts extended traditional lowcountry interests and institutions into the backsettlements; and this, more than any other single factor, produced a harmony of interests between the sections that set the stage for representation reform.

The fall elections of 1806 returned William Lowndes to the House along with most other incumbents, and the legislature elected Jeffersonian Charles Pinckney governor of the state. Among the new House members, hard-driving Langdon Cheves of the Charleston bar, returning to the legislature following a one-term absence, held the most promise. Another new man who drew immediate attention was Abraham Blanding, a widely respected attorney from Kershaw District. Joseph Alston, returned again to the Speaker's chair, extended a generous share of committee assignments to the experienced Cheves and the newcomer Blanding and elevated Lowndes to the important Committee of Ways and Means.[36]

With minor exceptions, however, the business of this session turned out to be fairly routine, a circumstance that allowed Cheves and Blanding to secure temporary leaves of absence for the conduct of other business. Considerable attention was devoted to establishing turnpikes and improving transportation generally, doubtless to facilitate the movement of cotton and other products from the interior to the seaports of Charleston, Georgetown, and Beaufort. The humanitarian spirit of penal reform, which was spreading southward from New York and Pennsylvania, stimulated a good deal of House committee activity toward revision of the penal code and eventual establishment of a state penitentiary. The rising spirit of democracy was evident in two other proposals. One called for the local election of county sheriffs and several other local officers currently being chosen by the legislature, and another proposed to eliminate property qualifications on the right to vote. The majority, however, would consider only one political reform at a time, and postponed both of these to the next session.[37]

As expected, upcountry petitions revived the issue of representation reform, and now the spirit of compromise began to surface. Speaker Alston named a committee of three upcountrymen, Joseph Gist of Union, Richard Johnson of Edgefield, and Thomas Edwards of Greenville, to manage the reform effort. Then Theodore Gaillard of Christ Church Parish persuaded the House to enlarge the committee so as to include one member from each election district, an arrangement that favored the upcountry with twenty-three election districts to the lowcountry's twenty-one. Even so, the wheels of political justice ground slowly. Chairman Gist brought in a reform bill on December 19, too late for serious discussion, so the House ordered five hundred copies printed to facilitate study of the bill over the summer and postponed any further action to the next session. Progress had been made, but it was much too methodical for upcountry militants. Edwards of Greenville moved that "all the members from the Back-Country have Leave of Absence the next Session, if they Choose to Stay at home [and] that there be no Election hereafter to take Place until a convention can be called." The majority, however, having caught a glimpse of compromise, voted his resolutions down and continued the question over to the fall of 1807.[38]

Events of 1807 not directly related to South Carolina's internal issues helped to promote intersectional unity by raising the prospect of war with England. Anglo-American relations, having deteriorated steadily since 1805, hit bottom in June 1807 when the British *Leopard* in American waters hard by the Virginia capes surprised the American *Chesapeake* with crippling broadsides and forcibly removed from the battered vessel four of her crew. The shocking news sent prowar reverberations throughout the Union. Reaction in Charleston, where throngs of citizens in a series of mass meetings denounced the outrage and vowed to defend national rights with force of arms if necessary, typified patriotic reaction all over the state.[39] President Jefferson's July appeal to Governor Pinckney for thousands of South Carolina troops to be made ready for emergency service sounded the call to arms. A few days later the president called Congress into early session, contributing to the general alarm. Consequently the state girded for war through the hottest summer in recent memory, planning for an army of more than thirty thousand South Carolina militia and volunteers.[40] Because the vast majority of these troops would come from the upcountry, everybody knew that if war came and the vulnerable lowcountry were invaded, its defense would depend to a great degree on upcountry cooperation. Sober reflection on such a contingency could not but have weakened further lowcountry resistance to representation reform.

When the House reconvened in November the alarming state of foreign affairs had the immediate effect of shunting aside plans for penal reform and directing substantial appropriations ($65,000 in the first bill) toward the purchase of arms and war materiel for the state's defense. Other problems had grown out of the rapid increase in slaves and in cotton production, requiring new laws to prevent frauds in the packing of cotton and to insure white supervision on every farm where slave gangs were employed.[41] On the reform of representation, the lowcountry was now prepared to compromise, but not in the form in which Gist had fashioned his bill. As presented to the Committee of the Whole on December 12, the bill compounded the issue by including a provision to eliminate property qualifications on the right to vote, and a motion to table carried. Immediately William Lowndes rose to offer the following motion: "Resolved, that on the Third Monday of June Next there be an Extra Session of the Legislature for the Special Purpose of Taking into Consideration a Reform in most parts of the Constitution of this State as respect the Representation in the Legislature thereof."[42] The members adopted the plan; authorized an immediate census, "as speedily as may be" completed, to provide population data necessary for reapportionment; and adjourned to the following June.

With the slave trade closed and the war scare having faded into economic coercion through the Embargo of 1807, the lowcountry members returned to Columbia for the special session in a most conciliatory mood.[43] The record of proceedings during this session reveals that William Lowndes played a central role in settling the representation issue, while newspaper reports indicate that Abraham Blanding had emerged as the principal upcountry advocate of compromise. Convened as scheduled on Monday, June 20, 1808, the House disposed of preliminary business and on Tuesday went into Committee of the Whole on Representation Reform, with William Lowndes in the chair. Here Blanding introduced "sundry resolutions, forming the basis of the future representation of the State, which were adopted in committee unanimously."[44]

These called for representation to be based in equal shares on white population and taxable property, with each election district to have at least one representative. Blanding's plan combined the lowcountry's familiar duality principle with the upcountry's often-expressed desire for equal representation from each election district. Further discussion, none of it reported, apparently joined the representation issue together with the question of universal white manhood suffrage, for when the committee rose on Wednesday and Chairman Lowndes duly reported, the House tabled the report.

At this point, on the motion of an unidentified member, the House approved a committee of ten "to bring in a bill for the amendment of such sections of the Constitution as respect the Representation in the Legislature . . . on the principles of Taxation and white population, with a provision securing one member to each election District." The selection of Lowndes to chair the committee points to him as author of the resolution. Named along with Lowndes were three lowcountrymen, Theodore Gaillard, Cheves, and Keating Simons; and six men from the upcountry, Richard Johnson, Joseph Gist, William Strother, Joseph Bellinger, Samuel Dunlap, and Blanding.[45] The next day Lowndes reported the bill out of committee and saw it passed through its first reading. Then on Friday the bill was discussed in Committee of the Whole, with Daniel Huger in the chair. When the committee rose, Speaker Alston directed Huger, Lowndes, and Gist to engross the bill for its second reading, which was done by Saturday when the House approved it and adjourned for the weekend.

On the following Tuesday the question was called on the decisive third reading, "Shall the bill pass?" In an unprecedented display of intersectional unity, all but 2 of 103 members present voted for passage. Even the fragment of last-ditch opposition was intersectional, with Alexander Starke of Saxe-Gotha (Lexington) and Richard VanderHorst of St. James Santee casting the only ballots against it.[46] Shortly afterwards the Senate gave its approval by a similar margin and Governor Pinckney added his signature on Wednesday. The constitution was thus amended, to take effect at the election of 1810. Having gained the compromise on representation, the upcountry reformers immediately pressed the issue of universal white manhood suffrage. They pushed a suffrage bill through the House over lowcountry opposition that included Lowndes, but it failed to win enough support in the Senate where it died on its second reading.[47] Refusing to consider any private business, the legislators adjourned forthwith, thus bringing to a close the session, "harmonious beyond example," which established a classically mixed and balanced constitutional republic in South Carolina that lasted throughout the antebellum period and the Civil War.

Authorship of the sectional compromise was generally attributed to Abraham Blanding following the newspaper report that he introduced the basic provisions of the settlement in Committee of the Whole on June 21. This view gained strength by a comment in 1841 from William Harper, who was not in the legislature in 1808, that "the measure was matured and introduced by ... *Abram Blanding*. ... With him, it is understood, that *William Lowndes* was associated, in the maturing of the bill."[48] Lowndes was too modest to advance a claim in his own behalf, especially since the idea was not his, only its articulation. After both he and Blanding had died, however, Alfred Huger, a close relative of Daniel Huger who served with Lowndes and Gist in putting the bill in final form, said in 1859 that "this plan undoubtedly originated with Mr. Lowndes."[49] Lowndes family tradition maintained that Lowndes fashioned the plan and persuaded Blanding to introduce it because of the latter's standing and influence among the upcountry men.[50] Contemporary evidence confirms the tradition. Established procedure required Lowndes, as author of the resolution that established the special session, to prepare a proposal for consideration when the session opened. His formulation of a specific proposal and circulation of it among his lowcountry colleagues, virtually all of whom annually came to town for the February races, would help to explain their going up to Columbia in an unusually positive frame of mind. It seems significant that the only extant manuscript copies of the plan, aside from the journal of proceedings, are in Lowndes's handwriting, one a preliminary draft with corrections written in, and the other in the form adopted by the legislature.[51] The most convincing evidence, however, is found in the behavior of Speaker Alston. He named Lowndes chairman of two of the most important committees dealing with the subject and member of a third that put the bill in final form, while relegating Blanding to a role so minor as to be unthinkable if he were the true author of the compromise.

Henry DeSaussure, writing to his friend Ezekiel Pickens in Pendleton, expressed the general satisfaction over the settlement: "It turned out as I told you it would. The Low Country Gentlemen went up in the most conciliating temper and consented readily to an arrangement of the representation which promises to Satisfy all Parts of the State, & to heal the differences which have so long diseased the body politic. We are now to learn if this medicine will produce the salutary effects expected from it."⁵² The heart of the compromise was the provision that kept House representation at 124 members but provided that thereafter 62 members would be elected on the basis of taxation and 62 on the basis of population:

> The House of Representatives shall consist of one hundred and twenty four members, to be apportioned among the several election districts of the state, according to the number of white inhabitants contained, and the amount of all taxes raised by the legislature, whether direct or indirect, or of whatever species, paid in each, deducting therefrom all taxes paid on account of property held in any other district, and adding thereto all taxes elsewhere paid on account of property held in such district; an enumeration of the white inhabitants for this purpose shall be made in the year [1809] and in the course of every tenth year thereafter.⁵³

Representation based on white population was a victory for the upcountry, while that determined by property in the form of taxes made the amendment acceptable to the lowcountry elite. The latter provision would control the transfer of political power rather like a valve that regulates the flow of ballast from one tank to another, providing stability during the process of change. This became more evident after the compromise went into effect in 1810.

The enumeration taken in 1809 gave the upcountry controlling majorities in the House and Senate for the first time in history. The lowcountry lost 16 House seats, dropping from a majority of 70 to 54 to a minority of 54 to 70. The compromise provision respecting Senate membership adopted the upcountry plan for equal representation of the election districts except for Charleston, which was assigned two, giving the upcountry a one-vote majority in the upper house, 23 to 22.⁵⁴

But while the compromise gave the upcountry districts control over the government of South Carolina in 1808, the "lowcountry interest" continued its usual domination over political, economic, and social affairs. William A. Schaper, in his reliable study of the representation issue in South Carolina, gave emphasis to this fact in concluding his discussion of the compromise:

In fact, it was only as a geographical section that the low country made any concession in 1808. It was only extending political power into those regions into which its interests and institutions were spreading. . . . There never was a time until the reconstruction days that the black belt, or the greater lower country did not absolutely control the government of the State. . . . as the institutions originating in the tide-water section, crept upon the up country, political power went with it. The concurrent majority principle was a success in South Carolina, because the minority, originally a distinct community having political power completely in its control, kept possession of it until it had won over the majority to its interests and institutions.[55]

Statistics on the rapid extension of slavery into the upcountry during this decade clearly support Schaper's conclusion. By 1810 slaves equaled or outnumbered the white population in Claremont, Clarendon, Orangeburg, Richland, and Kershaw. Moreover, slaves accounted for about a third of the population in Abbeville, Barnwell, Darlington, Edgefield, Fairfield, Lancaster, Lexington, and Newberry.[56] Considering the growth of upcountry slave population and the economic and institutional reorientation it produced, Orangeburg, Claremont, Clarendon, Richland, and Kershaw could properly be considered extensions of the lowcountry interest by 1810. If one calculates sectional voting strength on this basis, the lowcountry interest would have had eight-vote majorities in both the House and Senate (66 to 58 and 26 to 18) when the compromise first went into effect.[57] Afterwards the reapportionment that marked each succeeding decade reflected a steady expansion of the lowcountry interest, so that it always retained control of the state government. Even though universal white manhood suffrage went into effect simultaneously with the compromise in 1810, there was never a time before the Civil War when the planter class had to contend with the unchecked power of a popular majority in South Carolina. Although the democratic perspective of later generations would question the merit of this settlement, within the republican context of the times it would have been difficult to devise a more satisfactory solution to the dispute between South Carolina's numerical majority and her governing elite.

That the lowcountry interest continued to control the state following the compromise has been effectively demonstrated by Schaper, but its significance for the rising generation of South Carolina political leaders has not been fully appreciated. Never having to deal with a popular majority at the state level, men like Lowndes, Cheves, and Calhoun retained in varying degrees the traditional republican approach to government. Of the three, Lowndes provides the best example. He regarded public service as a duty attached to class and standing in the community, assumed the burden of government less as a public honor than a personal sacrifice in the public interest, and governed in behalf of the people as a whole rather than a narrow constituency, always keeping in view the rights of the numerical minority. Seeing himself as a man above party, he reserved a right to the free exercise of personal judgment, taking a breadth of view that transcended and at times conflicted with the interests of his immediate constituents. In time he would be elected to Congress, but his approach to government would remain the same and find expression in optimistic nationalism and altruistic support for nationalistic legislation. Not until 1819, toward the close of his career, would his traditional republican style of politics face a reckoning when the tariff and slavery issues raised sectional controversy on a national scale. By then the minority South had become in effect the national lowcountry, with interests and institutions traditional to the South Carolina tidewater but without an effective device to dissipate the numerical strength of the majority North. At that point Lowndes and his fellow Carolinians would confront for the first time the aggressive power they had always feared, "tyranny of the majority." Reverberations from that collision would echo down the decades to the Civil War.

But all that lay in the future. For the present, Lowndes went home to Charleston with every intention of returning to the legislature. He knew that the politics of his district were taking on a more partisan quality, fired by the rising spirit of democracy along with issues related to presidential politics and international affairs. He probably realized that this would make his reelection more difficult, but certainly he did not expect it to redirect the focus of his public career.

IV

Federal Republican

Producer of rice and sea island cotton for the European market, the lowcountry planter belonged to a great Atlantic community that bridged the ocean with commerce, correspondence, and periodic voyages to conduct business and to visit friends and relatives in the Old World and the New. Like others who raised produce for European consumption, his interest could not long be diverted from vicissitudes in international affairs that might affect the carrying trade, for an open sea lane was not less important in marketing the crop than favorable weather in producing it. His international concerns were respected by the editor of his newspaper, in which a few inches of local news vied for attention among several columns covering "Foreign Intelligence," ship "Arrivals and Departures," and "Prices Current," the financial section. With rare exceptions he depended on a Charleston factor to receive, warehouse, and market the crop and to supply tools, nails, cloth, medicines, blankets, shoes, and a variety of other imported goods as plantation needs required. Business between factor and planter was commonly managed through the factor's bookkeeping, with an occasional transaction in cash.[1] Because most rice plantations carried the fixed maintenance costs of a small community, few matters were of more practical concern to the average planter than those that affected the debit and credit balances in his factor's account book.

Carolina planters shared in the national prosperity that opened the nineteenth century. A decade of Anglo-American rapprochement dating from the Jay Treaty in 1794 blessed the first administration of Thomas Jefferson with the salutary benefits of peaceful commerce between England and her best customer.[2] The Peace of Amiens between England and France suspended the Napoleonic Wars in 1802 and offered neutrals, of which the United States was the largest, the temporary boon of trade with either belligerent without fear of reprisal. Even the resumption of

Anglo-French hostilities in 1803 appeared at first to have only positive results for America. It encouraged Napoleon to cede Louisiana to the United States, stimulated demand along with higher prices for American produce, and opened a booming business for American merchantmen in the French colonial trade, yet it did not seem to disturb Anglo-American cordiality. The combination of these factors helped to make Jefferson's first administration as popular, prosperous, and peaceful as his second would be factious, economically unstable, and stormy.[3]

South Carolinians took due note in May 1803 of the British declaration that reopened the European conflict, but another year passed before its negative consequences touched the Carolina coast. In March 1804 a French cruiser appeared off the Charleston bar and with bland indifference to American neutrality proceeded to demonstrate the ease with which outward-bound vessels carrying cargo for England could be intercepted.[4] With a competent pilot to negotiate the bar, the French might almost as easily have sailed into the bay and fired on the town, for the harbor defenses lay in a state of serious disrepair.[5] The cruiser's ominous presence raised from the *Charleston Courier* a salvo aimed at the Republican president whose parsimonious policies encouraged belligerent interference with the nation's neutral trade.[6] But the Napoleonic navy was needed elsewhere, and after diverting her crew and enriching her officers with this amusing interlude, the cruiser departed. A few weeks later the glorious lowcountry spring brought the inglorious news that the *Philadelphia* with a crew of 300 had been driven aground in a Mediterranean gale and subsequently captured by Tripolitans. This drew from the *Courier* another indignant essay on Jeffersonian stinginess that weakened the navy and deprived American ports of the protection of such "noble vessels."[7] Increasingly concerned over Charleston's neglected fortifications, the city council petitioned the legislature for improvements, but the fall session adjourned without providing any.

Even a hefty appropriation, though, could not have prevented an incident that took place the following spring and brought home to South Carolina the worsening state of international relations. In June 1805 a French privateer cruising off the Charleston bar seized the inbound merchantman *Two Friends*, a Charleston vessel burdened with a rich cargo of spring and summer goods for the state. After sending passengers ashore on a pilot boat, the privateer escorted the *Two Friends* southward toward the French prize court at Guadaloupe. The capture caused a sensation in Charleston, where its impact on numerous merchants was "injurious in the extreme." Flaming editorials in the *Courier* fairly roasted President Jefferson for pursuing policies that left American commerce exposed to lawless outrage.[8] Further developments in the *Two Friends* affair signaled a new departure in British policy. Word came in July that both privateer and prize had been taken by the British brig *Hunter* on the Florida coast; but to the dismay of Charlestonians, instead of returning the *Two Friends* to its owners, the *Hunter* dispatched vessel and cargo to Jamaica for eventual condemnation.[9] The Anglo-American rapprochement was over.

The shift in British policy that struck the neutral carrying trade without warning in the early summer of 1805 pivoted on Sir William Scott's May decision in the *Essex* case in the High Court of Admiralty. The question at issue was whether a "broken voyage" constituted an exception to the British "Rule of 1756," which held that trade between a colony and its mother country that was closed to neutral carriers in time of peace could not be opened to neutrals in time of war. The British had arbitrarily invoked the rule during the Great War for Empire to prevent neutrals from entering the normally exclusive French colonial trade and thereby releasing the French merchant fleet for belligerent employment. When British policy revived the unilateral doctrine during the Napoleonic Wars and enforced it with naval power, neutrals engaged in the trade adopted the device of the broken voyage, carrying French produce to a neutral port, paying customs duties on it, then receiving a rebate on the duties paid and reexporting the cargo to its original destination. Justice Scott in the High Court of Admiralty had ruled the broken voyage a legitimate exception to the Rule of 1756 in the *Polly* case in 1800. Afterwards American merchantmen and other neutrals enjoyed a shipping bonanza in the French colonial trade. Now Scott condemned the *Essex* by redefining his earlier decision so that the mere payment of duties in a neutral port no longer excepted the carrier from British seizure and condemnation, and the war against neutral commerce was underway.[10]

A lively discussion of British policy and neutral rights in the Charleston press brought young William Lowndes into the public forum for the first time. During the spring and early summer of 1806, the *Courier* published two series of essays that took opposing sides on the issue. Charleston Federalist William Loughton Smith offered a sympathetic defense of British policy and an able attack on the foreign policy of the Jefferson administration, published over the pseudonym "Phocion," the

Greek general and public leader of Plutarch's *Lives* who suffered ill treatment at the hands of his countrymen for giving them good but unpopular advice on foreign policy.[11] Lowndes countered with a closely reasoned defense of neutral rights based on fundamental principles of national independence and international commerce. To underscore his republican perspective, he selected an appropriately plain pseudonym, "Planter."[12] As the Planter essays provide the first and only detailed evidence of Lowndes's approach to public issues and his argumentative style prior to his entry into Congress in 1811, the discussion merits examination.

In defending England's aggressive application of the Rule of 1756, Smith relied on arguments previously laid down by James Stephen in his pamphlet *War in Disguise: or, The Frauds of the Neutral Flags*, published in England in late 1805. A member of the House of Commons and "spiritual father of the most aggressive attacks on American commerce," Stephen had designed his argument as the quasi-official defense of British policy on neutral shipping.[13] Subsequently published as a series in the New York *Evening Post* and again as a pamphlet in Charleston in March 1806, the work was familiar to both Smith and Lowndes.[14] America's neutral rights had received a vigorous defense from Secretary of State James Madison, whose argument had circulated through the country following its publication in pamphlet form in January 1806. Of the two, Stephen's greater clarity gave the advantage to *War in Disguise*, for Madison's effort suffered from "massive unreadability."[15] Lowndes apparently made free use of Madison's pamphlet, although his argument was essentially a rebuttal of Stephen, who had written in reply to Madison's views expressed in diplomatic correspondence earlier in 1805. Madison had hoped some talented lawyer would undertake the refutation of this British doctrine, and Lowndes was one of the first to attempt it.[16] Smith added to Stephen's argument the element of domestic politics, reducing his essays at times to the level of political diatribe. Lowndes adopted a more elevated tone and, until his last number, confined his essays to the subject of neutral rights.

Professing impartiality while betraying the strong pro-British bias of Charleston Federalists, Smith attacked Jeffersonian foreign policy. He condemned in particular recent legislation authorizing the president to withhold at his discretion the application of federal law against the belligerents, and he accused the president of brandishing this authority as an ultimatum during negotiations. The United States, according to

Smith, had never before claimed the right to engage in the trade of another nation, and Jefferson only claimed it for the purpose of "embroiling us with England." With President Jefferson and Secretary Madison espousing one set of principles before coming to office and another since then, administration policy, he said, was a scandal of inconsistency. Whatever trace of consistency one might discover reflected the president's longstanding hostility toward the British and his notorious sympathy for the revolutionary French.[17]

On the issue of neutral rights, Smith adhered closely to Stephen's thesis. He maintained throughout that Great Britain's vigorous enforcement of the Rule of 1756 was not in violation of international law. Because neutrals, especially the United States, had gained admission to the French colonial trade during the present war and as a consequence of it, American ships engaged in this direct trade were subject to the rule and therefore open to legitimate seizure and confiscation. The artificial device of breaking a voyage by unloading and reloading in a neutral port prior to delivery at the actual destination the British had patiently tolerated until this trade with her enemy began to threaten her very existence as a nation.[18] Convinced that the issue was so crucial to British survival that England would never yield to American demands without resort to arms, Smith warned that Jefferson's stubborn policy could only lead to calamitous war.[19] Smith buttressed his argument throughout the series with quotations from selected authorities on maritime law and illustrated points with frequent analogies, assuming the British point of view and finding that the United States would adopt the same or similar methods if its existence were similarly threatened.[20]

The first number of the Planter series appeared on April 23, 1806. Lowndes announced his intention to defend neutral rights without succumbing to Anglophobia:

> Let enemies' property be seized whenever it can be found; let the prostituted flag even of an imperial convoy be lifted to discover it; let it be torn by persevering investigation from the grasp of hired perjury. But the question which I propose to discuss is, whether articles which cannot be included in a list of contraband from any supposed utility or aptitude for war, and which are proved to be neutral property in a neutral vessel, can justly become objects of belligerent seizure, merely because purchased in ports of the adverse belligerent which had been closed upon the purchaser during peace:

—Whether the novelty of a trade under it (if commenced in war) is unlawful. This I consider a just statement of the controversy ... which threatens to marshall for mutual hostility the forces of two nations united in language, in blood, and I think in interest.[21]

Citation of authorities on maritime law, he said, could not justify the British Rule of 1756 nor admiralty decisions regarding the broken voyage because these were new questions of law uncontemplated by currently accepted authorities, Hugo Grotius, Samuel Pfufendorf, and others. (Lowndes's view of these authorities is discussed in greater detail later in the chapter.) England, "which usually sustains in their utmost rigor, the laws of war," did not consistently enforce her pretended right to exclude neutrals from the colonial trade of a belligerent power, "but its whole conduct can be vindicated only on the supposition of its being a right which has ... been relaxed but never abdicated." If England were conceded the right to prohibit this commerce, "who can consistently deny her that to regulate and to limit it?" On this supposition alone depended all the other British pretensions.[22]

Lowndes devoted his second number to those points he was willing to concede readily. He granted that any neutral trade with colonies of a belligerent power served to make the colonials more comfortable and patient with the war, and in this sense such trade could be construed as aid to the belligerent in wartime. He conceded further that in cases where a strong likelihood existed that a colony would be starved into capitulation, the belligerent had the right to confiscate cargoes shipped to that colony. He was also willing to concede that admitting neutrals to colonial trade during time of war could have the effect of relieving for war service ships and men of the belligerent otherwise needed to maintain its colonial trade. Lowndes then concluded that in effect each of these points could be applied to the British trade as well as the French and "would equally proscribe all neutral trade with either of the belligerents."[23]

At this point, when Lowndes had hardly defined his position and laid the basis for future argument, "Sedley" interrupted with a few remarks laced with sarcasm:

[W]hen we see a writer coming forward in all the pride of superiority and like Canute, pretending to command the intrusive waves to forbear their encroachments, we cannot but think his attempt deserves as severe reproof as that which the fawning sycophants received from their offended monarch. After this subject has engaged the pens of the most eminent civilians, without producing unanimity of opinion, "A Planter" promises to illumine our dull brains by his essays. But incredulity must be indulged in a smile, and Skepticism exclaims, "The ample proposition that Hope makes in all designs begun on earth below, fails in its promised largnes [sic]."

Accusing Lowndes of greater concern for elegance of style than correct principles, Sedley dismissed as idle sport the "war of words" on the subject, advised that the only decisive solution was in resort to force, and suggested that Lowndes "quit this studious retirement of the cloister for the anarchy of the tented field."[24] Lowndes was not insensitive to criticism but rarely allowed it to disturb his composure. Absorbing the sting of Sedley's barbs, he took no notice of the attack and in succeeding numbers continued with the elaboration of his thesis.

The third Planter essay defined *War in Disguise* as "an attempt to sustain by reasoning an argument erected only on power." The British case, Lowndes argued, rested on two assumptions: first, that neutrals had no right to benefit from circumstances produced by war; and second, that opening colonial ports during war which had been closed during peace must be attributed to the inability of the mother country to supply her colonies or to export their products.

> Have neutrals then a right to derive benefit from a state of things which is a direct consequence of a state of war? Has America the right by her utmost exertions to acquire the carrying trade of countries now neutral, though that trade be supposed to have been formerly monopolized by Holland, whose disastrous hostilities have alone thrown it upon our enterprise? Has Prussia a right ... to supply France with the manufactures formerly procured from England? These questions evidently admit not of different answers. A negative on the last would shock too rudely the interest and the common sense of every neutral power. An honest Yes must mark with reprobation the doctrine of the British judge.[25]

Regarding the British claim that a belligerent during war could not convey to neutrals "a right to institute a trade to his colonies not permitted during peace," Lowndes pointed out that England herself proposed to violate this principle in article twelve of the Jay Treaty, which would have admitted the United States, had the article met its approval, into the British West Indies trade.

> Answer then, ye advocates of British consistency, on what ground is the right of instituting a trade to the colonies of her enemies denied by that government, which invited us by a costly sacrifice to purchase even partial admission to its own? If we have no right now to trade to Martinique, we should yet have had none, though that article had been ratified, to trade to Jamaica. But perhaps the rule in question is to be wielded only by British tribunals.... Ambition is in either case the unceasing promoter. The sole end is in either case inordinate aggrandizement.[26]

Through numbers four and five Lowndes continued his closely reasoned argument without provoking further reader comment until May 9, 1806, when news of another sensational incident arrived from New York. The ship of war *Leander* from the British blockading squadron off Sandy Hook had fired without warning on the American sloop *Richard*, killing a member of the crew.[27] Receipt of the news in Charleston as elsewhere provoked strong hostility toward the British and sent the editor of the *Courier* into a transport of indignation directed toward President Jefferson and the impotence of his foreign policy: "Our ports are blockaded, and our citizens murdered at the mouths of our harbors, by foreign ships of war, and there exists not in the country a power to prevent or chastize them! Oh Washington! thou great and illustrious patriot, how would thy gallant soul have been grieved, if, during thy life, thy Country had been so insulted, and its innocent, inoffending citizens had been butchered in our harbors by lawless outrage!"[28]

Except perhaps for his exclamations to the departed Washington, already deified by the Federalists, the editor expressed the sentiments of most Charlestonians, for the incident caused a substantial shift in public opinion. Indicative of this change was Sedley's writing in to the *Courier* to admit the correctness of Lowndes's arguments and to denounce "the sophistry of menial advocates" such as Smith.[29] Nevertheless, the Phocion essays continued to the end of May.[30] Thereafter Lowndes found his Planter argument unopposed, the pro-British advocates having quietly retired from the contest. This did not, however, prevent his carrying the argument to its conclusion.

Through succeeding numbers Lowndes tied the knots of logic ever tighter in demonstrating that the same rule of self-preservation which Smith had invoked in justification of the Rule of 1756 would operate more directly to justify impressment of American seamen; that a relaxation of a right in favor of one belligerent would constitute an injury to the other; that there was no difference in the nature of injury caused by neutral trade begun in wartime and that begun at any other time; that the direct neutral trade between a colony and the mother country was lawful; and finally, that England could not be justified in confiscating a neutral vessel in consequence of any act committed before it had left the ports of its sovereign.[31]

In his concluding essay, published on July 9, 1806, Lowndes forcefully underscored the basic flaw in Smith's argument:

> The pretensions of England which you have defended can be sustained only on principles, which are equally capable of justifying the total destruction of our commerce. They cannot rest on the authority of impartial and distinguished publicists. In the retrograde motion which their admission would produce, nations would anew involve themselves in that belligerent tyranny which the philosophical spirit of two centuries had in some degree dissipated. When these obvious reflections shall be thrown into one scale, your ingenuity and your knowledge may fail in giving preponderance to the other.
>
>   A PLANTER[32]

Neither Smith nor anyone else attempted to answer Lowndes's Planter articles, with the single exception of Sedley's brief retort early in the series. Smith ridiculed his numerous critics in general terms in his last Phocion essay on May 31, but made no specific reference to Planter or his argument. A number of others, "Actius," "Anti-Brittanicus," "The American," "Cincinnatus," "Citizen," and "Junius" contributed to the discussion a mixture of Latin quotations, superficiality, condescension, ridicule, arrogance, and occasionally unorthodox grammar, but nothing toward the refutation of Planter. The only printed praise the Planter articles received came in a passing comment in an essay devoted to another subject.[33] To Lowndes the lack of public response to his effort was disappointing in the extreme: "These numbers were received with an indifference much more mortifying than the most insolent opposition— They were not refuted, they were not criticized, they were not probably read. I have consoled myself by considering that the discussion of a point in the laws of nations can never be rendered interesting to the body of the people except accompanied by frequent digressions which my plan did not permit."[34]

The plan that Lowndes sustained throughout the series excluded classical allusions, contemporary politics, frequent analogies, appeals to emotion, and other digressions from the rule of reasoned argument. As mentioned earlier, he excluded as well the citation of seventeenth-century authorities on international law on the ground that they had not covered such issues as the present one in their writings. The whole question of neutrality had been a hazy concept until well into the eighteenth century,[35] and the present dispute, Lowndes argued, represented a new departure in matters of international law, requiring examination not on the basis of past authority but on its own merits. Moreover, Cicero had taught that all law must meet the criterion of "right reason," and this standard of measurement was the one denominator common to all the great writers on international law from Albericus Gentilis to Hugo Grotius to Samuel Pfufendorf to Emmerich de Vattel. Whether expressed as right reason, natural reason, natural law, the law of nature, equity, fairness, or common sense, the fundamental standard in their writings never varied.[36] Gentilis, who strongly influenced Grotius, whose thought in turn dominated subsequent discussion of international law, held the Roman view that law was not a fixed set of principles but a living thing subject to change with changing conditions and circumstances. The test of reason, however, remained constant.[37] While Lowndes declined to accept arguments based on their writings as relevant to the current issue, he accepted their common approach to the issues they discussed. His principal contribution to the discussion of neutral rights was not the ideas he articulated, many of which Madison had argued before, but the "Ciceronian" clarity of his articulation.[38] What Lowndes ultimately learned from this debate Pfufendorf had already stated in another context: the problem of reconciling international differences on the basis of right reason lay in deciding whose reasoning was right.[39] And as subsequent events were to show, Lowndes saw the only alternative to right reason in the dispute over America's neutral rights as a resort to war.

By way of explaining apparent public indifference to the Planter series, and probably reflecting that their style would more readily have suited the Philomathean Society debates, Lowndes confessed, "After all, though as An argument I think well of the Planter, it was not adapted to its purpose, it was not adapted to the readers of a newspaper."⁴⁰ A better explanation might have been the universal tendency toward silent approval and vocal opposition. The critical response to Phocion was enough to confirm the popularity of Planter's position without public declarations of approval. It also heralded political difficulties for Smith in the fall elections and continued support for Lowndes among the Charleston electorate.

In September anonymous subscribers resumed the practice of nominating candidates for office through tickets published in the local papers. The *Courier* published two tickets on September 23, then took a new departure. Explaining that he had received far too many tickets to print, the editor advised that "writing out lists of competent persons for legislative duty is not the way to ensure the election of good and able Representatives." He urged his subscribers instead to busy themselves in getting out the vote on election day.⁴¹ Federalist apathy, subjected to post-election criticism in 1804, now drew repeated comment from the *Courier* without specific reference to party. Having abandoned the practice of printing all tickets submitted, the *Courier* printed on October 7 a list of thirty-three candidates for the legislature compiled from the tickets received by that date, omitting the names of those who had declined. Only in the last days of the newspaper campaign did the editor relent; he printed four more tickets, repeating the last on election day. The *Charleston Times* without public announcement followed the *Courier*'s example, publishing tickets so sparingly that only fifteen had appeared in its pages by election day.⁴² On the other hand, the Republican *City Gazette*, like the democratic constituency it represented, opened its columns to all submissions and printed a total of forty-two tickets.⁴³

The decision of Charleston's most conservative newspaper to depart in 1806 from the customary practice of publishing all the tickets submitted to it, printing a summary instead, precludes comparative study of the published tickets. Nevertheless, the tickets published give a fair indication of relative strength. Lowndes, for example, was recommended in twenty-eight of the forty-two tickets printed in the *City Gazette*, or two-thirds of the total; in eleven of fifteen published by the *Times*, again a two-thirds majority; and on all of the abbreviated number supplied by the *Courier*. Excluding the *Courier*, these figures are consistent with his final position in the election returns, in which he finished sixth among the fifteen elected candidates.⁴⁴ Considering his top-ranking position in the returns of 1804 and the growing strength of the Republican majority afterwards, the pattern of ticket support along with the election results placed William Lowndes in 1806 outside the mainstream, though not quite on the conservative fringe, of the Jeffersonian movement.

The election of 1806 furnished additional evidence of the character of South Carolina politics along with a clearer picture of the tendency to associate candidates for state office with national parties. On October 12 the *Courier* published a dual list of candidates "which are intended to be supported by the citizens of the different parties . . . omitting the names of those gentlemen who are on both of them." Submitted by "A CONSISTENT REPUBLICAN," the list was arranged in the following manner:

Federal Republican Ticket	Democratic Republican Ticket
Member of Congress	
William Loughton Smith	Robert Marion
Representatives	
John Dawson, jun.	William Rouse
John Rutledge	John Geddes
James Lowndes	Thomas Lehre
Adam Gilchrist	John Williamson
Henry Deas	Moses Glover
William Drayton	Doctor P. Moser
Keating Lewis Simons	Thomas Hinds
William Lowndes	Peter Freneau
Thomas Baker	Thomas Bennett, jun.
Thomas Campbell Cox	John Horlbeck, jun.
James M. Ward	Henry Bailey
Henry H. Bacot	William Clements

Judging from this dual list, of the legislative candidates elected in 1806, eight were associated in the public mind with the Federalist tradition: William Drayton, Henry Deas, William Lowndes, John Dawson, Jr., Keating Simons, James Lowndes, James M. Ward, and Thomas Baker; four were identified as Jeffersonians: William Rouse, Peter Freneau, Thomas Hinds, and John Horlbeck, Jr.; and three were acceptable to both political factions though clearly identified with neither: Langdon Cheves, Henry Middleton, and William Lee.[45]

The party alignment of legislative candidates suggested by CONSISTENT REPUBLICAN was confirmed by rival tickets that the *Courier* and the *City Gazette* recommended in the last days of the newspaper campaign. On

October 13 and 14, the *Courier* published in its editorial column along with editorial support identical tickets that included every winning candidate except the four identified as "Democratic Republicans" in the dual list. The *City Gazette* reversed this pattern, supporting through identical tickets published in the last three days of the campaign all the successful candidates for state office except the eight "Federal Republicans." The final election returns are equally suggestive. Cheves, Middleton, and Lee, who were identified with neither party, finished first, second, and third respectively. "Federal Republicans" claimed positions four through eight (Drayton, Deas, William Lowndes, Dawson, and Simons), followed by James Lowndes (tenth), Ward (eleventh), and Baker (fourteenth). The "Democratic Republicans" were clustered near the bottom, with Rouse, Freneau, Hinds, and Horlbeck ranking in order ninth, twelfth, thirteenth, and fifteenth.[46]

From this distribution of votes it seems conclusive that the Federalist party no longer functioned as an active organization at the state level of politics in South Carolina. Only William Loughton Smith, the party's congressional candidate, and James Lowndes, James Ward, Keating Simons, and Henry Deas among successful candidates for state office were well-known members of the Federalist party; yet all were described as "Federal Republicans," the conservative wing of the new Jeffersonian order. The poor showing of the "Democratic Republicans" suggests that active membership in the local party organization was perhaps more limited in 1806 than has been supposed and clearly did not include Cheves, Middleton, and William Lowndes, all of whom came to be considered Republicans. The two-to-one victory of "Federal Republicans" over their more democratic rivals, and the middle-range showing of the former in the election returns, can be misleading. Rather than showing evidence of Jeffersonian weakness or continued Federalist strength, the election results reflected the conservative character of lowcountry leadership within the Jeffersonian movement. Use of the contradictory misnomer "Federal Republican" was particularly revealing, demonstrating the difficulties inherent in attempts to relate traditionally conservative lowcountry politics to a national party with a liberal orientation. Actually, it appears that, except for the four "Democratic Republicans," virtually all the successful Charleston candidates attempted to remain aloof from party, as the popularity of the three front-runners implies. The assignment of party labels to the remainder resulted more from the individual candidate's personal viewpoint than direct party affiliation.

Federalist indecision wasted whatever chance William Loughton Smith might have had in the congressional race. Formerly a United States senator and minister to Portugal, Smith had actively promoted his prospects since returning to Charleston in 1804.[47] Following the critical reception of his Phocion essays, however, he appeared reluctant to challenge Robert Marion for Charleston's congressional seat. As a result, the Federalists put forward James Lowndes to contest Marion, and the *Courier* made the announcement on October 6, adding that Smith was not a candidate for the post. James Lowndes's candidacy lasted all of three days. When Smith reconsidered his decision and announced for the office on October 9, four days before the election, James Lowndes, "to his immortal honor be it recorded, withdrew his name."[48] Now the opposition press filled its columns with attacks on Phocion. Although several of his supporters denied that Smith had authored the series, the author himself remained silent on the subject. He made a final attempt to recover lost ground with a full page ad published in the *Courier* on election day, billing himself as the "Washington Republican Candidate." It was the familiar case of too little, too late; Marion won, carrying the city parishes by the slender margin of 38 votes, while James Lowndes took what consolation he could from his reelection to the state legislature.[49]

If national politics had not yet made a serious impact on the internal affairs of South Carolina, the changing nature of the European wars had become a source of steadily mounting concern. In the closing months of 1805 the British at Trafalgar swept the French from the seas but left Napoleon, after Austerlitz, virtual master of the continent. Unable to meet for a decision, the two great antagonists turned to economic warfare, each attempting to reduce the other to submission by cutting off or controlling its international trade. A Napoleonic decree in 1806 was answered by a British Order in Council and the process was repeated the next year, with the effect that neutrals could not trade with one without risk of retaliation from the other. Both inflicted serious damage on America's neutral carrying trade, which operated mostly out of Atlantic seaports northeast of Philadelphia. While the northeastern shipping trade lost hundreds of ships through seizure and confiscation and thousands of men forced into British naval service, the confiscated cargoes often originated in southeastern ports. Powerless to prevent these blatant violations of America's neutral rights, the Jefferson administration attempted to legislate the belligerents into a more respectful attitude by restricting their trade into American ports. This policy found its strongest support in the agricultural South, while the loudest complaints came from shipping interests and Federalist critics along the northeastern seaboard.[50]

Sentiment in Charleston was generally supportive of administration policy, with the *Courier*'s disposition to carp at anything Jeffersonian being balanced by the persistent loyalty of the *City Gazette*. Reaction from lowcountry conservatives such as William Lowndes was skeptical. After defending neutral rights in his Planter essays, Lowndes probably spoke for most of his peers when he expressed reservations concerning the policy of economic coercion:

> [W]hile I attempt to vindicate the claims of America, as founded in justice, and in policy, let me not be understood as pretending to vindicate the conduct of our government—It is a subject on which I write with reluctance. I am not insensible to the humiliation of my country; but believing our administration correct in its construction of our rights, we should endeavor to afford every aid and facility to the means which its wisdom has provided for their enforcement. The commercial restrictions which our Congress has opposed to the cannon of England appear to me, I confess, no substantial rampart. That the same quantity of goods as usual will be imported, and that the manufacturers and the merchants of England will derive from them very nearly the same profits as heretofore, I conscientiously believe. . . . all reflecting men must expect nothing but disappointment from this idle experiment.

Criticism of administration policy did not imply disagreement with administration objectives; but even a popular administration was not immune from the consequences of policy failure:

> [W]hatever opinions may be entertained in relation to the restrictions on our commerce with England, it is important that we should be convinced of the right which they were intended to protect. If when wielded by the general patriotism of the country, they prove to be mere weapons of lath, which flattered us into a confidence dangerous to our safety; if they are beheld by our enemies with contempt, and by our friends with bitter mortification, the men who proposed them may employ different measures, or the country may employ different men.[51]

Through all the years of Anglo-American tension, as economic coercion shifted from nonimportation to embargo to nonintercourse to Macon's Bill Number Two and on into the war itself, Lowndes's low opinion of the policy never changed. From any view of economics he considered the restrictive system unwise and effective enforcement impossible, but his strongest objection was that "its advantages would be too dearly purchased by presenting our government to its citizens in the constant attitude of repressing their enterprise, and punishing their industry."[52] He was ever willing to take up arms in defense of national rights, however, and in June 1807 the necessity appeared at hand when the *Leopard* mauled the *Chesapeake* off the Virginia capes.

As described in the last chapter, the national outrage the *Chesapeake-Leopard* incident provoked was mirrored in high excitement and indignation among Charlestonians. Mass meetings threatened war, demanded immediate reparation, and evoked pledges of lives, fortunes, and sacred honor in defense of American rights. Public prayer went up from lifelong Federalists: "Oh, sacred manes of Washington! Oh, hallowed spirit of Columbia's first and greatest Son! impart to our Councils that wisdom, judgment, fortitude and perseverence; that disinterested and pure patriotism which . . . so eminently characterized your illustrious career!"[53] City authorities lamented acts of violence against friends of Great Britain. Colors halted half-mast and citizens wore black crepe in "respectful tribute to the memory of the unfortunate seamen who were slaughtered on board the *Chesapeake*." When a lone dissenter from the public display of mourning contemptuously brought out his dog with crepe wrapped around the animal's leg, a mob seized him and "pumped him in the public streets."[54] The president's call for 5,700 additional South Carolina militia to be equipped and ready for marching at a moment's notice sent new units springing up all over the state, including the Washington Light Infantry of Charleston captained by William Lowndes. Speculation on the point of British invasion in the event of war ranged from New Orleans to Canada; and when a supply of cannon, muskets, and military stores arrived from Washington in August, General Charles Cotesworth Pinckney himself came out to supervise the military preparations.[55]

Public excitement over the threat of war soon diminished, however. Lowcountry belligerence waned rapidly in a stifling August heat wave and a September epidemic that took 328 lives, and then it disappeared altogether with congressional passage of the Embargo Act in December.[56] The state legislature strongly endorsed President Jefferson's leadership in December with the passage of two resolutions. On the first, that Jefferson "deserved well of his Country," William Lowndes voted with 84 colleagues in the majority. Only Benjamin Huger of Prince George Winyah and five "Federal Republicans" from Charleston disagreed: Dawson, William Drayton, James Lowndes, Simons, and Ward. The second resolution recommended Jefferson for a third term. A motion to strike out this resolution lost 21 to 73. Of the Charleston delegation, Cheves, Lee, and every "Federal Republican" except Baker and including William Lowndes voted against a third term.[57] Both Lowndes and Cheves evidently opposed a third term on the principle implied in Washington's precedent, but what appeared to be anti-Jefferson unity among Charleston's "Federal Republicans" would not be forgotten in the Charleston elections of 1808.

Charlestonians who expected termination of the foreign slave trade to quicken local commerce in the new year viewed with bitter irony implementation of the embargo on January 1, 1808. No sooner did the slave trade end than the export machinery shut down. Thereafter rice began to pile up in the factors' warehouses as cotton and forest products stacked up on the wharves, and incoming merchantmen, unable to secure cargo for export, dumped into the port city hundreds of unemployed seamen, "sturdy beggars" who wandered about the Charleston streets "begging for four pence to buy bread." The city council formed a committee to find work for the sailors, and this group persuaded masters of naval vessels in the harbor to give the men temporary employment on a daily basis.[58] The general stagnation of commerce encouraged several Charlestonians to establish the Homespun Company, a textile mill, to take advantage of federal restrictions on British imports. Correspondence from the upcountry told of similar hardships suffered by residents of the interior districts.[59]

Although Carolinians in general lamented the effects of the embargo, they gave overwhelming support to this latest expression of Jeffersonian policy. This was nowhere better illustrated than in the special session of the legislature in June 1808. After the sectional compromise on representation had been approved, James McKibben of Newberry offered several resolutions. The first called on every member of the House to wear to the next session "the manufacture of their own State," and the others declared that the president and Congress "deserved well of their Country" and pledged "at all hazards" to support "the late measures of our General Government." By unanimous vote the House adopted all four resolutions, giving the Jefferson administration a vote of confidence unprecedented in South Carolina.[60]

Without recording his reasons, William Lowndes did not run for office in 1808 either in Charleston or elsewhere. Nor did the usual published tickets mention his name. It is true the omission of his name could have resulted from the growing tendency of the *Courier* and *City Gazette* to publish quasi-official tickets as election day approached; but the *Courier*, promoting essentially the same group it had endorsed in 1806 and all the conservative incumbents, certainly would have recommended Lowndes had there been a chance he might be persuaded to accept. His return to the contest the following February fairly rules out the possibility that he expected defeat and retired from politics to avoid it. The only clue he ever gave that could explain his political disappearance in the fall of 1808 was a statement he made a decade later referring to attacks of his old illness as "decennial."[61]

Whatever his reasons, Lowndes's decision not to consider election in 1808 probably spared him the embarrassment of defeat. Comment in both the *Courier* and *City Gazette* hinted at a Republican party sweep. Prior to 1808 all balloting had taken place downtown at the Exchange, but the legislature had recently authorized a second poll at the Market and a third at the old "Tobacco Inspection" up on Charleston Neck, both of which would make voting more convenient for the more democratic element of the Charleston electorate.[62] Contributors to the *Courier* repeatedly criticized the change, warning the election managers to demand proof of property qualification on the right to vote. Numerous other complaints focused on apathy among conservatives and electioneering tactics of the Republican party faithful.[63] Cheves and Middleton evidently had moved into the Republican camp, for the *Courier* no longer found them worthy of endorsement. The *City Gazette* stressed party discipline, urging Republicans to vote the party ticket printed in the editorial column to insure the choice of Madisonian electors in the next legislature.[64] What remained of the Federalist party promoted General C. C. Pinckney for president and persuaded Thomas Lowndes to contest Marion in the congressional race, disdaining William Loughton Smith who dramatized his apostasy by entering, withdrawing, and finally throwing his support to the Republican Marion.

The election results gave a resounding victory to "those exclusive Republicans who take the *Aurora* as their oracle and Mr. Jefferson as their God."[65] Led by Cheves and Middleton, the party won every seat in the Charleston delegation, sending to the legislature four planters, three lawyers, a blacksmith, a bricklayer, a druggist, a printer, a storekeeper, a tanner, a "mechanick," and a final member obscure enough to have his occupation go unlisted in the city directory.[66] Numerical results, published for the first time in this election, revealed the extent of party discipline. Between Cheves, who finished first in the balloting with 802 votes, and Dr. Philip Moser, who finished last among the winning candidates, there was a difference of exactly 100 votes. The nearest conservative challenger was Federalist Henry Deas with 440.[67] In the congressional race and the contest for state senator, both Republicans routed their opponents by virtually identical two-to-one margins in the city parishes. Marion defeated Thomas Lowndes 775 to 391 while John Drayton won over Thomas Roper 770 to 389.[68] Taken altogether, the returns show that roughly two-thirds of the active Charleston electorate voted the Republican party ticket in 1808, demonstrating the correlation between the rise of organized parties and the decline of traditional patterns of political deference.

The older Lowndes brothers headed into permanent political retirement after this election, while three hundred of the Republican party faithful celebrated their victory at Meed's Hotel. The impressive display of party discipline should have discouraged William Lowndes, for clearly the days of patrician politics in Charleston were over. But his own politics never having embraced Federalism, he determined to reenter the political arena.

The opportunity came when the legislature in December elected John Drayton governor and Langdon Cheves attorney general of the state, opening up a Senate seat and a House seat in the Charleston delegation. As the by-election approached in February 1809, the usual anonymous subscribers nominated Federalist Henry Deas and political newcomer James Kennedy to contest the Senate post, and named William Lowndes to oppose banker William Turpin, who was making his debut in local politics, for the seat in the House. Shortly before the election, "FRANKLIN" in the *City Gazette* avowed his intention to vote for Kennedy and Turpin, "both of them known to be inflexible republicans," despite his admiration for Deas and Lowndes, "the federal gentlemen proposed."[69] Others further confused the distinction between a traditional republican and a known Federalist when one subscriber recommended Lowndes for the Senate and another pointed out that he was too young to qualify, suggesting instead, "His friends will therefore do well in supporting HENRY DEAS, esq., as Senator, and him as Representative."[70] In the face of that advice, the Charleston electorate, dominated by the strong

Republican party organization, regarded Lowndes and Deas as common opponents of the party candidates and sent them down to defeat by similar margins. Kennedy won 335 to 189, while Turpin defeated Lowndes by a slightly narrower margin, 308 to 208.[71]

William Lowndes would require no further evidence of the wisdom of republican tradition, which condemned parties and factions as incompatible with civic virtue. Loyalty to party compromised the personal freedom and independent judgment that republicans from time immemorial had considered essential to virtuous public service, and Lowndes knew that the "inflexible republicans" dominating Charleston politics had considered allegiance to party more important than his personal merit and legislative record combined. The narrow confines of partisan politics he always found too stifling to endure, although he was by no means unique in this respect.[72] Lowndes retained a residence in Charleston for the rest of his life, but never again would he offer his name for consideration in any election held in the Charleston District.

The election of 1808 followed by his defeat in 1809 might have driven Lowndes's traditional republican style of politics out of Charleston, but it would not drive Lowndes out of public life. As the election of 1810 approached, he was persuaded to allow his name to be entered as a candidate for Congress from his native district of Colleton. Once he shifted his political base out of Charleston to the lowcountry parishes, where party affiliation had scarcely begun to erode traditional republicanism and established patterns of deference, his political prospects improved while coverage of his congressional bid in the Charleston papers all but disappeared.

Although little detailed information on the South Carolina congressional elections of 1810 is available, enough exists to show that they could hardly be considered a revolution. Of the eight South Carolina incumbents in the national House of Representatives, three were returned. Another, Robert Witherspoon, declined in favor of his brother-in-law, David R. Williams, who replaced him. John C. Calhoun won election unopposed when cousin Joseph Calhoun, the incumbent, followed Witherspoon's example and withdrew in favor of his relative. For the three remaining seats there were only two real contests. In one, Elias Earle defeated Lemuel J. Alston in a struggle between old and bitter enemies, but no current issue was involved.[73] In the other, William Lowndes challenged the incumbent John Taylor of Columbia.

There was more similarity than difference between Lowndes and Taylor. Concerning national issues, both had spoken against the policy of economic coercion and both had advocated a more vigorous defense of America's neutral rights.[74] Moreover, they had served together in the legislature during the sectional controversies over the foreign slave trade and representation reform. Their principal differences related to the source of their political strength and the extent of their affiliation with the Republican party organization. Taylor was an active party man, one of the more important figures in state party councils, and being from Columbia, he would show strength in the upcountry districts. Lowndes, though holding quite similar political views, was indifferent to party affiliation and depended on the more traditional lowcountry parishes for his strongest support. Adoption of universal white manhood suffrage prior to this election should have given, and probably gave, an advantage to Taylor. But since the congressional district extended from St. Bartholomews and other parishes west of Charleston straight up through the heart of the Middle District to Richland and Lexington, Lowndes could expect to benefit from the recent expansion of the lowcountry interest into central South Carolina.

When the election was held on October 8–9, 1810, both Lowndes and Taylor ran well in the sections with which they were most closely identified. In his native parish, Lowndes ran ten to one ahead of Taylor, polling 318 votes to Taylor's 37, and piled up substantial majorities in St. Mathews on the Santee and in the Orangeburg District. Taylor reversed this trend in other upcountry districts, carrying Richland by a vote of 275 to 43 and Lexington by 365 to 75. The final returns, however, revealed that Lowndes had unseated Taylor despite the latter's high standing and influence in the party that then controlled the state.[75]

If the congressional elections of 1810 in South Carolina were not revolutionary, they nevertheless proved to be historic. Among the elected representatives, three were destined for outstanding careers in national government: Langdon Cheves, who had filled an unexpired term in the Eleventh Congress and now won election to the Twelfth; John C. Calhoun, the earnest young planter-lawyer from the upcountry with a captivating charm and an exceptionally powerful mind; and Lowndes himself. Calhoun had risen rapidly in state politics and promised to rise quite as rapidly in Congress. Lowndes had never met Calhoun, although both had studied in the same law firm and had served in the state legislature in succeeding sessions. More than once their paths had crossed, but they would not meet until both arrived in Washington to take their places among the "War Hawks" of the Twelfth Congress.

V
War Hawk

In October 1811 William Lowndes booked passage for Philadelphia on the *South Carolina Packet*, Captain Green. Although the congressman-elect possessed what his contemporaries would call enlarged views on national affairs, he had actually seen very little of the country itself beyond the borders of his home state.[1] Now he planned to spend several days touring about Philadelphia, then hire a carriage for an unhurried trip through the October countryside of Pennsylvania and Maryland and still be able to reach Washington before November 4, the day set for Congress to convene. After Lowndes came aboard accompanied by his manservant Thomas, the *Packet* crossed the bar on October 11 and set sail for Philadelphia.[2] The nine-day voyage gave Lowndes ample time to reflect on the paramount problems facing the nation.

The Twelfth Congress had been summoned to convene a month earlier than usual when President Madison "yielded to considerations drawn from the posture of our foreign affairs,"[3] that is, the failure of economic retaliation, the policy that presidents Jefferson and Madison had employed against England and France since the spring of 1806. Lowndes had anticipated this failure from the beginning, plainly stating in his Planter essays that year his doubts regarding the effectiveness of commercial retaliation against the major belligerents of the Napoleonic Wars. If he did not actually favor war with England as early as 1806, he left little doubt of his willingness to fight the British following the *Chesapeake* outrage in 1807, when he helped to organize and accepted command of the Washington Light Infantry of Charleston.

Even so, Lowndes agreed with the Jeffersonian construction of America's neutral rights and gave loyal support to the succession of pacific measures devised for their defense. In 1807 he publicly endorsed the embargo, but he was probably not surprised that it failed to gain its object nor that it generated widespread disaffection in New England along with economic hardship in all of the exporting states before Congress replaced it with the Non-Intercourse Act on March 1, 1809. Generally understood to be a face-saving gesture allowing Jefferson to retire with a semblance of his restrictive program intact, the new law was dismissed by the *Charleston Courier*, and probably Lowndes as well, as little more than "a *substitute* for the disease."[4] Its notorious weakness lay in how easily it could be evaded. In prohibiting trade with England and France, the law neglected to provide adequate safeguards against indirect trade with the major belligerents, so that a lively commerce in American goods sprang up in the ports of European neutrals.

Events of the spring and summer of 1809 gave Lowndes another opportunity to take a public stand on neutral rights. In April President Madison secured an agreement with David Erskine, the British minister in Washington, withdrawing the Orders in Council. Then by a proclamation of April 19, Madison suspended the Non-Intercourse Act against the British and resumed trade with them effective June 10, 1809. The proclamation and the joyous celebrations it provoked proved premature, however. After more than a thousand ships had sailed carrying $200 million in American produce, much of it before June, the British repudiated the agreement and recalled Erskine.[5]

South Carolinians highly indignant over what they called "British perfidy" quickly rallied to Madison's support. A mass meeting at St. Michael's Church in Charleston on August 29 declared their determination "to support the Union, Constitution, and Rights of the Country." To draw up formal resolutions, the throng elected Governor Charles Pinckney, Keating Simons, William Loughton Smith, Peter Freneau, Lowndes, Langdon Cheves, and a number of other political leaders. The committee reported to another mass meeting on September 5 with a resounding vote of confidence in the Madison administration. Lowndes and his colleagues vowed to silence the bickerings of party, pledging their "lives, fortunes, and sacred honor" in support of the government. Without a dissenting voice the throng roared its approval. The committee forwarded the resolutions on to President Madison and received from him a warm note of thanks.[6]

But the crisis passed. Administration leaders had seriously considered war in 1808 and Madison might have secured a declaration in 1809, a prospect certainly enhanced by the arrogant conduct of Erskine's successor, but neither Jefferson nor Madison was willing to abandon the restrictive system. The following year the Non-Intercourse Act yielded to

Macon's Bill Number Two. When the French appeared willing to rescind their decrees in response to this law, and the British declined to revoke their Orders in Council, Madison again placed England and her dominions under the ban of nonintercourse. British outrage at this turn of events, combined with American anger over the wholesale impressment of American seamen and England's continued abuse of America's neutral rights, heated Anglo-American hostility toward the boiling point. Congress added more fuel to the controversy in March 1811 by imposing further restraints on British trade.

This in brief outline was the posture of America's foreign affairs in the fall of 1811, the galling fruit of half a decade of diplomatic failure and national humiliation. Recent elections had turned out fully one-third of the old Congress, and now from all over the country a new generation of congressmen were descending on Washington. Sick of embargoes and nonintercourse and the whole bankrupt policy of economic coercion, these confident and determined young "War Hawks" shared a common objective: to exact from England a proper respect for the United States as an independent nation, even if it meant war.

William Lowndes arrived at Philadelphia on October 20 and took rooms for himself and Thomas at Mrs. Benson's, a boarding house favored by visiting South Carolinians. Among the Carolinians there Lowndes encountered fellow congressman Langdon Cheves, who was on his way back to Washington with his family, having filled out an unexpired term in the Eleventh Congress during the past winter. Lowndes had the highest respect for Cheves, as much for his character as for his superior talents and prodigious industry, and found his earnest and sincere manner particularly engaging. Even his attempts at humor had a certain awkward charm; as Lowndes explained it, Cheves joked so badly that he always hastened to add that he was only joking.[7] In the conversations between Lowndes and Cheves during their stay in Philadelphia, a genuine friendship grew, one that would gain strength from the mutual concerns and common efforts they would share as fellow congressmen.

This pleasant interlude was interrupted when the weather turned cold and damp, and Lowndes began to suffer attacks of fever and chills accompanied by violent headaches and periodic cold sweats. Alarm mounted when his heartbeat became irregular, causing friends to hurry off a messenger to fetch Dr. Physick, the most renowned physician of Philadelphia. After examining his patient, the doctor pronounced the irregular pulse to be the effect of costiveness and prescribed liberal doses of castor oil and rhubarb. Because of the treatment, or in spite of it, the patient improved enough to travel within a week. Lowndes later described the indisposition as "slight," but the irregular pulse, which always revived memories of his rheumatic childhood, was an ominous sign.[8]

His illness at Philadelphia forced Lowndes to abandon his plan for a leisurely trip to Washington. Instead he took the stage from Philadelphia and found himself traveling from Baltimore "with the elite of the Federalists," as he described congressmen James Emmot of New York and Josiah Quincy of Boston. Lowndes liked the little he saw of Emmot. Of Quincy he saw more and thought less: "He is always looking out for a prettiness in thought or language," he complained to Elizabeth, "always declaiming—he declaims ill; and even his language (which is doubly offensive in a *pretty* speaker) is very inaccurate."[9] Though few would deny that a traveling companion inclined to constant declamation can be trying in the best of circumstances, the usually mild and amiable Lowndes still suffered the effects of his recent illness and would not have encouraged even the company of friends. Whenever he was not feeling well he always preferred to be alone. By the time they reached Washington he had made up his mind that "these stages [were] not the things" for him, and had already begun considering other means of transport back to Carolina when the session should end.[10]

In Washington Lowndes took lodgings about a hundred yards from the Capitol building in a boarding house destined to gain fame in this session as the "War Mess," so named for the prowar sentiments of its boarders. Besides Lowndes, these included Henry Clay of Kentucky, Felix Grundy of Tennessee, Langdon Cheves and John C. Calhoun of South Carolina, and Senator George M. Bibb of Kentucky.[11] The decisive and ambitious Calhoun arrived two days after the session opened, and from their first meeting a firm friendship developed between him and the modest, soft-spoken Lowndes. In a letter to Elizabeth, Lowndes gave his first impression of Calhoun: "Mr. Calhoun of S. Carolina, has joined us within a day or two. I had heard a very favorable character of him; but skeptical as I am on the score of character, this did not at all lessen by preparing me for, the acquaintance of a man, well informed, easy in his manners, & I think amiable in his disposition. I like him already better than any member of our mess & I give his politics the same preference."[12] So rapidly did their friendship develop that within two weeks they were discussing plans to buy a carriage and horses to travel back to Carolina together at the end of the session.

Viewing the South Carolina delegation to the Twelfth Congress in retrospect, one is tempted to believe that fate rather than chance brought together in the War Mess the three young men whose combined efforts could revive the state's sagging influence in national politics.[13] During the heyday of Federalism, South Carolina had wielded through the Rutledge-Pinckney faction considerable influence in national affairs; but since Jefferson had come to power and Charles Pinckney had withdrawn from the national scene, the state had not produced a political figure of truly national potential. The other five representatives in the delegation were more indicative of the drought in political influence the state had suffered over the past decade. William Butler, Thomas Moore, and Richard Winn, all faithful Jeffersonians from the Carolina upcountry, had compiled uniformly undistinguished records since entering the House in 1801; all three would retire with their records virtually intact at the conclusion of this Congress. Elias Earle of the Greenville District had served a term in the Ninth Congress and would serve another in the Thirteenth without improving on the records of his erstwhile upcountry colleagues.[14] Considerably more notable was David R. Williams, the volatile "Thunder and Lightning" congressman from Society Hill northeast of Camden, now in his third and last term in the House. His unrestrained style of debate in the Ninth and Tenth Congresses had attracted a good deal of attention, gaining him perhaps more notoriety than influence along with a reputation for bitter hatred of the British.[15] In contrast to their colleagues in the delegation, Cheves, Calhoun, and Lowndes each possessed attributes of statesmanship and genuine leadership potential, qualities that the national temper in the fall of 1811 would give each of them an opportunity to display.

The Twelfth Congress, containing about seventy new members, convened as scheduled on November 4. Like Lowndes and Calhoun, who were both twenty-nine, and Cheves, who was thirty-five, most of the new men were young, the first generation born since the Revolution. In spite of their youth, however, they brought with them considerable legislative experience gained at the state level. On their very first day in the House they seized control, bypassing the senior men held over from the inactive Eleventh Congress and electing their boldest and most active leader, Henry Clay, to the Speaker's chair. Clay showed a similar disregard for seniority in making committee appointments and, in the process, thrust his South Carolina companions of the War Mess immediately toward the front rank of House leadership. Cheves was given preference. Clay named him chairman of the select Committee on Naval Affairs and second to Chairman Ezekiel Bacon of Massachusetts on the powerful standing Committee of Ways and Means. Calhoun but for his late arrival might also have received a chairmanship; instead Clay assigned him to the second position behind Chairman Peter B. Porter of New York on the important select Committee on Foreign Relations. Lowndes, the least promising of the South Carolina trio at this stage of their careers, was named second to Thomas Newton of Virginia on the Committee of Commerce and Manufactures. David R. Williams became chairman of the select Committee on Military Affairs, with Lowndes assigned to the fourth chair on his committee.[16] Clay stacked all the major committees to favor war unless England redressed America's grievances.

The House assembled the next morning to hear President Madison's opening message to Congress read. Its threatening tone doubtless surprised many who considered the president unalterably averse to war; it certainly warmed the hearts of the more ardent War Hawks. Charging the British with trampling on rights that no independent nation could relinquish, Madison outlined a program of legislation to prepare for war. New laws were needed to fill the ranks of existing military units and augment them with additional forces of volunteers and militia, to expand the production of arms, and to put the Navy in fighting trim. Further, Congress should take action, he said, to enforce compliance with the nation's commercial laws, to protect American commerce and industry, and to provide for a sufficient revenue.[17]

Taking the president's recommendations as a guide, the various committees went into session and remained occupied over the next few weeks with preliminary committee work. Lowndes gave his attention to scores of petitions referred to the Committee of Commerce and Manufactures. All were similar to the first of its kind received this session from William Dean, a merchant of Salem, Massachusetts, praying for permission to import certain goods purchased abroad before Congress passed the Non-Importation Act on March 2, 1811.[18] Lowndes was disposed to grant the petitions and would be prepared to explain why when the matter came before the House later in the session.

Aside from this routine committee work, Lowndes had very little to do of an official nature. The methodical pace of Congress was a far cry from the brief and busy sessions of the South Carolina legislature, and as the weeks wore on the lack of what Lowndes considered meaningful activity began to wear on his patience. "Everything concurs to make me wish to write frequently and I cannot complain of want of leisure to indulge my inclination," he wrote to Elizabeth; "There may be some difficulty in discovering the object we are pursuing, there can be none in seeing that we shall be very long in reaching it, whatever course our politics may run or rather crawl."[19] Again: "I write every Sunday and I shall certainly at no time of the Session be too busy to continue to do so. In fact I do not expect to be at all busy—I have not yet made any other effort at speaking in the house than an aye or no and I am not sure that these will continue to be the only specimens of my eloquence."[20]

Lowndes was only one of many War Hawks uncertain about their objectives and impatient with the slow rate of progress. This was a time of "slow groping towards common ground"; it would be some weeks before opinion among the War Hawks began to crystallize.[21] The Federalist minority were equally uncertain as to what course their opposition would take. As Senator Samuel Dana of Connecticut explained to Timothy Pickering, "the high priest of Federalism," Federalists in both houses of Congress had agreed "to abstain from opposing in debate favorite measures recommended in the President's message—to vote for such measures as might be comfortable to gentlemen's own views in relation to public defence—to allow to others the freedom of opinion which each might claim for himself—not to prevent or delay a decision on the menaced question of war."[22] Federalist indecision thus shifted the burden of opposition leadership to John Randolph of Roanoke and the Old Republicans, the dissident faction of Republican conservatives. The Old Republicans considered themselves alone the true keepers of the old Jeffersonian faith, which dictated a steady reliance on measures to keep the peace and preserve American virtues.[23] Randolph and his faction were prepared to spearhead resistance to the war party, but until the various committees brought in their reports, there was little to do but wait.

Lowndes, in the meantime, was hardly in the best frame of mind for patient waiting for action on the floor of the House. He still had not completely recovered from the indisposition suffered at Philadelphia, and he was beginning to feel the enforced separation from home and family quite strongly. His letters to Elizabeth, usually written by candlelight late at night, frequently revealed the depth of his feelings for his family. He would always inquire at length about the children. Rawlins, their firstborn son, was in his eighth year and, somewhat like his father, was prone to frequent minor ailments. Five-year-old Pinckney was just the opposite, rough-and-tumble and full of mischief. Becky, approaching her second birthday, was just beginning to explore the world beyond her mother's arms. Lowndes always offered suggestions and expressed solicitude for their care and for that of their mother. And soon he confessed to another sickness: "I wish myself at home—the wish is very childish—I know it and I wish myself at home."[24]

But the time was not altogether unpleasant. On the contrary, the War Mess was fast becoming the most congenial one in Washington. In fact, Lowndes found Clay and Calhoun so companionable that he seldom got to bed before midnight. Invited to the White House, he had dinner with "the great man," as he called the diminutive Madison, and he discovered the vivacious Dolley to be charming enough to encourage his attendance at their levees with some regularity. Lowndes went occasionally to other social functions, including a party given by the British minister which the whole War Mess attended, raising eyebrows all over Washington. He visited scenic areas around Washington such as the Falls of the Potomac, and one Saturday he borrowed a horse from Clay and set out on a leisurely ride to Alexandria. With knees high because of stirrups a foot too short for him and the crupper missing, the quixotic rider was not altogether steady in the saddle. Unfortunately the horse was even less steady, for on the way he stumbled, and as he tried for some distance to recover himself the loose saddle got nearly on his neck, and he went down, sending Lowndes sprawling on his face in the road. A fall that might easily have broken his neck luckily had no more serious consequences than bruises and a black eye. With characteristic humor, Lowndes said it looked "much more like the effect of a Virginian fray than a fall from a horse," so he chose not to show his face for a few days.[25] This odd circumstance explains his absence from the House when the first important debate of the session opened.

On November 29 Chairman Peter B. Porter delivered the report of the Foreign Relations Committee. Probably written for the most part by Calhoun because of Porter's "dearth of talents," the report opened the War Hawks' drive for a war declaration against England.[26] It followed the outline of Madison's recent message, reiterating the familiar story of British abuses, and offered six resolutions on preparations necessary for the anticipated conflict. The first called for the ranks of existing military units to be filled; the second would add to them ten thousand regular troops; the third and fourth would authorize the president to accept into service as many as fifty thousand volunteers and to call up state militia units at his discretion; the fifth would repair and put into commission the naval vessels; and the last would permit merchant vessels to arm.[27]

After turning aside a tabling motion by John Randolph, the House on December 6 approved the first resolution 117 to 11, with the entire South Carolina delegation in the majority. Three days later discussion opened on the second resolution to enlist ten thousand new regulars. Now Felix Grundy of the committee invited general discussion on this resolution, terming it the most vital part of the report. At this point the debate began in earnest.

Randolph led off with an assault on the second resolution in particular and the war party in general, grounding his attack on the unconstitutionality of a standing army in peacetime. In attempting rather ineffectually to answer Randolph, Grundy voiced widespread western sentiment by expanding the declared objects of the war to include the invasion of Canada, which he claimed could be easily conquered with the assistance of Canadians anxious to throw off the British yoke.[28] Grundy held impressive credentials as a lawyer and judge, first in Kentucky and more recently in Tennessee, but he was no match for Randolph on this day. His remarks drew from the Virginian one of the best speeches of the debate. As Randolph warmed to his subject, the War Hawks felt the power of his invective and biting sarcasm:

> This war of conquest, a war for the acquisition of territory and subjects, is to be a new commentary on the doctrine that Republicans are destitute of ambition—that they are addicted to peace, wedded to the happiness and safety of the great body of their people. But it seems this is to be a holiday campaign—there is to be no expense of blood, or treasure, on our part—Canada is to conquer herself—she is to be subdued by the principles of fraternity. The people of that country are first to be seduced from their allegiance, and converted into traitors, as preparatory to the making them good citizens. Although he [Randolph] must acknowledge that some of our flaming patriots were thus manufactured, he did not think the process would hold good with a whole community.[29]

Furthermore, the French were as guilty as the British in violating American rights; then why exclude them from the contemplated war? Worse still, the proposed military forces could not be raised and could not win if raised, and worst of all, an invasion of Canada would expose the cities along the whole eastern seaboard to certain destruction.

Richard Stanford of North Carolina echoed Randolph's arguments, while Cheves, Calhoun, and George Troup of Georgia rallied behind Grundy. Calhoun, easily the most effective, did not mince words. He stated bluntly that the resolutions had been recommended not as an empty menace but as deliberate steps in preparation for war. The nation had ample justification for war with England, "so much so as not to require the aid of logic to convince our reason, nor the ardor of eloquence to inflame our passions." Calhoun demonstrated a rare mastery of logical argument by proceeding in relentless fashion to refute Randolph's argument point by point.[30] The performance also served notice that here at last was a House member capable of meeting the brilliant Virginian on equal terms in debate. At times, though, Randolph could be considerably less than brilliant, as he proved on December 16 when he exhausted the House in a three-hour harangue that Lowndes described as "insufferably dull."[31] As soon as Randolph yielded the floor, the previous question was called and carried overwhelmingly, 110 to 22. Once again the South Carolinians all voted with the majority.[32]

The remaining four resolutions were dealt with in short order. The House quickly passed the third, fourth, and fifth by margins substantially the same as the first two. On the fifth, providing for the repair of naval vessels, David R. Williams voted nay, splitting off from the delegation for the first time. On the sixth, which passed a few days later, he was joined by Lowndes, who opposed the arming of merchant vessels on the ground that it placed the war-making power in private hands.[33] With the question thus settled until bills embodying the substance of the resolutions could be brought in, the House on December 24 adjourned for one day to observe Christmas.

Christmas Day in Washington dawned bitterly cold. The Potomac froze in a single night, and though the weather was clear and dry, the freezing winds seemed to Lowndes almost to take away the breath. As luck would have it, fuel for the fires in the War Mess failed them at the worst possible time; the boat bringing their coal sank in the river, and in that arctic weather they found wood a poor substitute. Lowndes apparently attended a Christmas party at the French minister's, enlivened by burgundy and champagne. But he lamented the custom that frowned on his going in boots to social affairs, protesting that "the exposure of a leg unprotected by flesh or leather in this windy place is a very uncomfortable thing."[34] The next day the members were back at work in the drafty House chamber, and, as Randolph would remark on a similar occasion, the southern men could hardly keep out of the fire.

Congress had been in session for almost two months now, yet Lowndes had still not risen to speak on any measure, a fact that began to evoke puzzlement among his friends at home. His old teacher, Dr. Gallagher, was growing impatient if not annoyed at his continued silence: "Why does he not speak? Let him speak and show what he is."[35] Actually Lowndes had already explained to Elizabeth in early December one reason for his reticence:

> I never have spoken, and I think I cannot speak without the expectation (perhaps always a mistaken one) of making some converts, but I am not vain enough to think of making a convert here in public debate. Something in this way is done in conversation; much, I think, has been done by the open declarations of the new members, behind which the timid may rally, and on whose opinions the lazy may in some measure repose; but this is something very different from conviction.[36]

There were other factors besides his natural reticence that Lowndes did not bother to explain. He had developed the custom, probably early in his legislative career, of biding his time in the course of a debate, silently taking the measure of his colleagues and the questions they raised, then rising toward its conclusion to state his own views when their impact could be expected to be strongest. And there was nothing like a wrongheaded argument to overcome his modesty.

On the last day of the year the House took up a bill from the Senate for raising an additional military force of twenty-five thousand men to serve for five years. Speaker Clay himself led in advocating the bill and succeeded in amending it to keep the number of officer appointments in proportion to the number of troops actually raised. Other and similar amendments were added by the time the bill passed through its second reading. When it came up for its third reading on January 3, Daniel Sheffey, a Randolph man from Wythe County in far southwestern Virginia, outlined his faction's objections to the bill. As Sheffey spoke, Lowndes listened in gaunt concentration, jotted down notes from time to time, and determined that his maiden speech in Congress would be a reply to the Virginian's remarks.

Sheffey admitted that the United States had sufficient cause for war with Great Britain, but he concentrated on injuries inflicted by the French. On the declared objects of the war, he charged the war party with deliberate deception. They were not after "the nominal repeal of the Orders in Council, when it was evident it would be unattended with a single practical benefit"; the truth was the War Hawks coveted "the unmolested commerce of France and her dependencies." He likewise condemned the notion of defending national honor:

> Sir, this nation's honor is the prosperity and happiness of the people. I cannot consent to purchase national misery, even should it be accompanied with what gentlemen call national honor. The abstract notions of honor which regulate the conduct of individuals, and which are valuable in private life, ought not to be a rule of action for wise men to whom are committed the affairs of nations—otherwise we might wage perpetual war.[37]

From this point Sheffey traveled over ground already covered by Randolph. Canada could not be conquered, for the men to do it could not be raised, and even if they could, the attempt would expose U.S. coastal cities to certain destruction. The national revenue could not support a standing army of such magnitude, which not only would violate the Constitution but would threaten fundamental liberties. Lowndes paid close attention to this passage:

> Sir, standing armies are always the same; the materials which compose them, and the subordination to which they are subject, fits [sic] them to become part of a machine regulated and moved by those who command them. And their interest generally happens to conflict with the rest of the community. If ever there was an army that possessed patriotism beyond others in their situation, it was the army of our Revolution. And yet I believe, had it not been for the virtues of that man to whom, under Divine Providence, we are indebted for our liberties—whose like, I fear, we shall never again see—the army who fought the battles of our independence would have been made the instrument in consigning us to a military despotism. "But the dark cloud which threatened to extinguish the beams of liberty . . . was dissipated by the guarding genius of our Revolution."[38]

Sheffey closed with the warning that England had never been driven from her purpose and, the War Hawk policy notwithstanding, she would not be driven from it now.

The next day Lowndes waited until Israel Pickens of North Carolina and John Rhea of Tennessee had spoken on the subject before he rose to address the House for the first time. He had not written out his intended remarks in any detail but spoke freely, using brief notes taken during Sheffey's speech as a guideline. An observer noted that "he spoke, however, in so low a tone as to render it impossible distinctly to understand him at a distance."[39] This defect in his speaking style resulted less from modesty than from the childhood illness that constricted normal thoracic growth, physically depriving him of sufficient vocal force in public address. If his voice was weak, Lowndes compensated for it in the clarity and logical force of his rebuttal as he methodically dismantled the opposition argument.

He began by agreeing with Sheffey on one point, that the nation had ample cause for war with Great Britain. From this agreeable opening he proceeded to disagree with practically every other point the Virginian had made, giving special attention to the matter of national honor in phrases that echoed his Planter essays of 1806:

> In acknowledging, sir, that we have cause of war, the gentleman from Virginia denies its object to be either important or attainable. That any importance should be attached to the object on the score of honor, is described as a romantic notion. But in the policy which it dictates, an enlarged view of national interest, usually concurs with a nice sense of national honor. It is impossible to compute the money-value of rights, like those in dispute between England and America. No rule of arithmetic will give you the answer as to the expense at which they may be worth defending. Let them be renounced and the loss will be felt, not for one year, but perhaps for the whole term of our existence as one nation. Let them be renounced, and every remaining right becomes more precarious by the encouragement which is offered for its infraction. Our object then, in resistance to England, is the preservation of that character without which neutrality would be a burden. Its duties would be exacted and its rights forgotten.[40]

On the contemplated invasion of Canada, he rejected the notion that it could never force concessions from the British ministry. As Sheffey had admitted, "[E]ven now it may be doubted whether the interests of England do not require a revocation of [the Orders in Council] while we patiently submit to them." Suppose, then, that the British were to be confronted with an invasion of Canada, "it should seem certain that it must be her interest to repeal them when their continuance involves the additional inconveniences which even the languid war which has been predicted would produce." The mournful prophecy that the proposed army could not be raised and, even if raised, could not secure Canada in less than five years Lowndes dismissed as "too humiliating to be admitted without proof."[41]

Turning to Sheffey's scornful condemnation of the military man in general and the American revolutionary army in particular, Lowndes spoke with deeper feeling. He had always had high regard for the military, even now preferring service in the field to his duties in Congress, and the eloquence of his defense reflects his feelings on the subject:

> From a military usurpation, such as the gentleman so much dreads, we were saved, he says, after the war of the Revolution, by one man. To the merits of General WASHINGTON, my feelings and my judgment equally subscribe. He had a mind too great to be bribed by title or by power. If a crown had been within his reach, he would have disdained it. But a Crown never was within his reach. The men who most loved and revered him, whose lives he might have commanded as the protector of his country, were incapable of becoming the slaves of any despot. I will not consent, sir, to demolish the fair fame of our Revolutionary Army, that its fragments may be employed in raising a monument even to Washington.[42]

The Randolph men found their leader's favorite weapon of ridicule turned upon themselves in Lowndes's closing remarks, as he addressed the alleged harmony of British and American interests within the context of the Napoleonic Wars:

> But there is yet, we are told, another danger, a danger to England. America, which cannot raise an army, and cannot pay one, which cannot injure her enemy at sea, nor in five years obtain possession of a country on its own borders, containing perhaps two or three hundred thousand inhabitants—America is to subvert the balance of Europe, and to destroy the nation which the same speech represented her as unable to resist. The Orders in Council, a continuance of which is required neither by the honor nor interest of England, our ineffectual hostility can furnish no motives to repeal. And from this ineffectual hostility we are to refrain, lest it subject her to

France. Such arguments, sir, if they were not inconsistent, would yet be inadmissible. We must leave the case of British interests to British statesmen.[43]

Although five other members spoke on the Senate bill that day, the *Alexandria Gazette* singled out Lowndes for special praise: "The Speeches ... consisted principally of a detail of British aggression so many thousand times repeated, with the exception of Mr. LOWNDES' remarks, which are said to have been uncommonly documentative and candid."[44] Indeed, his maiden speech in Congress was well worth noting. His argument was direct and to the point, his rhetoric refreshingly free of the florid oratory and classical allusions favored by so many of his colleagues. In this respect as in the logical flow of argument, his speaking style bore much similarity to that of his friend Calhoun, but there the similarity ended. Lowndes's manner was altogether unprepossessing, somewhat awkward and inelegant, standing in sharp contrast to the intense "tempest and whirlwind" of Calhoun's riveting eloquence.[45] These defects would tend to delay Lowndes's fair share of public recognition in his own time, while the weakness of his voice would contribute to his relative obscurity in future years. When the reporter was not especially diligent, which would prove all too often to be the case, Lowndes might speak for two or three hours on the subject at issue only to find his effort summarized in two or three sentences in the official record. But he was not so vain as to be disturbed by this sort of neglect. On the contrary, his indifference to public acclaim was such that he would almost invariably decline to write out his speeches for the record or for publication, even when a friend or the reporter appealed to him directly.[46] This attitude reflected his traditional republican approach to public service, a blend of duty and disinterestedness that formed the keystone of his public character and the foundation of his budding national repute.

On January 6, the Monday following Lowndes's Saturday speech, the War Hawks pushed through the Senate bill with amendments, 94 to 34, and sent it back to the upper house. Afterwards the two houses found it necessary to compromise minor differences over the amendments, then they approved the additional force of twenty-five thousand men, and the bill became law a few days later. Next the bill for a volunteer corps of up to fifty thousand men was taken up, debated for several days largely along the same lines, and passed on January 17, 87 to 23. The South Carolina delegation voted unanimously in favor of both bills.[47]

Turning immediately to consideration of the naval bill introduced by

Chairman Cheves, the War Hawks experienced their first serious disagreement over war policy. The split divided them essentially, but with exceptions, into sectional factions, with the northeasterners more disposed to strengthen the navy and westerners generally seeing little value in a military force that seemed more likely to benefit New England merchants than to be employed against Indians or to conquer Canada. Essentially the same considerations divided the South Carolina delegation. The upcountrymen, with the notable exception of Calhoun, generally cooperated with the western men, while Charlestonians Lowndes and Cheves became forceful advocates of American naval power.

As reported out of committee, the naval bill contained four major provisions: to repair the vessels on hand, to enlarge the navy to thirty-two warships, to purchase vital materials for repair and maintenance, and to construct a dockyard. In opening debate on the bill Cheves acknowledged its unpopularity within the war party, but he felt duty bound to advocate the measure, convinced that the United States was destined eventually to become a major naval power. Buttressing each of its major provisions with statistical support, he argued that the force proposed—twenty frigates and twelve seventy-fours—could give to American commerce adequate protection and to the United States naval ascendency in American waters without overburdening the national revenue. Moreover, if the opposition would consider that commerce benefited not only the merchant but in fact almost every part of the population, he felt they would find this branch of American enterprise entitled to the security of naval protection.[48]

Several War Hawks rose to answer Cheves with fearful declamations in lieu of reasoned argument. Seybert of Pennsylvania denied the possibility of protecting American commerce even with a greater force than that proposed. As the intent of the bill was to create a large, permanent naval establishment, Seybert could see with frightening clarity a ruinous succession of naval wars, a permanent public debt, national bankruptcy, and eventual revolution. Samuel McKee of Kentucky agreed. A nation possessed of a large navy was a nation always at war. A bloated naval establishment would become the tool of the commercial interest, raising up a moneyed mercantile aristocracy at the expense of republican liberties and leading eventually to their destruction. He was "decidedly opposed, and forever should be opposed, to the application of a cent to repair those old hulks of vessels which are fit only for fuel." Another Kentuckian, Richard M. Johnson, followed in the same declamatory strain, adding that throughout history navies had brought ruin and destruction to all nations attempting to maintain them. With respect to the present circumstances, he was content with the old Jeffersonian reliance on gunboats, perhaps augmented eventually by an intercoastal canal from Maine to Georgia.[49]

Lowndes rose to answer these extravagant claims with an appeal to reason. In condemning the navy as the tool of a narrow commercial interest group, his friends seemed to think that the profits of commerce were confined to the merchant. They had forgotten that "commerce implies an exchange of commodities, in which the merchant is only an intermediate agent. He derives, indeed a profit for the transaction—but so must the seller and the buyer, the grower and the consumer, or they would not engage in it. So must all those who are supported by their own industry in commercial cities—the clerk, the artisan, the common laborer." Knowing of no better instrument of maritime defense than ships of war, Lowndes offered a closely reasoned argument to show that the proposed naval force could and would achieve its intended objectives at less cost than the army required.

But there were limitations on applying the rule of reason in this debate even for Lowndes. McKee and Johnson had loudly declaimed western prejudice against the navy without supporting with rational argument their dire predictions of national ruin. McKee's blatant assertions were particularly vulnerable to critical examination:

> The honorable gentleman from Kentucky... offered objections to a navy, which if they were well founded, would supersede all further reasoning and calculation. He opposes a navy now—he will oppose it forever. It would produce no possible good and all possible evil. It would infallibly destroy the Constitution. Will the honorable gentleman tell us why? how? He sees the danger clearly. Will he explain it? An ambitious general might corrupt his army, and seize the Capitol—but will an Admiral reduce us to subjection by bringing his ships up the Potomac? The strongest recommendation for a navy in free Governments has hitherto been supposed to be that it was capable of defending but not of enslaving its country. The honorable gentleman has discovered that this is a vulgar error. A navy is really much more dangerous than an army to public liberty.... a navy would infallibly terminate in aristocracy and monarchy. All this may be very true. But are we unreasonable in expecting, before we give

up the old opinion, to hear some argument in favor of the new one? The honorable gentleman has asserted his propositions very distinctly. We complain only that he has not proved them."[50]

Lowndes drew numerous examples from history to answer Johnson. Nations such as Venice, Genoa, Holland, and England herself had come to prosper and wield power only with the development of their navies; other causes were responsible for the decline of those that had since lost their positions and influence. In the case of England, the world's greatest naval power, Lowndes said that she owed to her fleets her redemption from invasion for ages past: "While every other considerable nation of Europe has been bankrupt over and over again, she is not yet bankrupt. While nearly every other Government of Europe has been overset, hers yet rides out the storm. Should England fall tomorrow it should seem impossible to deny that her navy will have prolonged her independence for at least two centuries."[51]

Although Clay, Calhoun, and several others stoutly defended the bill, the old Republican fear of naval power proved too strong to overcome. On January 23, the House agreed to provide $480,000 for the repair of existing vessels, David R. Williams being among those opposed. On the twenty-seventh the section to fund construction of new vessels was struck out, 62 to 59, with three South Carolinians, Elias Earle, David R. Williams, and William Butler voting with the majority, providing the difference. The next section on building a dockyard suffered the same fate, 56 to 52, with the margin of difference this time being Butler, Thomas Moore, Williams, and Richard Winn. In this emasculated form the bill passed on January 29 by a vote of 65 to 30, with Williams in opposition to the last.[52]

The combined efforts of Cheves, Lowndes, and Calhoun could not prevent their friends from gutting the naval bill, but their stand on the issue made a significant impression on the Federalist leadership of commercial New England, where Republican refusal to enlarge the navy would raise strong protests. The very next day Senator Dana of Connecticut mentioned the South Carolina trio for the first time in his correspondence with Timothy Pickering, judging them "particularly entitled to consideration for talent and honorable principle," in contrast to "the mass of pulative sychophants."[53] John Randolph, leader of the Republican opposition, expressed a somewhat different view a few days later. Cheves he did not mention, but he paid Lowndes an unexpectedly high compliment in view of the latter's strong criticism of the opposition arguments. Randolph considered Lowndes "a man of great sense and modesty—of real worth." Calhoun was another matter: "That gentleman has not been educated in Connecticut for nothing. He unites to the savage ferocity of the frontier man all the insensibility of the Yankee character . . . all the cold unfeeling Yankee manner with the bitter and acrimonious irritability of the South."[54] Randolph evidently saw in neither Cheves nor Lowndes what many members including himself recognized in Calhoun: a direct threat to the Virginian's sway in the House. Yet the most influential newspaper in Virginia reflected neither Randolph's bias toward Calhoun nor his restraint regarding Lowndes; along with Langdon Cheves and David R. Williams, they constituted "a splendid constellation of talents."[55] The political stature of South Carolina was clearly on the rise.

After the January setback for the friends of the navy, the issues taken up during the next two months failed to draw Lowndes into debate.[56] During this interval he supported all measures advanced in anticipation of war. He voted in favor of the bill for arming the militia, which passed on February 21 over the opposition of his friend Calhoun, who objected to the states' being given power to distribute the arms. Four days later Lowndes gave his approval to the war party's scheme for financing the war, joining the majority in authorizing a government loan of $11 million for twelve years at 6 percent; and on March 4 he assisted by his vote the passage of a variety of war taxes to be laid on items ranging from salt to carriages.[57]

Outside of Congress Lowndes's fragile constitution was being subjected to a trial of endurance unique in his experience, that of withstanding the rigors of a winter uncommonly severe even for Washington. To make matters worse, at the onset of the coldest period in January, "some rogue in or out of the house" stole both his greatcoats from the House cloakroom. It was almost a month before he could have another made, and for weeks at a time he saw no other person on the windswept Washington streets without one. The bone-chilling winds were a genuine trial, so he took advantage of the snow to ride to and from the Capitol in a sleigh.[58]

In periodic blasts of arctic weather the protracted separation from home was wearing his patience thin. He wrote to Elizabeth in late February, "I am so much stupified by this long Session that I can scarcely write a letter intelligibly," and mentioned his plan to take a short leave of absence "to get out of the hum of Washington Politics." More importantly, he had begun to think of declining reelection:

> I am afraid that in the event of war Congress will be obliged to be almost always in Session and if this should be the case and if I find what without any extraordinary modesty I may expect that I am not of any use here and if I can decline without the appearance of wishing to avoid a situation of difficulty and responsibility and if I should feel as I do after hearing a long debate between Wright and Rhea—all these things being premises I shall certainly decline.[59]

Lowndes had not found an opportunity to slip away from the capital when the House received on April 1 a confidential message from President Madison which represented a definite stride toward war. The message called for an embargo of sixty days' duration, a move generally understood to be a necessary preliminary to a war declaration. The administration men formulated the bill, and then with Clay, Porter, and Calhoun in the lead, the War Hawks carried it over the stubborn opposition of the Old Republicans and the Federalist minority. The South Carolina delegation united with the majority in passing the bill on April 9, but Lowndes disagreed with the Senate's extension of its duration to ninety days.[60] Whatever hopes he entertained for an early end to the session suddenly vanished, for the embargo automatically extended the session into June and possibly July.

On that very day the House took up a bill from Lowndes's Committee of Commerce and Manufactures that would "authorize the importation of goods, wares, and merchandise, under certain circumstances, from Great Britain, her colonies or dependencies." The "certain circumstances" alluded to the Non-Importation Act passed on March 2, 1811, which trapped in England several million dollars' worth of goods purchased by American importers before the law passed. Most of the petitions his committee examined had come out of Federalist New England. Chairman Thomas Newton of Virginia explained in introducing the bill that he was too sick to discuss it, but before passing the burden of its advocacy on to Lowndes, Newton said he had always doubted the wisdom of excepting these imports from the nonimportation law.[61]

Under the disadvantage of such an introduction, Lowndes took a common sense approach to the issue, arguing that reason dictated a departure from the strict letter of the nonimportation law. The great bulk of the merchandise trapped in England was manufactured goods that would prove valuable in the war soon to be declared. The sensible course of action, then, would be to permit the movement of these goods to America. After all, the merchandise was now the property of American citizens for better or worse and its admission would mean a valuable addition to the nation's wealth at a critical time, especially since the embargo had stopped exports of specie normally used in the purchase of foreign manufactures. To admit as much of this merchandise as possible, Lowndes offered an amendment to suspend the nonimportation law through July.[62]

Lowndes had expected some opposition to the proposal because of the benefits it would bestow on the mercantile houses of Federalist New England, but he was unprepared for the storm of protest it provoked, mostly from the War Hawks themselves. It would violate an important point of administration policy, constitute a "breach of our plighted faith with France," subject America to ridicule abroad, and bring dishonor on the nation. John Rhea of Tennessee attempted to kill the bill with indefinite postponement. When this failed, James Pleasants of Virginia moved to postpone the measure for one week.

Astonished at the magnitude of War Hawk opposition to a bill so clearly beneficial to the projected war effort, Lowndes reluctantly agreed to Pleasants's motion, but not without reproving his colleagues for their doctrinaire stubbornness:

> He owed it to himself, he said, to state that his first opinion was unshaken. Without designing to trench on the rules of decorum properly observed in the House, he must say he was astonished at what appeared to him the blindness of the policy which required the rejection of this bill. Confirmed as he was in the opinion he . . . expressed in favor of the measure, he was only induced to refrain from pressing into decision by the single consideration that, if decided without further opportunity for reflection, it might not be carried. . . . Whatever might be its unpopularity elsewhere, he must, confiding in the good sense of the community, believe that feeling would be temporary. When the bill should be well understood, he had hopes it would meet a more favorable reception than now greeted it; and with that view alone consented to the postponement.[63]

Rhea attempted to answer Lowndes with a sarcastic retort only to find his effort negated by Cheves and Calhoun, both of whom rose to defend their Carolina colleague and the importation bill. Finally the House postponed the issue to April 20.

In agreeing to the postponement Lowndes had stated that if after a week's calm reflection there should appear to be no change in the opinion of his friends great enough to induce a majority "of those with whom he acted" to support the measure, he would not feel at liberty to call it up on the scheduled day. Apparently his friends could not be moved, for on the twentieth he announced that, although he thought its adoption would be wise and beneficial, to call it up now would in his opinion be a useless agitation that could benefit no one. In what amounted to acknowledgement of complete defeat in his first effort to push a measure through Congress, Lowndes declined to call it up for further consideration. He had no sooner resumed his seat than a message received from the Senate announced the death of Vice President George Clinton, and the House adjourned to pay its respects.[64]

As if his failure in managing the importation bill had not been embarrassment enough, Lowndes suddenly found himself the object of newspaper criticism for the first time in his congressional career. He professed indifference to the criticism in a letter to Elizabeth, but his explanation of its cause suggests a greater degree of sensitivity to public censure than perhaps Lowndes himself realized. He admitted that the sentence quoted against him—that he would not call up the bill "unless a change should take place in the opinions of a majority of those with whom [he] usually acted"—was susceptible to the construction his critics gave it. But what he found most disturbing was being criticized for lack of independence: "They represent me as accepting the principle of being implicitly governed by the majority of my own party.... the caucus principle which they impute to me is so abominable ... that I should have deserved all their censure if I had adopted [it]."[65] He usually cooperated with the administration men in their common effort to prepare the nation for war. Even so, the essential element of his old-style approach to politics was independence, and each measure that came before him would have to stand or fall on its own merits regardless of administration policy or party principle. It would be some time, however, before this basic principle of his political character became public knowledge.

After the embargo passed on April 9, the lag in interest became general as congressmen in large numbers began to absent themselves from the

House. Half seriously Lowndes had earlier suggested a recess. To his surprise it gained support, received consideration in the House and Senate, and narrowly failed passage on Saturday, April 25. Having changed his mind on the wisdom of a recess through May, Lowndes voted against it on Saturday and on Sunday rode off himself on a week's vacation trip to Philadelphia.[66]

The Philadelphia excursion reveals a facet of Lowndes's personality quite apart from his irresponsible neglect of congressional duties. As he explained it, "I determined suddenly upon the ride.... At Baltimore I paid the tavern bill out of some loose silver in my pocket and it was not till I got to the next stage that upon looking into my pocketbook I found that I had set out on my journey with merely enough money to pay my expenses to Philadelphia. I was obliged to borrow from Mr. Vaughan [factotem for a number of Charlestonians] who was entirely a Stranger."[67] The suddenness of his decision and hasty departure were not the only reasons for his forgetfulness. Other incidents of a similar nature reveal a habitual inattention to mundane matters of personal business. In January he had informed Elizabeth, "Among the inconveniences which I feel here too is that of being obliged to keep my own money. This I never could attempt without losing some of it, and my old fate attends me here. It appears from calculation that they allow us more than we require (certainly more than we deserve) for our expences [sic], but with all this superfluity of money I expect to draw on Mr. Kershaw in a day or two for more."[68] He was just as apt to forget he had worn his greatcoat somewhere and walk off without it. This doubtless explains why he had two hanging in the House cloakroom to be stolen. He left another behind in a North Carolina tavern along with his watch, both of which the honest tavern keeper sent on after his absentminded guest.[69] Nor are these the only examples that might be cited.

Lowndes joked that the embarrassments attending his Philadelphia excursion proved how unfit he was to live out of Carolina, and there was a good deal of truth in the jest. The protracted illness of his childhood and afterwards the size of his inheritance, especially in slaves (the Grove was staffed with fourteen servants), had developed in Lowndes habitual dependence on others to manage such matters. His manservant was expected to look after his wardrobe while his factor furnished such funds as routine affairs might call for. And like many another man of exceptional mental capacity, details of this sort simply failed to command his attention or even arouse his interest.

More importantly, Lowndes's indifferent attitude toward the responsibilities of office at this time raises serious questions concerning his maturity and fitness for congressional service in the circumstances of 1812. After his return from Philadelphia Lowndes showed even less interest in congressional affairs, becoming one of about forty congressmen who seldom attended the sittings of the House. On May 10 he confessed to Elizabeth, "I do not confine myself very strictly to the duties of my public station.... Of the plans of our Administration I know nothing and wish to know nothing."[70] Frequent practice was improving his skill at billiards, he said, and he had resumed cigar smoking, "the accidental result of the company which I keep."[71] Lowndes was restless, probably homesick, obviously bored, and generally dissatisfied with congressional service, hardly the characteristics of a responsible representative contemplating war with England. His behavior along with his admitted indifference to administration plans suggest a lack of maturity at this stage of his career as well as a lack of commitment to War Hawk objectives. For all his talents, Lowndes still lacked the resolution to apply them responsibly, quite in contrast to his colleague Cheves, who was hard at work on the preparations for war. What kept Calhoun at the center of War Hawk activity was a potent mixture of ability, patriotism, and ambition. Ambition also led Calhoun to engage in the presidential politics of the Republican party, an arena of public affairs that Lowndes always tried to avoid.

Lowndes declined, along with Cheves and Williams of the state delegation, to attend the Republican caucus that nominated Madison for a second term on May 18, but he did so on principle, considering the practice improper if not unconstitutional.[72] Throughout his career he would strictly avoid the machinations of party, as Senator Thomas Hart Benton of Missouri remarked, "from the approach of which he shrunk [sic], as from the touch of contamination."[73] Prior to the caucus nomination, according to an unsigned manuscript note in Lowndes's papers, Lowndes along with Calhoun, Cheves, Grundy, "and one other gentleman, it is believed from Virginia," called on the president "and advised him strongly to declare war."[74] Enemies of Madison later charged that the caucus nomination had been contingent on his pledging to recommend war. Irving Brant has convincingly demonstrated, however, that the president had already determined to call for a declaration, though not until he felt preparations for war were sufficiently advanced.[75] The very presence of Lowndes in the War Hawk delegation that called on the president, assuming the manuscript note to be accurate, would be enough to refute the charge of corrupt bargaining by Madison. If his companions had intended to bargain with the president in exchange for a caucus nomination, Lowndes would certainly have declined to accompany them. His object on such a mission, and therefore that of the delegation as a whole, could have been no more than to hasten the call for a declaration.

The president finally sent a war message to Congress on June 1, and for the next several days the momentous deliberations were carried on behind closed doors. The House referred the message to the Committee of Foreign Relations. Two days later Calhoun brought in their report recommending war. After Speaker Clay stifled Randolph's attempt to sidetrack the measure, it carried 79 to 49, with the South Carolina delegation in unanimous support.

Upon its arrival in the Senate on June 4, several senators attempted to change the nature of the bill so as to restrict the war to naval engagements. This unsuccessful attempt provoked from Lowndes the remark, "We determined to adjourn and go home doing nothing—or have a War in common form."[76] The War Hawks prevailed. The bill was received back in the House on June 18 where John Randolph made a last futile effort at delay before it received final approval and was sent on to the president. Madison signed it that day, and a report circulated that in the War Mess Lowndes and his colleagues improvised the "War Quadrille," dancing around the room in celebration of their achievement.[77]

Although much remained to be done, there was little more the exultant War Hawks could be persuaded to do. On June 26 they postponed Secretary of the Treasury Albert Gallatin's unpopular war taxes to the next session and resorted to the expedient of issuing $5 million in treasury notes and doubling the import duties.

And still the session dragged on: "I am miserably tired of my present situation" Lowndes told Elizabeth, "and wish I were honorably out of it."[78] The war declaration opened an honorable alternative to congressional service, a command in the army, which several of his colleagues including Porter of New York, Johnson of Kentucky, and Williams of South Carolina decided to accept. Lowndes investigated this possibility and received the promise of a field command as high as he should choose to accept. Finally he called on Secretary of War William Eustis to find out if he could be certain of being sent into action on the Canadian front. Eustis looked at the gaunt Carolinian and replied, according to Lowndes, "that he would not do it willingly and that if it were done at all it would be owing to the little political influence which I had acquired here ... which might therefore carry me to the Northern army without keeping me there. The Sec[retar]y's answer was quite sufficient to dissolve my military visions."[79]

Lowndes never bothered to explain the personal motives behind this implausible scheme, but the ease with which Secretary Eustis quashed it reveals that the Carolinian was not as ambitious for military distinction as he was simply dissatisfied with congressional service. Lowndes had gone through the whole session without firmly settling his mind on a congressional career and with one eye on a military appointment as an honorable and surely a more exciting alternative. All it took to settle the matter was an emphatic rebuff from the secretary of war that Lowndes had the good sense to accept: "For myself not engaging in the army now I must give up all expectations of ever leaving the pursuits of civil life. To make rice in Carolina and speeches in Washington must be the narrow limit of my ambition."[80]

Having resigned himself to such a fate with as much philosophy as he could muster after an exhausting eight-months' session of Congress, Lowndes was greatly relieved when the session finally adjourned on July 6, 1812. As Calhoun had since made other plans, Lowndes joined Senator John Gaillard of Charleston and the two set out on the long hot journey overland to Carolina and home.

VI

War in Common Form

The long first session of the Twelfth Congress significantly shortened the summer recess of 1812, giving William Lowndes less time to attend to personal affairs than he could have wished. His plans for the next session made the recess seem even shorter. Having finally settled his mind on congressional service, he decided to make the best of it by bringing his family to Washington in the fall. This necessarily required detailed arrangements on a variety of matters relating to family business that Elizabeth had capably managed in his absence. In fact, she had borne too many of the burdens arising in the operation of the Horseshoe, alarming her husband on one occasion by ignoring his advice and risking her health to supervise personally the care of slaves struck down by a fever epidemic that had ravaged the Horseshoe that spring.[1] Now he arranged with the firm of Kershaw and Lewis to furnish such supplies as the Horseshoe might require, to provide for disposition of the next crop, and in general to assume management of business affairs handled by Elizabeth during the past year. To visit the Horseshoe, leave detailed instructions for its operation, go over the accounts with Boineau, his overseer, and see to the multitude of details that only an owner can properly handle, there was perhaps time enough but little to spare.

The enjoyment of family and close friends was always a keen pleasure with Lowndes, and his children doubtless found their father a "good playmate" as he had promised in his letters. Afforded several opportunities to converse with his father-in-law, Thomas Pinckney, who had been recently commissioned major general and given command of the Southern Department, the congressman would not have failed to consult the general on military affairs and special problems involved in providing for defense of the southern coast. The two men would carry on an extensive correspondence on these matters during the coming year.

The recess was long enough for Lowndes to renew friendships temporarily interrupted by his absence in Washington and receive hearty congratulations from prowar Republicans along with more restrained compliments from his Federalist friends. His former comrades in the Washington Light Infantry showed little restraint in their approval of Lowndes and his Republican colleagues in Congress; they had "raised the sinking spirits of their constituents, and . . . secured the independence and sovereignty of their country."[2] "Diodorus Siculus" exemplified the confident enthusiasm of the *City Gazette* in a letter published on September 3, praising "the patriotic and distinguished Gaillard, the firm and inflexible Taylor, the learned Cheves, the solid Lowndes, the brilliant Calhoun and other worthies [who enable] South Carolina to claim a distinguished rank among the states of the union; a rank she will always maintain when represented by men of talents and inflexible republican principles."[3] Even the *Courier* gave its grudging approval; the time for argument had passed, and now all should carry on the war "with vigor, with unanimity, and we most sincerely pray with glory and success."[4]

As the October elections approached, Lowndes allowed his name to be entered for a second term and saw his enthusiastic neighbors of Colleton District press his candidacy against Federalist challenger Stephen Elliot of Beaufort. The incumbent "was one of those distinguished representatives of this State who voted for *war*, in preferences to degrading *submission* to British tyranny and injustice." He had rendered "immense benefit to his country, and . . . firmly maintained those rights which will ever be dear to America, and which can never be abandoned so long as we exist as a nation." In praising Lowndes so highly, his neighbors all but dismissed the candidacy of his opponent. They did not wish to detract from Elliot's character: "[H]e is certainly a respectable gentleman, but possessing little or no experience in political matters and in point of talents and general information is far inferior to Mr. Lowndes."[5]

Still in town when the *City Gazette* published this flattering notice, Lowndes remained there long enough to cast his ballot on October 12. By the time election returns began to come in, he was well on his way to Washington, traveling in his own carriage with his family.[6] To the surprise of nobody Lowndes routed Elliot, sweeping each of the four election districts of the Second Congressional District by a wide margin.[7] Neither Elliot nor anyone else ever again challenged Lowndes for his congressional seat. The state legislature had recently redrawn the boundaries of the Second Congressional District so that it contained only lowcountry parishes extending from St. Andrews immediately west of

Charleston down to Beaufort, and this, along with the quality of his service and his growing national repute, converted the district into the political province of William Lowndes.

Arriving in Washington without mishap despite a report to the contrary,[8] Lowndes installed his family in a comfortable Georgetown residence. Before the session was well under way the Lowndes home had become the favorite haunt of Calhoun, whose family had remained behind in Carolina, and it was almost as popular with the Cheves family. Mrs. Cheves and Elizabeth Lowndes became close friends during this session. Among the callers were a number of Federalist congressmen, encouraged by the legislative statesmanship of their amiable host and put at ease by the discovery that their well-informed and witty hostess held political views similar to their own. Other visitors included the James Monroes, with whom Elizabeth had established a friendship years earlier while accompanying her father on a diplomatic mission to Europe. Speaking fluent French and some Italian, and possessing in ample measure the social graces so carefully cultivated in the drawing rooms of Charleston, Mrs. William Lowndes moved easily into Washington society.[9]

Social affairs provided a welcome respite to the young men who assembled in Washington in the fall of 1812 and were faced with the sobering reality of the "War in common form" they had been so determined to have the previous session. The overly confident expectations and glowing visions of an easy conquest of Canada, which had accompanied the declaration and carried through the summer of 1812, rapidly faded in the fall as reports began to come in from the northern army. Beginning with the news of General William Hull's ignominious surrender of Detroit on August 16, ill winds from the North would continue to blow into Washington as Generals Stephen Van Rensselaer, Alexander Smyth, and Henry Dearborn, one after another, contributed to the growing evidence of unpreparedness, indiscipline, disorder, and incompetence along the Canadian frontier.

Quite in contrast to the army's dismal record thus far, the little United States Navy furnished Americans almost their only source of military pride during the early months of war. Through a combination of luck, skill, boldness, and determination, the navy brought home important early victories. The exploits of the *Constitution*, the *Essex*, the *Wasp*, and the *United States* between August 13 and October 25, 1812 demonstrated that in single engagements with vessels of comparable size and firepower, American ships and men were at least equal and more often than not superior to comparable British forces. Their exploits added the names of Isaac Hull, David Porter, and Jacob Jones to those of William Bainbridge and Stephen Decatur on the growing list of American naval heroes. Equally important, if not more so, "the old Jeffersonian jealousy of the navy vanished in the flash of Hull's first broadside."[10] Cheves, Lowndes, and other advocates of a larger navy could confidently expect Congress to be more friendly to the navy thereafter, but whether friendly enough to overcome ingrained western prejudice remained to be seen.

The second session of the Twelfth Congress opened on November 2, 1812. For this session Cheves succeeded Ezekiel Bacon as chairman of Ways and Means, David R. Williams again headed the Committee of Military Affairs, and at its first meeting Calhoun replaced ailing John Smilie of Pennsylvania who had succeeded Porter as chairman of the select Committee of Foreign Relations.[11] Lowndes still held his positions on Commerce and Manufactures and on Williams's Military Affairs Committee. Congress faced the primary task of providing men, money, and materiel for a more rigorous prosecution of the war. Calhoun, Cheves, and Lowndes believed that this could be done most effectively by pursuing a policy that would stimulate commercial activity. Such a policy would achieve a two-fold purpose in addition to increased revenue. It would help to conciliate commercial New England and afford economic relief to Charleston and New Orleans, the two cities, according to Speaker Clay, which had suffered more than any other "by the shackles upon commerce."[12] Hence the Carolina trio favored relaxation if not complete abandonment of the restrictive system that the president and administration forces led by Clay in the House intended to maintain. A collision between the Carolinians and the administration men over the restrictive system occurred sooner than expected. The issue was Merchants' Bonds.

The question of Merchants' Bonds had grown out of events that took place late in the previous session. During negotiations with the British prior to the declaration of war, the Madison administration had announced that nonimportation of British goods would terminate on suspension of the Orders in Council. On receipt of this news, American merchants in England prepared the several million dollars' worth of merchandise trapped there by the nonimportation law to be ready for shipment home upon repeal of the Orders. When the British announced suspension of the Orders on June 16, 1812, two days before the United States declared war, heavily laden ships raced for America only to find on arrival that a state of war existed and their cargoes were subject to confiscation under a new law. The law allowed them to sell their goods only after posting bond to the value of their cargoes. In the meantime, determination of the issue was referred, along with scores of petitions from the affected merchants, to the House Committee of Ways and Means.

On November 25 Chairman Cheves reported for the majority on Ways and Means "that it [was] inexpedient to legislate upon the subject, and that the petitions, with the accompanying documents, [were to] be referred to the Secretary of the Treasury."[13] This meant that Secretary Gallatin would review all cases with power to decide each on its individual merit. Cheves disagreed with the committee majority and yielded the floor to Johnson of Kentucky, who defended the resolution. Johnson claimed for the restrictive system full credit for pressing the British into a suspension of the Orders in Council. He had no doubt that the huge quantities of British goods imported in disregard of law and national policy had relieved economic distress in England to an extent that undermined the object of the nonimportation law and served to prolong the war. Having clearly violated an act of Congress, the merchants, he said, should be penalized accordingly.[14]

Speaking for the commercial interest, Samuel Mitchill of New York City heatedly denounced "the Shylock severity of demanding strictly the pound of flesh," objected to Gallatin's being permitted to decide alone an issue involving millions of dollars and the possible ruin of so many personal fortunes, and called for the remission of all forfeitures and penalties.[15] When Speaker Clay declared Mitchill out of order, Cheves took up the same line of argument. He agreed that the disposition of some $50 million in merchandise and bonds was a matter too momentous to be relegated to the secretary of the Treasury. To do so would prostrate the rights of their constituents and constitute an abdication of the legislative power to the executive. He proposed instead that Congress direct the remission of all penalties on bona fide American property and hold liable to forfeiture only foreign property imported in violation of the law, adding that in all doubtful cases sound policy recommended an act of grace.[16]

Speaker Clay defended what he termed "an essential system of policy" that he believed had won revocation of the Orders in Council. Clay viewed the restrictive system as "a powerful auxiliary of war" that, if persisted in, would break down the present ministry and lead to honorable peace. He proposed to limit relief only to those merchants who had purchased their goods before news of restriction reached England on February 2, 1811, and who shipped between the revocation of the Orders in Council and news of the declaration of war, about the first of August 1812.[17] Calhoun opposed Clay's resolution in a speech that reinforced the argument of Cheves and alluded to the foresight of Lowndes. Calhoun understood the intent of the law in question to be the punishment of negligent or willful violators, not those who had broken it through ignorance or necessity. He said,

> I am ready to acknowledge, that an act of grace will weaken the non-importation law; but that is a less evil [sic] than the alienation of the whole mercantile class. It is left to us to regret that the wise foresight of my two honorable friends and colleagues was not adopted last session. It was then proposed to suspend the law for the introduction of this very property; but it was borne down by the clamor of the day. Had that been done, we would not have been reduced to the present state. Our laws would have been saved and our merchants contented.[18]

Georgian William Bibb of the committee saw private interest motivating critics of the report. He thought repeal of the system would be "an act of unexampled inbecility and folly." Prosecute the war with vigor, he advised, "add non-exportation to non-importation, and I do verily believe you will have an honorable peace before the end of the year."[19]

At this point Lowndes took the floor, not to answer Bibb's unfounded charge but to demonstrate the injustice of such narrow limitations on relief that Clay's resolution called for. Consciously avoiding any reference to his proposal of the previous session that would have precluded this controversy over Merchants' Bonds, Lowndes pointed out that normal exportation under a policy of nonimportation had produced the unavoidable consequence of accumulating American wealth and property in England. To get this property home, Jonathan Russell, the American consul in London, had advised its shipment even after news of the war declaration had reached London, assuring the Americans that their property would be exempt from penalties of the law. As merchants of all nations "receive with deference such advice from their consuls," Lowndes urged the House to uphold the consul. He further justified the remission of all penalties in the most forceful argument of the debate and one of the finest examples of Lowndes's persuasive oratory:

Was the property which an American citizen had acquired in England in violation of none of your laws to be sacrificed without any possible advantage to his country? When he could no longer himself remain in England consistently with his allegiance, was he to intrust his fortune to agents over whom he could have no superintendence or control?—against whom by law he could not maintain a suit? And if he were obliged to leave England with his property, what other ports in the civilized world but ours could have been expected to admit him? Wherever else he had gone his cargo would have been confiscated as American property, or burned as English merchandise. Suppose him to have known that by the letter of your law his property would be liable to confiscation when brought into your country? By the letter of English law it was no less liable to confiscation while it remained there. To the mercy of the one or the other government he was obliged to trust. To which should he have trusted? To a declared enemy, or to his natural protector, his own Government?

Those who shipped before the war, shipped as the Speaker contended, on the reasonable expectation that their voyage and their profits would be lawful. But with those who shipped after war it was not merely the expectation of lawful profit. It was their only refuge from ruin.[20]

The combined opposition of Lowndes, Calhoun, and Cheves, an increasingly formidable combination in House debate, proved decisive on this issue as the House on December 11 rejected the Ways and Means report by the margin of their votes, 52 to 49. A few days later a bill came over from the Senate providing for the remission of all forfeitures on property owned by Americans and shipped before September 15, 1812, essentially Lowndes's proposal of the previous session with only the date changed. Advocates of less restrained commerce seized upon the Senate measure and pushed it through the House, 64 to 61. On this vote, which terminated the issue of Merchants' Bonds and went far toward conciliating the disgruntled commercial interests of New England, at least for the time being, the margin of difference was once again the votes of Calhoun, Cheves, and Lowndes.[21]

On December 16, the House took up another bill from the Senate which would receive Lowndes's wholehearted support. It proposed a substantial increase in the size of the navy, calling for the construction of four seventy-fours and six vessels to rate not less than forty-four guns.

With the knowledge of recent naval victories still fresh in mind, the House appropriated $2.5 million to build and equip the new vessels. Lowndes had the satisfaction of seeing the bill become law before he took leave over the Christmas holidays to accompany his son Rawlins to school in Philadelphia.[22]

Delayed to the second of January on his return, Lowndes arrived in Washington almost simultaneously with another blast of arctic weather so cold that John Randolph complained, "[W]e of the South can hardly keep out of the fire, and with minds scarcely less torpid than our bodies."[23] The issue now before the House, an act to raise an additional military force, heated enough tempers on both sides of the aisle to make several members, notably Josiah Quincy and Henry Clay, oblivious to the cold. As Lowndes explained, "[T]he Opposition selected it as the occasion of a general discussion of the war, its causes and the necessity of its continuance."[24] The bill called for twenty new regiments of one-year enlistees rewarded by new bounties. Lowndes alone of the state delegation opposed the measure, enduring the cold to speak at length against it in debate. The burden of his argument was that the creation of so many new regiments would prevent the ranks of the old ones from ever being filled. He might have saved his breath, for the bill passed on January 14, 77 to 42.[25] He then paid General Thomas Pinckney the courtesy of explaining his negative vote. The bill was not popular even within the war party—"there were not half a dozen men who approved of it" in the House—but because the opposition had broadened discussion into a general condemnation of war policy, "the vote by many was considered a vote of approbation to the war rather than the measure."[26]

On matters of finance, which next claimed their attention, Lowndes, Calhoun, and Cheves all voted with the administration. In late January they helped to secure passage of two bills authorizing the government to borrow an additional $16 million and to issue $5 million more in treasury notes, thereby leaving the neglected question of war taxes to the next Congress.[27] Little of importance was accomplished during the remainder of the session, but despite stubborn Federalist opposition, Congress had already given the president virtually all he had asked for in men and money to carry on the war.

The closing weeks of the session served to show that, although the South Carolina trio shared similar views on most issues, their thinking continued to be independent of a dominating personality. Cheves revived an old debate when he moved to suspend nonimportation in mid-February, but saw his bill fail when Lowndes voted with the majority to strike out its major provisions.[28] Later Calhoun introduced a bill to prohibit exportation of American goods in foreign vessels, and found himself on the opposite side of debate from Lowndes, who advocated the bill's rejection in an unreported speech. The satisfaction that Calhoun felt in seeing his bill pass on March 2, 1813, was doubtless lessened by the sight of both his friends, Cheves and Lowndes, voting against it.[29]

After agreeing to a special session to convene on the fourth Monday in May 1813, the Twelfth Congress adjourned about midnight on March 3. Their presence in Washington afforded the Lowndes family an opportunity to witness the next day the republican simplicity of Madison's second inauguration; nor would William, despite his distaste for dancing, have denied Elizabeth the singular pleasure of attending the inaugural ball on the evening of March fifth. Shortly afterwards they departed for home, for Lowndes felt such anxiety for the neglected state of his plantation affairs that until the special session was called he had planned to spend the whole summer at Walterboro near the Horseshoe to put its affairs in order.

In the account book of his rice factor and business agent, the firm of Kershaw and Lewis, the financial status of William Lowndes may be clearly traced. During his first year in Congress (from August 1811 to August 1812) Lowndes went $3,259.91 in debt to the firm; his expenditures for this year were $18,560.69, while his income amounted to $15,300.78. Selling 185 barrels of rice for $3,864.19 over the next four months enabled him to clear the account with his factor, but he still owed $12,000 to local banks.[30] By early spring, 1813, he was again running nearly $3,000 in debt to Kershaw and Lewis, who were paying off his bank loans as they fell due. In these circumstances the need to bring in a good crop claimed first attention when he arrived home in late March, 1813.

Lowndes thoroughly investigated conditions on his Horseshoe plantation, riding out from Walterboro daily to supervise personally the arrangements he found necessary to improve its operation. He made an inventory and had the list of his slaves brought up to date, giving their names and family relationships; this count revealed that he had 14 slaves at the Grove and 238 at the Horseshoe. The livestock numbered 178 cattle, 35 sheep, and 47 oxen besides numerous mules and horses, which were not listed in the plantation account book. When investigation showed that Boineau's management left much to be desired, Lowndes hired William Wilkinson in May to become his overseer at $400 a year. Leaving detailed instructions for Wilkinson and for Ellick, the slave driver at the Horseshoe, Lowndes was more hopeful of a successful crop when he returned to Washington for the special summer session of the Thirteenth Congress.³¹

House Members of the Twelfth Congress conspicuous by their absence in the Thirteenth were War Hawks David R. Williams, Richard M. Johnson, and Peter B. Porter, who had all resigned to accept commissions in the army, and John Randolph of Roanoke, temporarily unseated by John W. Eppes of Virginia. For a few weeks in April and May it appeared that Cheves, Calhoun, Lowndes, Earle, and Moore of the South Carolina delegation had involuntarily vacated their seats through failure to notify Governor Joseph Alston of their acceptance of election within the time required by law, but the governor showed the good sense to avoid this absurdity by issuing their commissions anyway.³²

For the session that opened on May 24, Lowndes arrived too late to receive committee assignments and thus had relative freedom while his colleagues quarreled with the opposition over Gallatin's tax program in the stifling heat of June and July. Gallatin's recent departure on a diplomatic mission to Europe rendered the task of passing his tax program much more difficult. Lowndes remarked, "For myself unless it shall be proposed to shoot Mr. Gallatin for desertion I shall maintain my accustomed silence during the Session."³³

Henry Clay, once again chosen Speaker of the House, named John Eppes chairman of the Committee of Ways and Means, and Eppes reported Gallatin's tax bills on June tenth. They proposed a direct tax of $3 million; taxes on salt, licenses, carriages, auctions, sugar, and alcoholic spirits; and a stamp tax as well as machinery for collection. Although this tax program meant that the Republican leadership were yielding doctrinal niceties to the necessities of war, it was hoped that the program might be pushed through Congress without excessive delay.³⁴

The hope for a short session soon faded, however, for the war leaders were to have their usual share of troubles, if not more. As Lowndes had feared, one of the "100 new members anxious to break a lance," Federalist Daniel Webster of New Hampshire, introduced resolutions suggesting Madisonian duplicity in respect to the French decrees and succeeded in enmeshing the House in two weeks of unprofitable debate. The Senate in a "factious" mood rejected Gallatin's diplomatic appointment. The president came down with a remittent fever, and not until July 7 did his recovery seem reasonably certain. Shortly thereafter reliable reports had a British fleet moving up the Potomac toward the defenseless village of Washington. Although Lowndes among others considered the alarm that this last intelligence raised to be groundless, the militia was put under arms and for a time all available manpower took the field, including the secretaries of state, war, and navy, before the fleet withdrew.[35]

Like most congressmen, Lowndes appeared to have little fear for the safety of Washington, but his concern for the safety of Charleston and the Carolina coast steadily mounted. The British appearance below Washington and a reported landing near Norfolk had demonstrated the ease with which the enemy could strike selected points on the navigable coastal waters of the South. Cautioning his wife to forego her usual summer stay on Sullivan's Island, Lowndes explained the basis of his fears: "They seem to have adopted the plan of alarming us by debarkations doubtless to prevent reinforcements being sent to the North as well as to increase the expense and unpopularity of the war. They have lately landed a considerable force in the neighborhood of Norfolk and I really do not see why they might not land near fort Moultrie [on Sullivan's Island] or Johnson [across the bay]."[36]

Free of burdensome committee assignments, Lowndes utilized his time in efforts to improve defense of the southern coast. Through June and July he carried on a triangular correspondence with General John Armstrong, who had succeeded Eustis as secretary of war, and General Thomas Pinckney, then in southern Georgia to prevent a suspected British invasion from Florida. Lowndes called frequently upon the secretary, besieging him in his offices in order to secure arms, supplies, and pay for the troops under his father-in-law's command. By July 31, he had succeeded on all counts and had persuaded Armstrong to heed General Pinckney's advice to break up the camp in south Georgia and use the troops to reinforce key positions along the coast.[37]

In the House Lowndes cooperated with the administration forces in pushing through the tax bills, anticipating an adjournment in late July, "if all general discussion be avoided—if we say nothing on either side of the origin of the war—do not accuse of moral murder or recriminate by charges of moral treason."[38] Fortunately leaders on both sides were tired of disputing in suffocating heat questions no longer worth debate. Lowndes explained it thus on July 6: "The Gentlemen of the Federal side of the house have intimated their wishes that a discussion of Foreign relations at this advanced period of the Summer should be avoided &

have promised not to begin it—I have employed all my activity in procuring a similar determination on the administration side of the house and have been authorized to [exact] assurances of the most talkative men there that they will not begin it."[39] Through Lowndes's activities as administration whip and the improved temper of both parties, the House avoided a general debate. The bills secured passage one after another and received the president's signature before Congress adjourned on August second.

Lowndes had felt such pressing need to be in Carolina to attend to his plantation affairs that he had written to Elizabeth in late June, "I never felt the same anxiety for a crop and it never indeed was so absolutely necessary."[40] Securing a leave of absence on July 11, he remained in Washington only long enough to vote for the tax bills, then left for home. August 1, the day before Congress adjourned, found him in Fayetteville, North Carolina, writing to Elizabeth that he regretted not traveling by stage, which had just passed him, but he was hurrying on and would "dine at the Grove on Friday."[41]

Time pressed in the late summer of 1813, for the family would return to Washington in the fall. Lowndes was obliged to go to Beaufort on public business and to attend to several matters in Charleston, but he spent most of his time at the Horseshoe where so much hinged on the success of his rice crop. Unfortunately, three months had been long enough to prove Wilkinson an incompetent overseer, so Lowndes replaced him with a Mr. Riggs.[42] Actually, if state law had not required the presence of a white man on every plantation employing slave labor, Lowndes might well have dispensed with overseers altogether and turned the Horseshoe's operation over to Ellick, his intelligent and reliable Negro driver, the true stabilizing force on the plantation year in and year out.[43]

Considering the recent change of overseers, one suspects that Ellick deserved most of the credit for the success of the new rice crop, which amounted to 756 barrels. At 1812 prices this would have brought something over fourteen thousand dollars. By September the Horseshoe had shipped more than five hundred barrels to the warehouse of Kershaw and Lewis in Charleston.[44] But from there the rice proved difficult to move. Cautious merchant shippers preferred not to attempt running the British blockade, and although some rice was being purchased in spite of this threat, the increased risk had cut the price in half. By the time Lowndes left for Washington in late November, none of his 1813 crop had been sold, and his account with Kershaw and Lewis showed him ten thousand dollars in debt.[45]

Lowndes crossed over the Potomac fifty miles below Washington to avoid the wretched roads in northern Virginia and arrived in the capital in time for the opening of Congress on Monday, December 6, 1813. On Tuesday President Madison's cheerful message recounted recent victories by Commodore Oliver Hazard Perry on Lake Erie and General William H. Harrison on the Thames in Canada, and reviewed General Andrew Jackson's energetic campaign against the Creeks. On Tuesday and Wednesday Speaker Clay named the heads of standing and select committees, including John Eppes for Ways and Means, Calhoun for Foreign Relations, George Troup of Georgia for Military Affairs, and William Lowndes for the Committee on Naval Affairs.[46] On Thursday by secret message the president asked Congress for a restoration of the embargo.

Few were willing to dispute the president's opinion that the present state of commercial and navigation laws tended to favor the enemy and prolong the war, but not all Republicans agreed that resort to embargo would prove more effective. The discontent of the New England states was becoming as notorious as their illegal trade with the enemy. The proposed embargo was obviously intended to operate against this illegal commerce, for the British blockade had effectively stifled the export trade elsewhere.

In secret session an embargo bill was drawn up and presented to the House on Friday, December 10. None who knew of their consistent opposition to restrictive legislation were surprised when Lowndes and Cheves voted with the Federalists and conservative Republicans against the bill the next day. Even so, the bill passed the House 85 to 57 and received subsequent approval from the Senate, and Madison signed it into law on December 18, to take immediate effect.[47]

The new embargo appears to have had little effect in curbing illegal intercourse with the enemy through Canada, but it halted the few efforts in the South to run the blockade, and for the next four months no shipments of rice left Charleston. The most significant effect of the law on New England was to increase public antagonism toward the war and the administration. Talk of disunion from this time forward became increasingly less guarded. No longer content merely to question the value of the Union, the more militant Federalists began positive moves looking toward a possible withdrawal from it.

The most promising Federalist in the House, Daniel Webster, led the resistance fight in that body. Arriving late in December, he opened an old wound and provoked a general debate in January, when on a measure to encourage enlistments, he called for an inquiry into the causes of military failures as well as the war in general. The Federalist strategy of obstruction combined with the pressures of war and embargo to strain nerves on both sides of the House. The tempers of Calhoun and Federalist Thomas P. Grosvenor of New York flared into threatened violence on one occasion and almost resulted in a duel before the affair was settled.[48] Lowndes joined in the discussion of various measures, but always maintained his composure and managed to avoid giving offense to members of the opposition. In the February debates on the $25 million loan bill, the administration's familiar answer to its pressing financial needs, he replied to the pointed sarcasm of Timothy Pickering "in his usual forcible manner, and eloquent language." Later he supported the same bill in a speech of an hour and a half, "during which he replied in that lucid and masterly manner which always characterize[d] his oratory, to various doctrines advanced by gentlemen in the opposition."[49] Pickering could be a devastating critic, but the worst he would say about his principal antagonist in this debate came close to flattery: "Even Mr. Lowndes of So Carolina, a mild and able and intelligent man, . . . *voted for the war*, altho in the last and present session, like his colleague Cheves, he has not taken very active part in its prosecution. . . . [T]hat pride which prompts a man to preserve a consistency of conduct even in error, may urge even the mild and amiable Lowndes."[50] The Federalist *New York Evening Post* took even more flattering notice of Lowndes in late March: "Mr. Lowndes is one of the most judicious, modest and imposing men in the House. . . . His voice and figure detract greatly from the pretensions which he might otherwise justly set up, and in claiming which he would be justified by the properties of his mind. He is reputed on all hands a scholar and a philosopher, and is universally allowed to be a most honorable man."[51]

In extending these compliments to the South Carolina congressman, both Pickering and the editor of the influential *Evening Post* were quite aware of Lowndes's recent success in strengthening American naval power. In the course of the session the chairman of the Naval Affairs Committee brought in bills to increase the pay of navy and marine personnel, to augment the Marine Corps, to construct several sixteen-gun vessels and build additional naval facilities, and to purchase the prizes captured by Perry's fleet on Lake Erie the previous September, all of which he guided successfully through the House.[52] The resounding success of the last measure, to purchase Perry's prizes, could not but have been deeply gratifying to Lowndes. The favorable vote may be attributed to the heroic nature of Perry's victory; but the extraordinary eloquence of his quiet-spoken advocate on the floor of the House should not be discounted. Recounting the manner in which Perry had snatched victory from the appearance of almost certain defeat, Lowndes proclaimed the exploit unrivaled in the annals of modern naval warfare and a valuable lesson for the future:

> Captain Perry and his gallant associates have not only given us victory in one quarter, but shown us how to obtain it in another yet more important. How deep is now the impression on every mind that we want but ships to give our fleet on the Atlantic the success which has hitherto attended our single vessels! We want but ships; we want then, but *time*. Never had a nation when first obliged to engage in the defense of naval rights by naval means—never had such a nation the advantages or the success of ours. The naval glory of other States has risen by continued effort—by slow gradation; that of the United States, almost without a dawn has burst upon the world in all the sudden splendor of a tropical day. To such men we can do no honor. All the records of the present time must be lost—history must be a fable or a blank—or their fame is secure. To the naval character of the country our votes can do no honor, but we may secure ourselves from the imputation of insensibility to its merit—we can express our admiration and our gratitude.[53]

The House endorsement of Lowndes's appeal not only expressed admiration and gratitude for Perry's victory but also reflected the fact that the administration was receiving pitifully little cheerful news. When an offer of direct peace negotiations came from the British in late December 1813, Madison accepted and appointed Speaker Clay to join the negotiating team. Clay's resignation in January to accept the appointment paved the way for Langdon Cheves to be elected Speaker. The prospect of peace negotiations and the recognized failure of the embargo soon led to repeal of the odious law. Recommended by Madison, introduced by Calhoun, and supported by Lowndes, the bills repealing the embargo passed the House early in April, 115 to 37; were approved by the Senate; and became law on April 14, four days before the session ended.

The summer of 1814 brought on the most critical period of the war. The collapse of France in the spring had released veteran British divisions for service in America. Reinforcements soon arrived in Canada for an invasion from the North. A fleet moved into the Chesapeake Bay and invaded Washington in August, burning the Capitol, Presidential Mansion, and other public buildings before departing for an abortive attempt on Baltimore. A third expedition was expected to strike some point on the southern coast between Charleston and New Orleans in the fall. Disaffection in New England had increased rather than diminished since the embargo's repeal and under pressure of an extended British blockade. Federalist leaders were preparing for an important convention at Hartford where secession was rumored to be among the subjects to be considered. Reports from the peace negotiators, quarreling among themselves, were discouraging, for the demanding British appeared to have already assumed American defeat.

The private affairs of William Lowndes were equally serious, though not yet critical. Through bank loans and the sale of 268 barrels of rice in the spring of 1814, he had reduced his debt with Kershaw and Lewis to less than seven thousand dollars, but the great bulk of his fine 1813 crop sat in warehouses, its value declining with age. Nevertheless, the hands could not remain idle, and a new crop was planted, doubtless in anticipation of early peace. Elizabeth was not too proud to market their rice by the single barrel or in smaller quantities, but her husband discouraged the scheme. When she suggested that his disapproval stemmed from pride, he was not altogether convincing in his denial: "I did not mean to express any disapprobation of your retailing plan any further than was implied in the doubt of your being able to derive any profit from it. If your experience have [sic] shown that my theory was wrong, I am very glad to have been so. I have no scruples of pride on the subject. These are in fact incumbrances which most people in these times must throw off."[54] He regretted that they could not do more for the comfort of their slaves and sent Ellick instructions to give them "as much beef as can be done without materially injuring the stock—Say any number of oxen which shall not exceed that of two year old steers."[55] He further directed that fifty barrels of rice be contributed to the public subscription to aid those suffering the consequences of war and blockade, explaining, "If there be no peace the rice if I keep it will be without value and if there be peace I hope we may be able to get along without it."[56]

The British burning of Washington shocked the nation and lent greater urgency to Madison's call for Congress to meet in extraordinary session on September 19. With deep misgivings and justifiable concern for the safety of his family—to say nothing of his plantation, state, and nation—Lowndes departed for Washington. Almost daily reports told of British naval movements, off Edisto Island, cruising off the Charleston bar, off Amelia Island, in the St. Mary's River, at Mobile and Pensacola.[57] When rumors spread of a major British invasion into the South, Charlestonians, expecting their city to be the target, held several public meetings, put the forts in order, and threw up works across Charleston Neck. A similar meeting of Lowndes's neighbors at Jacksonborough on September 19 prepared for the defense of the seacoast and parishes.[58] It is little wonder that Lowndes and his South Carolina colleagues arrived in Washington with minds as anxious for favorable news from home as they were for a solution to the nation's problems and an end to the war.

The session opened on September 19 in a room of the building housing the Post and Patent offices, the only public building left standing among the blackened ruins of the capital. Lowndes had suffered delays on the road and arrived five days late, having lost his watch and greatcoat on the trip.[59] Neither he nor Calhoun, who did not reach Washington until late October, was burdened with a committee chairmanship this session, leaving them relatively free to choose issues that most interested them.

The issue that claimed most attention this session was the National Bank Bill. The experience of war had proved the necessity of a national bank. With the government on the brink of bankruptcy, former opponents of the Hamiltonian institution were openly admitting its value. They were by no means in agreement on the details of the question, and would debate one point after another through almost the whole session. The starting point was the plan recommended by the new secretary of the Treasury Alexander J. Dallas and introduced in the House on October 18.

Dallas's plan proposed to establish a national bank along the lines of Alexander Hamilton's defunct Bank of the United States. To be incorporated for a term of twenty years and established at Philadelphia, it would have a capital of $50 million raised through the sale of 100,000 five-hundred-dollar stock certificates, three-fifths to be subscribed by corporations, companies, or individuals, and the remainder to be subscribed by the federal government.[60] Debate on the bill would most often revolve around the amount of capital, number and size of stock certificates, terms of sale of the stock, and participation by the federal government. Both Lowndes and Calhoun would figure prominently in the debates over this bill, and each would offer significant proposals for change.

Formulated by committee, the bank bill introduced on November 12 contained the essentials of the Treasury plan. A motion to reduce the capital to $20 million failed, followed by House rejection of several minor amendments. Then on November 16, Calhoun proposed a radical change in the provisions of the bill. Calhoun's bank, like that of Dallas, would also have a capital of $50 million, of which $6 million would be gold and silver, but there the similarity ended. Instead of accepting government bonds sold during the war in payment for bank stock, Calhoun would accept only future issues of treasury notes and specie. Advocates of the Dallas plan quickly pointed out that this would give all the advantage to those who now held specie, meaning New England Federalists, over those who had given financial support to the government during the war. Furthermore, by the Calhoun plan the federal government would be almost entirely excluded from participation in the operation of the bank, nor was its borrowing privilege guaranteed. The Dallas men were as thoroughly opposed to Calhoun's plan as the Carolinian was to the secretary's. Sentiment in the House divided almost evenly between the rival plans and changed little throughout the debate, with Lowndes a consistent supporter of the Calhoun version.[61]

From November 16, when Calhoun introduced his proposal, the House debated the rival plans for nine days without a decision. On Friday the twenty-fifth, Speaker Cheves referred the matter to a special committee headed by Lowndes; but by Monday he had to report that the committee could not agree, and dumped it back into the lap of the House. Objecting to both plans because of the large amount of capital, Lowndes succeeded in having it reduced to $30 million. The argument, continuing over the next few days, eventually saw Calhoun engage Federalist Alexander C. Hanson of Maryland in a sharp exchange. Then Richard Johnson of Kentucky, having returned wounded from the war, abruptly called the previous question and the bill failed.[62]

While the House wrangled over the bank issue, the war effort faltered toward certain defeat. The cheering news of Thomas MacDonough's victory on Lake Champlain on September 11 was giving way to the gloomy prospect of a British capture of New Orleans. Mobile had been taken in August, and by the end of October, a strike at New Orleans appeared certain and soon. Dispatches from the peace negotiators were not heartening, and rumors of the deliberations at Hartford added the likelihood of disunion to the prospect of defeat.

In Lowndes's extant correspondence there are almost no references to the peculiar problem presented by New England, but he wrote freely of the others. His letters reveal anxious concern over the possibility of an attack on South Carolina, then in December the probable fall of New Orleans, and always the serious condition of his economic affairs. He was sometimes optimistic about the conclusion of peace that winter and could usually take a philosophical attitude toward the state of his private affairs resulting from the war:

> If war should last many years I believe that the nation possesses resources which may enable it to support it with honor. As to *our* private interest I believe that if the war should last three years longer I shall not be worth more than fifty negroes after paying my debts. With these we must retire to some situation where we may enjoy health and tranquility. And then it will be some consolation to reflect that if in my public situation I have supported measures which have impaired the fortune of many of my Countrymen—at least I cannot be accused of having made my own.

But his sense of humor managed to keep matters in perspective. If things got worse, he told Elizabeth, "we can always live at Walterborough out of the reach of our Creditors or at least out of their sight.... The Aristocrats say that the best friends to republicanism are always to be found in a gaol, & I suppose they would acknowledge the second class to consist of those that expect to get into one."[63]

On December 23, 1814, the House again took up the bank issue on receiving from the Senate their version of the Dallas plan. After Christmas its features were debated until January 2 when Daniel Webster, outlining seven points such as he said his friends would support, failed in an effort to get the bill redrawn. Then the House appeared to pass the bill on its third reading, 81 to 80, with Lowndes voting for and Calhoun against it. Cheves, though, chose this occasion to exercise his right as Speaker to vote against the bill, producing a tie; so the bill was rejected. Recommitted and amended into the shape demanded by Calhoun, it passed on to the Senate on January 7, 1815. The Senate, however, preferred the Dallas plan; the two houses tossed the bank bill back and forth until finally the Senate yielded; but the president, supporting his secretary, vetoed the measure. A modified version was under consideration in the House on February 12, when the members, in the jubilant mood prompted by the news of Jackson's spectacular victory at New Orleans, postponed the bill at the suggestion of Lowndes.[64] Then came the glorious news of peace on the entirely acceptable terms of *status quo ante bellum*.

Throughout the nation joyful citizens celebrated the war's end. The war had not been won, but what now appeared more important, it had not been lost. Even Lowndes could not conceal his exultant pride in the stunning victory won in its last and greatest battle:

> When the war in Europe was over I sometimes expressed the opinion that it would perhaps be better for both nations that England should try her undivided strength against a power whose resources she probably little understood. But I little expected that a well apointed [sic] army of ten thousand veterans would have been foiled with the loss of half their number by men who two months before had left their ploughs—Orleans was our weakest point and the best effect of the war is the deep impression which our enemy must feel that on our own soil we are unassailable.[65]

Relief from the burden of war was universally exhilarating, except perhaps for the Hartford Federalists, now the objects of ridicule and jest.

The remaining weeks of the session were nothing if not anticlimactic. The House voted to retain the wartime double duties on imports but postponed the bank issue and most other questions to the next Congress. Now that the war was over, Lowndes, like most of his colleagues, was primarily concerned with the neglected state of his personal affairs; rebuilding the nation's strength could be dealt with in the years that lay ahead. He had already sent word for Thomas to meet him with horses at Fayetteville so he could go straight to the Horseshoe to supervise the spring planting. A mixture of elation and concern may be detected in one of his last letters to Elizabeth before the session adjourned on March 2: "The peace has given a new turn to everyone's thoughts and plans. Mine are very unsettled. But we shall have time enough to talk of them when we meet."[66]

VII

Federal Republican

The peace gave a far greater turn to thoughts and plans than Lowndes probably realized. It wrought profound change in the nation's self-image and in the primary focus of national attention. For the first time, in a manner of speaking, America turned its back on Europe, relegated foreign affairs to a position of secondary concern, and prepared to claim the riches beckoning her people westward. Inextricably fused in the national consciousness with Jackson's resounding victory at New Orleans, the restoration of peace generated a tremendous surge of national pride, which carried all but the most determined bastions of provincialism and smoothed the way for nationalistic legislation in the immediate postwar years.

In South Carolina, more so perhaps than in any other state, a generous infusion of state pride blended with the prevailing spirit of nationalism. Not since the Rutledge-Pinckney era had the state enjoyed such stature and influence in national affairs. The War of 1812 had been the vehicle and the state's House delegation the instrument that restored South Carolina to its old and fondly remembered position near the center of influence in national politics. During the course of the war the delegation had furnished chairmen for the four committees most directly concerned in prosecuting the war effort: Cheves for Ways and Means, Calhoun for Foreign Relations, Williams for Military Affairs, and Lowndes for Naval Affairs. By the time the war ended, Cheves held the Speaker's chair, John Gaillard was president pro tem of the Senate, and Calhoun, having emerged as a spokesman for the Madison administration during the war, moved among the select circle of political figures who commanded most influence over affairs of state. Cheves, Lowndes, and Calhoun were also marked out for early cabinet appointment. Cheves had already declined in late 1814 Madison's invitation to head the Treasury Department.[1] Soon Lowndes would have the distinction of declining offers of the War portfolio from both Madison and Monroe. Not until 1817 would a South Carolinian be persuaded to enter the cabinet, when Calhoun would consent to exchange his leadership position in the House for the office of Secretary of War.

Having its old position in the Union restored and resting with apparent security on such young and capable shoulders was not the only reason South Carolina faced the postwar years with confident optimism. Heavy demand in the export trade was driving the price of cotton and rice steadily upward.[2] The postwar boom, generating rapid expansion, especially in upland cotton, inflated the value of land along with that of slaves. With the lowcountry's black majority giving its usual appearance of stability and order, slave labor seemed ideally suited to the postwar expansion of southern agriculture. Nor did the national temper yet manifest much interest in attaching stigma to slave ownership or resentment over the system of congressional representation so advantageous to the slaveholding South. But the postwar boom and the apparent security of slavery affected the entire South. What set South Carolina apart from her neighbors, and produced in her congressional delegation more consistent support for nationalistic legislation, was the belief that her improved standing in the Union was assured, that the enviable record compiled by her "splendid constellation of talents" offered a standard for measuring her political future, perhaps even that South Carolina might once again provide the presidential nominee of a national party.

That half the "constellation" would not return to Congress in the fall of 1815 seemed not to disturb the state's nationalistic temper. David R. Williams, whose congressional disposition seemed better suited to war than peace anyway, turned his energies to state politics and textile manufacturing after the war, leaving his seat to a succession of men less talented than he. The loss of Langdon Cheves was more serious. Cheves had drawn the fire of Charleston Republicans for having in their opinion too stoutly championed the commercial interests so closely associated with Federalism. Rather than yield his judgment to theirs in submission to direct constituent instruction, he cut short a brilliant congressional career by declining reelection. After his return home, the state legislature in 1816 unanimously elected him judge of the Court of General Sessions.[3] Although widely regarded as too valuable a man for permanent retirement from national affairs, Cheves would not return to the House, nor did his constituents find a replacement of comparable ability. Charleston Republicans doubtless considered the wealthy and popular

Henry Middleton a worthy successor, but Middleton lacked Cheves's capacity for work and patience with routine. Two terms in the House would be enough to show that he preferred "honour with ease," a type of service he afterwards found in a diplomatic appointment.[4] Of the new men, only William Smith of Yorkville, who entered the Senate in 1817, had demonstrated more than ordinary ability, which he would employ more in pursuit of provincial than national interests.[5] Consequently, during the immediate postwar years, South Carolina nationalism depended heavily on the leadership of Calhoun and Lowndes.

Lowndes also considered retirement at the end of the war. He said he had tried civil life and found it "vapid,"[6] but the main cause of his discontent lay in his financial difficulties. With trade severely restricted by the British blockade, Lowndes had been unable to dispose of the great crop of 1813 at a price he considered reasonable. This circumstance had required his borrowing more heavily than usual from the Charleston banks, so that by the fall of 1814 his outstanding debts totaled almost twenty thousand dollars. With his affairs in such a critical state, he then consented to the sale of his old rice at the going price, about four dollars a barrel, which in normal circumstances would have brought three to four times as much.[7] He also returned to the possibility, mentioned as early as 1812, of selling his lowcountry property, paying his debts, and retiring to private life on a backcountry farm. He preferred to locate at Paris Mountain, the lofty terminus of a secondary range of the Appalachians which commanded a broad panorama of forest, fields, and meadowlands of the fertile piedmont. In that pastoral setting, surrounded by his family, his books, and such slaves as his creditors might leave him, he would live out the remainder of his days in Horatian serenity.[8]

A number of considerations combined to dispel the dream. Aside from relocation in a more healthful climate, the plan had little to recommend it for the family as a whole, suggesting that more romance than reason had gone into its genesis. Apparently Lowndes had idealized the experience of his favorite Latin poet. The rural isolation and pastoral pursuits of a Sabine farm might have suited him no less than Horace, but for Elizabeth the prospect meant protracted isolation from her lowcountry family and friends, to say nothing of the cultural stimulation of Charleston society. And what of the children's education, the subject of such anxious concern in Lowndes's wartime correspondence with Elizabeth?[9] The dislocations caused by the war had clearly demonstrated the difficulty of finding quality instruction outside of Charleston.

If familial duty discouraged removal to the upcountry, civic duty argued against immediate retirement. The mere restoration of peace could hardly free the War Hawks of all obligation concerning such postwar problems as the inflated national debt and the nation's uncertain security. But beyond duty, a more subtle and altogether human influence had insinuated itself into his thinking. That indefinable quality of political life that may at once repel and attract those engaged in it had begun to erode his resistance to further public service. In November he wrote Elizabeth,

> It would not be easy to say what it is which recommends public life and yet how few willingly quit it. I am sometimes a little surprised that I should have remained so long in it. Some men indeed want offices of honor or profit. And three years ago I should have been glad of military employment. But at present I am sure that there is no office from that of President to an ensigncy or collectorship of customs which I would accept. I cannot retain the place of member of Congress then from the hope of its leading to anything else and yet I have not *fully* resolved to decline.[10]

Within the month his constituents effectively settled the matter by electing him without opposition to a third term.

Prosperity quickly returned to South Carolina after the cessation of hostilities as cotton and rice factors prepared for resumption of the normal flow of trade. Fortunately the Horseshoe had produced a good rice crop in 1814, which Kershaw and Lewis now disposed of at prices above the prewar level. Between March 21 and June 19 they sold 500 barrels of Lowndes's rice for $7,615.26;[11] and prospects for the fall seemed even more promising as market prices continued to rise. In his improved circumstances Lowndes decided to bring his family with him when he returned to Washington in the fall, so there would be almost no letters to record his sentiments on the momentous issues of this session.

The House convened in temporary quarters on Monday, December 4, 1815. In the preliminary business the members again chose as their Speaker Henry Clay, recently returned to Congress after having figured prominently in the peace negotiations at Ghent. Clay promptly named Lowndes chairman of a committee to inquire into the state of the new building being hastily prepared for the accommodation of Congress. Lowndes toured the new structure and reported it ready for occupancy.

After Clay had made all major committee appointments, the House moved into its new quarters on December 11.[12]

The two most important committee chairmanships named this session were Lowndes to Ways and Means and Calhoun to head the special Committee on the National Currency. The most controversial issues during the remainder of Lowndes' political career, other than those involved in the Missouri question, would be concerned with proposals coming out of these two committees. The first would produce the Tariff of 1816 and, in the process, open an issue of intersectional volatility second only to slavery. The second would reestablish the Bank of the United States, the most powerful and most controversial financial institution of the antebellum era. No other issues would so clearly demonstrate South Carolina's commitment to postwar nationalism than those promoted by her two most influential congressmen.

The choice of Lowndes to head Ways and Means resulted in part from the departure of Langdon Cheves and John Eppes of Virginia, who had chaired this powerful committee in the Thirteenth Congress. Cheves had declined reelection and Eppes had been unseated in his second try against John Randolph. A tried and proved administration man, Eppes had labored with exceptional energy as chairman of Ways and Means in order to strengthen his bid for reelection.[13] Had he succeeded, there seems little doubt that Clay would have returned the incumbent to that chair. In the absence of this trusted lieutenant, the Speaker named Lowndes to the post.

But the Speaker's choice was by no means ill-considered. A southern nationalist untainted by sectional bias and a consistent supporter of administration policy, Lowndes was widely regarded as one of the most able political economists in Congress. Midway through the session, Thomas Robertson of Louisiana, a member of Lowndes's committee, declared that the chairman was "better acquainted with the fiscal concerns of the nation than any member of this House."[14] To an acute observer of the Washington scene, Lowndes had "discovered a very general, profound and extensive knowledge of finance; a subject in itself dry and difficult, and to which very few citizens of this country have devoted much of their leisure. To Mr. Lowndes, however, it appears to be a branch of political science peculiarly pleasing, and to which he is much devoted both from inclination and habit."[15] A modest demeanor and an amiable disposition could be definite assets in cushioning the impact of tax proposals on disparate elements in the House, and Lowndes had displayed increasing skill in the management of legislation. Whatever misgivings the Speaker might have harbored concerning the appointment would most likely have arisen out of certain weaknesses suggested in a contemporary portrait of the chairman, which described "the imperfections of his person and figure, his quixotic countenance, lank, lean and rueful; his tall, slender and emaciated form, and all the inelegancies and defects of his body. . . . His memory is powerful and retentive, and furnishes him, in an instant, with whatever he may have wished to retain; but he is no orator; his voice is low and feeble, his gesticulation awkward and inelegant, and his whole manner unprepossessing and defective."[16] Even so, Clay could hardly expect Lowndes to become a creature of the administration; as the same Washington observer noted, Lowndes "never takes up an opinion or adopts a theory that has not been sanctioned by his own judgment, or that cannot bear the test of logical analysis. His mind possesses a mathematical tact, and every subject which presents itself and which cannot be demonstrated is rejected or admitted with hesitation and doubt."[17] Clay knew that Lowndes could be counted on to promote administration objectives, but the Speaker understood from the outset that the revenue program to come out of the Committee of Ways and Means would bear the clear mark of its chairman.

The bulk of national revenue was expected, as always, to come from taxes laid on foreign goods imported into the United States. The unique circumstances of 1815, however, suggested a broader objective for tariff legislation than revenue alone. Three years of war had revealed profound national weaknesses that demanded remedy. The most critical problems concerned bad currency, bad roads, and infant American industries. These industries had been nourished by embargo and war only to be exposed to the cut-throat competition of British manufacturers now dumping their goods on the American market. To remedy these problems, the Jeffersonians in power, having always been more apprehensive of Federalist power than Federalist policy, prepared to embrace Hamiltonian solutions. A national bank and a system of internal improvements were looked upon as remedies for problems concerning currency, communication, and transportation, while Congress was expected to provide a measure of protection for the industries the war had fostered.[18]

President James Madison directed the attention of Congress to these matters in his Seventh Annual Message read in the House on December 5, 1815. To facilitate fiscal matters and commercial exchange, he pointed to the need for a uniform national currency and suggested the consideration of a national bank. The revenue flowing into the treasury under the existing program of Ways and Means he declared sufficient to provide for present needs. On this point he noted that the deluge of British imports since the peace had brought a shower of gold—$12.5 million in nine months—pouring through customs into the empty coffers of the Treasury. But additional provision would have to be made for reduction of the national debt, which stood at $120 million. Nor should Congress overlook the necessity of improving transportation and communication facilities by establishing roads and canals throughout the country. Most of the funds for these purposes the president felt could be provided by a revenue-producing tariff that should at the same time afford for industry a "protection not more than is due to the enterprising citizens whose interests are at stake."[19]

Following the president's recommendation, the Committee of Ways and Means set to work on the revenue program. As its centerpiece would be a new tariff law, the crucial issue concerned the degree of protection to be recommended. Named to Ways and Means with Lowndes were James Burwell of Virginia, John W. Taylor of New York, Jonathan Moseley of Connecticut, Thomas B. Robertson of Louisiana, Samuel D. Ingham of Pennsylvania, and William Gaston of North Carolina.[20] Ingham, a manufacturer of paper, was the only strong protectionist on the committee, with Taylor being his most consistent ally.[21] Robertson stood ready to cooperate with Ingham and Taylor but only in return for support for Louisiana sugar. Their efforts were balanced by Gaston and Burwell, who consistently stressed limitations on the rates considered, while Moseley and Lowndes occupied the moderate center.

In formulating the revenue program in 1816, the Committee of Ways and Means generally followed the outline and schedule of rates suggested in the annual report of the secretary of the treasury, Alexander Dallas. The report showed that under the laws in force, the Treasury Department anticipated a net annual revenue of $25,278,840; the changes recommended by the secretary were expected to yield an additional $90,660. Estimated annual civil, diplomatic, military, naval, and miscellaneous expenses amounted to $9,628,669, to which would be added $6,150,000 representing the interest on the national debt, bringing the ordinary annual expense of operating the government in 1816 to $15,778,669.[22] These figures provided the basis on which the committee report would rest.

Historians who have evaluated Lowndes's management of the revenue program in 1816 have differed on his views regarding the protective principle. Edward Stanwood stated that Lowndes "accepted fully and frankly the principle of protection." More recently Norris Preyer, in a seminal essay on southern support for the postwar tariff, maintained that Lowndes harbored a hostility toward manufacturing but supported protection primarily with a view toward national defense. William Freehling reiterated Preyer's thesis and agreed with Stanwood that the duties of 1816, "while designed to be protective, were actually too low to protect."[23] An examination into the background of the Ways and Means report reveals that each of these judgments stands in need of correction.

In July 1812 Congress doubled import duties for the duration of the war and later extended the law one year beyond the cessation of hostilities. After the war officially ended on February 17, 1815, the House called on Secretary Dallas to recommend a tariff schedule to the next Congress in time for action before the double duties expired in February 1816.[24] Complying with this request, Dallas adopted what seemed to be the most sensible procedure. He decided to base his recommendations on as much information as he could gather from a balanced variety of sources and sent out a circular letter calling for data on the current state of manufacturing and on other areas of economic enterprise.[25] The response, according to his report, was disappointing. As he explained to the House, "The attempt . . . to obtain detailed and accurate information upon the subject has only been successful in a very limited degree; and consequently, the result must be presented to the view of Congress rather as an outline and an estimate than as a complete and demonstrative statement of facts."[26]

The significance of this research effort in 1815 lies not so much in its limited result as in its objective approach. If the information received was disappointingly thin, it was nevertheless the best Dallas could compile through the fairest method of inquiry available to him. Lowndes especially lauded the secretary's approach and repeatedly reminded his colleagues of the conscientious effort made to base the rates of 1816 on objective research. Moreover, the chairman of Ways and Means found the information compiled by Dallas, supplemented by letters, petitions, and other materials consulted by the committee, to contain "substantially, and indeed much more fully than he should require it, all the information in respect to the state of our manufactories in 1816."[27] The fact that both the secretary of the Treasury and the chairman of Ways and Means compiled data to demonstrate need for the degree of protection recommended opens a neglected avenue of understanding of southern support for the protective principle when first applied. The guiding principle of protective legislation under the direction of Lowndes was the golden mean of moderation applied for the good of the whole. This fact becomes more evident in further examination of the secretary's report.

In recommending his tariff schedule to Congress, Dallas explained how the rates had been determined: "The amount of duties should be such as will enable the manufacturer to meet the importer in the American market on equal terms of profit and loss. . . . There still, however, remains a diversity of opinion as to the amount which will be competent . . . , and the aim of this report will be to strike the medium which appears to be best established from all the information that has been collected."[28] Here Dallas articulated the prevailing view of what constituted adequate protection in 1816, which is to say, a schedule of rates high enough to negate the importing merchant's current advantage over the American manufacturer without giving the manufacturer an advantage over the American importer. The secretary's reference to the "diversity of opinion as to the amount which will be competent" probably anticipated disagreement between himself and Chairman Lowndes, because Dallas wanted not merely a protective but a growth-promoting tariff. Finally, Dallas cautioned Congress against exclusive reliance on import duties for the nation's revenue, suggesting the retention of internal taxes somewhat reduced from their wartime rates. In view of President Madison's assurance that American manufactures required a reasonable degree of protection as well as the declared intention of Secretary Dallas to limit that protection to the minimum necessary for balanced competition, it seems plain enough how the reasonableness of such a program might appeal even to southern representatives whose constituents would bear the heaviest burden of protective duties.

The rates that Dallas recommended, though, seemed to be at variance with professed objectives. Claiming "national independence in the department of manufactures" as the long-range goal, Dallas assured the agricultural community that "inconveniences of the day will be amply compensated by future advantages," most notably an expanded home market for the great staples. But the rates he proposed offered protection in inverse proportion to need. He divided American manufactures into three classes according to their ability to withstand foreign competition, then recommended the highest protection for those industries most securely established and the least protection for those least able to compete. The crucial issue concerned textiles. Cottons and woolens of the coarser kinds generally produced in America fell into the middle class. Textiles of this class had been taxed at 12.5 percent ad valorem before the war. Now Dallas recommended duties of 33.33 percent on cottons and 28 percent on woolens, higher in both cases than the wartime double duties and on cottons almost three times the prewar rate.[29]

How Dallas arrived at this relatively high level of protection is not apparent from documents preserved in the public records relating specifically to textiles and known to have been consulted in formulating the revenue program. Of the many petitions calling for tariff protection, three on the subject of textiles were selected for official publication, which justifies the presumption that they typified others not preserved. Two of these petitions came from New England cotton manufacturers. Both recommended a virtual prohibition of cheap cottons from India and suggested higher duties on foreign cottons generally, but neither ventured to specify what cotton manufacturers might consider adequate ad valorem protection. On the other hand, the third petition, from woolens manufacturers in New Jersey, Pennsylvania, and Delaware, expressed satisfaction with the existing rate of 25 percent under the double duties. Here the key passage read, "[I]t seems certain that the present duties may maintain the present manufactures of the country, but that unquestionably nothing less will do it."[30] Isaac Briggs, owner of a Delaware cotton mill, proved more opportunistic. He wrote Dallas in November 1815 a densely argued letter based on figures that seemed to support no more than a 20 percent duty on cottons. After the Treasury Department report with its higher schedule appeared in February 1816, Briggs revised his figures upward and wrote Chairman Lowndes that "although less than is proposed in the [Dallas] tariff might possibly sustain them—less would not do it with certainty."[31]

Of these petitions, only that of Briggs attempted anything like statistical support for generalizations on the need for protection, and even he weakened his case by comparing British cotton goods of the first class with American cottons of the second class. The upshot was that the Ways and Means Committee could find in these documents no adequate justification for Dallas's higher schedule. The committee concluded that if woolens manufacturers believed 25 percent would "maintain the present manufactures of the country," cottons should fare as well if not better with a similar degree of protection. After all, cottons enjoyed the additional benefit of an abundant home-market supply of raw material, to say nothing of the technological advantage of the power looms of Lowell. Lowndes believed 20 percent would be enough to restore competition in the textiles market, but he yielded to the committee majority so that by unanimous vote the committee settled on a tax of 25 percent on both cottons and woolens. The schedule Lowndes reported was designed to achieve Dallas's first objective: to restore competition. The Dallas schedule was designed for the second: to promote manufactures.[32]

The chairman of Ways and Means laid the committee report "from the polished pen of Mr. Lowndes" before the House on January 9, 1816.[33] Aside from revenue to meet the usual expenses of government, the report embraced three distinct objectives blending Hamiltonian principles with traditional republican doctrine. The first objective envisioned a peacetime military force strong enough to discourage the British from reopening the war. Not only Lowndes and the committee majority but most administration leaders as well considered a resumption of hostilities not at all unlikely. As Lowndes phrased it with the British clearly in mind, "It is impossible not to see that Europe is more military than ever, . . . [and] her Governments have acquired a power which makes preparation more difficult and more necessary on the part of every State exposed to the chance of their hostility."[34] Consensus among postwar nationalists held that ten thousand men should be kept under arms for the time being and a comparable measure of strength retained in the postwar navy.

Compensating for this departure from traditional republican principles, the report rejected the Hamiltonian view that a national debt gives stability and order to a nation and recommended as its second objective "rapid extinguishment of the public debt." Lowndes articulated the traditional republican view in pointing out that interest payments on the debt, "to be received by the few, must be paid by the many," who would be giving "to the stockholder what would be reserved for supporting the seaman and the soldier."[35] As Treasury Department figures projected an annual surplus after 1816 of almost $10 million, the committee recommended that $7 million annually be added to the fixed appropriation for interest on the debt. This would form an annual sinking fund of $13,150,000 which could extinguish the debt in twelve years. Jefferson himself might have written Lowndes's closing admonition on this point: "Government . . . neglects one of its first duties when it allows the season of peace to pass away without an adequate provision for removing every encumbrance on its effective revenue."[36]

Lowndes employed his pen with obvious caution in treating the third objective, tariff protection for American manufactures. Indeed his phrasing of this passage seemed to preclude protectionist construction. For the considerable revenue required to attain the first two objectives, the committee expected duties on imports to furnish the principal supply: "Cheap and easy in their collection, paid like all indirect taxes, when it is convenient to pay them, they will be found, under a system of prudent moderation, to discourage no branch of national industry." Although taxes on imports were "the natural resource" of thinly peopled countries like the United States, moderate rates were necessary to discourage smuggling. Moreover, recent experience had demonstrated that, in the event of war, "the liberal provision which [import duties] are capable of making in peace, disappears in the moment when war requires larger contributions." Hence the committee agreed with Secretary Dallas that the internal tax system should be retained and ready for expansion in case of war.[37]

On the whole, Lowndes's rationale for the moderate tariff schedule fashioned by his committee was quite conventional. It neither betrayed sectional bias nor appealed to sectional interests. More importantly, it furnished neither explicit nor implicit justification for a protective system. And not at all incidentally, it denied more ardent protectionists a valuable precedent for future exploitation. The tenor of the report left little doubt that Lowndes considered the competitive position of American manufacturers in 1816 a temporary difficulty to be dealt with on terms that should carry no implications for future tariff policy.

Twelve resolutions that concluded the Ways and Means report outlined the revenue program. The first five would continue in force several revenue laws, including a temporary extension of the wartime double duties in addition to taxes on salt, on refined sugar, and on notes and bonds. Other resolutions called for reduction of internal taxes, the most important being a proposal to cut the direct tax in half, from $6 to $3 million. Three other resolutions proposed repeal of certain wartime emergency taxes. Every member of the House recognized the explosive potential of the tenth resolution, which recommended an average increase of 42 percent over prewar tariff rates after June 30, 1816.[38]

On Monday, January 15, the House in Committee of the Whole took up the Ways and Means report. Lowndes assumed the burden of exposition and defense. He read the first resolution, to extend the double duties law "until the 30th day of June next, and until an act shall be passed establishing a new tariff of duties," and followed with "a general explanation of the views of the committee."³⁹ Unfortunately, the reporter chose to summarize the chairman's remarks, a practice employed with such frequency throughout these debates that Lowndes's own views are not readily apparent. Opposition surfaced immediately as several members, southern planters for the most part, objected to the protective principle generally and the double duties in particular. Except for Benjamin Huger, Lowndes's Federalist colleague from the Georgetown District who immediately objected that the proposed tariff would saddle the staple-producing South with higher taxes for the benefit of northern manufacturers, members of the Federalist party joined the silent majority that adopted in quick succession the first five resolutions rather than risk a government without revenue by mid-February.

At this point, with seven resolutions yet to be acted on, Lowndes suggested a departure from established procedure so bills could be introduced in time for passage before the affected laws expired.⁴⁰ This unorthodox maneuver brought John Randolph out of his chair to instruct Lowndes both on the rules of the House and on correct republican principles. The Virginian's main concern was the clause in the first resolution regarding a new tariff. From his Old Republican perspective Randolph could see in the protective system the corrupt Age of Walpole reborn in America, with government twisted after the British fashion into a cornucopia of special favors feeding private interests at the expense of the public good. In patented Randolph style he assailed the committee program through the remainder of that day and much of the next, finally moving for recommitment on the ground that this was "the first time a committee of that or any other legislative assembly had ever made a report in part." The House majority, however, upheld Lowndes. Then a motion to strike out of the first resolution the clause relating to a new tariff brought Randolph back to his feet to ridicule the report, and by clear implication the committee chairman, with more than usual severity:

> Mr. Randolph asked the Speaker, if the question were not on striking out of the resolution the words "and until an act shall be passed establishing a new tariff?"—and on the Speaker answering in the affirmative—so I thought, said Mr. R., and yet I could not help doubting my understanding on the case. This is a limitation I have never before known or heard of. A law to remain in force not to a

particular time, but until a particular contingency shall have happened; until another law now in contemplation shall have passed! This, sir, is such a curiosity in legislation as I have not only never witnessed or heard of but, never so much as imagined; and as not only myself, but, I do most potently believe, no man living, or that ever lived, did hear of.[41]

To Randolph, the young nationalists had abandoned the guiding principles of their own party. The revenue program was clear proof "that the time is come when the system of Mr. Jefferson, though it was the ladder by which the present Administration mounted into power, is to be departed from, both in practice and theory," to be replaced by "old Federalism, vamped up into a something bearing the superficial resemblance of Republicanism." If abandonment of principle were not enough, these young "Hyper-federalists" would betray the yeoman farmer, the honest practitioner of all the old virtues and the bulwark of true republicanism. Under the new system, the cultivator, with "his property, his lands, his all, his household gods to defend," would be "like that meek drudge, the ox, who does the work and ploughs the ground, and takes for his reward the refuse of the farmyard, the blighted blades and the mouldy straw, and the mildewed shocks of corn for his support," while the manufacturer, "the citizen of no place, or any place [but] always on the Rialto," could "skip into a coffee house, and shave a note with one hand, while with the other he signs a petition to Congress, portraying the wrongs, the grievances, the sufferings he endures, and begging them to relieve him out of the pockets of those whose labors have fed and enriched" him.[42]

For all his brilliant imagery, Randolph weakened the republican cause he espoused by indulging too freely his penchant for ridicule, further isolating himself from the group in power. According to family tradition, William Lowndes "so resented some of Mr. Randolph's attacks, that . . . he for years never offered him his hand, and never addressed him except on the business of the House."[43] The young nationalists could hardly ignore their chief critic, but his best efforts generally left them unmoved. After Randolph yielded the floor, the question was put on the first resolution, and by Thursday, January 17, all five had passed. Chairman Lowndes brought in the bills on Friday and pushed them through. With Senate approval and the president's signature, they became law on February 9, just a week and a day before the old laws expired.[44]

Urgent need for the laws in question had eased the work of Chairman

Lowndes thus far, but consensus gave way to serious division on the sixth resolution concerning the direct tax, more commonly referred to in debate as the land tax. Due to the complexity of the issues involved, Speaker Clay decided to permit wide latitude of discussion here, launching a broad and extended debate on tax policy.[45] The sixth resolution proposed to continue indefinitely the wartime tax, though reduced by half so as to bring in $3 million of revenue annually. The Ways and Means report had justified retention of the internal revenue system on the basis of the need for rapid reduction of the national debt and for internal tax machinery capable of rapid expansion in the event of war. Besides raising the issues of the war itself and the postwar military establishment, the direct tax also raised the question of tariff rates, for reduction of the one would justify raising the other. By unanimous agreement the Ways and Means committee had struck what they considered a reasonable balance between the two, and the principal effort of Chairman Lowndes in this debate would be to retain the balance the committee had achieved.

Discussion of the sixth resolution opened on January 20. Chairman Lowndes explained the committee's justification for it in terms of debt reduction and support for the postwar standing army. Afterwards he avoided set speeches and responded to the efforts of his colleagues, relying on his talent for persuasion through force of reasonable argument based on detailed information. Throughout the debate he was on his feet daily and often several times a day, although the reporter continued to record virtually useless summaries of his remarks.

As his erstwhile Federalist allies remained silent, John Randolph again spearheaded the opposition. He accused "the Ministry" of conjuring up "pretenses for laying their hands on the public money," advocated retrenchment as the honest republican solution, and denounced a revenue system that would send American labor "supperless to bed" in order to support "an overgrown Military Establishment."[46] Speaker Clay, the chief administration advocate of higher protection, would reduce the land tax even further and make up the revenue deficiency by raising the tariff. This provoked Benjamin Hardin, a new member from Kentucky, to complain of the dictatorial legislative process and the great power of standing committees. He would scrap the whole internal revenue system, which he considered a vast preserve of corrupt placemen, and reduce the army to six thousand men. Clay responded with allusions to current troubles with Spain over West Florida and the possible need "to aid in the cause of liberty in South America." Randolph would not be frightened by "the raw head and bloody bones of Old Spain"; the Speaker had "snuffed the carnage" at Waterloo on his European mission and caught the infection of war.[47] After a spirited exchange between Randolph and Clay, the Virginian sorely tried the patience of administration men with a speech that began on Thursday and ran through Saturday, railing against the revenue program, the peace establishment, and the huge debt run up in the recent "unnecessary" war.[48]

Clay replied to Randolph's marathon effort with a speech that constituted a major policy statement. He reminded the opposition that, however contracted, the public debt did exist, and the faith of the nation was pledged for its redemption. He rejected retrenchment as a reasonable solution, for reduction of the army below ten thousand would only encourage British hostility. He expected war and would have the nation prepared to defend itself: "My policy is to preserve the present force, naval and military; to provide for the augmentation of the Navy; and if the danger of war should increase, to increase the Army also. . . . In short . . . I would act seriously, effectively act, on the principle that in peace we ought to prepare for war—for I repeat, again and again, that in spite of all the prudence exerted by the Government, and the forebearance of others, the hour of trial will come." Clay also wanted to commence the great work, too long delayed, of internal improvement. He wished to see a chain of turnpike roads and canals from New England to New Orleans, intersecting the mountains and binding the nation together. Funding of these projects could be supplied by a combination of internal taxes and tariff duties. The tariff also would achieve the beneficial object of protecting American manufacturing, "not so much for the sake of the manufacturers themselves as for the general interest."[49] When he closed with a patriotic flourish on national gains won in the recent war, all that remained to complete this early formulation of Clay's "American System" was a reference to the bank bill then under the guidance of Calhoun.

Now the discordant voice of northern Federalism began to sound. Speeches by Joseph Hopkinson of protectionist Pennsylvania and Cyrus King of commercial Massachusetts demonstrated conflicting interests within the party. Hopkinson instructed Clay that the United States had actually gained nothing from the war, that in fact the War Hawks had been lucky to escape with restoration of the status quo. Still, he rejoiced to see that their bungling had at least taught them correct principles and urged his Federalist colleagues not to oppose the traditional Federalist program simply because Republicans now embraced it as their own. Cyrus King took the opposite view, extolling the wisdom of Randolph and reiterating the Virginian's arguments against "this burdensome system of duties" and "overgrown expensive Military Establishment" whose only object was war.[50]

John Calhoun, burdened with management of the other major piece of nationalist legislation this session, had not yet joined the debate on the land tax, although his views were hardly distinguishable from those of Lowndes. Both considered the revenue program essential to make the nation "free from external danger and internal difficulty."[51] They shared a mutual concern that growing opposition to the land tax threatened the whole revenue program. But in a larger sense, extending far beyond the issues immediately at hand, they held in common a vision of national purpose and public duty grounded in the classical tradition of republican government and civic virtue. When Calhoun took the floor on January 31 to deliver one of the truly great speeches of his career, he gave eloquent expression to this vision.

Calhoun began by observing that there are, in the affairs of nations, moments "on the proper use of which depend their fame, prosperity, and duration."[52] He believed such to be the current situation of the United States, recently emerged from war and finding itself in possession of great physical and moral power. With political institutions resting on justice and reason, he believed that national policy should be not only moderate and just, but that "as we render justice to all, so we should be prepared to exact it from all." He warned against the natural disposition of a free people to relax their vigilance:

> In the policy of nations, said he, there are two extremes; one extreme in which justice and moderation may sink into feebleness; another, in which that lofty spirit which ought to animate all nations, particularly free ones, may mount up to military violence. These extremes ought to be equally avoided; but of the two, he considered the first far the most dangerous—far the most fatal. . . . I consider the extreme of weakness not only the most dangerous of itself, said Mr. C., but as that extreme to which the people of this country are peculiarly liable.

Calhoun dismissed any threat of national danger from maintaining strong military forces; and, naming England as the major threat to national security, he urged strengthening the navy as the safest, cheapest, and most effective means of defense. Stressing the theme of national security, he advocated construction of a system of roads and canals, not merely to improve internal communication and trade but to facilitate the rapid movement of troops to points threatened by invasion. The promotion of manufactures as a means of defense he believed to be a national duty, especially those that provided clothing and essential war materiel, and he would strengthen coastal defenses and key points along the nation's boundaries. As to finance, he envisioned a future not too far distant when internal taxes would furnish the principal supply of national revenue:

> This nation, Mr. C. said, was rapidly changing the character of its industry . . . becoming, to a considerable extent, a manufacturing nation. We find that exterior commerce . . . is every day bearing less and less proportion to the entire wealth and strength of the nation. The financial resources of the nation will, therefore, daily become weaker and weaker, instead of growing with the nation's growth, if we do not resort to other objects than our foreign commerce for taxation.

With Jeffersonian confidence in the intelligence and virtue of the American people, Calhoun believed they would bear the burden of taxation cheerfully if convinced that the measures were necessary and wise. On the wisdom of national policy embraced in the revenue program Calhoun had no doubt. He saw the nation charged by divine Providence not merely with the happiness of its own people but "in a considerable degree with that of the human race." America, with a government resting not on authority or prejudice or superstition but on reason, represented a new departure. Its success would open a new era in human affairs, for "all civilized Governments must in the course of time conform to its principles." It was this unique opportunity to wield great and far-reaching moral power that would thenceforth be the principal determinant of national policy:

> This nation is in a situation similar to that in which one of the most beautiful writers of antiquity paints Hercules in his youth. He represents the hero as retiring into the wildernes [sic] to deliberate on the course of life which he ought to choose. Two Goddesses approached him; one recommending to him a life of ease and pleasure; the other

of labor and virtue. The hero adopted the counsel of the latter, and his fame and glory are known to the world. May this nation, the youthful Hercules, possessing his form and muscles, be inspired with similar sentiments and follow his example.

John Randolph was impressed, even moved by Calhoun's powerful speech, which, like that of Clay a few days earlier, received glowing praise.[53] In a reply of some length, Randolph complimented the Carolinian on his abilities, integrity, and guiding principles. Knowing as well as Calhoun the value of moral power, the Virginian agreed in the abstract with Calhoun's principles but feared they would lead to consolidation of political power and destruction of the state governments. The Carolinian was "too deeply read in Aristotle, too well versed in political lore" to deny that the great value of this government lay in the "federative character of the Constitution," which balanced opposing interests within a harmonious whole. Randolph called on his colleagues to consider current policy from this perspective:

> As the gentleman from South Carolina has presented the question to the House, they and the nation cannot have the slightest difficulty in deciding whether they will give up the States or not; whether they will in fact make this an elective monarchy. The question is whether or not we are willing to become one great consolidated nation, under one form of law; whether the State governments are to be swept away; or whether we have still respect enough for those old respectable institutions to regard their integrity and preservation as a part of our policy? I, for one, said Mr. R., cling to them. . . . I am not for a policy which must end in the destruction, and speedy destruction, too, of the whole of the State governments.[54]

Although the debate ran on for several more days, the most incisive speeches had already been delivered by Clay, Calhoun, and Randolph. Lowndes contributed more to the discussion than the record reveals. Two days after Calhoun and Randolph spoke, "Mr. Lowndes then addressed the Committee [of the Whole] in defense of the report under consideration and in reply to the objections urged against it in the course of debate."[55] On February 6, the House approved the land tax of $3 million for one year, and within two weeks more had passed bills in conformity with all remaining resolutions except the tenth.

Taken up on February 8, the tenth resolution of the Ways and Means report read: "*Resolved,* That it is expedient to amend the rates of duties on imported articles, after the 30th of June next, as that they shall be estimated to produce an amount equal to that which would be produced by an average addition of 42 percent to the permanent rates of duties."[56] Agreed to without a dissenting vote, the resolution went back to Lowndes's committee, who spent the next six weeks fashioning a tariff schedule into a bill that the chairman reported to the House on March 20. The schedule generally followed the recommendations of Secretary Dallas, with one major exception: the committee recommended rates on cottons and woolens at 25 percent.

No sooner was the bill read through than Solomon Strong of Massachusetts moved to tax cottons at 33.33 percent and woolens at 28, according to the Dallas schedule. Chairman Lowndes took this opportunity to present to the House a full exposition of his views. The reporter noted that he spoke against the motion, "taking a clear and comprehensive view on the subject of protecting duties generally," and explained why the committee had reported smaller duties on these articles than the secretary had recommended.[57]

When Strong withdrew his motion the next day, Speaker Clay moved again to raise the tax on cottons to 33.33 percent, "to try the sense of the House," he said, "as to the extent it was willing to go in protecting domestic manufactures—assuming there was no difference of opinion on the propriety of such protection, but only on the degree." Clay disagreed with the basic premise of the Ways and Means report. To him the purpose of protective duties was not merely to restore competitive balance in the American market but to stimulate the growth of American manufactures. For this purpose, which he took pains to identify with the national interest, the duties offered by Ways and Means were, he said, too low. To stimulate growth, Clay would raise the rates high enough to give American manufacturers a clear advantage over merchants who imported foreign goods.[58] Lowndes adhered to his committee's view of what constituted adequate protection and restated their position. He "entered into an ample and particular defense of the system reported by the committee," and the Speaker's motion failed, 43 to 51.[59]

Clay was undaunted. He still favored "thorough and decided protection by ample duties" but offered a compromise resolution of 30 percent on cottons. Ingham of Pennsylvania spoke at length in its support, borrowing from the Dallas report his main points of argument. Admitting that higher tariff rates would raise the cost of consumer goods, Ingham argued that this was a small price to pay for a more balanced and diversified economy, increased employment, and the nation's economic independence. He believed Americans had acquired a degree of skill in the mechanical arts that could become through encouragement "a source of inexhaustible wealth to the nation" or be lost for centuries if not forever through neglect. Renowned for his statistical expertise, Ingham buttressed his appeal with facts and figures except on the point most crucial to his argument, the alleged need for higher protection than the committee recommended. Opponents of higher duties called repeatedly "for estimates and calculations to show the precise amount of duty that would enable the American manufacturer to come into the market upon equal terms with the importer."[60] In answer, Ingham could only complain that such demands were "unreasonable and unfair" because "they could not be answered with any kind of certainty."[61] Samuel Smith, the great Baltimore merchant, disagreed. In "that minute and technical manner . . . peculiar to him," Smith supplied figures to show that when insurance, freight, commissions, and other costs were added to this tariff, the manufacturer would enjoy a competitive advantage in excess of 47 percent over the importer.[62] Chairman Lowndes "replied, in detail, to the arguments of Messrs. Ingham and Clay," but a slight majority found 30 percent an acceptable duty on cottons, so Clay's motion carried, 68 to 61.

The degree of opposition strength indicated that the question was far from settled. On March 23, Daniel Webster, with the approval of the nation's leading manufacturer of textiles, moved to set the duty on cottons at 30 percent for two years, 25 percent for two more years, and 20 percent thereafter.[63] Lowndes assented to the motion. "Satisfied that twenty-five or even twenty percent was a sufficient protection," he accepted the graduated plan, "persuaded that it would eventually produce the state of things which he thought most desirable."[64] The chairman's concession encouraged high protectionists to press for more. Clay wanted to extend the 30 percent tax to three years, which John Hulbert of Massachusetts quickly endorsed. Hulbert's colleague, Artemus Ward of Boston, wanted to go even further, with "substantial and permanent support" for the manufacturing interest. Timothy Pitkin of Connecticut agreed; wishing the bill to "encourage additional establishments," he said two years at 30 percent hardly gave a man time to erect his buildings. But the opposition stiffened. Calhoun, Smith of Maryland, and John Ross of Pennsylvania each declared 20 percent to be ample protection, although Calhoun said he would support the Webster amendment. Speaking for his rural constituency, Ross saw a powerful combination of selfish interests at work. Unwilling "to see one class of the community enslaved by another," the Pennsylvanian proclaimed the "great necessity for a strong country party to withstand the manufacturing and commercial parties here."[65]

Following this exchange, Webster's graduated tax passed with the support of Lowndes and Calhoun, but tactical blunders cost northern protectionists the advantage just won. They lost some southern support by voting with the majority to cut protection recommended for Louisiana sugar from four to two cents a pound, then alienated wool-growing interests of the middle states by supporting a similar reduction of the 15 percent duty recommended for raw wool. To Hardin of Kentucky, "their policy seemed to be to get all they could and keep what they got." Timothy Pickering, the influential spokesman of New England commerce, argued against "an extravagant duty" on textiles, "not believing that the existing manufactures required a duty of twenty-five per cent for two years." John Forsyth of Georgia denounced the high protectionist's display of sectional partiality and moved for a flat 20 percent duty on both cottons and woolens, which lost by less than five votes.[66] At that point Thomas Grosvenor of New York reminded his colleagues that "it had been admitted on all hands that present protection only was necessary" and even the manufacturers "had acknowledged that twenty-five per cent was sufficient."[67] The House finally fixed the rates on both cottons and woolens at 25 percent for three years and 20 percent thereafter.

Discussions on other articles produced considerably less interest than those on textiles, but this hardly lessened the labor of the committee chairman. Scores of resolutions were introduced to alter the rates recommended by the committee on the multitude of items to be taxed. On almost every one Chairman Lowndes found it necessary to rise and explain a point, to clarify a misconception, to reiterate the committee's position, or to defend its recommendations, quietly but firmly resisting all efforts to alter the limited purposes of the bill.

Lowndes's opinion carried great weight with the House majority, and usually only a few words from him determined the success or failure of a proposal. Henry Southard of New Jersey proposed to increase the duty on gunpowder from six to ten cents a pound; "after a few words from Mr. Lowndes in reply . . . the motion was negatived." William Milnor of Pennsylvania moved to reduce the rate on tin plates; "Mr. Lowndes offered a few arguments in support of the duty proposed by the bill, and in opposition to the amendment; after which the motion was negatived." Isahel Stearns of Massachusetts wanted the provision regulating the duty on woolens broadened; his suggestion was approved, "being accepted by Mr. Lowndes." Ingham moved that the duty of six cents a pound on gunpowder be raised to eight cents, "which was assented to by Mr. Lowndes, and agreed to by the House." Nathaniel Ruggles of Boston would have had copper sheets included in the list of copper articles protected by a duty of four cents a pound. "This motion was supported by the mover, Mr. Milnor, Mr. Stearns, and Mr. Webster, and opposed by Mr. Lowndes; and ultimately negatived, without a division."[68] Gradually it became clear that while the views of Chairman Lowndes regarding specific rates remained flexible, he intended the Tariff of 1816 to offer the American manufacturer no more than an equal opportunity in the marketplace.

Reported by the Committee of the Whole, on April 4 the amended bill was on the point of final passage when Randolph moved to strike out the section that fixed a minimum valuation on imported cotton goods. This provision, recommended by Secretary Dallas, provided that "all cotton cloths, whose value shall be less than 25 cents per square yard, shall be taken and deemed to have cost 25 cents per square yard, and shall be charged with duty accordingly."[69] Designed to give protection against cheap cottons produced by the cheap labor of India and the power looms of England, the "minimum principle" had originated with Francis W. Lowell, whose Boston Manufacturing Company, utilizing power looms invented by Lowell, was to derive the greatest benefit from it.[70] Randolph argued "with some invective" that this "scheme of public robbery" would destroy the East India trade and levy "an immense tax on one portion of the community to put money in the pockets of another." Ward of Massachusetts agreed with Randolph, stressing the injustice of a proposal that would destroy a valuable commerce, created altogether out of New England enterprise, to benefit American producers of cheap cottons.[71] The issue was compromised, however, when Webster, Ingham, Hulbert, Hopkinson, and Pitkin joined in support of an amendment from Timothy Pickering, which postponed the effective date of the minimum principle to March 1817, allowing ships in the East Indies trade a year of grace to bring their cargoes home. Then a final vote taken on April 8 passed the tariff bill 88 to 54.[72] Slightly amended by the Senate, the Tariff of 1816 received final approval on April 27 and went into effect on July 1.

Sectional distribution of votes on Forsyth's motion a few days earlier, to cut textile rates to a flat 20 percent, and on the final House vote that passed the Tariff of 1816 profiled the distribution of protectionist sentiment. On the naked question Forsyth presented, New England endorsed the reduction 14 to 13, showing fairly equal division among the region's commercial and manufacturing interests and evidence of commercial discontent over the minimum principle. Only five members from the Old Northwest and the manufacturing middle states, "the mushroom interest which had sprung into favor," as Randolph described them, considered 20 percent enough protection. Agricultural interests of the South Atlantic seaboard, where geography reinforced tradition to preclude any serious prospect of developing even regionally marketed manufactures in the near future, approved a 20 percent rate 41 to 7. The western South (Kentucky, Tennessee, and Louisiana), with high hopes for internal improvements financed with tariff revenue and needing protection for sugar and hemp, voted 7 to 4 against the lower rate.[73] On the bill's final passage, the margin of support increased in each of the four sections. After the House modified the minimum principle slightly and postponed its effective date, New England voted 17 to 10 in favor of the bill. The middle states, gratified by elevation of textile duties to 25 percent for three years, supported passage 47 to 5. Almost every third congressman from the South Atlantic states found the temporary increase acceptable, as this section voted 35 to 15 against the bill. From the western South, Louisiana's only representative voted against the bill after the House majority had cut in half protection recommended for sugar, but Kentucky and Tennessee voted 9 to 3 for passage.[74]

In one of these four sections, the South Atlantic states, support for the Tariff of 1816 has been misunderstood. The standard interpretation until 1959 was that southerners expected the law to promote the growth of manufactures in the South. Norris Preyer so effectively refuted this interpretation in his 1959 article on the subject that William Freehling dismissed the theory as resting on nothing more substantial than "the historian's faith in economic causation."[75] Preyer found southern motives in what he termed "patriotism, prosperity, and promises." Genuinely concerned that the British might reopen the war, southerners cooperated to establish the necessary degree of national self-sufficiency; the postwar boom made higher prices occasioned by the law more easily affordable; and the "promises" lay in the provision that would lower textile rates in three years to the level of a tariff for revenue only.[76]

The findings here confirm those of Preyer, although his list might be expanded to include four other points: (1) the clear understanding on the limited purpose of protection in 1816, to restore balanced competition, explicitly stated by Chairman Lowndes of Ways and Means and implicit in the bill itself; (2) the disinterested recommendations of southern leaders, President Madison, Chairman Lowndes, and Calhoun; (3) the objective research effort to establish proof of need; and (4) rates held to the necessary minimum that even manufacturers admitted to be fair. As for Lowndes's management of the bill, he sustained a spirit of moderation, balance, and fairness through its final passage that created an atmosphere conducive to altruistic support for a national objective. A substantial southern minority subordinated southern interests for the good of the whole. South Carolina, alone among the states of the southern seaboard, cast a majority vote, 4 to 3, in favor of protection.

Whether disinterested southern leadership could sustain a spirit of intersectional harmony on the tariff issue beyond 1816 remained to be seen, but the *National Intelligencer* showed little restraint in praising the quality of that leadership thus far. The editor said, "It is gratifying to the friends of government founded in reason, to discover, that real merit, however unobtrusive, attracts, in due time, the public regard." He took pleasure in reprinting a tribute from the *Baltimore Patriot*, "not without some fear of offending that modesty" which "would retire from so public a notice," but "justice to the gentleman named" required mention of "the arduous, useful, and brilliant discharge of his legislative duties" for the several years past. It was the public's misfortune "that Mr LOWNDES has not filled the space in their view to which his distinguished services have invariably entitled him. A voice of very moderate capacity unable to fill the large hall of Representatives, and, of course, not to be well heard by the reporters, has ... ably maintained the cause of his country [but] prevented that justice from being done to his abilities and merit, which they have always deserved." The Baltimore tribute declared that if Secretary Dallas should leave the Treasury Department, "no one could be selected to preside over that department more capable of administering its affairs than Mr Lowndes. He is universally admitted to be a statesman of the first order of talents, of unsurpassed patriotism and integrity."[77]

Such flattering notice of one South Carolina congressman could quite as readily have been directed to another. The second major piece of nationalistic legislation produced by the Fourteenth Congress was the act that incorporated the Second Bank of the United States. Formulated in the special committee Calhoun chaired, the bill provided for a bank capitalized at $35 million, one-fifth to be subscribed by the federal government and the remainder offered for public sale. Headquartered in

Philadelphia with branches in other cities, the Bank would have twenty-five directors elected by the stockholders, so five of the directors would be appointed by the president of the United States. Throughout the twenty years of its chartered existence, it would serve as the repository for federal revenue and surplus funds, which the Bank might use for ordinary business transactions free of charge. In exchange for this exclusive privilege, the Bank would pay to the federal government a bonus of $1.5 million and handle all its financial transactions without charge. Debate on the bank bill extended from the end of February to the middle of March, with Calhoun serving as its principal advocate and Daniel Webster its chief critic. Opposition arguments claimed excessive capitalization and condemned the government's role in the Bank's direction. On these grounds Webster made a final effort to defeat the bill on March 14, shortly before it passed 80 to 71.[78]

Lowndes had little to do with the bank bill, for throughout the debate he was heavily engaged with the revenue program and the general appropriations bill. Even so, he and Calhoun cooperated closely on these two momentous pieces of legislation, each lending support to the other's bill through its final passage. Their only significant point of disagreement this session concerned the party caucus held on March 18, which nominated James Monroe for the presidency by a vote of 65 to 54 over William H. Crawford, Georgia's rising political star recently appointed secretary of the Treasury. Calhoun attended the caucus, but Lowndes, as expected, declined.[79]

Before this session closed, the Congress passed a relatively insignificant act upon which the career of many a representative would turn. Introduced by the colorful war veteran, Richard M. Johnson of Kentucky, the bill changed the pay of congressmen from six dollars a day to a sum of fifteen hundred dollars a year. Few members seemed to attach much significance to the bill or anticipate unfavorable reaction from their constituents. Lowndes never expressed his opinion on the change, but when it passed 81 to 67 on March 8, he voted against it.[80] Not until Congress adjourned at the end of April and the members went home did they discover how fully they had aroused the wrath of their constituents. To defend the law or yield to the popular clamor was a question virtually all would have to decide during the summer. Fall elections loomed, and the aroused electorate would not always distinguish between those who voted for the bill, such as Calhoun, and those like Lowndes who opposed it.

VIII
Nationalist

The summer of 1816 brought Lowndes a welcome respite from public cares but in his private affairs it gave him anything but relief. To demonstrate the lowcountry planter's vulnerability to fluctuations in the weather, perhaps no better example could be found in the immediate postwar years than the record compiled by the Horseshoe plantation. Beginning that summer Lowndes suffered a sharp and sustained reversal of fortune. His account with Kershaw and Lewis showed on April 27 a credit balance of $4,985.90. After that date the account noted a steady accumulation of entries in the debit column but nothing under credits for the remainder of the year. By December 31, instead of almost $5000 to his credit, he found himself $4,855.70 in debt to the firm.[1]

What went wrong may be gathered from the weather reports. Indeed, observers throughout the nation from this summer through much of the next year noted such strange and unexpected fluctuations and temperature extremes as to excite universal wonder. This "Year Without A Summer"[2] chilled the northeastern states while the southern seaboard endured sweltering heat and a crop-killing drought. July temperatures in the Carolina lowcountry were "the warmest in years," hovering consistently near "98 in the shade." Drought conditions continued into August with no rain to relieve the oppressive heat and sunstroke beginning to appear among the causes of lowcountry fatalities. News from the upcountry in early September told a similar story of steady heat and no rain and great rivers falling to unheard-of levels.[3] All across the South, from Louisiana up through the Carolinas, crops sustained serious damage.[4] Reports of impending disaster came down from North Carolina and Virginia where the corn crop stood a shriveled ruin in sunbaked fields.[5] As lowcountry water reserves covering thousands of acres ran dry, rice threatened to go the way of upcountry corn. And all the while, diminishing supplies of foodstuffs drove prices steadily upward.[6]

A violent squall accompanied by thunder and lightening struck Lowndes's Grove on September 17, heralding a break in the lowcountry drought and the apparent salvation of the rice crop. When the rains came, though, it seemed as if the summer's accumulation of moisture would be dumped on the parched landscape before they stopped, for a great storm extending from the mountains to the sea was moving through the South. Commencing on Friday, September 21, torrential rain with gale force winds lashed the Carolina lowcountry. Relief was general and gratefully received as water supplies were replenished and rivers rose toward normal levels. But a week of heavy rains with no letup transformed general relief into general concern. By September 30, with the fields ready for harvest, the worst lowcountry fears were realized. Swollen rivers backed up by the tides spread over the landscape, submerging whole plantations in a brackish mixture of salt and fresh water, destroying a third of the total anticipated rice harvest and wrecking the intricate systems that controlled normal water flow to the fields.[7] The Georgetown area suffered heavy losses from flooding. To the southwestward losses in the Edisto basin were no less severe if not indeed worse, judging from the Horseshoe's unfortunate example. Crop failure at the Horseshoe was nearly total; Lowndes sent only twenty-five barrels of rice to market and found it necessary to purchase food supplies to carry the Horseshoe population through the coming winter.[8]

As the Horseshoe's example suggests, the vaunted postwar prosperity of lowcountry rice planters, described by one historian as "the days of jubilee, when there seemed no limit to South Carolina's prosperity,"[9] actually lasted one year, then disappeared in a bewildering sequence of drought, flood, and pestilence. Following the banner year of 1815, which produced for export almost 83,000,000 pounds of rice, the 1816 crop fell to 47,578,000 pounds. Although the short crop drove up the average price per hundred weight, the increase was too small to compensate for diminished production.[10] And for planters like Lowndes, it offered almost no compensation whatever.

Lowndes lost, in addition to his rice crop, at least ten thousand dollars in 1816. The reversal helps to explain his decision to sell almost a third of his slaves. Fortunately, the bountiful harvest of 1815 had provided enough cushion against the forced sale of his chattel property so that he was able to impose a condition on the sale. The condition, which ultimately prevented the sale, shows a regard for his slaves consistent with the more humane traditions of lowcountry paternalism. His advertisement in the *Courier* read,

PRIME NEGROES

FOR SALE, an entire gang of between seventy and eighty Country born Negroes; among them are Carpenters, Coopers, Sawyers, and Ploughmen. The owner is unwilling to separate them. They will be delivered at any time most convenient to the purchaser. For terms, apply to

Kershaw & Lewis
No. 264, East Bay[11]

Even though four major sales ranging in number from fifty to seventy-six lowcountry slaves took place between September 1816 and March 1817, no purchaser came forward who could meet Lowndes's approval or was willing to meet his terms.[12] After Lowndes returned to Washington, his attorney arranged the sale of two families of five members each, who went as units to neighboring plantations, and a skilled craftsman named Flander, bought by Charlestonian John Farr. Lowndes realized $5,270.00 from these sales excluding fees, just enough to clear his debt with Kershaw and Lewis, whose own business affairs were adversely affected by the diminished harvest.[13] After this disastrous summer, the income Lowndes received for congressional service began to assume a humbling significance.

The issue of congressional pay dominated the fall elections of 1816. Public wrath over the "salary grab bill" was all but universal, and to congressional incumbents, astonishingly strong. Richard M. Johnson, the Kentucky congressman, said the Compensation Law "excited more discontent than the alien and sedition laws, the *quasi* war with France, the internal taxes of 1798, the embargo, the late war with Great Britain, the Treaty of Ghent, or any one measure of the Government, from its existence."[14] To the average voter, the law smelled of congressional self-indulgence bordering on corruption, in blatant contradiction to the ideal of civic virtue at a time when the nation was still heavily burdened with debt and the revenue program demanded of the general public personal sacrifice for the common good.[15] Consequently the voters repudiated two out of every three House members and replaced more than the usual number of Senators.

In South Carolina, sixteen candidates took the field to contest the nine incumbents for their seats. Of the nine, only three were returned: Middleton, Calhoun, and Lowndes. Middleton and Lowndes, having voted against the measure, felt no necessity to defend the controversial law. Calhoun took the issue to the people and successfully defended his vote without departing from his initial stand. William Mayrant, attempting to follow Calhoun's example, was so overwhelmingly defeated that he resigned immediately. On the other hand, Federalist Benjamin Huger lost election even though he had "strenuously and ably" opposed the Compensation Bill. Significantly, none of the challengers cared to test the loyalty of Lowndes's constituents, and he alone won reelection unopposed.[16]

When the Fourteenth Congress convened for its second session on December 2, the members were "mortified, angry, and defiant, disgusted alike with the public and the public service."[17] In one of their first actions, they considered and flatly rejected a motion to repeal the Compensation Law. After Speaker Clay had appointed standing committees—Lowndes being named again to chair Ways and Means—the House resumed discussion of the issue. Johnson of Kentucky, author of the original bill, now introduced a motion for repeal. To Johnson, the sovereign people had spoken; their representatives had but to obey.[18] The House wrangled over the issue to the middle of January, then disposed of it by voting to leave the law undisturbed to the end of the session when it would expire, leaving the next Congress to set its own rate of pay. During the course of debate, Calhoun delivered a stern lecture on meek submission to popular clamor; as for constituent instruction, the Constitution was his only "letter of instruction."[19] Lowndes never rose to speak on the issue, in part perhaps for personal reasons that might well be imagined, but also because the duties of his office already occupied most of his time and interest.

The revenue program had proved bountiful in its first year of operation. President Madison in his annual message pointed out "with great gratification" that revenue for 1816 would reach $47 million while expenditures would amount to not more than $38 million, leaving a surplus in the Treasury of at least $9 million.[20] This news inspired opponents of internal taxes, the least popular feature of the revenue program, to mount a campaign for their repeal. Lowndes, though, saw in the surplus an opportunity to hasten further reduction of the public debt, a favorite project with him and a fundamental tenet of republican economy. On the fourteenth day of the new year he reported a bill that would apply to the debt all surplus funds above $2 million remaining in the Treasury at the end of each year.[21]

Through the balmy October-like weather of January, little opposition to internal taxes or the Sinking Fund Bill surfaced. Then, opposition restraint and the weather broke almost simultaneously, a combination that taxed the precarious stability of Lowndes's health more than he realized. In early February, "the climate of Canada, we had almost said of Lapland," moved down over the eastern seaboard and for weeks held the region locked in its grip. It drove temperatures well below the zero mark, dumped more than a foot of snow over a vast area extending from North Carolina through New England, closed ice-bound ports to the northward, and bridged the Potomac with ice up to twenty-six inches thick. "Such cold, of so long duration," the *Intelligencer* noted, "has not been experienced here, it is believed, for thirty years."[22] When the House continued to sit in an uncommonly frigid chamber, prudence dictated that Lowndes keep to his quarters. But on February 14, Lewis Williams of North Carolina moved to repeal the internal taxes, and for the remainder of the session the chairman of Ways and Means was locked in a struggle for the survival of his program.

The chairman's habitually mild and courteous manner belied his determination to defend his program, nor was he above the use of parliamentary maneuver to stifle its critics. In the midst of discussion on Williams's repeal motion, Lowndes suddenly moved to proceed to the orders of the day. Carried by a single vote, the deft maneuver brought James Johnson of Virginia to his feet complaining of the chairman's excessive power over tax legislation:

> How long . . . has it been settled that the rights and interests of the American people shall be exclusively confided to a few members of this House who compose its standing committees; or more peculiarly, to the still smaller number appointed to preside over these committees? Is it presumptuous, or criminal, in any member of this body, to submit a proposition, which he believes calculated to promote the interest, the prosperity, and the happiness of this nation? Are the laws imposing taxes to remain fixed and unalterable except by the will and pleasure of the Chairman of the Committee of Ways and Means . . . ?[23]

Williams, too, found cause for protest when the chairman exposed the blunt side of his customary courtesy:

> That gentlemen, Mr. Speaker (pointing to Mr. LOWNDES), at all times and on all occasions, has conducted himself in this House so

as to secure not only the confidence and esteem, but I believe the admiration of every member on this floor; but while I pay this just tribute to the merits of that gentleman, I must be allowed to say, that I think he was incorrect when he stated, in reply to the remarks I made on Friday, that I had failed to show any sufficient reasons in support of the resolution then under consideration.[24]

At other times Lowndes spoke "on various grounds and at some length," or "replied very fully to the arguments of gentlemen who supported the resolution . . . and showed how inconvenient a moment this was to agitate this question." Ultimately he succeeded. A few days before adjournment the House postponed further consideration of the resolution to March 2.[25] As this date fell on a Sunday, the repeal measure was dead. Shortly afterwards the Sinking Fund Bill passed, and Lowndes could relax in the knowledge that his revenue program would remain intact for another year.

In the meantime, two measures of constitutional significance arose in the House. One of these, the Bonus Bill, originated in a motion from Calhoun to establish a fund for the improvement of transportation and communication throughout the nation. The proposal would set apart for such internal improvements a bonus of $1.5 million, paid by the Second Bank of the United States in exchange for its charter, in addition to dividends on stock in the Bank held by the federal government. The Bonus Bill narrowly passed the House (86 to 84) and the Senate as well, but President Madison, in one of the final acts of his public career, vetoed the bill on constitutional grounds. Resuming the strict constructionist stance of his congressional years, Madison could find "the power proposed to be exercised by the bill" neither among the enumerated powers nor in the clauses of the preamble, "without a latitude of construction departing from the ordinary import of the terms" and "contrary to the established and consistent rules of interpretation."[26] The views of William Lowndes, though unrecorded in the debate on the Bonus Bill, differed from those of Calhoun on the one hand and the president on the other. Lowndes favored internal improvements financed with federal funds, and he would have much to say on the subject at a later time; but he disagreed with the specific allocation of the bonus for this purpose and voted against Calhoun's bill both before and after the veto.[27] The House majority favoring the bill proved too thin to override the veto but too strong to consider the issue settled. It would be revived in the next Congress.

The second issue of constitutional significance grew out of a bill to enforce neutrality. The issue came before the House when John Forsyth of Georgia, chairman of the Committee of Foreign Relations, introduced a bill to halt activities in port cities of the United States carried out by sympathizers of the Spanish American colonies,[28] which had been in revolt since 1808. The rebels had captured the imagination of American citizens who saw in the struggle a repetition of their own revolution against British tyranny. President Madison had issued in September 1815 a proclamation of neutrality enjoining citizens to maintain strict impartiality toward both Spain and her rebellious colonies. In practice, American neutrality proved more beneficial to the insurgent colonials, for ships flying the rebel flags enjoyed free use of the ports of the United States just as other foreign vessels did. As sympathy for the Spanish Americans grew, unneutral activity in their behalf became notorious, especially in Baltimore and New Orleans. Forsyth's bill would prevent American citizens from "selling . . . , arming and equipping vessels of war" in American ports intended for use "against nations in amity with the United States."[29]

After Forsyth explained its details, John Randolph endorsed the measure, dubbing it "a bill for making peace between His Catholic Majesty and the town of Baltimore."[30] Randolph saw the revolts as internal struggles with which outsiders had no right to interfere. Here Henry Clay took the floor to champion the Latin American cause, expressing a view he would reiterate repeatedly in the years ahead. Condemning the bill as an instrument calculated to assist a European despot in his efforts to suppress the independence movement in Spanish America, Clay entreated the House to take a liberal view of the neutrality issue. Forsyth rejoined that the success or failure of the rebel cause had little to do with the question; the central issue was whether the honor and good faith of the United States would be upheld in the face of notorious violations of its neutrality and evasion of its laws.[31] Debate on the bill revolved around these opposing points of view. Lowndes concurred with Forsyth's position and supported the Neutrality Bill through its final passage, but he reserved detailed comment for a more spirited review of the subject in the next Congress.

About midnight on March 3 the Fourteenth Congress adjourned. The next day James Monroe was inaugurated. Lowndes, although anxious as usual to see to his affairs in Carolina and caring little for state occasions, would not have considered slighting the Monroes by declining to attend the inaugural, which was held out-of-doors on a fine spring day.[32] A similar regard for the feelings of Elizabeth doubtless led him to join in the social affairs surrounding the inaugural, fittingly concluded with a brilliant ball at Davis's Hotel. Afterwards a siege of rainy weather turned the wretched roads of northern Virginia into quagmires, delaying to early April the family's departure for home.[33]

Prospects of April and May for a successful rice crop in 1817 dissolved in an almost continuous summer downpour. By the end of June the entire lowcountry was waterlogged after twenty-six days of rain. And still it continued to fall—five more inches in July—and on into August the "heavy and continual rains" filled the rivers to overflowing, flooding the lowcountry for the second successive year. Damage to Lowndes's parish and most of the country south and west of Charleston was heavy, with crops drowned and "most of the bridges carried away."[34]

When the rains stopped, the "fevers" came, not only the "stranger's fever" but the dreaded scourge of yellow fever, to which no one seemed immune. With surprising suddenness it spread through Charleston, claiming 16 victims in the second week of August. Natives and newcomers alike fled the city as the epidemic spread. By the end of August more than 60 had died, and within another week the number approached 90. The city council set apart September 11 "as a day of Humiliation and Prayer to Almighty God," and yet the grim toll continued to mount. Finally in October it began to diminish and terminated abruptly on November 20 with the arrival of the "long looked-for and welcome visitor, Jack Frost."[35] It was the worst yellow fever epidemic in South Carolina history, claiming, by final reckoning, 270 lives.[36]

Discounting lives lost in the fever epidemic, the summer of 1817 proved slightly less destructive than the previous one. Rice production rose to 52,909,000 pounds,[37] still 30,000,000 pounds short of the harvest of 1815, but a welcome increase nonetheless. Production at the Horseshoe also improved; it could hardly have done otherwise. Lowndes produced enough rice to feed his people and send 139 barrels to market, hardly enough to cover operating costs, but at least he did not have to purchase food supplies to carry them through the second successive winter.[38] Forced to depend on credit from his banker friends for another year, he still had abundant reason to be thankful, for the great fever epidemic had passed over both the Horseshoe and the Grove.[39]

Lowndes arrived in Washington in time for the opening formalities of the Fifteenth Congress on December 1, 1817. The tone of this session was determined in substantial degree by President Monroe's cabinet appointments of the previous spring. The key appointment had been that of John Quincy Adams to the highly coveted post of secretary of state, generally considered the stepping stone to the presidency. Chairman Forsyth of the Foreign Relations Committee, "speaking as if he personally knew it," explained to Lowndes how domestic politics had influenced Monroe's choice. Henry Clay and William H. Crawford of Georgia, late American minister to France whom Madison had recently named to succeed Dallas as secretary of the Treasury, were regarded as the leading competitors to succeed Monroe as president. Forsyth said that "Mr. Monroe would have been quite willing to make Crawford Sec[retar]y of State if Clay had been willing. The difficulty was to give no decided advantage to either Clay or Crawford as competitors for the Presidency. The expedient employed was to make Adams Sec[retar]y of State because as Mr. Monroe said it was impossible he should ever be President."[40] Quite aware of the New Englander's personal qualities and his tenacious defense of American interests in dealing with European diplomats, Lowndes commented, "I confess I do not exactly see the impossibility."[41] Clay was so disappointed at losing the cabinet prize to Adams that he turned down a consolation offer to head the War Department and used the House Speakership to launch an undeclared and none-too-subtle war against the Monroe administration's foreign policy. Crawford agreed to continue as Treasury secretary under Monroe so that he could employ the patronage of his office to enhance his future presidential prospects.

Had William Lowndes been willing to compromise his republican principles, he would have become secretary of war under Madison and subsequently under Monroe as well. Madison tendered the offer to Lowndes in October 1816, but the eminent Carolinian declined with the explanation that he felt he could be more useful in the House. Monroe also offered the post to Lowndes, but the first public announcement gave the president's choice as Isaac Shelby, after whose refusal John C. Calhoun accepted the appointment.[42] Lowndes had repeatedly stated that he had no ambition for office outside the House, and he meant what he said. He would receive several offers of appointment in the coming years and refuse them all.[43]

Two exceptionally knowledgeable observers of the Washington political scene, one a perceptive though uncritical admirer of Lowndes, and the other a tough-minded realist, together offered a balanced analysis of Lowndes's ambition as a public figure. George Watterson of the Library of Congress, anonymous author of a series of penetrating sketches of contemporary political leaders published in 1818, said of Lowndes,

> [H]is ambition is the ambition of virtue, and he aspires to the lofty and imposing elevation of a statesman and a patriot. The contracted, and paltry intrigues of party are beneath the dignity of his mind and revolting to the virtues of his heart: and he labors not for adventitious and fleeting reputation, but for the permanent good and lasting glory of his country. When he addresses the house every ear is attentive lest anything should escape, and every mind is satisfied because the truths which have been uttered were recommended by the charms of virtue, and arrayed in the simple beauty of moral worth.... I know not what station destiny has designed for him, but his mind would qualify him for almost anything; he realizes the idea which Mirabeau has formed of a statesman.[44]

John Quincy Adams, after he had become well acquainted with the modest Carolinian, recorded similar sentiments in his diary two years later.

> Lowndes is a man of fine talents, of good principles, of mild temper, and placid manners—grave, but cheerful, and always inoffensive. ... He has more personal influence in the House of Representatives than any other member, and is generally friendly to the present Administration. But, as much of his influence rests upon the general impression of his independence, he is rather over-solicitous to maintain that reputation. To be very sure of standing erect, he leans a little backward.[45]

For Lowndes, to accept a political office of any kind, except by vote of his constituents or the people at large, would be to abandon the old classical ideal of civic virtue, the polar star of his public life. That this was also the abstract ideal of the age in which he lived accounts in substantial degree for his growing political influence and public esteem.[46] In what might be termed his purist approach to politics, he differed from his friend Calhoun, who entered Monroe's cabinet as secretary of war in 1817, leaving Lowndes the last of the "splendid constellation of talents" from South Carolina still serving in the House.

The House organized, routinely electing Clay to the Speaker's chair, and Clay once again appointed Lowndes chairman of Ways and Means.

Aside from the routine legislation annually formulated by his committee, most of the questions engaging Lowndes's attention had been carried over from the last Congress. President Monroe now recommended repeal of the internal taxes that Lowndes had skillfully maneuvered to save during the previous session. Lowndes brought in a bill to this effect on December 9, explaining that he had not altered his opinion on the propriety of retaining the taxes for speedy debt reduction, but as the necessity for their retention seemed to have diminished, he had no desire to remain obstinate in view of a general expectation that the unpopular measures would be repealed.[47] The delighted representatives sped the bill through the House in two days, and it became law before Christmas. Early in January the House took up the controversial issue of congressional pay left deliberately unresolved by their predecessors. With almost no debate, the members settled on a per diem allowance of eight dollars, a modest increase of two dollars above the original rate, which the general public found acceptable.

The Committee of Roads and Canals reopened the constitutional issue of federally financed internal improvements, and for a time the question appeared to be a private quarrel among the Virginians. Madison's veto of the Bonus Bill and Monroe's subsequent statement of agreement with his predecessor might have initiated action for the constitutional amendment Monroe suggested had Virginian George Tucker, chairman of the committee, been willing to accept the doctrine of presidential infallibility. But on March 6, Tucker brought in and stoutly championed a superficially altered version of Calhoun's vetoed bill. This aroused Philip Barbour and several colleagues of the state delegation to take the floor in defense of strict construction, bearing down on the danger of reading into the Constitution authority not specifically granted in its articles, denying to the federal government the right to appropriate money except to carry out the enumerated powers, and citing the *Federalist* essays in support of their narrow constitutional doctrines.[48]

In response, Henry Clay spoke for the developing West in calling for liberal construction on this issue. Leaning heavily on the clause, "Congress shall have power to establish post offices and post roads," the Speaker attempted to demonstrate that throughout the Constitution the term "establish" meant to make or to construct rather than to employ preexisting facilities and arrangements. He stressed the constantly growing need for roads and canals to bind the nation together, a need that future growth would render absolutely imperative. He would guard the rights of the states but maintained that the only constitutional restriction on federal power to construct roads and canals was the requirement that the government make adequate compensation for the confiscation of private property.[49]

When Lowndes rose to speak, his calm detachment contrasted sharply with the earnest intensity of Clay's appeal, nor was that the only difference between them. Lowndes had prepared his remarks with meticulous care, adopting the higher ground and more elevated tone befitting a respectful dissent from a presidential veto on constitutional grounds. His analysis of the fundamental questions involved in the proposal reflected the clarity of his thought, his analytical powers, and the magnitude of his nationalism.[50]

Lowndes observed that the resolution as presented to the House tended to confuse the issue of federally funded internal improvements because it entangled the principle of constitutionality with the expediency of establishing the fund recommended: "After the adverse opinions of two Presidents had been expressed, [he] thought it was proper to settle the Constitutional question, and in so doing it was best to present it free from the question of expediency, or from any embarrassments of detail." Moreover, he felt it was necessary to "distinguish between the right of appropriating money to the construction of canals and roads, where the necessary rights of soil were obtained by contract with its owners, and the high power which a Government could only exert, of taking private property for public use, and making the canals or roads, which the public necessities might require, without the consent of the owners of the soil, upon paying to them a just indemnity."

Lowndes believed the national government possessed the constitutional authority at issue here in not one but two essentially different rights. The first was a civil right, embracing the rights of contract, purchase, sale, or holding of land or other property and of employing it as the public interest might require. The other, a political right, "the power of taking private property, for public service, of making a road or a canal, without purchasing the land from its owner, was one of the highest attributes of Government." Lowndes found it most strange that the government's civil right of contracting, purchasing, or holding land was not only "vehemently contested, but viewed as a subject of suspicion and alarm." He saw nothing to fear in this right: "Has the General Government, then, under the Constitution, those rights of acquiring property, and using it, which are enjoyed by every legislative body in the Union; by every municipality; by every individual citizen of the United States?" He conceded that the federal government possessed only delegated powers, "and will it be whispered, that there are in this country any governments which draw their powers from a different source?" The general government, like that of the states, was created by and for the people who also animated and controlled it. He believed these civil rights belonged equally to both kinds of governments, and even to towns and villages whose very act of incorporation gave them these rights. He illustrated that while Philip Barbour denied to the general government the right to appropriate money except to carry out the enumerated powers, in the state of Virginia cities such as Richmond and Norfolk doubtless appropriated funds "on objects neither specified by their charters, nor anticipated by their framers," nor had their constitutional authority to do so been questioned. All governments by exercising this civil right acquired property; the corresponding right of employing the property to some useful purpose was implicit in the elementary notion of property itself and could not be denied.

Lowndes pointed out that the three primary political powers, raising armies, navies, and money, were among the enumerated powers of Congress. As the national government possessed undisputed authority to raise these three great instruments of control, Lowndes presumed it also had the right to employ them. He rejected Barbour's argument that their employment was constitutionally limited to the execution of the enumerated powers. The Virginian had formulated a new rule of construction, an interpolation of a principle found neither in the Constitution nor in any political instrument ever written: "It was a question, then, not of constructive power, but of constructive limitation." Were the army and navy limited to "the objects of the other enumerated powers—to raising taxes, and passing naturalization and bankrupt laws?"

> [N]o man would maintain the fanciful rule that each power was to be limited to the objects of other enumerated powers, who should, with any patience, examine the result of this reciprocal application. And if each power was not to be so limited, why any? He thought himself justified in concluding that, where there was no express limitation in the Constitution, the Federal Government might employ army, navy, or money, for any purpose which might promote the public welfare without impairing the rights of States or individuals.

Lowndes illustrated the unreasonableness of strict constructionist claims that the government could acquire land only for certain specified objects, such as a fort or a dockyard or a seat of government, and yet be constitutionally restrained from building military roads. A road to a fort was as necessary as the cannon on its bastions; but according to the strict constructionist,

> the General Government has a right to make the ditch, and rampart, and platform of a fortification, but that the road which is necessary to supply it with reinforcements, or provisions, or munitions of war, cannot be constitutionally made by it, even with the consent of the owners of the soil. The State, indeed, or the people of the neighborhood, may do the work and keep it in repair; and upon this contingence must depend the power of the United States to maintain a garrison for the protection of the country which it was established to defend.

Furthermore, the federal government had purchased an immense amount of territory. If by this narrow construction it had no right to acquire title to this vast area, the result would be something infinitely worse than mere pecuniary loss. The doctrine simply could not be admitted. Nor would he accept *The Federalist* as the highest authority for narrow constitutional doctrine, for the celebrated authors of those essays were then the most zealous of advocates, "men yet warm from debates, in which all their ingenuity and talent for refinement had been employed to prove, that the powers which the Constitution gave were not great enough to be dangerous."

By way of summary, Lowndes stressed that to deny to the national government the common rights of purchase and contract was to impute to the Constitution a gross defect. While neither the national nor state governments possessed any but delegated powers,

> he had no doubt that the State governments had the right to make roads and canals; and it would be to him an inscrutable mystery that a people should, in their State constitutions, give to their Representatives the power of levelling houses and taking private property, that the street of a town might be widened, and its convenience and beauty promoted, and that the same people should refuse to their Representatives, in the National Government the same power; not to promote the symmetry, but to secure the defence of their towns.

In concluding, Lowndes admitted the probability of abuse. He conceded that interested and enterprising individuals might build roads and canals with greater economy than the government. He conceded further that states might, as a rule, handle such projects better than the national government could. "But there were military and national roads that had to be made by the Government of the United States, or not at all. To these he would be willing to apply a part of the public income." Nowhere in the world, to his knowledge, were roads and canals left entirely to voluntary undertakings and individual interest. The most sensible policy was to make roads and canals the objects of attention by the national government, a policy adopted by every civilized country, to the mutual advantage of the nation and the individual.

Committee Chairman Tucker judged Lowndes's arguments "powerful and overwhelming," in fact, unanswerable; and as the debate continued, Tucker accused opponents of the resolution of taking great care to avoid meeting them.[51] Clay spoke once more before the debate ended, to show that the doctrine of the power belonging to Congress, by virtue of the "necessary and proper" clause, had been utilized by Madison himself in the Virginia Resolutions on the Alien and Sedition Acts.[52]

Lowndes introduced four resolutions that put the issue in final form when brought to a vote on March 14. The resolutions actually reduced the question to two points: whether Congress had the power under the Constitution "to appropriate money" for construction of internal improvements, as phrased in the first resolution; and whether it had the constitutional authority "to construct" internal improvements, as stated in each of the remaining three. The resolutions permitted a clear delineation of sentiment on the issue. By a vote of 90 to 75 the House accepted the constitutionality of the power to appropriate money for internal improvements. By a vote of 84 to 82 the House denied that Congress had the power "to construct post roads and military roads." On the power "to construct roads and canals necessary for commerce," the majority again disagreed, 95 to 71. The fourth resolution, that Congress had the authority "to construct canals for military purposes," failed also, 81 to 83.[53] So the House majority decided that Congress possessed the constitutional authority to appropriate money for internal improvements but not to construct them. There the matter rested. Lowndes dispelled all doubt that he approved broad-ranging congressional power in these areas, voting in favor of all four resolutions.[54]

In failing to persuade the House majority to his liberal point of view, Lowndes's closely reasoned argument may be deemed a failure.

Although he neglected to record his personal opinion, Lowndes thought well enough of it to consent to its publication in pamphlet form, the first of only three such occasions in his public career. While circulation of his views beyond the Washington community and his immediate constituency would broaden his reputation and enhance his stature as a national figure, Lowndes doubtless intended the wider distribution of his speech to reinforce internal improvement efforts in his home state.

South Carolina in 1817 embarked on an ambitious program designed primarily to facilitate the movement of upland cotton and other exports from the interior downriver to the coastal ports, with a reciprocal flow of plantation and farm supplies into the Carolina hinterland. The state legislature authorized the expenditure of $2 million over the next decade to deepen channels and clear obstructions from navigable streams, construct multilock canals at the Fall Line and rapids, and lay out additional roads into the backcountry. More ambitiously, the plan envisioned interstate transport through an intercoastal canal connecting the lowcountry with North Carolina, Georgia, and perhaps beyond, as well as upstate canals linking South Carolina rivers with the Ohio Valley through the New-Kanawha-Ohio river system as well as the Tennessee River. Under a Board of Public Works headed by General Superintendent Abraham Blanding, crews of stonemasons, quarrymen, and engineers were brought down from New England to build the canals. The extremely wet year of 1817 retarded progress, but the drought of 1818 drove the water table down to near ideal levels for the work, especially for river clearance. Along with the state's heavy financial commitment to develop the intrastate system, the provisions for interstate connectors encouraged a liberal view of federal authority under the Constitution to promote the grand design.[55] Few would have doubted that a broad-visioned nationalism shaped the contours of Lowndes's position on public affairs, but he could hardly deny that on this issue he spoke for South Carolina.

Lowndes and Clay having demonstrated close harmony on the domestic issues of internal improvements, the two House leaders differed sharply on the foreign policy question that next claimed their attention. Clay had given notice on the third day of the session to expect a forceful move in favor of the Spanish American rebels. The Speaker genuinely desired to assist the rebels in their quest for independence, but unfortunately for their cause, he chose to employ the issue of their recognition as a base from which to harass the Monroe administration. By 1818 his concern for the cause bore all the earmarks of a single-minded obsession, which claimed as its first casualties the Speaker's customary charm, conciliatory disposition, and prudent leadership. Lowndes regarded the issue with his customary objectivity from the constitutional perspective of the separation of powers.

The deliberate nature of administration policy on recognition served only to sharpen Clay's irritability. Lacking reliable information on conditions in the rebellious provinces, Monroe had sent a fact-finding mission to the area in December and considered any action prior to receipt of more precise information unadvisable at best. To complicate matters, the Neutrality Act of 1817 had proved inadequate, and energetic activity in American ports, fitting out ships and filibustering expeditions to assist the rebels, or to capitalize on conditions in the area, continued apace. When Monroe called on Congress to strengthen the enforcement power, the Committee of Foreign Relations responded with a comprehensive neutrality bill that Chairman Forsyth introduced on March 17, 1818.[56]

Forsyth had hardly concluded his introductory remarks when Speaker Clay derided "the offensive nature of the bill, which . . . instead of an act to enforce neutrality, ought to be entitled, an act for the benefit of His Majesty the King of Spain," and commenced a wholesale condemnation of its details. When Forsyth interrupted to express dismay at the Speaker's rejecting the bill out of hand after having himself instructed the committee to bring it in, Clay retorted that the bill was an unnecessary extension of the "superfluous" neutrality act of the previous session, upon which he recalled with pleasure that he cast a negative vote. Clay chose to view flagrant evasion and defiance of the law as the voice of the nation pronouncing doom on an uncivilized act passed at the remonstrance of a foreign power, leaving Congress nothing to do but repeal it.[57] Robertson of Louisiana, whose constituents were among the most active in the Spanish-American cause, agreed with Clay and moved a repeal of the act of 1817.

At this point William Lowndes joined the argument, denying Clay's charge of oppressive provisions in the existing law and foreign influence in its passage. There had been very little difference on principle between members who voted for or against it. Clay himself had conceded the illegality of activity the law was designed to prevent: "[T]he only difference between us," said Lowndes, "is that for the prevention of these unlawful acts we propose a remedy, which they will not accept." Lowndes stressed that the position of Congress and the country "must be that, so long as we profess neutrality, we ought to observe it; . . . our neutral obligations should be fairly and honestly fulfilled."[58] Clay found himself "with very painful regret" differing with Lowndes and Forsyth, but he pursued nonetheless his assault on the law. At one point he charged Lowndes with inconsistency, provoking the Carolinian to instruct the Speaker that a proper argument could hardly be established on a sentence fragment from a speech. As the debate wore on, support for the repeal resolution failed to materialize. When the House voted against repeal, Clay declared that until the United States recognized the "Southern independent governments," their friends could not find justice in its courts; but he would soon propose a remedy.[59]

The dramatic move came on March 23. The House was considering a clause in Lowndes's appropriations bill providing $30,000 to compensate the fact-finding commissioners sent to South America in December. Now Clay moved an amendment to appropriate $18,000 to outfit and pay one year's salary for a minister to be "deputed to the independent provinces of the River Plata, in South America." He followed up his proposal with a lengthy speech, giving free rein to his masterful talent for vivid visualization, painting in lurid colors the horrors of life under Spanish rule.[60] Forsyth attempted to refute Clay's arguments on the Speaker's own grounds. Then Lowndes took the floor to address the constitutional issues involved.

Lowndes observed that in the separation of powers the Constitution had specifically assigned to the executive branch the administration of foreign affairs. Therefore, communications and negotiations with foreign powers could be properly transacted only through the office of the Executive. The House had no right to interfere in such matters except in cases of proved culpable negligence or unreasonable delay in sending a minister. Neither exception obtained in the present case. For the House to approve the Speaker's proposal would violate the separation of powers by authorizing an unconstitutional intrusion of the legislative authority upon that of the Executive. Less significant but nevertheless worthy of note, such an act would cast censure on the conduct of the Executive. With the affairs of the provinces in their unsettled state, recognition would be at best unwise and at worst could involve the nation in war with Spain.[61]

Clay's reply, derisive and sarcastic, accused Lowndes of being inconsistent, lacking candor, and construing the Constitution to suit his immediate purpose, maintaining one day that there existed "a sweeping right in Congress to appropriate money to any object," and the next "that Congress has no right to appropriate money to a particular object." Lowndes spoke no more on the issue, and though the Speaker strove with great intensity to gain passage of his proposal, it lost overwhelmingly, 45 to 115, on March 28.[62] There the matter ended on a note of discord, to the relief of President Monroe and Secretary Adams and the frustration of Clay, who would carry on through the next three years his peculiar style of guerilla warfare in the cause of independence for the Spanish American colonies.

Through the remaining weeks of the session Lowndes wrapped up the routine business of his office including the annual appropriations bill along with minor adjustments in the tariff schedule. Then Congress adjourned on April 20, and Lowndes headed homeward to turn his attention for a few months to the chronic problem of his financial affairs.

IX

Constitutionalist

As William Lowndes headed homeward in April 1818, Major General Andrew Jackson pushed through the wilderness of Spanish East Florida with two thousand Tennessee militia and volunteers in pursuit of Seminole Indians. After the close of the Creek War in 1814, bands of Seminoles augmented by runaway slaves and dispossessed Creeks had raided southwestern Georgia from the Spanish Florida sanctuary. By 1816 the border had become a virtual no-man's-land. Troops sent to the area that year had successfully intimidated the Seminoles and removed the menace posed by the runaways by blowing up their Apalachicola River fort. Quiet had returned to the frontier until November 1817 when General Edmund P. Gaines, commanding troops along the border, attacked and burned the Indian village of Fowltown. The Indians had retaliated with a massacre of captured soldiers, and the Seminole War was under way.

Wishing to restore peace in the area, President Monroe in consultation with Secretary of War Calhoun had decided to move General Gaines to Amelia Island on the Atlantic coast and call Andrew Jackson down from Nashville to take command of the Apalachicola region. The key document in the controversy over Jackson's subsequent invasion of Spanish Florida was Calhoun's order of December 16, 1817 assigning Jackson to the command. The vital passage read: "With this view you may be prepared to concentrate your forces and to adopt the necessary measures to terminate a conflict which it has ever been the desire of the President . . . to avoid; but which is now made necessary by their settled hostilities."[1] Although restrictions that had been imposed on Gaines remained in effect—they authorized the commander to reduce the Indians by force, pursuing them into Florida if necessary, but on no account to molest a Spanish fort or garrison—Jackson had construed the passage quoted above as authorizing a latitude of action agreeable to his aggressive disposition. To secure presidential confirmation of his design, he had written directly to Monroe offering to secure the Floridas within sixty days. His later claim that he received that assurance, indirectly through Tennessee Congressman John Rhea, became a subject of controversy when Monroe denied the story.

Nevertheless, in April 1818 Jackson stormed into Florida with all the self-assurance of a man who had the entire nation at his back. By the end of May he had routed the Indians, taken every Spanish post in the region except St. Augustine, captured and executed two British subjects, deposed the Spanish governor, and extended the laws of the United States over the territory. He then departed for home, leaving behind a diplomatic problem of the first order for the Monroe administration.

When the cabinet assembled in July to discuss the problem, Calhoun recommended a reprimand on the ground that Jackson had violated orders. Monroe, however, yielded to the persuasive arguments of Secretary of State Adams, who advised an aggressive defense of the audacious general as an expedient that might pry Florida loose from the ineffectual grasp of Spain. To give the appearance of presidential sanction for the invasion, reconcile the general's conduct with his orders, and skirt the constitutional issues involved would require some nimble phrasing through three long paragraphs of explanation in Monroe's address to Congress in the fall.[2]

Along with the rest of the country, Lowndes followed news accounts of the Tennessee general's exploits but devoted most of his attention to the repair of his disordered finances. With the cooperation of his creditors and the first decent harvest in three years, he succeeded. He cleared his account with Kershaw and Lewis by giving bond for more than $7,000, converting the short-term obligation into a long-term, interest-bearing debt.[3] Scorching heat and a long summer drought that ran through August cut lowcountry rice production to 45,914,000 pounds, the lowest since the war,[4] but fortunately for Lowndes, water reserves at the Horseshoe held out long enough to produce the best crop since 1815. The 620 barrels sent to market brought a return of $11,402.44. They might have brought $4,000 or $5,000 more, but not one barrel of his 1818 crop had been sold before agricultural prices broke in January and began their downward slide into the depression of 1819.[5]

Of more immediate concern was Lowndes's health, which had shown signs of marked deterioration during the past year. From the latest Washington winter, with February cold "so excessive as to prevent the members from remaining in the House, without great inconvenience to themselves," Lowndes had come home to "an almost unexampled continuance of steady heat."[6] The necessity of traveling north in winter and south in summer and being regularly exposed to the worst of both seasons could break the health of stronger men than Lowndes. His had so weakened during the past few months that his doctors advised a leisurely vacation in Europe for its recovery. Entreated by Elizabeth to follow their advice and assured that she could manage plantation affairs in his absence, Lowndes began to make plans for a summer in Europe after the close of the next session of Congress. The state of his health helps to explain his delayed arrival in Washington in late November, after Congress had been in session almost two weeks.[7] Indeed the delay might have been deliberate. When he arrived committee appointments had already been made. This relieved him of the taxing burden of the chairmanship of Ways and Means, leaving him free to regulate his attendance as the state of his health might require.

One of the first questions taken up was General Jackson's invasion of Florida. Following Monroe's attempt to defend the general in the president's annual message on November 16, the House experienced some difficulty deciding whether to refer the matter to the Foreign Relations Committee or to the Military Affairs Committee before finally dividing it between them. The Military Affairs Committee confined its attention to issues surrounding the two British subjects, Alexander Arbuthnot, a Scot trading with the Seminoles, and Robert Ambrister, a British soldier of fortune, who were captured in Spanish territory and then tried and executed on Jackson's orders. On Tuesday, January 12, the committee brought in its report censuring the popular hero.[8] On the following Monday the House went into Committee of the Whole on the subject, and for the next three weeks national attention focused on the debate that followed.

Thomas W. Cobb of Georgia, a political ally of Treasury Secretary Crawford, led off with a speech in support of the report, broadened the issue by calling for House disapproval of the capture and occupation of Pensacola and Fort St. Marks, and closed with resolutions to prevent such controversial military action in the future.[9] Two days later Speaker Clay assumed leadership of Jackson's critics. Ranging over Jackson's military career in search of flaws, the Speaker found fault with the general's earlier Treaty of Fort Jackson and almost every aspect of the Florida campaign. He concluded with a solemn warning that the ambitions of a modern military chieftan could be as dangerous to liberty as Caesar's had been to Rome.[10] Friends of the general heard political overtones ringing through the speeches of Cobb and Clay and understood their efforts as an attempt to stifle the presidential prospects of the Hero of New Orleans. This diverted attention away from the questions at issue and gave a decided political character to the debate as a whole.

Of Jackson's many defenders in the House, three of the most effective were James Tallmadge of New York, George Poindexter of Mississippi, and a member of the Military Affairs Committee, the war veteran Richard Johnson of Kentucky. Johnson had introduced in the committee a minority report in Jackson's favor that failed by one vote. Jackson himself arrived in Washington during the debates, and his presence was not without effect on their course. Before a House so crowded with spectators that it was feared the structure might not stand the strain, the general's friends extolled his virtues, his selfless patriotism, and his great contributions to the country. It was crowd-pleasing oratory in the grand manner, replete with all the colorful flourishes and classical allusions at the members' command, as this passage from a speech by Alexander Smyth of Virginia illustrates:

> Had this man lived before Hesiod wrote and Homer sung, temples would have risen to his honor, altars would have blazed, and he would have taken his stand with Hercules and Theseus, among the immortals, as the preserver of a nation; the vindicator of the rights of suffering humanity; the avenger of our matrons, our virgins, and our little ones.
>
> And shall we see him depart from this city in disgrace; censured and dismissed from office by Congress; and like Camillus, imploring Heaven so to direct human affairs, that his country may never have occasion to regret her treatment of him? No; it cannot be. Forbid it, every power that guards the protectors of innocence! Forbid it, policy! Forbid it, gratitude! Forbid it, peace![11]

William Lowndes attended the House with admirable regularity considering the state of his health and the fact that most of the speeches, in his view, dealt with questions altogether beside the point. Regarding the issue from his customary constitutional perspective, Lowndes saw the central question as a conflict in the separation of powers. He considered the question too important to permit his friendship for the president or his respect for the general to interfere with his duty to defend the constitutional prerogatives of Congress. Through the early part of the debate he was occupied with the chairmanship of two special committees. After he made their reports in January, one on weights and measures and another on coinage, he turned his full attention to the debate. On January 30, he took the floor to deliver another respectful dissent from presidential opinion on a major issue.[12]

Lowndes saw the fundamental issue in Jackson's Florida campaign as an infringement of executive authority on that of the legislature. He conceded that the Constitution authorized the president to order troops to pursue the Seminoles beyond the boundary of the United States, and that Congress could order the occupation of Florida; but the seizure of Fort St. Marks and Pensacola from the Spanish authorities was an act of war that neither the general who accomplished it nor the president, who claimed "by an ingenious construction of vague and general phrases" to have authorized it, possessed the right to commit. Not being in the possession of such authority himself, the president could not delegate it to a subordinate officer:

> The power of declaring war is given only to Congress. To employ the army of the nation for the purpose of taking possession by force of the territory, the towns, and even the forts, of a foreign State, seems to fulfil every condition which can be necessary to constitute an act of war. If such an act be done by an officer who has the authority to do it, it is war. It is war, then, if General Jackson was authorized by his office, or by the legal orders of the President, to take possession of Pensacola; and to say that he was authorized by neither, is at once to admit the truth of the position taken in the resolution.

If the explanations in the president's annual message were accepted at face value, Monroe, rather than Jackson, had exceeded his authority. But, Lowndes reminded the House, another speaker had already proven that Jackson occupied Fort St. Marks and Pensacola without authority or instructions from President Monroe. In fact, the president had issued orders "the obvious import of which forbade" occupation of these places. To Lowndes it was clear that the general had not merely exceeded but violated his orders:

> But the violation of the orders of the Executive Government by General Jackson would not . . . form a case which would require the

interposition of the House, if it had not been combined with an assumption of powers belonging neither to the President nor the General. It seemed, indeed, to be thought by the opposers of the resolutions, that, independently of the orders or powers of the President, the commanding General, as an attribute of his station, had the right to attack the Spanish fort under the circumstances in which he acted. The argument would not avail, unless he had a right, not only to do it without orders but against them.

To those who argued that the character of General Jackson was implicated in the resolutions, Lowndes replied that for the House to suppress its disapproval, if merited, would not raise the character of the general but lower that of the House. He could think of no case in which an unconstitutional assumption of power should be passed over in silent acquiescence. He would therefore vote for the resolution disapproving the occupation of Pensacola and Fort St. Marks.

On the execution of the two British subjects, Lowndes took a different view. Here Jackson had not exceeded his military authority, but he had assumed a high responsibility, and both he and the military court had erred on the assumption of jurisdiction. Astonished at the indifference displayed throughout the debate to important principles of international law, Lowndes pointed out that jurisdiction in such cases was confined to the nation in whose territory the crimes were committed, with the injured government obliged to seek redress from the nation that permitted the crimes to go unpunished. This question, though, was of minor importance compared to the assumption of authority that the Constitution had reserved to Congress, and he hoped the House would limit its vote to that subject.[13]

When the votes were taken on February 8, the Military Affairs Committee's original resolution of censure for the executions had been divided in two, one for each execution. The House rejected both by almost identical votes, 108 to 62 and 107 to 63. Lowndes made the difference, voting for censure in the case of the trader Arbuthnot but against it in the case of Ambrister, the soldier of fortune. The resolution disapproving seizure of the Spanish posts also lost, 70 to 100, with Lowndes voting again with the minority.[14] This vindication by the House majority was a resounding triumph for Jackson, who immediately set off on a northern tour to receive the adulation of an admiring public. It proved no less a triumph for Secretary of State Adams, whose aggressive defense of the Florida invasion soon paid a handsome dividend; two weeks after the debate ended he signed a treaty with the Spanish minister in Washington ceding Florida to the United States.

The House debate on Jackson's Florida invasion turned out to be less a clash of principles than jockeying for position in the presidential sweepstakes to succeed Monroe.[15] Moreover, the public desire to acquire Florida was too strong and Jackson himself too popular to cause many House members to quibble over constitutional issues. Lowndes himself shared in the spirit of national expansion; when Spain later balked on execution of the treaty, he would recommend presidential authority to order immediate occupation of the territory.[16]

Following their warm endorsement of Jackson's gunbarrel diplomacy, the House took up the profoundly disturbing question of the Second Bank of the United States. The Bank had enjoyed strong public favor during its first eighteen months of operation, and with good reason. From the day its doors opened in January 1817, the Bank appeared in the role of public benefactor, pursuing liberal policies regarding loans and currency exchange that pumped millions of dollars into the economy.[17] Easy credit and the ready acceptance of state bank notes in exchange for specie helped to prolong the postwar boom, fueled additional expansion, and stimulated speculative mania in newly opened areas of the South and West. Then in August 1818 the Bank suddenly began a general contraction of credit, which had the effect of reversing its flow. State banks and businessmen in debt to the Second Bank had to follow suit. As the pressure mounted, overextended firms came crashing to ruin, carrying with them an ever-increasing number of debtor merchants, farmers, and speculators who turned on "the monied monster" as the chief cause of their distress. William Jones, president of the Bank, was singled out as the principal villain. He was accused of having managed the Bank's affairs with a cavalier if not criminal disregard for charter regulations and fundamental principles of sound banking, driving the institution to the brink of insolvency, which ultimately triggered a financial panic and national depression.[18]

Widespread condemnation of the Bank's administration was not only much too severe but basically unjust. Jones and the board had made errors both minor and serious, but in a very real sense, they no less than the general public had been victimized by Treasury Department policy. One of the principal objectives in rechartering the Bank had been to force resumption of specie payments throughout the banking system. In 1816 three-fourths of the nation's bank reserves were in the form of some $16 million in treasury notes issued during the war, most of them overdue for retirement from circulation. State bank notes were used for hand-to-hand transactions while the banks paid out treasury notes rather than hard money on demand for specie. Secretary Crawford of the Treasury Department reasoned that to force hard money into circulation the treasury notes must be retired. Accordingly, more than $15 million in these notes were removed from circulation by the end of 1817. To cushion the shock of such severe depletion of bank reserves, the Treasury Department expected and received the Bank's cooperation in the form of a liberal loan policy as well as indulged state banks that claimed inability or simply declined to redeem their own notes in specie after using them to secure specie from the central Bank. When these practices brought the Bank into a precarious financial position in the summer of 1818, the board ordered the curtailment of loans and credit contraction that precipitated a chain reaction of business failures.[19]

Popular wrath against the Bank was rising when Congress convened in November 1818. On Lowndes's first day in the House John C. Spencer of New York moved that a general investigation be made into the records and practices of the Bank to determine "whether the provisions of its charter have been violated or not." Spencer gave as his reason the agitation in the public mind and loud complaints against the Bank's officers. When friends of the Bank expressed doubts concerning House authority to conduct such an investigation, Lowndes rose to lend his support to the resolution. He said the House was fully empowered to prosecute the inquiry and entirely justified in doing so. He considered such an investigation "not only interesting to the public, but necessary to the bank. Many imputations had been thrown on the bank, the result of disappointed expectations, where the expectations themselves were unreasonable; and it was the interest of the bank that a full inquiry should take place." On the recommendation of Louis McLane of Delaware, the investigating committee was to be left unfettered by specific instructions and given, in Lowndes's phrase, "*carte blanche*" to examine the Bank's whole proceedings.[20]

On November 30 Spencer's resolution passed, and being the mover, he was named chairman of the committee. Lowndes accepted the second position, followed by McLane of Delaware, Joseph H. Bryan of North Carolina, and John Tyler of Virginia. McLane and Lowndes had spoken in defense of the Bank, but Bryan and Tyler were known conservatives, and they with Spencer gave the committee an anti-Bank complexion.[21]

Proceeding forthwith to Philadelphia, the committee members were courteously received by the officials of the Bank and for the next three weeks were provided every facility in examining the books and conducting their research. Upon completing their work in Philadelphia the day after Christmas, they separated to examine the branches in Baltimore, Richmond, and Washington before returning with their report.[22]

On Saturday, January 16, 1819, Chairman Spencer laid the report before the House.[23] The committee had decided to avoid speculative opinions and confine themselves to questions relating to management of the Bank and violations of its charter. Nevertheless, the report appeared to confirm the suspicions of the Bank's enemies and the worst fears of its friends. Officials and directors at Philadelphia, including President Jones himself, were reported to have been engaged in personal speculation in the institution's stocks and mismanagement of its affairs to an appalling degree. The extent of fraud and mismanagement in the Baltimore branch was not yet known, but it threatened to be worse than that at Philadelphia.[24] Various specific examples of fraudulent practice and mismanagement were recounted and supported with a mass of facts pertaining to the Bank's operation. The report closed with a summary statement of the committee's findings, that the Bank had violated its charter in four instances: (1) by speculating in the public debt, (2) by failing to enforce provisions requiring payment of specie for its stock, (3) by paying dividends to stockholders who had not completed payment for their stock, and (4) by permitting multiple voting for directors in violation of regulations governing voting by proxy. The committee refrained from offering any opinion on whether the violations would warrant forfeiture of the charter, but left the House entirely free to use its own judgment in the matter. Their only recommendation was a measure to regulate more closely the elections for directors, as the committee considered the secretary of the Treasury fully empowered to take prompt and adequate remedy for the other evils exposed.[25]

In view of the magnitude of fraud and mismanagement alleged by the investigating committee, its conclusions were exceptionally weak. This can be explained by the fact that, while all its members vouched for the facts presented in the report, they disagreed on its conclusions. Lowndes and McLane, the only members on the committee who possessed more than a smattering of knowledge on banking and currency questions, disagreed with the majority. And Spencer, who proved unequal to the task before him, relied too heavily on his own inadequate knowledge of money and banking in writing the report.[26]

In the wake of the committee's revelations, opponents of the Bank had no intention of leaving the matter to the secretary of the Treasury. On January 19, David Trimble of Kentucky, believing that the Bank lacked the power or means to regain the confidence of the nation, moved that it be made to show cause why its charter should not be revoked.[27] The House proved more deliberate, however, and voted to postpone discussion until the issue could be taken up in Committee of the Whole on February 18. In the meantime, the cause of the Bank suffered when agricultural prices broke in January and began to swoon downward. The volume of criticism against the Bank soared, and before the month ended, President Jones had resigned. By the middle of February the state of Maryland had initiated legislation to tax the Baltimore branch out of existence.[28]

On February 8, James Johnson of Virginia moved that the Committee on the Judiciary be instructed to report a bill to repeal the charter altogether. His resolution was the first taken up in Committee of the Whole ten days later, and the debate commenced. Johnson held the Bank completely responsible for the current economic distress. Emphasizing the institution's power, he struck a chord that would provide the dominant theme of opposition rhetoric as long as the Bank remained in existence:

> What, now, is our condition? Surrounded by one universal gloom. We are met by the tears of the widow and the orphan. Pictures of highly wrought suffering, of misery, and of distress, are crowded upon us. Our sympathies are assailed. We are pointed to the Bank of the United States, and gravely told, that destroy but this corporation, and you dissolve the charm which secures to the people of this nation prosperity and happiness. And is it possible . . . that the ten millions of people in this country depend for their prosperity, their happiness, and their repose, on the conduct of the directors of this bank? This corporation, which by its very first act put our authority at defiance, by the first step which it took, violated the charter which created it. Sir, I should consider this country in the most deplorable, the most melancholy condition, if the proposition be true, that by the act to incorporate the subscribers of this bank, which gives them exclusive privileges for twenty years, we enable them to direct the destinies of this nation, and make it happy or miserable as they shall choose.

A strict constructionist, Johnson was among many who believed the Bank was unconstitutional. He called for immediate revocation of the charter, so as not to "permit this violated act to remain in the Statute Book a disgrace to the nation."[29]

James Pindall of Virginia buttressed his colleague's effort with a lengthy exposition of the Bank's brief history. He questioned the motives of those in the Fourteenth Congress whose votes had established the Bank. He implied that their chief purpose had been to destroy the state banks, which he contended were then on the point of resuming specie payments:

> At this juncture of their convalescence of the paper currency, when the danger and dread of war were gone, and when our Government found it unnecessary to importune to the State banks for further loans, the projectors of the United States Bank urged the National Government to call into existence a mighty corporation, to overawe and correct the local institutions, that had dealt themselves almost out of breath in supporting the Government in times of peril and adversity.

Pindall endeavored to show that the incorporation of the Bank had been unnecessary to begin with and positively harmful in its effects. He closed with a warning that the Bank, with awesome power wielded by a moneyed aristocracy, "would devour the State banks, intimidate the State governments, and swallow the annual revenues of the country."[30]

When Pindall finished his speech, William Lowndes, with his own health less stable than that of the Bank, rose to deliver perhaps the greatest speech of his career. An acknowledged authority on financial matters, Lowndes demonstrated in this speech that, among the members of the investigating committee including the former banker McLane, he best understood the intricate questions involved in the Bank's affairs.[31] The practice had already developed that whenever he rose to deliver a speech on an important subject, members in all parts of the House would leave their seats and gather near to hear him.[32]

Lowndes took scant notice of the two speakers who had preceded him, dismissing Pindall's attempt to impugn the motives of the Congress that chartered the Bank: "If the reputation of the fourteenth Congress, or of the late Administration, could be impaired by observations and circumstances like those which had been adduced, he would say of both, that they were not worth defending." Instead, Lowndes concentrated on the findings of the investigating committee and delivered what amounted to a minority report and a powerful defense of the Bank.[33]

Lowndes reminded the House that the great object in chartering the Bank had been to provide a stable currency of uniform value. While perfection of this ideal lay beyond the power of human wisdom, he knew that the Fourteenth Congress had not aimed at perfection but had wished only to combine the conveniences of bank circulation with a uniformity of value equal to that possessed by precious metals. At the present time, he said, the price current indicated that the greatest discount on notes of any branch of the Bank was less than 1 percent, "a value much more uniform than that which coin could be expected to have in so extensive a country." The currency, he said, was more uniform in value than coin and everywhere readily convertible into silver. He admitted that the distribution of its loans had been unwise and that greater care should be exercised to avoid this in the future. It was nonetheless clear that the institution had succeeded in meeting the primary object of the government in chartering it.

Lowndes explained how the Bank had performed its great duty of restoring and maintaining specie payments. Furthermore, no one could deny that it had faithfully fulfilled its obligation of transmitting the public money without charge wherever it was required. Among the advantages of the Bank, the bonus of $1.5 million he considered worthy of mention, to say nothing of the convenience of facilities that the institution would afford in all future loans.

That the Bank had made mistakes, both minor and serious in their consequences, he freely admitted. Importations of precious metals from Europe had resulted in substantial losses for the Bank, and the committee had been quite critical of these dealings. Lowndes made the pertinent observation that while they had been injudicious they certainly were not criminal. The effect had proved injurious to the stockholders, but he could not see where the country had cause to complain. He recounted several other mistakes that had been committed by the institution's officers and listed by the committee.

But one of the institution's greatest errors, in Lowndes's opinion, the committee had failed to comment upon. This was the attempt to pay the notes of all branches at any office where they might be presented. In attempting to do this, without strictly regulating the issues and controlling the amounts of discounted paper at each branch, the Bank had rendered the public a great convenience at the expense of serious injury to itself. This policy had permitted the West to drain specie from the East, placing a serious strain on the eastern branches. He demonstrated this with a simple illustration:

> A bank note is an order for the payment of money; and if the holder has the option of drawing this money at different places, he will draw it where money is most valuable. If the discounts of Lexington were larger than the business of the place required, and the notes which were issued there were redeemable nowhere else, the bank at that place would immediately discover its error by the drafts upon its specie, and its discounts would accordingly be contracted. But if the notes of the Lexington branch are payable at New York, however profuse may be its discounts, the directors themselves discover, within the limits of their observation, no inconvenience from their liberality. . . . the specie in their vaults remains untouched, and the income of the institution is increased by the large amount of their loans.

When the Bank announced that this practice would be discontinued, "the loudest complaints [came] from the States in which the disproportionate and excessive issues had been made." This evil, overlooked by the committee, was responsible for many others that they had censured.

As the question before the House proposed the destruction of the Bank, Lowndes thought it wise to consider the probable consequences. One of the first results would be the disappearance from circulation of its currency, and any expectation that it might be replaced by coin he pronounced visionary: "[I]n destroying the Bank of the United States, then, we must do it, because we prefer the currency which will be afforded either by the notes of local banks or by Government paper." All members of the House, he said, were well-acquainted with the evils of local currency; and of the other kind he would only remark, "The inequalities and inconveniences of bank paper would not be removed by Government paper." There would be other temporary evils, individual losses, a decline in property values, and a corresponding rise in the value of money, all of which would certainly follow destruction of the Bank.

But was destruction of the Bank necessary? Even if the Bank had disappointed reasonable expectations, was there no remedy short of its destruction? The charter had given the government powerful means for restraining and controlling the institution, means that its officers could neither disregard nor resist. Lowndes asked, "Would it be wise to destroy a constitution because you disapproved of its first administration? Would you even break up a machine, because in its first experiment there had been some mismanagement?" The committee had declared that the illegal methods employed in voting for directors were the greatest evil in the system, "the origin of all the others," and had proposed a remedy in the form of a bill. If the greatest evil in the Bank's operation could be corrected by a simple legislative act, would it not be great folly to destroy an institution that could be so easily cured?

The most serious charges against the Bank were the four specific allegations of charter violation. On this part of the report Lowndes differed from all other members of the committee. In his opinion, none of the alleged acts amounted to a violation of the charter, and he proceeded methodically to refute, one after another, the committee's allegations.

On the first, the purchasing of government stock, Lowndes informed the House that the Bank had acted merely as agent for the government at the instance of the secretary of the Treasury. The stock had been purchased in Europe and immediately transferred to the commissioners of the Sinking Fund. At no time during the transaction did the Bank own the stock. Any fair interpretation of the provision forbidding the Bank to purchase public stock could not, in his opinion, find the Bank in violation of the charter in these circumstances. He could not believe that the purchase in question had been seriously submitted as just cause for the institution's dissolution.

He disposed of the other allegations in rapid succession. The second had found the Bank violating its charter in not requiring specie payments on purchases of its stock after the first installment. To this he replied that once the Bank opened its doors, it correctly considered its own notes as specie. Because they were convertible into specie on demand, he could not see how anyone could seriously contend that the Bank should not have accepted its own notes in payment for stock. He dismissed the charge concerning payments of dividends to delinquent stockholders by informing the House that the total amount involved was only $360, paid out by a subordinate officer without knowledge or consent of the directors. The fourth alleged violation concerning illegal votes for directors he felt had been sufficiently answered and left the charge without further argument to the decision of the House.

Lowndes found himself too fatigued to discuss further the resolutions before the House but said he intended to vote against all of them. He concluded his great effort in behalf of the Bank by declaring that its dissolution, as a measure of policy, was not wise; as a penalty, it was not legal; and from any other consideration, it was unjust.[34]

When Lowndes finished, John Tyler of Virginia claimed the floor to deny the constitutionality of the Bank, and the debate ran on for several more days. When the House finally voted on the two resolutions on February 25, the issue appeared never to have been in doubt. Johnson's call to repeal the charter lost 30 to 121; Trimble's proposal for a "show cause" order met a similar fate, 39 to 116; and the House declined to take any action against the institution except to prevent stockholders from casting illegal votes in future elections of its officers.[35]

For this triumphant vindication of the Bank, John Quincy Adams gave credit to one congressman: "Lowndes was the Atlas upon whom alone the support of the bank rested in Congress. He was its only disinterested defender in the House."[36] Even so, Norman Risjord is doubtless correct in stating, "Despite the revelations of the investigating committee, it was unlikely that any action would be taken against the bank."[37] This was true not so much because the government needed it, as Risjord maintains, but because the Bank had been, in Secretary Crawford's phrase, a "passive agent" guided by and acting in harmony with Treasury Department policy.[38] One of the more interesting features of Lowndes's speech was the skill with which he defended the Bank without exposing the Treasury Department to public censure for the severe depletion of bank reserves caused by massive currency contraction that in turn brought on the banking crisis. The overwhelming House support for the Bank is a fair indication that the members generally understood its essentially passive role, but many a vote might have turned on the authoritative exposition delivered by William Lowndes.

Lowndes's old friend and former House colleague Langdon Cheves was called from South Carolina to become the Bank's new president. Cheves increased the stringent measures Jones had begun to return the institution to a secure financial position. The effort proved only too successful, for in the process Cheves earned for the Bank the cordial hatred and abiding hostility of the people, who had ample reason to expect a more liberal policy from the federally chartered institution.[39] Lowndes, though, endorsed the austerity program, writing to Cheves in November 1819, "I concur with you entirely in the opinion that there is no remedy for our money difficulties, but a steady perseverance in old-fashioned principles."⁴⁰ The statement illustrates his laissez-faire view of political economy. Adhering to the doctrines of Adam Smith, Lowndes felt that neither the Bank nor the federal government should interfere with the ebb and flow of natural economic forces. Consequently he warmly supported the beleaguered Cheves and at the same time failed to consider the possibility, let alone the propriety, of reissuing the recently contracted treasury notes to ease pressure in the money market. He believed the depression should run its natural course. As this conservative view predominated among administrators of both the Bank and the national government, neither lent assistance as the nation struggled through the first great depression in American history. Of course, the Bank rode out the storm, but as Bray Hammond has remarked, "Its survival damned it worse than failure would have done," for its enemies would neither forget nor forgive when its day of reckoning came.⁴¹

An entry in the account book of his rice factors dated June 8, 1819 requires mention here.⁴² It reveals that six months before Lowndes advised Cheves to persevere "in old-fashioned principles," the Bank had loaned Lowndes four thousand dollars. As subsequent entries show, the loan was regularly renewed on payment of interest through the period of rigorously contracted credit between 1819 and 1822. Had this fact become public knowledge, there seems little doubt that his motives in defending the Bank would have been called into question, nor could he have denied that the Bank had given him preferential treatment. The Bank extended favorable treatment to its influential friends as a matter of policy, one that would become notorious under Cheves's successor. By traditional republican standards, Lowndes was no less corrupt in accepting the loan than the Bank in making it. That he did so reveals not a fundamental flaw in his public character but the elitist character of his commitment to republicanism.

The lowcountry elite of South Carolina were long accustomed to deferential treatment from the business community, as well as the public at large; and the deference they enjoyed never implied an exchange of favors although such reciprocation might now and then take place. To expect it, however, was to impugn the character of the lowcountry elite and consequently to lose their business. The services of a banker were as essential to the business affairs of Lowndes and his lowcountry peers as the services of a factor, and credit from both was a way of life involving no obligation from the borrower beyond repayment on mutually agreed upon terms. This is what lay behind Lowndes's comment on how unfit he was to live outside of Carolina. And this is why he evidently saw no inconsistency in defending the Bank, supporting its stringent credit policy, then routinely borrowing money from its Charleston branch.[43] Lowcountry elitism had its privileges.

Lowndes's preparations for his voyage to Europe were most likely the reason that he took no active role in the opening stage of a far more important issue raised in the House in February 1819. It began with a routine petition for statehood from the citizens of the Missouri Territory. Routinely referred to the Committee on Territories, the petition resulted in an ordinary enabling bill that the House took up on February 13. When James Tallmadge, Jr., of New York introduced the following amendments, however, the bill became anything but ordinary: "That the further introduction of slavery or involuntary servitude be prohibited, except for the punishment of crimes, whereof the party shall have been convicted; and that all children born within the said State, after the admission thereof into the Union, shall be free at the age of twenty-five years."[44] The amendments threw into immediate focus sectional differences over the institution of slavery and provoked a brief though intense debate. Speaker Clay led the opposition, basing his argument on the unconstitutionality of restriction. Tallmadge was supported by his New York colleague, John W. Taylor, who challenged the whole system of slavery. As the debate grew more heated, Thomas W. Cobb of Georgia warned that Tallmadge had "kindled a fire which all the waters of the ocean cannot put out, which seas of blood can only extinguish."[45]

On February 16, the two clauses of the Tallmadge amendment were put to separate votes. Both passed the House but were rejected by the Senate, after which neither house would yield. There the matter rested when Congress adjourned. Whether the issue would be revived in the next Congress seemed doubtful when it subsided in late spring and early summer. Lowndes set off on his European voyage apparently anticipating nothing of this sort to disturb the usual summer doldrums at the nation's capital, unaware of the thunderheads building for a storm over the Missouri question in the fall.

X
The Confrontation

Following a rough Atlantic voyage, William Lowndes arrived in Liverpool on March 30, 1819 and through the next six months made a leisurely tour of Europe,[1] though his idea of leisure included little thought of idleness. Wherever he went he recorded in a small notebook observations of things he found interesting. And almost everything attracted his interest: characteristics of the people, the British Parliament, the French Chamber of Deputies, canal and road construction, bridges, factories, crops, and especially machines and mechanical devices of various kinds—pumps, windmills, or whatever his alert and inquisitive mind observed that he thought might be useful back home. He took care to see that his weakened body received the prescribed rest, confining travel to the morning hours, resting during the heat of the day, then riding through the countryside and visiting points of interest or acquaintances in the late afternoon and evening. In this manner he made his way across Europe, traveling to London, Paris, Milan, Geneva, and finally to Scotland before departing for home in October. The summer of rest and travel proved so beneficial that on his return in mid-November he could announce to his relieved family that his health had been completely restored.

During Lowndes's absence the national economy had sunk into a deep depression, and the Missouri question had become increasingly ominous. Public excitement over both issues mounted through the summer of 1819. Antislavery elements of the free-state North, holding mass meetings in every major northern city, drummed up massive support for congressional action to restrict the admission of Missouri and halt slavery expansion. The popular crusade drew strength from two potentially disruptive sources of northern discontent.[2] The first was resentment over the three-fifths clause in the Constitution providing for representation based on slavery, which by 1819 gave the slaveholding South eighteen additional seats in the House. This had been a central point of New York senator Rufus King's speech in support of the Tallmadge amendments the previous spring. The second was mounting free-state concern over the expansion of slavery, not only into the western territories but also into states carved out of the Northwest Territory, presumed to be a free-state preserve by virtue of the prohibitory ordinance of 1787. Inclined to reason backward from result to cause, an inclination whose growth would parallel the westward march of slavery, many advocates of restriction found in these circumstances evidence of a concerted effort to perpetuate southern dominance over the national government.[3] From this perspective, the unchecked expansion of slavery threatened to upset the traditional balance of free and slave states within the Union. The admission of Indiana and Illinois since the war, counterbalanced by that of Mississippi and presently Alabama, had maintained the balance thus far. But the intrusion of slavery into states of the Old Northwest aroused fears that free-state expansion could be circumscribed, tilting the balance permanently toward the slaveholding South.[4] Consequently, the majority of northern congressmen returned to Washington in the fall of 1819 determined to make their stand on the admission of Missouri.

But the Missouri question was only half the story in 1819. The onset of hard times throughout the land aroused widespread agitation for governmental action to relieve economic distress. The West and the western South, where expansion and speculation on borrowed capital had been most active in the postwar boom, demanded cheap money to repay debts and stay laws to postpone debt collection. When neither the federal government nor the Second Bank responded to the debt and currency problems, these issues devolved by default on the state governments. Meanwhile, manufacturing areas of the Middle Atlantic states and New England clamored for higher tariffs to remedy the imbalance of supply over demand in a depressed market. When much of the Ohio Valley joined the protariff chorus, including producers of hemp, wool, iron, and other raw materials for manufacturing, protectionist agitation mushroomed into the first large-scale lobbying campaign for special interest legislation in American history. Except for representatives of northern commerce and a few others, the northern phalanx that was determined to restrict the admission of Missouri also stood together in support of higher tariffs.[5]

Both the tariff and Missouri questions threw the South on the defensive. Having always traded their exports for imports of manufactured goods and preferring British manufactures because of their acknowledged superiority over American-made products, southerners regarded protective tariffs as special interest legislation imposing a tax on southern agriculture for the benefit of northern manufacturers. At the same time, agitation of the Missouri question threatened the South's slave labor system, which, when considered as property, had an estimated value of $600 million. Like a double-edged sword, sectional promotion of these twin objectives in the first session of the Sixteenth Congress, the one perceived as an unprovoked assault on a distinctly southern interest and the other a distinctly northern interest promoted at southern expense, cut through the ancient republican assumptions undergirding southern nationalism and laid bare the "Machiavellian moment" in southern history, "the confrontation of 'virtue' with 'corruption.' "[6]

The Sixteenth Congress opened on December 6, and in its preliminary business the House reelected Henry Clay Speaker. On the eighth, William Lowndes appeared, was qualified,[7] and took his seat. Immediately there followed a petition, a resolution, and an announcement embracing subject matter of great significance for the future of the South. John Holmes of the Maine District of Massachusetts presented a petition from a convention recently held in his district, with the approval of the Massachusetts government, praying the admission of Maine as a separate and independent state "on an equal footing with the original States." This petition was referred to a select committee headed by Holmes. John Scott, the delegate from the Missouri Territory, next moved the referral of Missouri's application for statehood to a select committee of which he was named chairman. Immediately thereafter James Strong of New York announced his intention to introduce a bill "to prohibit the further extension of slavery within the Territories of the United States."[8] Three fundamental elements in the great Missouri Controversy thus came before the House on the third day of the session.

With an antirestrictionist majority in the sectionally balanced Senate, the principal arena for the contest over Missouri became the floor of the House, where free-state representatives outnumbered their southern colleagues 105 to 81. Of the House members destined to play significant roles in the contest, the most influential were Speaker Clay, John Taylor of New York, and William Lowndes. Clay's influence could be crucial, although it had grown less through the management of legislation, or of the opposition to it, than through his judicious management of the committee system of government.[9] Clay consistently exercised the Speaker's appointive powers to select balanced committees that reflected each member's standing in the House, the interests of his constituents in the subject at issue, and the opposing point of view. Clay candidly and actively opposed restriction without departing from his usual fair-minded exercise of the Speaker's power over committee appointments.

Taylor of New York, the leading exponent of the Tallmadge amendments in the Fifteenth Congress, assumed leadership of restrictionists in the Sixteenth. His New York colleague, having won legislative immortality by introducing the controversial amendments in the last Congress, had declined reelection to this one but still maintained a parent's interest in his "offspring" and gave warm encouragement to Taylor. Restriction, Tallmadge wrote, "is *our Child*, and with me a Darling favourite"; "You have in this business a monument to your fame"; "It is a great and glorious course,"[10] one that Taylor would pursue with such resolute determination that even Vice President Daniel Tompkins considered his fellow New Yorker "too zealous and unyielding."[11] Taylor's strategy was first to establish the principle of slavery restriction by act of Congress. This might be accomplished with less difficulty, he reasoned, by applying the principle to the western territories. Once established, the principle could be applied to Missouri, or, for that matter, to any subsequent territorial application for statehood. In this effort Taylor would find a worthy opponent in William Lowndes.

Lowndes, like most of his southern colleagues, thought he recognized in the agitation over Missouri northern impatience "to put the gov[ernmen]t into the hands of Northern men."[12] Even at the height of the controversy he could discuss the prospect of northern control over the national government with a detachment unique among southern congressmen, but he could not countenance the conditional admission of Missouri as the means to achieve it. His stance on the Missouri question remained consistent with his congressional record, which had been confined almost exclusively to the constitutional issues. As he read the Constitution, restriction represented an intrusion of federal authority into the authority constitutionally reserved to the states. Hence he opposed restriction and supported the right to move slave property into the Trans-Mississippi territories. His constitutional perspective also led him to regard the morality or propriety of slavery as a matter of personal sentiment or judgment and consequently improper ground for congressional action involving rights sanctioned by the Constitution. The abstract nature and elevated tone of Lowndes's approach, and the persuasive style of calm and amiable rationality with which he presented his arguments, tended to separate the issue of slavery from the issue of constitutional rights and consequently to encourage antislavery moderates to vote against restriction on constitutional grounds. Lowndes assumed the principal burden of defeating Taylor's strategy by preventing slavery restriction in the territories from coming to a vote before the House could take up the Missouri Bill.

On December 9, Delegate Scott brought in a bill to authorize the people of Missouri to form a constitution and state government and to admit "such State into the Union on an equal footing with the original States." Here Strong withdrew his restrictive resolution so as not to "embarrass the question" on the Missouri Bill. Taylor had no such qualms. When the House had not found time to take up the bill by the fourteenth, Taylor moved "that a committee be appointed to enquire into the expediency of prohibiting by law the introduction of slavery into the territories of the United States west of the Mississippi." Explaining his purpose, Taylor said he deeply regretted the sectional animosities that the debate of the previous session had provoked. He did not know whether conciliation was now possible, but he thought it should be tried. This might best be achieved, he said, by separating the question of slavery in the territories from the expediency of admitting Missouri to statehood. Let the issue of slavery in the territories be first examined by a committee of seven, who might work out a compromise to avoid another general and unprofitable debate on the subject.[13]

As the resolution implied neither approval nor disapproval of slavery, the House accepted it without debate and Speaker Clay appointed the committee. He named Taylor chairman, along with Arthur Livermore of New Hampshire, Philip Barbour of Virginia, Lowndes, Timothy Fuller of Massachusetts, Benjamin Hardin of Kentucky, and Thomas Culbreth of Maryland. Taylor, Livermore, and Fuller were decidedly restrictionist. Culbreth opposed restriction but with more moderation than Barbour and Harden, both determined advocates of slavery expansion.[14] Lowndes, though opposed to restriction, was willing to compromise in the interest of intersectional harmony.

At this point the thrust and parry of parliamentary maneuver began. Taylor moved that the House postpone consideration of the Missouri Bill to the first Monday in February, to give his committee, he said, sufficient time to work out a compromise. Lowndes countered at once that the committee should be able to determine in considerably less time whether they could compromise the issue. Besides, he hesitated to delay its consideration unnecessarily in view of the "glimpse of the possibility of a compromise, which had appeared."[15] The House sustained his objection and moved the date of postponement up to the second Monday in January.

The committee of seven no sooner began their deliberations than their chairman's intentions became clear, and the antirestrictionist members set about blocking his moves. His proposal to exclude the further introduction of slavery from the entire Trans-Mississippi West got nowhere. Subsequent attempts to exclude slavery from the western territories fared no better. At one point Taylor suggested a boundary between slave and free territory along rivers that would divide Missouri itself. Lowndes made a counter proposal. Maintaining that the freehold population of settled territories had vested rights beyond the legitimate control of Congress, he suggested that the boundary line of congressional jurisdiction over slavery should run along the western edge of frontier settlement through both the Arkansas and Missouri territories, conceding the right of Congress to regulate slavery beyond the line. The concession pleased neither faction. Taylor's allies rejected it as a gesture as empty as the vacant lands to which it applied, while Barbour and Harden considered it a surrender of principle that could lead to congressional interference with slavery elsewhere.[16] Eventually the committee deadlocked and on December 28 were discharged from further consideration of the subject.

Frustrated in committee, Taylor turned to the House where his views enjoyed greater support. After reporting the deadlock, he moved that a bill to prohibit slavery in the Trans-Mississippi territories be drawn up without the usual formality of debate. Lowndes immediately rose to suggest that Taylor's motion be modified so as not to express any opinion of the House in adopting it: "If a committee could not agree, as has just been stated, it certainly could not be expected that the House would adopt such a form of expression, without debate." Moreover, established procedure called for open discussion of the principles involved prior to formulation of a bill. Again the House sustained Lowndes and postponed consideration of Taylor's motion, to be taken up on the same day as the Missouri Bill.[17]

Two days later Holmes of Massachusetts added the second major ingredient to the developing ferment over Missouri when he reported the enabling bill for admission of Maine into the Union. Upon completion of Holmes's report, Speaker Clay offered some observations for consideration. Addressing his remarks to the advocates of restriction, Clay asked, "If beyond the mountains Congress can exert the power of imposing restrictions on new States, can they not also on this side of them?" If not, Clay said, "[P]roclaim the distinction at once; announce your privileges and immunities." He pointed out a comparable circumstance in 1791 when the admission of Kentucky and Vermont had been combined in a single bill, and he asked whether this precedent might not serve the present case.[18] Having anticipated one part of the Senate compromise proposal shortly to be offered, the Speaker did not press the issue, and the Maine Bill passed the House without a roll call on January 3.

Attention now shifted to the Senate, for the House would not resume consideration of the Missouri question until January 24. The Senate took up on January 13 the House Maine Bill together with an amendment from the Senate Judiciary Committee authorizing Missouri to form a constitution and state government without slavery restriction. An attempt to insert an antislavery proviso in this amendment provoked considerable debate before the antirestrictionist majority voted the proviso down. Senator John Walker of Alabama explained their strategy to a friend:

> The Senate have rejected the restriction, and will continue to reject it. The question now before that body is, on concurring with the amendment of the judiciary committee to the Maine bill: which amendment is a bill for the admission of Missouri, thus linking the two states together. This is the only measure which can save us. You will recollect that the Bill to admit Maine has already passed the house. Should it pass the Senate, likewise, without the amendment, Missouri may "hang her harp upon the willows." In the present temper of the House, the restriction would be imposed, and both houses adhering to their respective opinions, her admission will be again postponed. Whether we shall succeed in this coadmi[ss]ion is a good deal feared, but it is believed that we shall by a majority of one or two. If we succeed in that, we hope to carry Missouri thro' the House, without the restriction, by the representation of Maine.[19]

They succeeded. On February 18, the Senate majority shackled Maine to Missouri, to enter the Union together in unrestricted equality or suffer mutual exclusion. To facilitate compromise, Jesse B. Thomas of Illinois offered an amendment to prohibit slavery "forever" in the remainder of the Louisiana Purchase north of 36°30', the line of Missouri's southern boundary. The Senate added the Thomas amendment also to the House Maine Bill and on February 18 sent the legislative package to the House for concurrence.[20]

The House in the meantime had become enmeshed in a rancorous and seemingly interminable dispute over its own Missouri Bill. When taken up on January 24, Taylor promptly moved its postponement. The motion touched off an unreported debate of some length. The reporter's summary named Lowndes and Scott of Missouri as leaders of the opposition that narrowly defeated the motion, 87 to 88. Two days later Henry Storrs of New York moved to exclude slavery from the territories north and west of Missouri, essentially the compromise amendment of Senator Thomas without the compromise. This provoked another unreported debate with Lowndes and Scott again leading the opposition to ultimate success.[21] The defeat of Storrs's motion marked the end of preliminary skirmishing. Taylor's initial strategy had failed, but the contest had only begun.

Reading of the Missouri Bill proceeded as far as the fourth section when Taylor again rose and offered an amendment providing that "there shall be neither slavery nor involuntary servitude in the said State, otherwise than in the punishment of crimes, whereof the party shall have been duly convicted." In the words of the reporter, "the main question of the restriction on slavery in the future State of Missouri, being thus fully before the House," the great Missouri debate began.[22]

The Missouri debate raged for the next thirty-seven days, to the exclusion of all other business in the House. The magnitude of the issue and the sectional collision it produced created an atmosphere of high tension, sometimes awe. Crowds flocked to the Capitol, filling the galleries to overflowing and invading the floor itself, to hear speaker after speaker discuss the question of slavery restriction from every conceivable angle. As the debate waxed hotter, angry members hurled threats of violence and disunion back and forth across the House. Dire rumors abounded. Even Lowndes, according to one report, had joined Clay, Barbour, and other southern leaders in threatening that, if the North had its way, "they would merely pass the appropriation bills, and then adjourn, to consult their constituents whether they should ever come back again! A dissolution of the Union was spoken of as certain."[23] As the debates wore on they became repetitious, for both sides advanced arguments in patterns that soon became familiar.

Assuming the burden of proof, restrictionists ransacked the Constitution in search of congressional authority to make a state's admission conditional, and through what one southerner called "strong squinting" at the document, came up with four clauses in its text and another in the preamble.[24] To all of them, restrictionists gave the most liberal construction: The new states clause, providing that Congress "may" admit new states into the Union, meant that Congress possessed discretionary power to impose conditions on such admittance; the territories clause, by giving Congress power to "make all needful Rules and Regulations" respecting the territories, authorized congressional regulation of slavery in, or exclusion of it from, the territories. The term "migration" in the slave importation clause, which restrained Congress from prohibiting the foreign slave trade before 1808, implied congressional authority to restrict slavery expansion since then. The provision guaranteeing to each new state a republican form of government authorized Congress to exclude slavery because of its incompatibility with republican institutions. On even broader grounds, Congress might restrict slavery expansion in order to "promote the general welfare." Although restrictionists invoked the Declaration of Independence and laws of God for additional support, probably their strongest case rested on the restrictive precedent established in the Northwest Ordinance of 1787.

Opponents of restriction, no less disposed to squint at the Constitution from a different angle, strictly construed each of the five clauses. Phrasing of the new states clause implied only that Congress may or may not admit new states; to impose conditions would violate the constitutional guarantee "that the Citizens of each state shall be entitled to all Privileges and Immunities of Citizens in the several States," or as statehood enabling acts commonly phrased the guarantee, "on an equal footing with the original States." Moreover, the terms of the Louisiana Purchase treaty that embraced the Missouri Territory had specifically reiterated this constitutional guarantee. The "needful Rules and Regulations" passage in the territories clause referred only to the land itself and not to the settlers nor to such institutions as they might see fit to establish. Congress derived no authority to restrict slavery expansion from the term "migration" employed in the slave importation clause because, by definition, the term meant voluntary movement and so could not have been meant to include slaves. The guarantee of a republican form of government for each state, if construed to prohibit slavery in the territories, must by extension authorize the abolition of slavery in the original states. Finally, to admit the general welfare clause as grounds for curbing slavery expansion would legitimate a dangerously broad doctrine capable of infinite abuse.[25] The majority of southerners and northerners alike agreed that slavery was an evil; but while northern critics advocated containment, southerners professed a desire to ameliorate the evils of the institution through diffusion.

The reporter recording these arguments proved consistently inconsistent. Glover Moore, commenting on the shipshod reporting, remarked, "Sometimes the reporter was absent, sometimes he might arrive late, and again he would merely record the fact that a congressman spoke in an inaudible tone."[26] The speeches of the two "most powerful of those opposed to restriction" went unrecorded: Clay's four-hour speech against the Taylor amendment on February 8, and Lowndes's three-hour effort on February 18.[27] There had been no little competition to secure a favorable position in the speaking schedule. Lowndes followed his customary practice of waiting to deliver his views toward the end of debate, but either through defective delivery or the reporter's neglect, his effort did not receive even the usual summary.

Allowing for the fact that Lowndes's strongest points usually went unanswered, the essentials of his argument may be surmised from scattered references to it in rebuttal arguments. On February 20, William Plumer, Jr., of New Hampshire alluded to the quality of Lowndes's effort: "We have had many speeches in our House since [February 12], but none very able—except that of Mr. Lowndes—I was indiscreet enough to take the floor immediately after him."[28] In the course of his own speech, Plumer said that Lowndes "founded his chief objection to this measure, on the supposed inability of Congress to acquire, by compact with new States, federal powers not conferred by the Constitution on the General Government, to be exercised over the other States; and thus, in effect, to alter the Constitution in a manner not provided for by that instrument." Furthermore, Lowndes "said that the people, and not Congress, possessed the power to impose conditions on States about to be admitted into the Union."[29]

Five days later, Timothy Fuller gave a fuller exposition of the Carolinian's principal argument. Lowndes had maintained

> that, if Congress should admit into the Union a body politic, possessing powers or attributes different from those possessed by the original States, it would be an assumption of power not conferred by

the Constitution. The power to admit States . . . means to admit other bodies politic with political powers exactly commensurate with those of the States then existing and consequently, to admit other and different bodies politic, must be a usurpation. Hence . . . such an innovation might lead to the most dangerous consequences; to compromises and conditions on the part of the new States, which might keep them in a state of vassalage and dependence on the General Government, and make them ready instruments to subjugate and oppress the original members of the Confederacy.[30]

Lowndes interrupted Fuller at one point to correct a misstatement of his views on the issue of congressional control over slavery in the territories. Lowndes explained that he considered territorial settlements to have vested rights beyond the control of Congress; but because unsettled areas had no vested rights, Congress might exclude slavery in territories where no settlements existed. At another time he indicated, without actually saying it, that the word "forever" in the Thomas amendment excluding slavery north of the compromise line meant forever during the region's territorial status only. Daniel Cook of Illinois put the following question to him: "But are we to understand gentlemen as conceding the point that Congress has the power to make that restriction or territorial prohibition perpetual and binding on the States hereafter?" The reporter recorded, "Here Mr. Lowndes smiled and shook his head."[31]

Their brevity notwithstanding, these fragments are sufficient to show that Lowndes, like most of his southern colleagues, grounded his argument on the "Privileges and Immunities" guarantee of the new states clause. But what gave his argument distinction was the way he utilized time-honored republican assumptions to make his case. His reference to the "vassalage and dependence" of conditionally admitted states was the key phrase. The fundamental imperative for self-government was independence, because only independence could guarantee freedom. Just as property secured independence for the individual in society, the "Privileges and Immunities" guarantee of the new states clause secured for each state equal partnership and independent standing within the Union. No restriction could be imposed on a new state without compromising its independence, the essential attribute of statehood. Political bodies shorn of independence were not states at all but political dependents. History had repeatedly demonstrated, most recently in the notoriously corrupt British example, that dependents, whether individuals or corporate bodies, were obliged to do the bidding of their master. The master in this case being the "General Government" and the restrictive principle being capable of far-ranging application unrelated to slavery, Lowndes evoked the specter of new Trans-Mississippi states held in perpetual thralldom to federal authority, and as its creatures, augmenting its power to "subjugate and oppress" the older states, North and South alike. To adopt the restrictive principle, therefore, would be to alter fundamentally and forever the nature of the Union. The authority to do so, according to Lowndes, lay not among the powers delegated to Congress but among those embraced by the Tenth Amendment, "not delegated to the United States" but "reserved to the States respectively, or to the people." His "vested rights" argument and narrow construction of "forever" in the Thomas amendment followed the same line of reasoning: to preserve intact the constitutional right of new states to equal partnership and independent standing within the Union.

Fuller dismissed as "utterly chimerical" the notion that a dependent class of new states would help the federal government to unhinge the Constitution and reduce the old states to dependence.[32] The point of Lowndes's argument, of course, was not the probability of such abuse but the possibility, which neither Fuller nor anyone else effectively challenged. Two antirestrictionists who followed Lowndes in debate, George Tucker of Virginia and Scott of Missouri, elaborated on this point.

Tucker said that if Congress had the right to impose one condition, it had the right to impose another:

> [T]his power must appear to be the more dangerous, when we recollect how large a part of our territory west of the Mississippi is yet to be laid off into new States, and that every new State which enters into the Union, with restrictions on its sovereignty, as was well argued by a gentleman from South Carolina, (Mr LOWNDES) becomes at once an example and an advocate for further restrictions on others. In this way, that Constitution, whose component parts were so cautiously adjusted and so skillfully balanced, would be effectually destroyed.

It was no answer to this argument to say, "such an exertion of power is highly improbable." Even the founding fathers found it necessary to guard against remote possibilities, as witness constitutional prohibitions against feudal titles and bills of attainder, neither of which then seemed remotely probable.³³ To Scott the term *state* had a precise and technical meaning: "Its attributes were freedom, sovereignty, and independence." At the moment of admission, Missouri "must be considered free and independent"; otherwise the compact could not bind her. And once this restrictive principle should be established, each conditional admission must further distort the nature of the Union:

> If Missouri was [sic] admitted under restrictions and conditions that did not exist in relation to any of the States then existing, ... it was not into "this Union" she was incorporated, but into another Union, formed by special compact in that particular case. And thus every State that was admitted might be required to submit to some extraordinary condition, until the original principles of the Constitution were entirely lost, and it would become a matter of contract, in which each party would make the best bargain they could, and "this Union" would be no longer "this Union," nor would the term State be any longer intelligible, because it would give you no idea of what were its powers, its privileges, or its attributes.³⁴

Throughout the controversy, Lowndes never deviated far enough from this constitutional line of argument to discuss slavery. Given his premise the slavery question was neither central nor peripheral but merely incidental to the controversy, and all the impassioned rhetoric expended on the subject was beside the point. On the other hand, the nature of the controversy required restrictionists, regardless of personal disposition or motive, to condemn slavery in terms strong enough to justify application of the principle to Missouri. This entailed an assumption of moral superiority that many among the northern majority appeared to flaunt with imprudent relish. The more militant southerners found the assumption hypocritical and the criticism proceeding from it insufferably provocative. Their varied responses ranged from icy sarcasm to vehement denunciation and threats of war. Lowndes remained aloof from this rhetorical violence, appealing instead to the reason, moderation, and virtue of his colleagues. Through this statesmanlike approach he managed to retain his customary position of influence in the House. As one congressman explained it, "Mr. L[owndes] stands, as it were, on the isthmus between the contending parties in the hall—and by means of the influence, which he has obtained, is able to moderate the dashing of the billows on either hand."³⁵

But no man could stand "on the isthmus" in this controversy and expect to speak for South Carolina, where the crisis impelled a sudden shift toward militant sectionalism. Although his constituents continued to revere Lowndes as the personification of civic virtue, it was not he but Charles Pinckney who gave voice to their deepest concerns.

Charles Pinckney was the living embodiment of the rise and fall of South Carolina nationalism. To his fellow Carolinians, his career bordered on the legendary. Member of the Confederation Congress in his twenties and, at thirty, of the Constitutional Convention of 1787, Pinckney had advocated the growth of centralized authority with all the enthusiasm and confidence of youth. He afterwards claimed and at home was generally credited with a larger role in formulating the Constitution than surviving evidence would support. Elected United States senator and four times governor of the state, he became "Blackguard Charlie" to his Federalist cousins, Thomas and Charles Cotesworth Pinckney, when he abandoned Federalism to promote the election of Jefferson in 1800. A year later he gave up his senate seat and retired from national politics, but he continued to head the Republican party in South Carolina. Pinckney's disillusionment with Federalism dramatized a general trend among South Carolinians, but it did not signal a diminution of nationalist sentiment within the state. South Carolinians overwhelmingly endorsed Republican efforts to defend the nation's neutral rights through the War of 1812, as well as the postwar nationalism of her "splendid constellation of talents." Pinckney did not significantly alter his nationalist stance nor reappear on the national scene until the Missouri Controversy erupted.[36] Elected to the Sixteenth Congress, the sixty-two-year-old political veteran rose in the House on February 14, 1820 to deliver his valedictory, an embittered voice from out of the past sounding the principal themes of South Carolina rhetoric for decades to come.[37]

Pinckney nodded briefly in the direction of debate formalities, then with belligerent candor arraigned his northern colleagues in a classic display of southern belief in northern conspiracy. One needed only to glance back over the nation's brief history to recognize a pattern of northern conduct that would "strip away the thin, the cobweb veil" from the restrictionist crusade, "as well as the pretended [motives] of religion, humanity, and love of liberty." The true motive "for all this dreadful clamor throughout the Union, this serious and eventful attack on our most sacred and valuable rights and properties" was, he said, "to gain a fixed ascendency in the representation in Congress." The festering sore in the northern political conscience was southern representation based on slavery, "the great ground on which the Northern and Eastern States have always, and now more particularly and forcibly than ever, raised all their complaints." Northerners had been quite content with the three-fifths bargain as long as they controlled the government. They began to complain only when rapid growth in the West and South had "torn the sceptre from the East." The restrictive principle was simply the latest and most sinister manifestation of northern envy, a device contrived for the recovery of power and for "laying the foundation of forever securing their ascendency, and the powers of Government" in northern hands.

Pinckney denied claims that the three-fifths bargain had been a concession to the South. Actually, the North got the better part of the bargain, he insisted, citing figures from the latest Treasury Department report as proof. These showed that exports from Pennsylvania and states to the northward had during the previous year amounted to about $18 million. On the other hand, southern exports produced by slave labor amounted to some $32 million, nearly double that of the free-state North. As everyone knew, a nation's exports paid for imports received in exchange; simple arithmetic showed that the slave states added almost twice as much as the North to the nation's wealth. Moreover, through duties paid on the goods imported, the source of all but a small fraction of the national revenue, the slave states nearly doubled the contribution of the northern states to support the national government. All this meant that "the labor of two or three [slaves was] more valuable to [the Union] than the labor of four or five of their inhabitants in the Eastern States," and yet the slave population was denied representation "but for three fifths on this floor." The North with its numerical majority enjoyed all the advantages under this system of representation, he said, while the minority South carried the heaviest burden of federal taxes. Pinckney believed representation "ought always to be equally founded on population and taxation." South Carolina had adopted this duality principle in the compromise of 1808, which recognized "the contributions of our citizens in every way, whether arising from services or taxes," and offered protection against the tyranny of numbers under majority rule.

Turning to the constitutionality of restriction, Pinckney strictly construed each of the points raised in debate and denied the right of Congress "to legislate at all upon the subject of slavery." Then he undertook to defend the institution, finding biblical sanction for it in the scriptures and specific examples from the Old Testament. He claimed the southern slave was better off than the lower classes of England and Europe, the Russian serfs, and nine-tenths of the populations of Asia and Africa. As to free blacks in the northern states, their wretched circumstances observed daily in New York, Philadelphia, and elsewhere "proves that a state of freedom is one of the greatest curses you can inflict on them." The misery of free blacks stood in sharp contrast to the happy condition of southern slaves.

> Every slave has a comfortable house, is well fed, clothed, and taken care of; he has his family about him, and in sickness has the same medical aid as his master, and has a sure and comfortable retreat in old age, to protect him against its infirmities and weakness. During his whole life he is free from care.... Being without education, and born to obey, [for the slave] moderate labor and discipline are essential.... In this state they are happier than they can possibly be if free.... The great body of slaves are happier in their present situation than they could be in any other, and the man or men who would attempt to give them freedom, would be their greatest enemies.

The attempt of northern congressmen to legislate on slavery had "shaken the very foundations" of property in slaves. Had the North no idea of the value of slave property? "At least, sir, six hundred millions of dollars." He added, "If we lose them, the value of the lands they cultivate will be diminished in all cases one half," for a loss of at least another $600 million in the value of southern real estate. Should the North persist in its course and force on the South property losses of such magnitude, the result "may be the division of the Union, and a civil war." Even so, he could not "on any ground" agree to compromise Missouri's admission:

> However we all may wish to see Missouri admitted, as she ought, on equal terms with the other States, this is a very unimportant object to her, compared with keeping the Constitution inviolate—with keeping the hands of Congress from touching the question of slavery. On the subject of the Constitution no compromise ought ever to be made. Neither can any be made with the national faith ... which gives to all Louisiana, to every part of it, a right to be incorporated into the Union on equal terms with the other States.[38]

Although it may be doubted whether Pinckney's effort won a single convert on the floor of the House, his speech marked a departure of no small significance for the history of his state. In defiant disavowal of his lifelong attachment for the Union, Pinckney spoke with unique authority for the citizens of South Carolina, heralding a new era of militant sectionalism. And to a considerable degree, the arguments his successors would employ in the years to come—such as Calhoun's *Exposition and Protest*, his concurrent majority theory, and his "positive good" speech of 1837; George McDuffie's "forty bale theory"; the scriptural defense of slavery; and the widely credited charge that the northern majority like the tyrants of old would suffer no constitutional restraint to check its arbitrary will—all could be considered variations on one or another of the themes Pinckney outlined in his speech of February 14, 1820.

Even as Pinckney spoke, the Senate was turning the tables on the House majority. Five days later the House Maine Bill came back hobbled by a restriction of its own, the Senate amendment to admit Missouri on equal terms, with the Thomas compromise appended to ease the antislavery conscience and Missouri's admission.[39] Restrictionist reaction ranged from stunned disbelief to outrage, as if few had imagined that the crusade to restrict Missouri could jeopardize the admission of Maine. The emotions of Ezekiel Whitman of the Maine District "were stronger than he could find proper language to express . . . he could scarcely trust himself to speak on the subject of the amendments." McLane of Delaware condemned the Senate maneuver as "a dangerous mode of Legislation," whose object, added Henry Storrs of New York, was "to coerce this House, by operating on those members particularly interested in the admission of Maine into the Union." To Ezra Gross of New York, "the conduct of the Senate in this affair . . . did not deserve the respect of this House," which statement brought a sharp rebuke from the House Speaker. Arthur Livermore of New Hampshire denounced the attempt to bond Maine to Missouri, entreating the House to consider "the claims which Maine has to admission without delay" and "the feelings of irritation which such an unkind course would produce in her citizens." Holmes of the Maine District explained the peculiar basis of their anxiety. The Massachusetts law authorizing Maine's application for statehood would expire on March 3, 1820. This left Maine only twelve more days, excluding Sundays, to gain congressional approval, or "all that had been done would be lost."[40] Taylor of New York moved immediate rejection of the Senate amendments, but the House had them printed instead and resumed their consideration two days later. In the ensuing discussion John Randolph spoke several hours against the exclusion of slavery north of the compromise line; Randolph would not support the restrictive principle in any form. The following day, February 23, the House majority rejected the amendments in quick succession. Lowndes supported the Senate's effort at compromise, but after the majority struck out the Missouri amendment, he voted with them in rejecting the Thomas amendment.[41]

After sending the Maine Bill back to the Senate, the House resumed debate on Taylor's amendment to the Missouri Bill, with some thirty speakers yet to be heard. Time was running out for Maine, and the supply of original arguments had long since run out. On the twenty-fifth, Mark Hill of Massachusetts, weary of discussing a subject "stamped with all the marks of eternity," moved to terminate debate. Lowndes took the floor at once and gently persuaded Hill to withdraw his motion: "Mr. Lowndes said, that, if the gentleman from Massachusetts insisted on his motion being put, he would cheerfully vote in favor of it; yet if he would consent to withdraw his motion for the present, to give two or three gentlemen more an opportunity to speak to-day, he thought it might be a saving of time, and the motion could be renewed again, if necessary, tomorrow morning, which would then, he thought, receive a decided support."[42] Hill acquiesced, and the debate continued for a few more hours. Scott made one last plea for the unrestricted admission of his territory. After four others took their turns, the House had heard more than enough. When Felix Walker of Buncombe County, North Carolina rose to "make a speech for Buncombe,"[43] his effort was lost in calls for the question all over the House. The question was put and the Taylor restriction passed, "by from 12 to 18 votes."

On the twenty-eighth, the secretary of the Senate sent over a message informing the House that the senators "*insist*" on their amendments to the House Maine Bill. Taylor moved that the House "*insist on its disagreement*" with the amendments. Lowndes moved to table the matter until the Missouri Bill could be voted on, but the majority were as stubborn as their Senate colleagues and rejected all their amendments.[44] With the issue thus deadlocked, the Senate requested a conference on the twenty-ninth. The House agreed and Clay sent Taylor, Lowndes, Charles Kinsey of New Jersey, and two Massachusetts moderates, James Parker and Holmes of the Maine District, to confer with the Senate delegation. The next day the House passed the Missouri Bill including the restrictive

Taylor amendment, 91 to 82, and sent it to the Senate for concurrence. The Senate struck out the Taylor restriction, replaced it with the Thomas compromise, and sent the altered bill back to the House on March 2.[45]

Then came on the most crucial hours in the long contest over Missouri. On the motion of Chairman Holmes of the joint compromise committee, the House tabled the amended Missouri Bill to consider the committee report. With the single exception of Taylor, the joint committee unanimously recommended that the Senate strike its amendments from the House Maine Bill and the House strike the Taylor restriction from its Missouri Bill and replace it with the Thomas compromise excluding slavery north and west of Missouri.

Four restrictionists were absent: Henry Edwards of Connecticut and three New Yorkers, Caleb Tompkins, Walter Case, and Hermanus Peek.[46] The friends of Missouri glimpsed an opportunity to push the compromise through, while their opponents, no less adept at counting heads, now maneuvered for delay. Philemon Beecher of Ohio moved to print the report, a customary procedure that would postpone action to the next day. Lowndes immediately rose to oppose printing on the ground that it would "imply a determination in the House to delay a decision of the subject to-day, which he had hoped the House was fully prepared for." Taylor rose in support of Beecher, and the two opposing leaders engaged in a conversational exchange.[47] Taylor questioned the propriety of acting on the committee recommendations before the Senate had fulfilled its pledge to strike all amendments from the House Maine Bill. Lowndes thought

> it would be wrong to put in jeopardy a satisfactory settlement of this question, from an adherence to a mere point of etiquette and order; that the House could not fear that the Senate would adopt the recommendation to recede from their amendments, as the committee of conference was unanimous in their report, with the exception of one member of this House, (Mr TAYLOR) and became us further, as the disposition of the Senate to admit Maine could not be doubted, they would have no motive to adhere to their amendments if this House should adopt their report.[48]

Beecher withdrew the motion.

Proceeding to the recommendations, the House took up first the one to strike the Taylor amendment from the Missouri Bill, the key to a compromise solution. Lowndes was the first to speak. The time for argument had passed, and he would be brief. He appealed to his colleagues not as partisans of a cause but as statesman in the ancient republican tradition, revealing in the earnestness of his appeal his depth of commitment to timeless republican virtues: "Mr. Lowndes spoke briefly in support of the compromise recommended by the committee of conference, and urged with great earnestness the propriety of a decision which would restore tranquility to the country—which was demanded by every consideration of discretion, of moderation, of wisdom, and of virtue."[49] Committee members Holmes and Kinsey reinforced the effort of Lowndes, then a call for the question terminated discussion. The absence of the four restrictionists proved decisive as the House killed the Taylor amendment by a margin of three votes, 90 to 87. Southern moderates then joined their erstwhile opponents in quick passage of the Thomas compromise, 135 to 42, and two days later the enabling acts for the unrestricted admission of Maine and Missouri became law.[50]

President Monroe had intended to veto the proposed restriction on Missouri on the same constitutional ground that Lowndes and most of his southern colleagues had taken in the debate. Before adding his signature to the Missouri enabling act, Monroe consulted his cabinet on the Thomas compromise amendment. With Adams the lone dissenter, the cabinet concurred in the opinion Lowndes had expressed earlier, that the word "forever" in the amendment meant forever during the region's territorial status only and was not to be binding on applications for statehood from the region north and west of Missouri. When Monroe added his signature to the Missouri enabling act of 1820, he had no intention of binding future generations under a "sacred pledge" to exclude slavery forever north of the compromise line.[51]

Lowndes had reason to suspect that Missouri's path to statehood might yet be difficult. On the last day of February, Taylor had attempted to insert the following condition before the "equal footing" clause of the Missouri Bill: "[A]nd if [the Missouri constitution] shall be approved by Congress, the said Territory shall be admitted into the Union as a State."[52] Opposition led by Scott and Lowndes marshaled 125 votes to defeat the proviso, but 49 congressmen voted for it.[53] The restrictionist crusade had been thwarted, but it was by no means dead.

XI

The Protectionist Crusade

Like the eye of a hurricane, three weeks of relative calm followed the storm over Missouri. The House welcomed the interlude to clear the calendar of neglected business. Months had passed since the subdivisions of Monroe's opening message were referred to appropriate committees, but the Missouri question had delayed committee reports. William Lowndes, now chairman of the Committee of Foreign Relations, found an opportunity on March 9 to bring in his committee report on the Adams-Onís Treaty. What followed was one of the more awkward episodes of his congressional career.

The terms of the treaty had appeared reasonably satisfactory to both parties. East of the Mississippi, Spain ceded to the United States East Florida, which had proved ungovernable under Spanish rule, and gave up all claim to West Florida. In exchange the United States assumed responsibility for settling claims of her citizens against Spain up to $5 million. West of the Mississippi, the treaty surrendered claims of the United States to Texas and those of Spain to the Oregon country by establishing a mutual territorial boundary that ran up the Sabine River from the Gulf coast, then northwestward in stair-step fashion to the forty-second parallel, thence due West to the Pacific. Spain thus gave up a vexing and unprofitable colony for a generous definition of the northern boundary of Mexico. The United States emerged with an unbroken coastline from Maine to Louisiana, and beyond that, a transcontinental southern boundary sanctioned by a major European power. That Spain had been prepared to yield further on the Texas boundary hardly diminished the brilliance of Secretary Adams's diplomatic achievement.[1]

Concluded on February 22, 1819, the treaty allowed the two heads of state six months to ratify. Monroe added his signature three days later, but Ferdinand VII of Spain permitted the deadline to pass without signing. A major dispute had arisen over last minute grants of Florida lands to royal favorites which, Monroe explained, "conveyed all the lands which till then had been ungranted."[2] The administration had planned to use the vacant lands to discharge the $5 million in assumed claims. Efforts to resolve the issue through traditional diplomatic channels produced new evidence of Spanish recalcitrance and dissimulation. Finally in the fall of 1819, President Monroe asked Congress for a grant of discretionary power to take possession of Florida, which would strengthen his hand in dealing with Spain.

Having conferred repeatedly with Monroe and Adams on the matter, Chairman Lowndes knew that what the president wanted from Congress was a bargaining tool, but what the chairman called for in his report was something else again. In terms surprisingly bellicose for Lowndes, his report gave King Ferdinand fair warning that, because of his wholesale give-away of Florida real estate, he "must expect us to look westward" for territorial compensation. Then Lowndes offered a resolution that the president be forthwith "authorized and required, to take possession of, and occupy, East and West Florida."[3] Adams confided to his diary his opinion as to why Lowndes gave this personal twist to the president's request. The Carolinian's great influence in the House, Adams wrote, rested on his reputation for independent judgment, a reputation he took special care to protect:

> Supporting the administration in the main, he is apt to seek for differences of detail. He joins in no factious opposition, but loves to devise ways and means of his own. So, in this case, he proposes not what the President recommended, but a substitute; not a power which the Executive might have held up "in terrorem" in negotiation with Spain, and the very possession of which would probably have rendered its exercise unnecessary, but a positive direction to the President to take possession at all events. Lowndes, finding it doubtful that either of the proposals would pass, produced one differing from that of the President, to manifest at all events his independence.[4]

To avoid the encumbrance of a House mandate for reprisals, Monroe found an excuse to back away. On March 27, he sent over another message informing Congress that friendly overtures from England, France, and Russia gave him reason to believe the issue could be resolved peaceably through continued forbearance.[5]

At this point Lowndes would have dropped the matter, but Speaker Clay seized the opportunity to exchange the swampy Florida peninsula for the potential cotton kingdom of East Texas. Taking his cue from the reference to western compensation in Lowndes's own report, Clay introduced resolutions declaring that only Congress could dispose of territories belonging to the United States, that Florida was inadequate compensation for the loss of Texas, and that it would be inexpedient to make a transfer of Texas to any foreign power or to renew the treaty. Arguing as if Texas were a territorial possession of the United States rather than a region subject to conflicting claims, the Kentuckian declared the treaty aborted and called for specific congressional instructions to prevent future alienation of the land of milk and honey west of the Sabine.[6]

Here Lowndes rose to defend the treaty, assuming the broader perspective of the Monroe administration. In the first place, he argued, a congressional attempt to place limitations on diplomatic negotiations would constitute an intrusion of the legislative authority into that constitutionally reserved to the Executive. As to the relative desirability of Texas and Florida, the latter's strategic importance along with free access to the Gulf coast strongly recommended retention of the treaty. Without Texas, Spain would have no motive to cede Florida. The opportunity to acquire the strategic peninsula could be lost forever if Spain's unstable control over her Mexican possessions should collapse or if Florida should fall into the hands of a third power. Moreover, the future of Texas was yet to be decided, and to considerable degree, by patterns of western settlement. At his suggestion the House agreed to limit discussion of this topic to points that would not jeopardize continuing administration efforts to complete the ratification process.[7]

This constraint effectively muzzled the advocates of southwestern expansion. Even so, David Trimble of Kentucky, speaking for Americans "residing on the Western waters," chided the committee chairman for his hasty retreat from belligerence to "cautious prudence." If Lowndes, said Trimble, "did not advance with the boldness of Alexander, he displayed in retreat all the skill of Xenophon. . . . [H]e carried everything with him; had left no spoil for his pursuers; no point exposed; no barriers undefended. The honor of the nation could not be placed in better hands, or safer keeping; and no one could defend its interests with superior ability."⁸ The rebuke was not unmerited. By denying that his colleagues should presume to specify limits on treaty negotiations, after having himself presumed to instruct the president to take possession of Florida at once, Lowndes invited the charge of inconsistency. But the House majority, overwhelmingly favoring the treaty and thus sympathetic to Lowndes's point of view if not to his awkward position, extricated the committee chairman by voting to table the matter to the next session. Their patience paid dividends in Spanish ratification of the treaty and the peaceful annexation of Florida the following February.

This interlude of relative calm ended on March 22, 1820 when Chairman Henry Baldwin of Pennsylvania reported out of the Committee of Manufactures a bill to raise tariff duties to an average of 33.33 percent ad valorem. Baldwin advocated his bill with a wholesale condemnation of the existing tariff. In the process, he accused Lowndes of narrowly sectional motives and hostility toward manufactures in framing the 1816 law, which was a partisan interpretation of Lowndes's role that has found its way into modern scholarship.⁹ An examination into the background of the Baldwin Bill helps to clarify Lowndes's position and suggests a fundamental consistency in his support for protection in 1816 and his decision to join the opposition leadership in 1820.

The Baldwin Bill represented the culmination of a sustained and concerted lobbying campaign that singled out the moderate Tariff of 1816 as the principal cause of the nation's economic distress. Although no permanent lobbies were yet established in Washington, lobbying by individuals or by ad hoc groups had been practiced since 1789. By 1815 interest groups had begun to assess members to send lobbying agents to Washington, establishing a practice that became increasingly common in the postwar years.¹⁰ Francis Cabot Lowell and Nathan Appleton of the Boston Manufacturing Company had demonstrated the potential rewards of skillful lobbying in their effort of 1816. Utilizing the power loom he invented, Lowell set up his factory "to imitate the yard wide goods of India, with which the country was then largely supplied."¹¹ He brought Appleton into the firm, and the two came to Washington and persuaded the Fourteenth Congress to adopt Lowell's proposal for a minimum valuation of twenty-five cents a yard on imported textiles. Under this minimum principle, as it came to be called, India cottons worth about nine cents a yard were valued at twenty-five cents and taxed at the ad valorem rate of 25 percent. This added six cents to the market price of India cottons when Lowell's firm could market its own cottons at three or four cents less and still make a profit.[12] The company found the results gratifying. By 1819 India cottons had disappeared from the American market, and as the depression brought a rise in consumption of cheaper grades of cotton cloth, it also cut the price of raw cotton in half. Dividends paid to company stockholders began to soar: 12 percent in 1819, 17 percent in 1820, 20 percent in 1821, 28 percent in 1822, 25 percent in 1823 and again in 1824, and finally a postwar peak of 30 percent in 1825.[13]

Customs house returns showed other positive though less dramatic developments under the Tariff of 1816. Imports dropped from a postwar high of $130 million in 1816 down to $80 million the following year, then climbed to $103 million in 1818, the last year of the postwar boom. In parallel fashion the excess of imports over exports plummeted from $65 million in 1816 down to $12 million the following year, then rose to $29 million in 1818.[14] These figures represented a 20 percent reduction of imports under the existing tariff while the trade deficit had been cut in half. Although the influence of tariff duties in producing this result could be debated, the improved condition of America's trade balance testified to the effectiveness of the 1816 law within the moderate limits William Lowndes and his colleagues had intended: to restore competitive balance in the American marketplace.

The minimum principle and other benefits notwithstanding, the Tariff of 1816 failed to satisfy more ardent protectionists. This was especially true of Mathew Carey of Philadelphia and Hezekiah Niles of Baltimore, the two men most responsible for continued agitation for higher duties after the law went into effect. Their efforts helped to persuade Congress in 1818 to revise upward the rates on selected iron products and to cancel the scheduled reduction of textile duties promised in 1816. Then the Panic of 1819 brought the deluge.

Operating out of Philadelphia and Baltimore, Carey and Niles launched a massive campaign for tariff reform. Joined by other protectionists, they drew up and printed large petitions, very broad in their requests, which were then circulated for signatures mostly in Philadelphia, New York, and Baltimore. When a number of protectionist organizations sprang up in the Middle Atlantic states and New England, Niles opened the columns of his influential *Weekly Register* to give their views national exposure. Carey and seven of his Philadelphia friends joined forces to give the protectionist crusade centralized direction. Styling themselves the "Society for the Promotion of National Industry," these eight men organized the prototype of the nineteenth-century lobby.¹⁵ During the tariff debate, Congressman Ezekiel Whitman of Massachusetts critically appraised the lobby's success in molding public opinion in favor of tariff reform:

> An association in Philadelphia, calling itself a Society for the Promotion of National Industry, has its branches in every part of the Union, with which it corresponds, and which it directs, and instigates, and sets in motion, by the means of pamphlets and newspaper essays. Its inflammatory and unfounded statements have pervaded every part of the Union. Each member of the present Congress has been favored with enough to make two large volumes at least. And these have, for the moment, deluded the people, and made them believe it is wise to annihilate commerce, in order to build up great manufactories. "If they can do this in the gristle, what will they do in the bone?"¹⁶

While the society's "addresses" educated the public through the *Weekly Register* and other sympathetic journals, protectionists bombarded Congress with petitions. Crying with one universal voice that the rates of 1816 were too low to protect, the petitions bore a marked similarity to those of 1816. They begged Congress for protection from ruinous foreign competition, resting their case on generalized accounts of unemployment, falling prices, and general industrial distress and relying on widespread unrest brought on by the depression to strengthen popular support for tariff reform.¹⁷ The train of evils Mathew Carey recounted in the petition he wrote in 1819 for a New York convention of delegates from New England, the Middle Atlantic states, and Ohio was typical:

> [T]he United States . . . find themselves in a state of great embarrassment and difficulty, involving almost every description of our citizens: our commerce is greatly prostrated; our shipping has sunk in value to one-half of its original cost; real estate is depreciated, in most parts of the country, in an equal degree; numbers of our merchants, manufacturers, and farmers are reduced to bankruptcy . . . ; a great portion of our mechanics and artists are unemployed; . . . our great staples are so far reduced in price as most seriously to affect the interests of the agriculturists. . . . [W]hile so many of our manufacturers are thus ruined, our working people destitute of employment and of the means to support their families, our manufac-

turing establishments falling into ruins . . . , our cities and towns are filled with the manufactured productions of other nations, by which we have been, and are, ruinously drained of our wealth. . . . [T]hose complicated evils which oppress us . . . evince that there is something unsound in our policy, which requires a radical remedy, in the power of the National Legislature alone to apply.

The solution?

First. To abolish credits on import duties.
Secondly. To impose a restrictive duty on sales at auction.
Thirdly. To alter and increase the amount of duties on imported goods.[18]

The "radical remedy" that Carey outlined here represented a radical change in protectionist objectives since 1816. Together the three proposals would create such serious problems for importing merchants as virtually to eliminate their competitive position in the American market. The petitions as well as the debates of 1820 revealed that "protection" was taking on a new and broader meaning. No longer content with a protective system which gave them competitive equality in facing foreign competition, high protectionists now were moving to convert the American marketplace into the exclusive preserve of the American manufacturer. Toward this end, their petitions expounded at length on the theme of national independence, attempting to demonstrate that the interests of manufacturers and the national interest were one and the same, and claiming that agriculture and commerce would benefit from the closed economic system they proposed.[19]

Finally, when Henry Baldwin's Committee of Manufactures began to formulate a new tariff bill, Carey secretly financed a trip to Washington taken by his friend Condy Raguet, a zealous and persuasive advocate of high protection, "for a week's talk during recess with Baldwin . . . and others."[20] How well Raguet accomplished his mission may be judged by the committee report. Baldwin offered three proposals for tariff reform straight out of Carey's New York petition of 1819. The first would abolish credits on import duties. The second would impose a prohibitive duty of 10 percent on sales at auction, the standard method of disposing of imported merchandise. And the third would increase import duties to 33.33 percent ad valorem.[21]

When Baldwin laid his tariff bill before Congress in 1820, the motivating factors behind southern support for protection in 1816 no longer obtained. Prosperity had vanished with the Panic of 1819; the current Anglo-American rapprochement removed patriotism as a plausible pretext for encouraging the growth of domestic manufactures; and protectionist assurances that duties would be lowered to the revenue level, once the massive dumping of British goods passed, had proved a delusion. Nor were these the only contrasts. Others pertaining to purpose, recommendations, reasonableness, and research soon became evident.

President Monroe gave a qualified endorsement for a tariff increase in his opening message to Congress in December 1819. After surveying the effects of the Panic he said, "It is deemed of great importance to give encouragement to our domestic manufactures." On the other hand, he continued, the great reduction in the cost of labor and raw materials had created conditions "favorable to the success of manufactures." The president therefore left to the wisdom of Congress "how far it [might] be . . . practicable to afford them further encouragement, paying due regard to the other great interests of the nation."[22] Three days later Secretary Crawford of the Treasury Department offered a similarly qualified recommendation in his annual report. "It is believed," he said of manufactures, "that the present is a favorable moment for affording efficient protection to that increasing and important interest, if it can be done consistently with the general interest of the union." Quite aware of the vigorous campaign to exclude British textiles from the American market, Crawford said the state of the revenue gave Congress a choice, either to increase taxes or to cut expenses. Should Congress elect to augment the revenue, he warned, any attempt to give American cottons and woolens a monopoly of the home market through prohibitive duties would leave the government no choice but to resort to internal taxes, which "would be severely felt by the great mass of our citizens."[23]

The administration's qualified endorsement of higher duties brought alarmed reaction from northern commerce and southern agriculture. In January 1820, the House received two counterpetitions, one from the Agricultural Society of Fredericksburg, Virginia and the other from importing merchants and seafaring men of Salem, Massachusetts.[24] Both petitions stressed the merits of free trade, called for retention of the existing law, and in strikingly similar language, condemned the drive for tariff reform as a self-serving attempt to promote private interests at the expense of the people as a whole. The similarity of these petitions reflected a harmony of interests between agriculture and commerce, the producer and the carrier, while differences were revealed less in content than in a marked contrast of tone. And each furnished the main lines of opposition argument for the interest group it represented.

Sniffing corruption and tyranny in the tainted protectionist breeze, the Virginians grounded their protest on the principles of traditional republicanism.[25] They opened with a reference to the constitutional right of petition, then moved directly to the heart of their argument: "That hostility, resulting from true republican principles, to partial taxation, exclusive privileges, and monopolies created by law, was the primary cause of [the] revolution." To this form of oppression they felt an aversion equal to that of their fathers; and while neither they nor their sons after them would hesitate to make whatever sacrifices the public good might "obviously and necessarily require," they had been taught to believe that "a Government founded upon the immutable and sacred principles of truth, justice, and liberty—if she required sacrifices at all from those whom she is so solemnly bound to protect, would make them such as should operate equally upon every member of the community." Hence they viewed with great concern attempts of manufacturers and their friends to increase tariff protection. These attempts were "sustained under the plausible pretext of 'promoting national industry'" but actually were calculated to produce a tax "highly impolitic in its nature, partial in its operation, and oppressive in its effects . . . to be levied principally on the great body of agriculturists . . . who are the chief consumers of all foreign imports." Taxes of any kind, "to be rightfully levied, must be equal, and . . . for the support of Government alone."

A policy of high protection would be "a flagrant violation of the soundest and most important principles of political economy" because it would destroy competition, exposing the consumer to extravagant prices and allowing the manufacturer exorbitant profits. Only through free and open competition, they said,

> can the benefits of good government be equalized among the various orders and classes of society, the prosperity and happiness of which depend . . . upon the unfettered exercise of talent, skill, and industry, directed and employed in whatever manner, and upon whatsoever objects of pursuit, each individual may select for himself; provided, always, that such objects be not incompatible with the public good; for so to use your own rights as not to injure the rights of others, is not less the dictate of common sense and common honesty than it is a cardinal maxim of all legitimate government.

Manufactures, always the last of the three great industries to arise in countries favorably situated for agriculture, would arise naturally when "the wants of the people" should create the necessary demand. In the meantime, "any legislative interference to force either this or any other class into existence by the strong arm of power . . . contrary to the wishes and interests of the other members of the community, is not only bad policy, but oppression." The Virginians reinforced their laissez-faire argument with several additional points on the advantages of free trade. They also disavowed any hostility toward manufacturers "or any other useful description of our fellow citizens," and then they reaffirmed their stand in the language of civic virtue confronted with corruption:

> We ask no tax upon manufacturers for our benefit; neither do we desire any thing of Government to enable us to cultivate the soil as profitably as we could wish, but to leave us free, so far as it depends on them, to carry our products to the best market we can find, and to purchase what we want in return, on the best terms that we can, either at home or abroad. We will ever support the Government of our choice in all just and rightful undertakings, both with our fortunes and our lives; but we will never voluntarily contribute to maintain either manufacturers, or any other class of citizens, by the payment of unequal and partial taxes, by awarding to them exclusive privileges, or by sustaining them in the enjoyment of oppressive monopolies, which are ultimately to grind both us and our children after us "into dust and ashes."

The Fredericksburg petition set the tone for all future discussion of the tariff issue in the exporting states of the antebellum South. With few exceptions, their congressmen concurred with the Fredericksburg viewpoint, cast themselves in the role of defenders of traditional republican values, and gave expression to the moral disgust, outrage, and defiance that resonated through the Virginia protest. The assumption of republican purity entailed in the southern reaction rested on the widespread conviction that the exporting South remained untainted by the corrupting effect of special interest legislation. The two points on which such an assumption seemed most vulnerable to challenge were the Fugitive Slave Act of 1793 and a specific duty of three cents a pound on imported raw cotton dating from 1789. Southerners always maintained that passage of a fugitive slave law had been a condition on which the slaveholding

South agreed to enter the Union. As recently as 1819, this argument had received apparent confirmation from the chief justice of Pennsylvania, who held that the law represented the fulfillment of a contractual obligation made by the founding fathers out of "historical necessity."[26] In any event, southerners had difficulty finding a basis for comparison between a law that might burden the conscience of the North and another that would burden the economy of the South. As for the specific duty on imported cotton, it had indeed benefited southern planters in the early years and still served as an effective bar to imports of foreign cotton. But after the cotton gin brought about a substantial surplus in 1794, the law had no apparent impact on domestic cotton prices. The annual surplus amounted to 128 million pounds in 1820, two-thirds of the total crop.[27] The stern reality of a market glutted with three times as much cotton as it could absorb left little room for illusion about the effect of a three-cent tax on imported cotton. Hard experience taught the southern planter that what once might have been special interest legislation favoring the South had long since become a dead letter on the statute books, imposing no burden whatever on domestic consumers of raw cotton.[28] These considerations strengthened convictions of republican purity in the South and sharpened the edge of southern response to the drive for high protection.

Just as the Fredericksburg petition had done for representatives of southern agriculture, the petitioners of Salem, Massachusetts, suggested the main lines of opposition argument for northern commerce. But unlike the Virginians, the men of Salem were hardly in a position to condemn outright federal aid to the manufacturing interest while they themselves enjoyed the benefit of federal laws specifically designed to facilitate maritime commerce and give American shipping interests an advantage over foreign competition. These laws included discriminating tonnage duties in American ports and the credit system, which could delay payment of import duties until the goods were sold.[29] The moderate Tariff of 1816 did not seriously hinder America's maritime commerce except in one important particular: the minimum principle had deranged the Far Eastern trade. To this major grievance protectionists were now preparing to add higher tariffs and a prohibitive duty on sales at auction. Because all citizens appeared to benefit from the promotion of international trade through the high percentage of federal revenue it provided, general consensus had held the policy to be nationalistic both in purpose and effect. But being the direct beneficiaries of that policy, the Salem petitioners employed the more temperate approach of an interest group competing for federal favor with a new and powerful rival.[30]

The men of Salem expressed surprise and regret at seeing measures, "advocated by respectable portions of the community," that would reduce American commerce from its globe-girdling greatness to the narrow confines of the coasting trade.[31] They believed manufactures deserved "to receive the fostering care and patronage of the Government," but could it ever be sound or safe policy to build them up on the ruins of commerce?

> Is it just, is it salutary, is it politic, to abandon a course which has so eminently conduced to our welfare, for the purpose of trying experiments . . . founded upon mere theoretical doctrines . . . ? Cases may possibly arise in which the interests of a respectable portion of the community may be justly sacrificed; but they are cases of extreme public necessity, not cases where the rivalry and the interest of one class of men seek to sustain themselves by destruction to another. In a free country, too, it may well be asked if it be a legitimate end of government to control the ordinary occupations of men. . . . Nothing, however, can be more obvious than that many of the manufacturers and their friends are attempting, by fallacious statements founded on an interested policy, or a misguided zeal, or very shortsighted views, to uproot some of the fundamental principles of our revenue policy, and to compel our merchants to abandon some of the most lucrative branches of our commerce.

Building their case on the beneficial effects of free commerce, most notably its contributions to the federal revenue, national wealth, and naval support in the event of war, the petitioners argued at length the necessity of retaining intact the present system, including the moderate tariff duties of 1816. That the existing tariff law was "singularly favorable to manufacturers" they supposed would have been freely admitted. The law, they said, had all but destroyed the trade in East India textiles, and, when freight costs were included, the tariff provided a protective rate of 30 to 35 percent against British textiles. These advantages notwithstanding, manufacturers, "blinded by a partial view of their own interests," were clamoring for more.

> Why should the farmer, and the planter, and the merchant, and the mechanics, and the laboring classes of the community, be taxed for

the necessaries of life a sum equal to more than a quarter part of their whole expenditures on these objects, that the manufacturers may put this sum into their own pockets?

In sum, high protection could be expected to produce a multitude of evils:

> to impair our naval strength and glory; to injure our most profitable commerce; to diminish . . . the public revenue; to promote unjustifiable speculation; to enhance the price of manufactures; to throw the great business and trade of the nation into the hands of a few capitalists . . . ; to introduce general distress among commercial artisans and agriculturists; to aggravate the present distress of the other classes of the community; to provoke fraud and smuggling; and, in fine, to destroy many of the great objects for which the Constitution of the United States was originally framed and adopted.

After the January counterpetitions came in, Secretary Crawford added a significant caveat to his original recommendation on the tariff. In early February he informed the House that even in cases where tariff rates were not prohibitive, "revenue will frequently be diminished by an increase of duty" because, as rising taxes reduce the capacity to pay for foreign imports, the point is soon reached where smuggling "upon an extensive and systematic plan, commences." Again, Congress would have to impose direct taxes to make up the loss in revenue.[32] To William Lowndes, and doubtless the House generally, the implications were plain enough; Crawford's arguments "were prepared for a different conclusion," retrenchment.[33]

The third significant recommendation came in late March from the House Committee of Ways and Means chaired by the Baltimore merchant Samuel Smith. Finding the Treasury secretary's ambivalence compatible with his own views, Smith brought in a report devoid of any reference to the manufacturing interest or to the tariff. It counseled rigid economy and continued dependence on the existing law, supplemented by loans, to meet the fiscal needs of the government.[34] Heretofore such a report would have settled the matter, as tax legislation was the exclusive prerogative of this powerful committee. But Henry Clay, as House Speaker, skillfully circumvented the Ways and Means Committee in one of the more adroit parliamentary maneuvers of his career.

Evidently anticipating a negative report from Ways and Means, the Speaker moved early in the session to divide into two separate committees the standing Committee of Commerce and Manufactures chaired by Thomas Newton of Virginia. Newton was not an opponent of protection, but his committee as a whole lacked the protectionist zeal necessary for the Speaker's purpose. Over Newton's objections, the House, with a protectionist majority of roughly nine to seven, divided his committee in two, creating a new Committee of Manufactures and leaving Newton in charge of the Committee of Commerce. Clay promptly staffed the new committee with high-tariff men headed by Henry Baldwin, the Pittsburg manufacturer of glass products.[35] As Baldwin later explained, nobody knew whether his committee actually had the authority to draw up a revenue measure: "[T]he Committee of Manufactures was a new one; its powers and duties were undefined by any rule; the various subjects referred to them related as well to the revenue and commerce of the country, as its manufactures."[36] Notwithstanding dubious authority and the lack of positive instructions to act on, the new committee wrested the initiative from Ways and Means and set about drawing up a bill of its own.

In contrast to the research effort Lowndes employed to formulate the tariff bill in 1816, the Baldwin committee declined to consult the Treasury Department for information or advice and made no effort to establish through research proof of need for protection on any given item listed in the schedule.[37] Lowndes immediately discovered on reading the report that the Baldwin method of writing tax law was simplicity itself. Having taken Mathew Carey's New York petition as a guide in structuring the three parts of their legislative package, all Baldwin and his committee had to do was fill in details. The committee supplied the principal items of their tariff schedule with similar ease, taking the old Dallas rates of 1816 and writing them with minor alterations into the Baldwin Bill of 1820.[38]

If any mystery remained concerning protectionist objectives, Baldwin's opening speech in defense of this bill removed all doubt.[39] The speech, like the lobbying campaign, rested on the premise that the rates of 1816 were too low to protect. Baldwin asserted this allegation as indisputable fact requiring no further proof than the wretched state of the national economy. Had Lowndes not committed the deliberate error of scaling down the schedule Dallas recommended, said Baldwin, the Tariff of 1816 would have given American manufactures the protection necessary to withstand foreign competition and avert the present crisis.[40] Lowndes and his colleagues had written a revenue tariff, pure and simple. They had "wantonly abandoned" such crucial industries as iron, so that numerous flourishing ironworks had been "destroyed apparently by design."[41] The Committee of Manufactures had recognized the urgent need to correct the mistakes of 1816; and when neither Ways and Means nor any other committee would take action, Baldwin and his colleagues, "left thus alone," saw no alternative but to supply the remedy themselves.[42]

In making his case, the committee chairman adopted the strategy of the lobbying campaign, relying heavily on broad generalizations and giving special emphasis to the restrictive policies of other nations in contrast to the self-destructive openness of the American market.[43] To justify an increase on a particular item, he would frequently compare it with the old Dallas schedule, invoking the authority of the former secretary in behalf of the Baldwin Bill. On the one article that he thought required special justification, the generous rate of protection for glass manufactures of his home district, he claimed special need on the ground of fierce foreign competition and stressed, as if the attribute were unique to the industry, that glassmakers made something out of nothing, for the raw materials of this product were otherwise worthless.[44] But Baldwin offered no evidence on the impact of the depression on wages, the price of raw materials, and other costs of production in this or any other industry which could demonstrate special need for a given rate increase. This was a fundamental weakness in his argument that the opposition was certain to exploit. Another was the uncertain consequences of his revolutionary plans for funding the national government.

According to Baldwin, the three-part legislative package his committee offered represented a comprehensive system designed to secure the nation's economic independence. He insisted that this would require a historic shift in the nation's revenue system from a primary reliance on import duties to a system depending principally on excise taxes.[45] The state of the Treasury and the national depression were sufficient proof that "this miserable system of impost" had failed. The glaring flaw in the existing revenue system was that it always failed precisely when it was most needed, during time of war. Moreover, no nation could claim to be independent while it continued to rely on others to supply its own people the basic necessities of life such as clothing and even the means to equip its army in wartime. Given proper encouragement, American manufactures could supply these basic needs and halt the ruinous drain of the nation's wealth to Europe. He would achieve this by giving American manufactures such a clear advantage over foreign imports that excise taxes on American-made goods would displace tariff duties as the principal source of national revenue. "Restore the confidence now destroyed," he urged; "bottom your revenue on the manufactures of the country; then both are placed on a foundation which combines the support of the Government with the best interests of the nation."[46] His program contained no actual provision for excise taxes because, he said, tariff reform was necessarily the first step toward economic independence. The rest would come later.

The revolutionary character of the Baldwin program, the highly sectional allocation of its benefits and burdens, and the conviction among southerners especially that it violated fundamental republican principles aroused intense controversy. The issue divided Congress along lines that tended to sunder the nation's midsection from its southern and northeastern extremities. Except for the Louisiana sugar country, many a winter storm blanketed virtually all areas of protectionist sentiment with snow that came out of Missouri, spread a broad front across the Ohio Valley as far south as Tennessee, moved eastward up the valley, and passed through Pennsylvania and northern Maryland, Delaware and New Jersey, New York and the industrial areas of New England.[47] Representatives of northern commerce and southern agriculture bonded together in stout opposition to the Baldwin program. Lowndes worked to strengthen this defensive alliance, but the coalition was still some twenty votes short of a majority when the tariff bill came up for discussion in mid-April.[48]

XII

The Politics of Special Interest

The opposition counterattack began on April 14, when Arthur Livermore of New Hampshire condemned the proposed shift to an excise-based revenue as a change for the worse and moved to kill the tariff bill through indefinite postponement. Clay ruled Livermore out of order, but when Lowndes and Philip Barbour of Virginia challenged the ruling, the Speaker consented to a vote on the motion and it lost.[1] The next day Lowndes introduced a resolution of the first importance to this stage of tariff history:

> *Resolved*, That the Committee of Manufactures be instructed to report to this House such evidence as it may be in their power to present, showing the several rates of wages given, and expense of all kinds incurred in the different branches of manufacture which, in their opinion, require additional encouragement, with the prices of their product, so as to exhibit the profit which, at the present prices of subsistence, materials, and labor, and the present value of land, buildings, and machinery, may be obtained in such manufacture, skillfully and economically conducted.[2]

Lowndes's principal objection to the bill was the committee's failure to conduct research into the relative condition of manufactures in the American economy, as his committee had done in 1816, in order to demonstrate actual need for higher protection. Then in the process of preparing a speech on the bill, Lowndes had collected information showing that the decline in wages and the cost of raw materials had more than offset the depressed prices of manufactured goods.[3] Because all branches of the American economy had suffered in the Panic of 1819, he said, it was incumbent on the committee to prove that manufactures had suffered greater injury than had commerce and agriculture, both of which stood to be injured by this bill. Surely the friends of the bill did not expect Congress to intervene in order to save from ruin manufacturing establishments whose difficulties arose from poor management or bad judgment in their directors, or marginal operations erected for speculative purposes on borrowed capital that had suddenly become dear. Suppose that Congress should supply a reasonable degree of protection to well-managed operations, how was the House to determine what that degree might be without the information he called for?[4]

The antiprotectionist coalition rallied behind Lowndes. Timothy Fuller of Massachusetts attacked the Committee of Manufactures as "a private committee, acting on the private petitions of individuals, who sought support and encouragement from the Government, at the expense of the nation."[5] Another critic accused Baldwin of writing "a Pittsburg . . . cut glass bill, local [and] partial in its operations."[6] Virginian John Tyler echoed Lowndes in language equally plain: "Are the present manufacturers in the United States really entitled to your aid? Where is the proof of it?" All classes were greatly depressed. He wanted such information as would enable him "fairly to contrast the condition of the manufacturing with the other interests of the country . . . , to be informed whether that interest only suffered in the same ratio with the others, and whether its sufferings were produced by similar causes."[7]

Baldwin, his Pennsylvania colleague John Sergeant, Ezra Gross of New York, and Peter Little of Maryland responded. According to the reporter's summary, they said the committee had structured their bill "from considerations of national policy, and not from a minute investigation of details; that the information asked was not such as a committee of this House ought to be required to give, and which each member could as well procure for himself as a committee for him."[8] Lowndes disagreed. The point of his resolution was that the committee should furnish not the House but themselves with this information for use in constructing a rate schedule of proved necessity. He reminded the House that the rates of 1816 were based on precisely such information as he now called for, collected by the Treasury Department through a circular letter sent throughout the nation. He quoted from the 1816 report of Secretary Dallas to show that the duties subsequently recommended by the Committee of Ways and Means "were founded on evidence of the degree of encouragement which would enable 'the manufacturer to meet the importer.' That evidence was laid before the House. It contained, substantially, and indeed much more fully than he should require it, all the information in respect to the state of our manufactories in 1816, which it was the object of his resolution to obtain in 1820." This proved, he concluded, "at least that the object of his resolution was practicable, and had hitherto been considered important and necessary."[9]

Baldwin's answer to Lowndes captured the essence of the entire protectionist campaign.

> We have been called on by the gentleman from South Carolina for the evidence on which the committee have acted. Of the description referred to in his resolution we have none; and I tell the gentleman plainly, that the Committee of Manufactures have not acted, and would not act, on the statement, or even the affidavits, of interested persons. Others may make motives for us—but we shall not avow what we disdain. I refer him, for the information on which we have acted, to the commercial codes of other countries—our own official documents from the Treasury; to the able reports of the Committee of Commerce, of the Secretary of the Treasury, and to one which deserves particular notice, from being presented by himself; the bill reported by the Committee of Ways and Means in 1816. I repeat it, that the profits of manufactures had not been our leading motive, but the public national interest; this nation must command its own consumption and the means of defense.[10]

The protectionist majority required no further persuasion. They rejected the research resolution, 90 to 72, with the pattern of their votes following the storm track across the nation's midsection.[11] The result drew from Lowndes the observation that the majority "had refused all evidence as to the proper degree of encouragement, and left the defense of the bill to the same vague considerations which would support a duty of one hundred percent as well as one of forty. They took they knew not how much from the people; they gave they knew not how much to the manufacturer."[12]

On Friday, April 21, the House went into Committee of the Whole to examine the particulars of the Baldwin schedule. Smith of Maryland questioned the wisdom of an excise-based revenue and moved for a rate reduction on more than two dozen items.[13] Clay spoke against the motion. In the process, he warmly praised Baldwin and his committee for the comprehensive system they had fashioned and warned its friends not to tamper with a part of the overall plan lest they "lose the whole."[14] The warning had the desired effect. The remainder of the day was spent in considering one amendment after another, all ultimately defeated. The House spent all day Saturday at the same business with the same result except on three items. The majority added prunella shoes and butter to the duty list and, in their only concession to the opposition, agreed to adjust downward the rate on scholarly books.[15] The majority having carried the Baldwin schedule through the amendment process intact, on Monday John Tyler moved to strike out its first section, to kill the bill, and the tariff debate began.

Tyler opened with an argument so ill-advised as to strengthen the protectionist case. He said the bill was designed to draw capital and labor away from commerce and agriculture into manufacturing. All the clamor "has this for its object and nothing else." But manufacturers were grossly deceived in thinking the plan would bring them permanent relief, he went on, because their higher profits would naturally attract more capital and labor, which would increase competition, drive down prices, and ultimately bring manufacturers back to their present condition. Evidently it had not occurred to Tyler that this meant the burdens of the program would be temporary, a point protectionists had repeatedly stressed.

The Virginian was more effective in addressing the home market issue. The bill would double the three-cent tariff on raw cotton and place a protective duty on imported tobacco. Tyler wondered if Baldwin intended to deceive the South: "Did he really imagine that the members from Georgia and South Carolina were to be entrapped by the first, or the Virginians by the last? . . . Look at the list of annual exports of cotton and tell me if the cotton planter has anything to fear from foreign competition? And is it not well known that the Virginia tobacco planter fears no competition on earth? No other tobacco comes into competition with it." Drawing a familiar comparison, Tyler said Baldwin might as well have been legislating for Newcastle by placing a high duty on coal imported there. Unless the committee chairman could figure out a way to increase the number of domestic consumers, protective duties on cotton and tobacco were "futile, nay a perfect mockery." And would "this Chinese system" actually secure the nation's independence? True independence for a nation of free men rested not on manufactures but on land, the only kind of property "which war cannot destroy or fire consume."[16]

Two New Yorkers rose to defend the bill. Henry Storrs consumed an hour extolling its merits and contemning "this rotten system" of impost revenue. Ezra Gross confessed he should have thought Tyler "in favor of the bill did I take his remarks instead of his motion, as the test of his sentiments." But in advocating the new tariff, Gross followed the familiar example of the lobbying campaign, avoiding specifics and stressing generalities:

> A spirit of inquiry has gone forth, and the progress of public opinion in favor of a change of policy is not to be arrested, but, if the Government does nothing, years of suffering and embarrassment may pass before the evil will be completely cured. Let us not permit the distresses of our fellow-citizens to be the sole cause of reformation; the skilful [sic] physician follows the indications of nature, and assists all its operations in throwing off the disease. Let us follow the example, and afford a seasonable encouragement to the manufacturing interest, which is now struggling between hope and despair.[17]

When Gross finished, the House rejected Tyler's motion, 75 to 48.

At this point the House suspended discussion of the tariff to take up the bill to abolish the system of credits on revenue bonds, and debate on this bill occupied the House for the remainder of this day and the next. Baldwin explained how the measure constituted an integral part of his program. He advocated this bill on the general ground that the credit system, perhaps necessary during the nation's infancy, had long since outlived its usefulness. It now served, he said, as a bounty extended to the foreign importer at the expense of his American competitor and produced long delays in collecting the nation's revenue.[18] After Clay and Trimble of Kentucky defended this measure, Nathaniel Silsbee of Salem, Massachusetts, moved to kill it by striking out its first section and supported his motion with a largely factual exposition of arguments from the Salem petition.[19] Lowndes, James Johnson of Virginia, and Ezekiel Whitman of Massachusetts gave additional support to Silsbee's motion, but the Tuesday session adjourned with the issue still unresolved.[20]

Debate on the tariff resumed on Wednesday and continued through Friday. Few of the speakers added much of substance to the principal arguments from the Fredericksburg, Salem, and New York petitions. Barbour distinguished himself with a lucid and balanced presentation of the Virginia point of view. In the process, he gave emphasis to a familiar republican assumption, that the rise of manufactures would draw the independent yeoman farmer away from the land that secured his personal freedom and convert him into a dependent mill operative obediently responsive to the mill owner's will.[21] Henry Clay displayed once more his masterful talent for popularizing an issue, using colorful imagery and homespun eloquence to show that "home industry" was "the cause of the country."[22] On Friday Louis McLane of Delaware devoted almost his entire speech to a theme destined to dominate protectionist rhetoric in the years ahead: how protection would provide full employment for American labor.[23] Then William Lowndes took the floor to deliver what protectionist historian Edward Stanwood has called the "weightiest" speech against the Baldwin tariff bill.[24]

What gave weight as well as a detached and timeless quality to Lowndes's speech was the republican simplicity of its content; for, unlike the Virginians, he appealed neither to emotion nor theory nor dogma but to the unwavering rule of reason resting on fact. Lowndes said the question was not whether manufactures were useful; "a great deal of trouble had been taken to prove what nobody denied." Nor was the question whether the policy of the federal government should be to encourage manufactures by duties on foreign imports, "a subject on which they had, perhaps, already gone too far." The fundamental issue was whether the relative condition of manufactures within the national economy warranted the legislation proposed in their behalf. He believed "the encouragement already afforded was as great as could reasonably be granted." In elaborating this point, Lowndes asked:

> Had it ever been contended, not merely that manufactures should be encouraged, but that the bounty to be given should not be limited by any determined relation to the necessity of the manufacture, or the fair profits to the manufacturer? You say that it is important to encourage the manufacture of cotton. Be it so. We know that, however it be disguised, this can only be done at the expense of other classes of society. Is it not proper to inquire what expense is necessary; what would be adequate?[25]

Lowndes explained that when duties were laid on imports that faced no domestic competition, the additional price paid by consumers went into the public treasury. When duties were laid on imported articles of a type produced within the country, the price of both, domestic and foreign, would rise. Whichever he purchased, the buyer would pay a higher price, but in this case, only part of the additional cost to the consuming public would go into the Treasury. The other would go to the manufacturer who produced the domestic article. It was hardly by chance that Lowndes selected the sugar industry to illustrate his point.

> If, for instance, one hundred million of pounds of sugar were consumed annually in the United States, and three-fourths of this amount were furnished by domestic industry, an additional duty of one cent the pound would cause the consumers of sugar throughout the country to pay one million of dollars more in the price of the article, than they would otherwise do—would impose upon the people a new tax of one million; but of this sum, less than $250,000 would be received by the Government, and $750,000 by the sugar planter.[26]

Lowndes said this example explained the principal difference between himself and those who supported the bill. In his view, if Congress determined to encourage the production of an article by an additional bounty, then they were duty bound to inquire carefully what sum would be necessary for this object.

> To justify the tax, it was necessary to determine that the nation had such an interest in the establishment of the additional sugar plantations to which the bill was expected to give rise, that it was worth its while to contribute annually seven hundred and fifty thousand dollars to their support, and that a contribution of less than seven hundred and fifty thousand dollars would not cause their establishment. If the bounty in question were greater than the value of the object justified ... we applied the money of the country injudiciously; but if a less bounty [sic] would produce the effect which we desired, we gave it away without object and without excuse. It was in this view that he had asked the Committee of Manufactures information to show what were the duties upon foreign importation which would give to our manufacturers a reasonable profit on their capital and labor. Everything beyond this was not a liberal encouragement of manufactures, but a profuse and capricious donation of the public money.[27]

Who could say whether the House would be guilty of such a breach of public faith in passing the bill when the information that could answer the question had been withheld?

Having researched the subject in a limited way through correspondence with merchants and manufacturers, Lowndes presented to the House the information they supplied. This revealed several fallacies in protectionist claims. One example was the common practice of claiming diminished profits and operating losses based on the price structure prior to the Panic, rather than on current prices that actually favored the manufacturer. A typical case was that of a candlewick maker whose inventory had been fabricated out of cotton purchased before the general price decline and who had delayed selling it as prices began to fall. When finally sold the inventory brought approximately half the original cost of production, and the candlewick maker calculated his losses accordingly. Lowndes pointed out that losses from this cause were not unique to the manufacturing industry but common throughout the population and altogether unrelated to tariff duties. Manufacturers cited such losses in calling for higher duties, although the greater decline in the cost of raw materials and labor would now permit the candlewick maker to replace his inventory at less than half the original production cost. In short, his relative position was better now than before the Panic.[28] As Lowndes made several other points of a similar nature, Baldwin interrupted with a call for the names of his informants, but the Carolinian declined to reveal them.

Lowndes devoted fully one third of his speech to a refutation of other protectionist arguments. On the attempt to apply the popular phrase "home industry" exclusively to manufactures, he said that "the phrase had no small influence on the discussion" and explained in some detail how, in foreign trade, "if it be the industry of Europe which produces, it is the industry of America which acquires" the goods through "the exchange of what we wanted less for what we wanted more." Nor was American commerce any less American industry for effecting the exchange.[29] To the protectionist argument that because certain federal laws favored maritime commerce, manufacturers were also entitled to federal favor, Lowndes answered, "If the nation had been taxed to encourage commerce, it was a poor indemnity, (it was not exactly a compensation of errors,) that it should be taxed for the support of manufactures." Protectionists overlooked, however, an important difference between the two cases: "Taxes for the support of Government were laid upon commerce; these were paid by the consumers of foreign merchandise, and whatever the expenses on account of commerce may have been, they were expenses which commerce herself was made to pay." The merchant or purchaser received some relief from credit currently allowed on payment of duties, "but he certainly received nothing from contributions which were paid by any other class in the community."[30] The most eloquent passages in his speech concerned the intended proscription of the East Indies trade on the ground that the trade was a one-way drain on the nation's wealth because the Far East took no American produce. Lowndes countered that many an American merchantman sailed from New England without capital, acquired it by carrying the produce of other peoples, invested it in other saleable produce, and through multiple exchanges and reinvestments, finally arrived back home with a valuable cargo of Far Eastern goods, which the advocates of this bill would not allow to be entered, or condemned as contributing to an unfavorable balance of trade.[31]

Lowndes expressed surprise that many people involved in agriculture had believed the home market argument, which maintained that higher duties would cause a rise in the domestic price of agricultural produce. The argument was entirely fallacious, he explained, because whatever might be the domestic demand, the supply would always exceed it, and no buyer would give a higher price than the surplus could command. Consequently, "when there is an export trade, although the quantity exported may bear a small proportion to that which is consumed in the country, the price of that small proportion must determine that of the whole. He did not say that this was a reasonable theory, but a notorious fact." As long as supply exceeded demand,

> how perfectly illusory all duties upon importation must prove for the protection of our agricultural industry. The price of our agricultural products must be determined by that part of them which is exported, and must in consequence be absolutely unaffected by duties, or even prohibitions. Gentlemen might, therefore, lay duties, or withdraw them from cotton, wheat, or tobacco, and they would change nothing but the words of their statute book.[32]

Lowndes thought that "if it were ever right that Government should impose its duties, with a view to the encouragement of particular branches of industry," the fairest policy would be "to lay a very small and equal duty upon all manufactures, which would leave the relative inducement to engage in each unchanged." Quite apart from its effect on commerce and agriculture, the Baldwin tariff threatened injury to every part of the manufacturing community not in competition with foreign producers. Every part would share its burdens while its benefits went to the fortunate few:

> Admit that it is in our interest to manufacture articles which we could procure at cheaper rates from abroad, it must be still more to our interest to manufacture such as prove themselves adapted to our circumstances by being able to bear foreign competition. Our capital and labor are limited, and in directing the largest amounts of these into branches which require most encouragement, we really divert them from those into which they would flow with most advantage. Thus every branch of industry which is entirely safe from foreign competition ... must be injured by the encouragement of those which draw from them their resources of capital and labor.[33]

The matter that most troubled Lowndes was not the prospect of higher duties nor even the broader meaning of "protection" in 1820, but the protectionist majority's evident determination to set up rates that could rest on no rational basis. What he regretted most in the course pursued by the Committee of Manufactures, he said, was "that they suggested no standard by which the sufficiency of the encouragement which they proposed could be tested, and promised, therefore, no limitation to the burden which might be imposed on the country."[34] This complaint would reach the level of prophecy within a dozen years when the protectionist majority in Congress would pursue their numerical advantage to the brink of disunion. But for the present, the advantage existed only in the House.

On Saturday, following some last minute maneuvers to postpone it, the tariff bill passed the House 91 to 78.[35] Speaker Clay sent the bill over to the Senate for concurrence and the House adjourned for the weekend. The tide suddenly turned on Monday, however, when the Senate, as it had done two months earlier on the Missouri question, proved the nemesis of the northern majority. The senators by a majority of 1 voted to postpone further consideration of the Baldwin tariff bill to the next session.[36] This began the collapse of the whole Baldwin program, for the House, on Silsbee's original motion, now voted 86 to 60 to kill the bill to abolish the credit system on import duties.[37] With two parts of his ambitious program gone, Baldwin maneuvered to salvage the third, the prohibitive tax on sales at auction. By Thursday, though, the House had cut the tax to 5 percent. At this point Baldwin declared that the lower rate would not serve the committee's purpose. On the chairman's own motion the House postponed this bill to the next session, and for all practical purposes the ambitious Baldwin program was dead.[38]

The tariff controversy of 1820 added a powerfully disruptive dimension to intersectional relations already strained in the controversy over Missouri. The dominant trend of modern scholarship on this stage of tariff history has been to discount tariff protection as a legitimate southern grievance and to attribute the surge of southern discontent to concern over the future of slavery aroused in the Missouri question.[39] In a significant counterpoint to this trend, historian Daniel Walker Howe has convincingly argued for the recognition of a substantial degree of genuine conviction in contemporary rhetoric.[40] Judged by this standard, the tariff issue in 1820 represented an honest and irreconcilable difference of opinion among Republicans themselves on the legitimate limits of governmental power.

The emergence of an aggressive majority of northern Republicans in the Sixteenth Congress, actively hostile to a fundamental southern interest on the one hand while promoting a particular northern interest on the other, demonstrated in terms unmistakable to the slaveholding, antiprotectionist South its minority status in the Union. Southerners responded with the rhetoric of classical republicanism because republican principles were the natural resort of opposition minorities. Moreover, the protectionist majority almost to a man professed adherence to the republican ideal, which had always made specific provision for the protection of the minority from the abuse of majority rule. By traditional republican standards, the democratic principle of majority rule represented the degeneration of legitimate government into one of its corrupt forms.[41]

To the southern minority, the conduct of the protectionist majority of Republicans in 1820 marked an alarming departure from republican tradition into the unstable realm of democracy and potential tyranny under majority rule. From the first Fredericksburg appeal to "common sense and common honesty" to Lowndes's final plea for a rational approach to tariff legislation based on research, the protectionist majority remained as steadfast in their refusal to furnish specific proof of need for higher duties as in their apparent indifference to the negative impact of their program on minority interests. Such conduct violated republican principles as ancient as Aristotle and as current as the Fredericksburg petition: the good of the whole citizenry was the supreme law, and the pursuit or promotion of special interests in public office was the very definition of corruption.[42]

It was to be expected that the southern appeal to republican tradition would invoke the authority of the revolutionary generation, for the founding fathers had had no intention of creating a democracy. The republican system of values had furnished the main lines of argument leading to revolution as well as the ideological foundation of the new nation. The abuse of majority rule at the state and local levels of government during the confederation period had destroyed the illusion that Americans could be trusted to practice self-government within the voluntary constraints of civic virtue.[43] These abuses of majority rule had supplied a powerful motive for restructuring the national government on the republican model.

Although the Constitution incorporated the Lockean principle of majority rule in the House and Senate, the tripartite separation of powers and the federal division of governmental authority into state and national spheres created the illusion of a mixed and balanced constitutional republic capable of protecting minority interests from a determined majority. The formidable series of arguments that comprised the *Federalist* essays encouraged the belief that the powers of the national government were not great enough to threaten traditional republican liberties. Among southerners the youthful Madison was the most persuasive advocate of the new system, offering confident assurances that the diversity of interests within so large a republic virtually precluded their combination into a majority capable of tyranny.[44] When southern dissenters warned that the new Constitution would permit the northern majority to exploit the minority South, southern Federalists brushed such warnings aside, leaving to their Republican sons the realization of southern fears.

Scarcely a decade later the dominant Federalist majority demonstrated that the founding fathers, for all their checks and balances, had established in the form of a republic the substance of a democracy. Controlling all three branches of the federal government and wielding the Alien and Sedition Acts with partisan zeal, they drove their Republican opponents into the only apparent refuge from democratic despotism, the constitutionally vulnerable citadel of state rights shored up in the crisis by a compact theory of union.⁴⁵ After the crisis passed and the Jeffersonians came to power in 1801, a combination of factors encouraged southerners still to regard the government as republican in the traditional sense. The first was a tendency to attribute the abuse of majority rule in 1798 not to a deficiency in the governmental system but to a lack of republican virtue in those who governed.⁴⁶ Other factors were the preponderance of southern leadership in the Republican majority and consistent restraint in the exercise of potentially despotic power, for throughout the period of Republican rule under the Virginia dynasty the majority controlled the executive branch and both houses of Congress. When New Englanders among the Federalist minority felt the heavy hand of majority rule in the policy of economic coercion and war with the British, the Republican majority justified their measures on the ground of extreme public necessity and dismissed the Federalists' ultimate resort to the Hartford Convention as an unpatriotic aberration inspired by an unrepublican faction.⁴⁷

The immediate postwar years brought the nation perhaps as close as it would ever come to realization of republican ideals. With the discredited Federalist party dwindling toward extinction and the very idea of a party system on the wane, the public man who approximated the ancient ideals of civic virtue and personal independence was assured a generous measure of public esteem.⁴⁸ These ideals encouraged a substantial minority of southern nationalists to support the Tariff of 1816, offering persuasive evidence of their commitment to the good of the whole in the classical republican tradition. Among their leaders, Lowndes and Calhoun took scrupulous care to preserve the constitutional balance of federal powers but otherwise construed the Constitution with a liberality that betrayed no more fear of federal power than one might expect from men who had never felt nor expected to feel its abuse.

The collision between the Republican majority and the Republican South in 1820 dramatized the divergence of traditional republicanism into two distinctive and increasingly antagonistic ideological streams. Historian Joyce Appleby has credited this divergence to men of the revolutionary generation who found their inspiration and their hopes for American greatness not in the stasis of classical republicanism but in the vigor of Jeffersonian liberalism, with its emphasis on the unique character and future promise of this "empire for liberty." Freedom for them meant liberation from past oppressions and the constraints of old systems: "They did not look to the past for wisdom; they did not yearn for a government of balanced estates in a society of established relationships. ... The conceptual language of classical republicanism had little relevance to their social realities and positively impeded their political purposes."⁴⁹ They believed in progressive change both in human institutions and social development. Recognizing that "spiritual and material advances depended upon free initiatives and creative intelligence," they invoked democratic values and espoused limited government not so much to give the individual citizen a larger voice in government as to afford him greater freedom from traditional authority and liberty to act in his own behalf.⁵⁰ Even so, traditional Republicans and their more liberal colleagues shared a mutual commitment to limited government, and through the War of 1812, or as long as they faced a common opponent in the Federalist party and a formidable challenge in Old World abuse of America's neutral rights climaxed by British invasion of the nation itself, they stood shoulder-to-shoulder in unity, with only the uncompromising posture of John Randolph and the Old Republicans giving evidence of serious Republican dissent.

In the aftermath of war, however, the bonds of Republican unity loosened in ways that enlarged the liberal progressive share of the Republican spectrum. The rapid decline of the Federalist party deprived Republicans of the unifying influence of a strong opposition, while erstwhile Hamiltonians crossed over to swell the liberal Republican ranks. Continuing concern over British hostility soon faded in Anglo-American rapprochement, but not before it broadened Republican agreement on a larger role for the national government in the postwar years.

It is not the least irony of southern history that, in their consistently liberal construction of federal authority, probably no congressmen of this era except Henry Clay did more than two South Carolinians, Lowndes and Calhoun, to weaken the constitutional case for traditional republican limits on the exercise of federal power. The reckoning came with arresting clarity in the Missouri Controversy and the protectionist crusade of 1820, when the liberal Republican majority left no doubt of their determination to enlist the powers of the federal government in pursuit of their individual and collective goals. The governing elite of South Carolina having carefully hedged themselves in from the stern political reality of majority rule at home, no state in the Union would find the sobering fact of an American democracy more difficult to accept. And for the remainder of his life, all the theoretical writings of John C. Calhoun would constitute an ultimately fruitless search for an acceptable alternative, in the Aristotelian spirit of classical republicanism, to the democratic despotism of majority rule that confronted the minority South in 1820.

After 1820 more militant southerners would require no further evidence of the aggressiveness of power and classical corruption. Fortunately for purposes of intersectional harmony, the Senate, in defeating both the attempt to restrict the admission of Missouri and the drive for high protection, took the cutting edge off southern anxiety and forestalled a more rapid shift to militancy among southerners in general. With that performance the Senate elevated its importance for the future defense of southern interests, and realization of this fact encouraged a significant movement of House leaders into the Senate chamber over the next decade.

The Missouri and tariff controversies undermined the middle ground on which Lowndes and other southern moderates stood. Lowndes's reaction was characteristically moderate, more expressive of regret than of anger or outrage. One suspects that what he really regretted most about the tariff controversy was the degree to which he had been responsible for encouraging the campaign for higher protection. From the perspective of traditional republicanism, the great error of 1816 was adoption of the minimum principle, a measure conceived by and intended for the direct benefit of a special interest group, manufacturers of cheap cottons. In giving his sanction to this measure as chairman of Ways and Means, Lowndes surrendered a fundamental republican principle and, in a very real sense, unlatched the gate to what a later generation would call "The Great American Barbeque."[51] By 1820 he knew as well as anyone that the rising clamor for similar favors from the national legislature had only just begun, and the task of future congresses would be not so much to prevent special interest legislation as to balance one interest against another. For a South Carolinian who had charted the course of his public career by the polar star of civic virtue, the part he played in producing this result was genuine cause for regret.

Perhaps because he held a consistently moderate view of public affairs, but more likely because he had grown accustomed to the inner circles of governmental power, Lowndes was more inclined than his southern colleagues to underestimate the divisive impact of these controversial issues, and especially their effect on his personal influence in the House. Before Congress adjourned on May 15, Clay announced that personal affairs requiring his attention dictated that he resign the Speaker's chair.[52] Several of his colleagues then approached Lowndes promising their support if he would stand for the Speakership in the fall. But with the Missouri Controversy apparently resolved and having no personal desire for the office, he declined. In the privacy of family correspondence he told Elizabeth that he had no doubt of his election had he agreed to stand.[53] He would discover soon enough that the best judge of a man's public image and personal influence may not always be the man himself.

XIII

The Politics of Geography

Henry Clay and William Lowndes had more in common in the spring of 1820 than either congressman wished. The "financial obligations and burdens" that compelled Clay to resign the Speaker's chair proved heavy enough to keep the Kentuckian away from Congress for the remainder of the year. The financial affairs of his South Carolina colleague were hardly less compelling. Informed in the fall of 1819 that his latest rice crop had failed, Lowndes wrote his father-in-law, "anxious to know," he said, "how much I owe and to whom."[1] General Pinckney directed Kershaw and Lewis to furnish Lowndes with information on the state of his account. The figures were disheartening. The Horseshoe produced 620 barrels of rice in 1818, which would have brought more than $18,000.00 at 1818 prices, but none had been sold before prices collapsed in the Panic of 1819. When finally sold the average price per barrel had fallen to $18.40, almost $11.00 below that of the previous year, for a total return of less than $12,000.00. Moreover, although his latest crop had not completely failed, production at the Horseshoe declined almost two-thirds in 1819 while the price per barrel fell another $5.00 to $13.53.[2] The Horseshoe sent only 232 barrels of the 1819 crop to market, sold for a total of $3,126.13. As for how much he owed and to whom, his account showed a steadily mounting deficit that by the fall of 1820 would exceed $13,000.00 due Kershaw and Lewis, a bonded debt due the firm of almost $8,000.00 more, and bonded indebtedness to others of at least another $7,000.00.[3]

In these straightened circumstances, the Lowndes family decided "to come home and be prudent."[4] They packed up their furniture for shipment south, for Lowndes would return to Washington alone in the fall.

Then the family traveled by carriage to Philadelphia where they boarded the *Georgia Packet* and sailed for home. The summer of 1820 gave Lowndes his first opportunity in two years to attend personally to his plantation affairs and to other business matters. Through the sale of selected livestock, another bank loan, and collection of two outstanding debts, he raised almost $8,000.00, enough to stabilize his finances through the fall harvest season.[5] It is worth noting that Lowndes did not attempt, as he had done in 1816, to sell off a gang of his slaves even though he had more than the Horseshoe's operation and productivity could justify. Reduced prices in the slave market were certainly an important consideration. The condition he placed on the contemplated sale of 1816 offers another plausible explanation for his decision now to keep the population of the Horseshoe intact: he was unwilling to separate them. He seriously considered following Clay's example and taking a similar leave of absence to devote more attention to the Horseshoe's management. And he might have done so except for his continuing concern over the tariff issue.

Lowndes regarded the recent defeat of the tariff bill as no more than a temporary check on the campaign for high protection. He had said as much to Secretary Adams before leaving Washington and had written to Timothy Pickering on the need for greater New England unity for the contest expected in the fall.[6] Protectionist reaction to the bill's defeat strengthened his convictions. An immediate outcry arose from the industrial North, gathering volume as the news spread westward down the Ohio Valley.[7]

Hezekiah Niles showed little enthusiasm for a renewal of the lobbying campaign, but in the *Weekly Register* of June 3 he warned opponents of protection

> that if the sufferings of the country and the wants of the treasury, shall not compel congress, at their next session, to do something in favor of a home-market for the products of agriculture, and to find employment for the laboring capacity of the people of the United States—the congress which shall be chosen *after* the next census will do all that is necessary to rescue the nation from its present poverty and distress.

In this same issue, Niles published Henry Baldwin's major speech from the recent tariff debate, calling the Pennsylvanian's effort a "rich treat" for the reader. "We are really anxious to see in what manner its arguments were *answered*," the editor added, as if no effective answer were possible. Niles had hardly expressed this wish, he said in his next issue, when he received a copy of the *Southern Patriot* of Charleston, South Carolina containing Lowndes's rebuttal speech of April 24. Niles published it without comment and let the two speeches stand as representative of the debate as a whole.[8]

With the notable exception of Baldwin himself, who began to prepare an elaborate argumentative report for the next session of Congress, protectionists in general paid no more heed to opposition arguments than if the tariff debate had never taken place. Instead, they turned their anger and resentment on the slaveholding South, erecting out of materials that were not entirely new a framework of accusatory argument, which they and their successors would embellish and refine over the coming decades into a full-fledged "slave power conspiracy." The editor of the *Public Advertiser* of Lexington, Kentucky, mourned "the death" of the Baldwin tariff, "*murdered*" by a majority of one vote in the Senate. "Mourn, oh, ye sons and daughters of Kentucky," he cried. "Oh, ye inhabitants of the United States, put on sackcloth and ashes, for the great enemy of your independence has prevailed."[9] Protectionist journals across the free-state North, as Glover Moore has amply demonstrated, left no doubt that the "great enemy" was the slaveholding South. The manufacturing North, they said, had only exchanged British oppression for the "black despotism" of a southern oligarchy, whose policies were calculated to hold national industry in "the iron grasp of slavery," refuse to the rest of the nation the means of prosperity, treat northern interests with contempt, make tributaries of the manufacturing states, impoverish the free people of the North and West, and entail misery on the black population of the South.[10] With this outburst, protectionists began to construct a thoroughly unrepublican stereotype of the southern planter, and they made increasingly effective use of the slavery issue to infuse a self-serving sense of moral outrage into an intersectional disagreement over economic policy.[11]

The rising volume of protectionist protest in the spring of 1820 promised a revival of the Baldwin program and consequently stimulated a flurry of antiprotectionist activity, especially among Virginians and South Carolinians and chambers of commerce in the major northern cities. Each of these groups prepared to memorialize Congress against higher duties, mostly along the lines of the Fredericksburg and Salem petitions of the previous session.

The South Carolina petition, originating in Charleston and endorsed by resolutions from the Colleton District and elsewhere, bears the unmistakable stamp of William Lowndes. This is evident not merely from its argumentative content. With printed copies of his recent speech readily available, it is not surprising that the petition followed the lines of argument marked out by the state's most influential congressman. But internal evidence on tone, syntax, and usage from start to finish leaves little doubt that Lowndes had been prevailed upon to write the petition himself. Throughout its seven thousand words, its author sustained a calm, unemotional appeal to reason, justice, and moderation, scrupulously avoiding the increasingly popular trend toward emotion-charged recrimination and theoretical discussion of economic principles. The petition's opening paragraph set the tone for the whole:

> The citizens of Charleston have seen, with deep regret, the efforts which were made at the last session of Congress to impose a high rate of duties on all manufactured articles imported into the United States—efforts made for the express and avowed purpose of creating, encouraging, and supporting, in this country, great manufacturing establishments; of modifying and curtailing extensively our mercantile intercourse with foreign nations; and of forcing from their present employments much of the labor and capital of our fellow-citizens.[12]

The petition's only reference to the constitutionality of tariff protection was equally moderate, stating that the Baldwin program "departs equally from the spirit of our constitution and the best established principles of national economy." This restrained and rational response to the resurgent protectionist campaign would be the last South Carolina petition of its kind on the subject. The course of tariff history would soon thrust the constitutional question into the center of tariff discussion and charge the issue with a greater degree of emotion than the South Carolina leadership could resist; and in their subsequent writings not even the relentless, unemotional logic of Calhoun could recapture the calm rationality of Lowndes.

At this early stage of the protectionist controversy, it was the Virginians who took the more militant stance. Short, terse, and belligerent, the petition from "the United Agricultural Societies" of the Old Dominion pointed an accusing finger at proponents of protection. The opening paragraph called for congressional "protection against the wild speculations and ruinous schemes of an association denominating themselves the friends of national industry." The Virginians structured their argument after the Fredericksburg pattern of the previous year except on the point of constitutionality, which they flatly rejected in language calculated to evoke strong emotions: "That the despotic power of driving any class of citizens from the employments of their own choice, and forcing them into others . . . has been delegated to the Federal Government, we can no more believe, than that the authority to divide our people (like the Hindoos) into castes has been conveyed under the form of powers to regulate trade."[13] The secretary who put the phrasing of this protest in its final form was a twenty-six-year-old agricultural reformer destined to gain greater fame for his implacable hatred of all things northern: Edmund Ruffin.

In the meantime, at least well into July, the Missouri question appeared to be settled. That South Carolinians thought so was clearly apparent in the correspondence of Calhoun, who had been writing of it in the past tense since April, and in Independence Day toasts. One such toast typified South Carolina's generous assessment of Lowndes's role in settling the controversy: "The Honorable William Lowndes—He who preserved the life of the Roman citizen was rewarded with a civic crown. What honors shall we pay to him who has saved the Republic?"[14] But the people of Missouri would not have the republic so easily saved. Later in July came word that Missourians in convention had drawn up a constitution that included a provision to prevent free blacks and mulattoes from immigrating into the new state. News of the controversial clause in the Missouri constitution flashed like chain lightening across the free-state North, bringing thunderous denunciation from northern strongholds of restrictionist sentiment and renewed activity to challenge Missouri's admission. Reaction in the South was mixed, ranging from the undisguised delight of proslavery militants to the dismay of southern moderates. The *Charleston City Gazette* expressed Lowndes's view, pointing out the needlessly provocative nature of the offending clause, because after admission to statehood the Missouri legislature would have full power to pass laws to achieve this purpose even if the state constitution remained silent on the subject.[15] But now it was obvious the battle of the previous session would have to be fought all over again. And when Lowndes headed northward in November for the opening of the second session of the Sixteenth Congress, he could expect to bear a larger burden of House leadership, for Clay had officially resigned the Speaker's chair in October.

Clay's resignation set the stage for an unprecedented contest for House

Speaker between opposing factions of the revived Missouri Controversy. Over the weekend before Congress convened on Monday, November 13, a good deal of maneuvering took place in behalf of four candidates, two from each faction. The Federalist lawyer and humanitarian, John Sergeant of Pennsylvania, an uncompromising restrictionist and a forceful orator, enjoyed the support of men committed by conscience to oppose slavery, but his identification with the Federalist party was an insurmountable liability. The other restrictionist candidate, John Taylor of New York, commanded a broader basis of support because of his leading role in the restrictionist effort during the previous session, but there was opposition to Taylor in the New York delegation for reasons concerned not with the Missouri question but with the internal politics of New York.[16] A dozen or so Marylanders and their personal friends preferred Samuel Smith of Maryland in spite of his connection with the financial scandal surrounding the Baltimore branch of the Bank of the United States. The overwhelming choice of southern moderates was William Lowndes.

Lowndes suffered all the disadvantages of a reluctant candidate. When he declined offers of support at the close of the last session, some of his colleagues persuaded Smith to stand for the office and consequently committed their votes to him. Calhoun wrote Lowndes in October urging him to reconsider, but Lowndes still preferred not to be a candidate after he returned to Washington, and he declined another offer of support on Sunday, the day before the session opened.[17] It was not until Monday morning that he agreed to stand, after a delegation of his colleagues "from the West and South" persuaded him with the assurance "that no other member could combine the Southern interest." It was eleven o'clock before the news of his candidacy spread, with the House scheduled to convene at noon.[18]

For three days balloting for Speaker occupied the House. Seven ballots were taken on Monday. On the first ballot, Taylor led with 40 votes followed by Lowndes with 34, Smith with 27, Sergeant with 18, Hugh Nelson of Virginia with 10, and 3 scattered. On the second ballot Hugh Nelson dropped out. Taylor still led with 49, Lowndes followed with 44, while Smith dropped to 25 and Sergeant to 13. By the third ballot it became clear that the contest was between Lowndes and Taylor, the Carolinian leading the New Yorker 56 to 50 with Smith a distant third. Sergeant dropped out on the fourth ballot, strengthening Taylor's position, although Lowndes still led by 1 vote. Through the remainder of the day the votes for Smith added to those for Lowndes could have elected

Lowndes, but Smith, though he never polled more than 15 votes, declined to withdraw.[19]

John Quincy Adams, commenting on the first day's balloting, said Smith had "conceived a passion to be speaker, and had personal friends and Maryland members enough adhering to him to defeat the election of Lowndes."[20] That Smith partisans would eventually defeat the southern moderate became evident on Tuesday when 12 more ballots were taken. With 73 votes necessary for a majority on the seventeenth ballot, Lowndes received 72 and Smith 17. The Marylander never gave up the contest, and as support for Lowndes began to wane, Smith supporters bargained with both sides for additional votes and ran their candidate into a temporary lead.[21] But southern moderates steadfastly voted for Lowndes, and on the twenty-second ballot on Wednesday, Taylor was elected. The result drew this comment from a disappointed Marylander: "[T]he Southern men have outwitted themselves ... by obstinancy which is not to be accounted for, on principles of prudence."[22] That was a judgment in which Lowndes most certainly concurred.

The strong sectional character of his opposition from Maryland northward took Lowndes by surprise. As he explained to Elizabeth,

> You will no doubt see in the papers the poll of yesterday which makes it certain that I cannot be elected—If there be anything mortifying in the disappointment of presumptuous confidence I have reason to be mortified for I entertained no doubt of success—My great reason for agreeing to be a Candidate was that I thought that the vote would be less sectional & the decisive objection to me is that I come from the South of the Potomac—Once a Candidate I certainly wished to be elected but I mistake myself very much if I do not regret much more the strong sectional feeling which produces my exclusion than the fact itself.[23]

He was made quite aware of strong sectional feeling during the balloting on Tuesday. According to a Smith partisan, "The South and West had not sufficient strength. They required in aid Maryland, and a portion of Pennsylvania. A majority of the Pennsylvanians were willing to go as far south as Maryland—further they declared they would not go. This was made known to the friends of Mr. Lowndes."[24] The geography of slavery, Lowndes could only conclude, had become more important than reputation and republican principle combined.

Lowndes considered the alignment of votes that elected Taylor "proof of a fact that I have been aware of for some time that the Northern States differing in everything else are impatient to put the gov[ernmen]t into the hands of Northern men."[25] He was hardly alone in this conviction. Southern leaders in the federal government from the president downward, including Calhoun, Crawford, Clay, and a chorus of southern congressmen, agreed with Senator John Walker of Alabama that the whole Missouri Controversy was "a mere contest for power, the free states striving for control of the union under the mask of affected humanity."[26] Crawford thought Lowndes had judged the meaning of his defeat correctly. It had "produced an impression that a geographical party ha[d] been formed which for several years would control the course of events."[27] Excongressman Salma Hale of New Hampshire also saw the election as a harbinger of things to come. Hale told Taylor, in reference to his victory over Lowndes, "It is an event of more than ordinary consequence as it indicates what may be expected to follow. The sceptre is departing from the South. The North and West begin to feel their power, and power once felt and experienced is too agreeable to man to be freely surrendered."[28] But Hale was not speaking for the many true humanitarians in the restrictionist majority. What tended to blind Lowndes and his southern colleagues to humanitarian motives in the recent contest over Missouri was the contest over the tariff that immediately followed.

On the day he lost the election, Lowndes confided to Elizabeth a sentiment that distinguished him from most of his southern colleagues. Convinced by the manner of his defeat that the political objective of the controversy over Missouri was "to put the gov[ernmen]t into the hands of Northern men," he said, "[E]very consideration of prudence in my judgment recommends that this should be done & that we should submit with good grace."[29] Beyond this veiled reference to slavery, Lowndes did not elaborate because he felt no elaboration was necessary. The danger inherent in antislavery agitation and its potential for disrupting the previous stability of southern society gave southerners a choice between political preeminence in the national government and social stability in the slaveholding South, for they could no longer expect to have both. Unless they yielded the one, they risked losing the other. As Lowndes saw it, political leaders of the free-state North had recognized the popular appeal of antislavery argument and meant to use it as an avenue to power, as the rhetoric of the resurgent protectionist campaign seemed to say. Southerners might counter with proslavery argument, as some had already attempted to do, but the proslavery defense in a democratic society was ultimately doomed to failure. Nowhere in the extant record of his life, neither in public address nor in private correspondence, had Lowndes ventured a defense of slavery for the obvious reason that he found it intellectually indefensible. He was not unaware of the evils of slavery and the dilemma it posed for men like himself, but he had the wisdom to see that a debate on its merits was one the slaveholder must lose. To Lowndes, the logic was inescapable: the South would be wise in this contest for power to yield to the North with grace. By this he meant to concede the presidency at once. That few of his peers shared his vision was not the least tragedy of his era.

Southerners by general consensus identified conservative Governor DeWitt Clinton and Federalist Senator Rufus King of New York as the two northerners most anxious to grasp "the sceptre" from the South. Both had zealously promoted restriction. Southerners thought they did so for the purpose of polarizing national politics along geographical lines that would isolate the South, revive Federalism, and transfer political control into northern and presumably Clintonian hands.[30] After all, New Yorkers had made no secret of their growing resentment over southern preeminence in the national government; and the extent of Federalist leadership in the restrictionist crusade lent credence to suspected Federalist designs.[31] Then there were the Clintonian connections of James Tallmadge, Jr., who introduced the restrictive amendments, and of John W. Taylor, who had seconded them and subsequently pressed for their passage with unexpected zeal. And what of the fact that the only members of the New York delegation who voted against restriction and who also voted against Taylor's election were anti-Clinton?[32] Each of these considerations served to strengthen southern belief in a northern conspiracy to gain control of the national government. As Congressman Thomas Cobb of Georgia said, "I remember I was laughed at last year for suggesting that Clinton originated this question. Everyone *now* thinks the same."[33]

The intrusion of New York politics into the House election for Speaker could only have deepened southern convictions. Those who voted against Taylor through twenty-one of the twenty-two ballots included several New Yorkers, members of Martin Van Buren's Republican faction commonly known as Bucktails, who opposed the conservative faction of Governor Clinton.[34] The Bucktails insisted on a committed and disciplined membership with unswerving loyalty to the party. Taylor not only lacked the requisite loyalty; he was all too cordial to Clintonians. The *New York National Advocate*, principal organ of the Bucktail faction, predicted factional opposition to Taylor the week before Congress convened. Ignoring the great national question at issue in the Speaker's election, the *Advocate* said Taylor's conduct toward the Bucktails since Clinton's election was such that Taylor could not expect their support.[35] When Taylor won the election, rumors circulated in New York that only through bargaining with his Bucktail colleagues after the twenty-first ballot had he succeeded on the next. Taylor's answer confirmed the intrusion of state politics into the election but denied the alleged bargain. "It is true," he said, "that some members from our State informed me that they had hitherto opposed my election solely on the ground that they considered me devoted to the fortunes of DeWitt Clinton and his adherents and hostile to the Republicans of New York." Taylor told them they were mistaken. He had become detached from factional alignments in the state, he said, through preoccupation with national concerns over the past eight years of congressional service. His Bucktail colleagues found his explanation acceptable, and he won on the next ballot.[36]

In significant ways, this quiet conversation on the floor of the House between members of the New York delegation carried implications for the future course of American politics hardly less profound than the Missouri and tariff controversies. Its significance lay not so much in what it said about the Missouri Controversy or Clinton's alleged ambition, but in the way the conversation presaged a whole new era in national politics based on the party principle. Van Buren and his Bucktail faction, and later the Albany Regency they dominated, were in the process of marking out guidelines for the rise of the second party system over the next decade. Preaching the gospel of party loyalty and the disciplined subordination of personal judgment to the collective party will, the party leadership would decide what constituted the good of the whole, and the party member who clung to old fashioned notions of republican independence could expect ostracism for his reward.[37] The intrusion of this political system into the House election for Speaker in 1820 heralded the imminent decline of traditional republicanism as a practical approach to congressional service. The patrician politics of William Lowndes were on the downward slope to obsolescence, while civic virtue on the classical model ascended toward the realm of venerable abstractions, to be admired from a distance like a prized antique whose utilitarian function was gone.[38]

No sooner had Taylor taken the chair than he ascended toward "Olympian heights of objectivity and disinterestedness."[39] One of his first acts was to appoint a committee of three to bring in a report on the Missouri state constitution. For this task he named his defeated opponents, Lowndes, Smith, and Sergeant, with Lowndes to serve as chairman. Appointment of a committee favorable to admission complied with the custom of the House and illustrated at the outset Taylor's determination to be impartial according to the custom of the chair.[40] Lowndes and Smith as the committee majority cooperated in drawing up the report, with Sergeant a minority of one in dissent. The committee members were well aware that Missourians had already set up their state government. After receiving the enabling act and writing their state constitution, they had elected a governor, a legislature, and other state officers. They had also elected two senators and a representative, who were now in Washington ready to take their seats in Congress.[41] The committee report reflected these facts when Chairman Lowndes presented it to the House on November 23.[42]

The report took the position that Missouri had complied with all requirements of the enabling act of the previous session and was therefore already a state. Lowndes explained the basis of their decision. The committee, he said,

> have not supposed themselves bound to inquire whether the provisions of the constitution referred to them be wise or liberal. The grave and difficult question as to the restraints which should be imposed upon the power of Missouri to form a constitution for itself was decided by the act of the last session, and the committee have only to examine whether the provisions of the act have been complied with. In the opinion of the committee, they have been.

Missouri, then, had "performed the act which makes them sovereign and independent," and it could not constitutionally be restrained from entering the Union on an equal footing with the other states.

The report next addressed the controversial clause in the Missouri constitution and advanced the opinion that its constitutionality was a matter for the judiciary to decide. On this point the report showed that other states including Delaware had similar restrictions against the entry of free blacks and mulattoes, and their citizenship was ambiguous under the laws of most states. Moreover, the constitutions of states in every section of the Union provided "that a State has a right to discriminate between the white and the black man, both in respect to political and civil privileges, though both be citizens of another State." By introducing the controversial clause into their constitution, the people of Missouri had violated none of the provisions governing admission of states to the Union, so the state could not be denied admission on constitutional grounds. Lowndes concluded the report by reiterating the committee's opinion that the clause in question could be admitted or rejected only by the courts or the people of Missouri; and despite any action that Congress might take in the matter, the state of Missouri could not be returned to the status of a territory. Lowndes then introduced the following resolution: "That the State of Missouri shall be, and is hereby declared to be, one of the United States of America, and is admitted into the Union, on an equal footing with the original States, in all respects whatsoever."[43]

This view of the question pleased the friends of Missouri, of course, but left the restrictionist majority unpersuaded. Two weeks later on December 6, the House opened discussion on the subject in Committee of the Whole. The subject was announced, the resolution read, and William Lowndes rose to deliver the last important speech of his career.

Lowndes's first remarks were lost to the reporter in the clatter and confusion of members' leaving their seats from all over the House and gathering near to hear him.[44] His speech was in general an elaboration of the arguments stated in the committee report and a defense of the position the committee had taken. He addressed himself to the good sense and moderation of his colleagues in considering whether questions once decided by the legitimate authority of the country should be left open. Majorities in the House and the Senate of the Sixteenth Congress had decided this question by passing the Missouri enabling act. If that decision was not binding on the minority, then all their legislation was void. Were future congresses not bound by the contract to pay the national debt?

> And were all the members of this and the other House not *equally* bound by the act of the last session respecting Missouri? Whether we ought or ought not to have given to the people of Missouri the power to form a constitution and State government we *have* given it. Whether or not we individually wished Missouri to form a constitution, the authority to do so was given by Congress. The constitution

was formed, and Congress were now asked to declare that it was so. For himself, he believed that the law of the last session gave Missouri a right to form a constitution; and that, having done so, she is now a state.

In elevating territories from their dependent status to that of a state, he continued, Congress emancipated them from its control and possessed no authority to return them afterwards to their previous territorial condition. The very act of allowing the territory to form a constitution determined that it was an independent state. Ohio, for example, was never admitted by congressional resolution but proclaimed by Congress to be a state by virtue of its people's having formed a state constitution. Kentucky had been admitted by an act declaring that when it had formed a constitution it should be a state, and it was admitted without further legislation. The resolution before the House, therefore, could have no effect in determining the actual statehood of Missouri. It was an act of declaration, he said, "mere surplusage."

Taking up the controversial clause in the Missouri constitution, Lowndes elaborated at length the position stated in the report. Some members had expressed doubt on the point of constitutionality, which, he implored, "the interest of the nation, justice to Missouri, and respect for itself, required that the House should not undertake to decide." The House had no duty even to declare an opinion on the clause, much less a decision on its constitutionality:

> If, in all other cases of Constitutional questions, it has been provided that they shall be decided by the Judiciary, the reason must apply and be conclusive why this body should not undertake to decide a Constitutional question in the case of Missouri. Justice requires that those who have the same rights, shall have their rights decided by the same tribunal.

To do otherwise would constitute an invasion of the legislative authority into that constitutionally reserved to the judicial branch.

At this point Lowndes concluded his defense and conceded a point for the purpose of compromise. If the primary objection to passage of the resolution were that an inference might be drawn "from the silence of Congress," that the majority approved the controversial clause, he said the House might adopt some mode by which the objection could be explained. He would only consent to do this with the utmost reluctance, considering such a step "exceedingly unwise." He admitted that cases could possibly arise in which the duty of Congress might require their interposition at the time a new state was to be admitted. If, for example, a state should attempt to control its congressmen in such a manner as to render judicial action powerless to correct it, Congress might properly intervene because the state law in such a case would infringe on the legitimate authority of Congress. But, he concluded, the duty of Congress began only where that of the judiciary ended. The constitutionality of the clause in question lay well within the purview of the courts and clearly beyond the authority of Congress to decide.

William Plumer, Jr., of New Hampshire doubtless spoke for other restrictionists, and some southerners as well, when he said Lowndes's concession "gave up the whole argument."[45] Actually Lowndes conceded nothing essential to his objective, the unrestricted admission of Missouri. The friends of Missouri knew, as Plumer would soon discover, that a concession of some sort was essential, and the one Lowndes offered marked the limit they were willing to go to effect a compromise. That members of the House and Senate had prearranged this concession became evident this same afternoon when Senator John Eaton of Tennessee introduced in the upper house a resolution to the same effect and with the same limitations.[46] Both Lowndes and Eaton offered the more moderate restrictionists a way to concede Missouri's constitutional right to unrestricted admission behind a rhetorical and essentially meaningless facade, a public declaration condemning the controversial clause.

Lowndes's concession made no apparent impression on the opposition. The next day John Sergeant delivered his minority report, a speech of two and a half hours condemning the committee report and disputing the chairman's argument. Sergeant rejected the contention that Missouri was already a state and argued that the power to admit or refuse admittance to new states was one of the most important powers Congress possessed. Congress had not only the right but the duty to decide whether constitutions submitted in the statehood process were repugnant to the Constitution of the United States. He found the Missouri constitution so repugnant that any respect for the federal Constitution and every consideration of humanity demanded that Congress deny admission to Missouri until her people removed the obnoxious clause and furnished guarantees against similar offenses in the future.[47] Henry Storrs of New York spoke for those who had voted for the compromise but now opposed admission because of the controversial clause. Since Missouri had not kept her part of the bargain as he understood it, he felt no longer bound by the terms of the compromise and planned to vote against admission. He might be persuaded to reconsider, though, should the House adopt a proviso that would overcome his objections. Philip Barbour of Virginia supported the committee report in a detailed exposition on various state laws to show the contrast between northern objections to the Missouri constitution on the one hand, and on the other the laws of northern states that denied citizenship and other civil rights to free blacks.[48] The debate in general revolved around the points made by Lowndes and Barbour in support of admission and Sergeant and Storrs against it, with the additional restrictionist suggestion that admission might be postponed to the next Congress, giving Missouri time and reason enough to correct her error. Lowndes took the floor again to defend his resolution before it came to a vote on December 13. He might have saved his breath, for the northern majority rejected admission, 93 to 79, producing outrage among the more radical advocates of slavery expansion, who gave vent to their wrath in threats of defiance and disunion.[49]

The vote left Missouri in unique circumstances, having passed beyond ordinary territorial status but denied admission to statehood. Lowndes called attention to Missouri's peculiar situation when he addressed the House immediately following the vote. With undisguised disappointment he said "he did not wish to be disrespectful to a majority of the House, as declared on the vote just taken, but he now felt it to be his duty to call on them, having rejected the resolution proposed by the committee of their appointment, to devise and propose to the House the means necessary to protect the territory, the property, and all the rights of the United States in the Missouri country."[50] Though disappointed, Lowndes was not surprised by the defeat of his motion, and his next tactic was to counsel delay. Some restrictionists saw the advantage to be gained in taking up immediately Eaton's Senate resolution before their unity broke down, but their opponents succeeded in putting off that question. Antislavery advocates like Plumer especially feared the debilitating effects of delay. As the idealistic young congressman explained to his father, "We are strong now, but every day will take something from our strength."[51] When the House adjourned for the day, Plumer asked Lowndes why he wanted to delay further consideration of the issue. After some hesitation Lowndes confessed that he wanted to give restrictionists time "to cool down," as he put it. "You are excited now," he said, "and I think it good policy to wait until the antagonist muscle relaxes."[52] But as December gave way to January without further action on Missouri, the antagonist muscle held firm.

Christmas brought no joy to Lowndes in 1820, for reasons other than his separation from home and family. The December weather turned cold and damp, with one day of snow generally followed by two days of rain. Then an epidemic of influenza spread through the city and into the halls of Congress, killing three congressmen before Christmas and leaving the recovery of several others doubtful.[53] Among the dead was Senator James Burril, Jr., of Rhode Island. Burril, a widower, had become good friends with Lowndes through his son, who was a friend of the Lowndes boys and had often stayed with the Lowndes family when his father was out of town.[54] Lowndes usually took his turn sitting up with his sick friends. If he sat up with Burril, which seems more than likely, that could explain something about the future course of his own health, for Burril suffered from tuberculosis. With that deadly lung condition complicated by influenza, Burril died on Christmas Day, 1820.[55]

In January the House took up the tariff issue according to the postponement of the previous session. Chairman Baldwin of the Committee of Manufactures brought in a long argumentative report that addressed most opposition arguments raised in the spring. He also included an effective defense of the constitutionality of protective duties and corrected the major defect of his first effort with a proposed system of excise taxes on American manufactures.[56] But for several reasons his best opportunity lay behind him. The passage of time, added to renewed concern over Missouri, had taken its toll on protectionist hopes for this session. After their angry outburst in May and June, which aroused such concern in the South, protectionists had been unable to sustain the vigor of their previous lobbying effort. The prospect of excise taxes on their manufactured goods dampened protectionist enthusiasm for the Baldwin program, which also received a serious setback from a new committee. The Speaker, responding to complaints that among the three great economic interests only agriculture lacked committee advocacy, had appointed a new Committee of Agriculture chaired by Thomas Forrest of Pennsylvania. The new committee countered Baldwin's report with a report of its own opposing any change in the existing tariff and proclaiming tax legislation "strictly the province of the Committee of Ways and Means."[57] Baldwin might have overcome these disadvantages had

Henry Clay been there all along to give more disciplined direction to the protectionist majority. In the circumstances Baldwin faced, the protectionist effort faltered, an unpropitious beginning to a decade of unprecedented success.

Clay's absence was felt in the Missouri admission effort as well. A wrangle over indirect recognition of Missouri's statehood developed in the House on January 12, when Lowndes introduced petitions from Missouri concerning land titles and Cobb of Georgia moved to insert the pregnant phrase "the State of" before the word "Missouri." The House consumed the whole day disputing this point in one form or another. Plumer of New Hampshire, observing the younger members with "hot and hasty tempers" who were taking the lead, said, "They want the guidance of such a man as Mr. Clay, who, with all his violence and impetuosity, knew better how to control and direct their party, than any man they now have here."[58] Nathaniel Macon of North Carolina, on the other side as uncompromising as Plumer, was equally critical, writing to a friend that the whole Missouri business had been managed "rather badly, nor is it certain that any management whatever could have succeeded; a fixed and settled majority is hard to move, especially if power is the object."[59]

To the extent that either congressman had Lowndes in mind, and there can be little doubt that both of them did, their criticism underscored the limitations of his old patrician style of leadership. Lowndes lacked both the art and the temperament for the sort of political management that seemed so natural to Clay, the ability to line up votes and marshal majorities through such bargaining and intimidation as might be necessary short of surrender of principle. Clay could be threatening and abusive or mild and humble as the occasion required. Plumer captured the essence of the Kentuckian's political style shortly after he returned in mid-January: "[H]e begs, entreats, abjures, suplicates [sic], and beseaches [sic] ..., ready to vote for anything, and everything we may propose, short of restriction."[60] Clay was at his best in committee management, for no congressman of his generation knew better than he how to isolate and intimidate a wavering colleague behind closed doors.[61]

There are enough tributes to Lowndes's influence in the House during the controversy to leave little doubt of its magnitude, but it was influence of a different sort, personal rather than political.[62] Although he was capable of adroit parliamentary maneuver to stifle opposition and knew how to wield the power of a committee chairmanship to gain his object,

Lowndes consistently led through force of character and personal example, relying on the art of gentle persuasion by reasoned argument to bring his colleagues to his position. This approach reflected a deeper commitment to traditional republican principles than his Kentucky colleague displayed. The problem with commitment to republican principles was that it limited tactical options and allowed less flexibility in moving toward political objectives. This style of leadership had been popular for as long as anyone could remember, but it was essentially the style of a passing era, unsuited to the demands of the decades to come. That it would continue to flourish in the slaveholding South should not have been surprising, for the natural resort of a political minority was an appeal to republican principles, and the appeal itself entailed a commitment to principles that limited tactical alternatives. As Lowndes's faltering leadership in January 1821 illustrated, beyond appeals to reason and principle, how was "a fixed and settled majority" to be moved? The man best qualified to answer that question strode into the House chamber on January 16 in the person of Henry Clay.

Clay brought with him a seige of freezing cold so severe that it froze over rivers from the James at Richmond to the Charles at Boston, but it did not interrupt congressional business.[63] A few days after he arrived the Senate sent over their resolution to admit Missouri while withholding approval of her constitution until the constitutionality of its controversial clause could be determined. This provided a basis for renewed discussion when the House took it up on January 29. Now Clay took charge of the compromise effort and within a month the issue was settled.

Despite its caveat on Missouri's admission, Clay advocated the Senate resolution as a basis for further discussion. Lowndes gave wholehearted support. When John Randolph moved to strike out the restriction, Lowndes opposed the motion as "going to present to the House the naked question it had already decided in the negative."[64] The House agreed and discussion continued. By Friday, February 2, more than a dozen different resolutions had been offered and rejected. At this point Clay moved to refer the Senate resolution to a committee of thirteen. This was agreed to, and Taylor named Clay, Lowndes, Sergeant, Smith of Maryland and nine others to constitute the committee.[65] Through the next seven days the committee labored to work out a compromise acceptable to a majority of the House. When the committee came in on Saturday, February 10, to present its report, William Lowndes was conspicuously absent.[66]

Those who realized the seriousness of the reason for Lowndes's absence knew that his labor in behalf of compromise was over. Sometime Friday night or Saturday morning he had been struck down by his old and familiar enemy, the "Rheumatic fever," and he lay for several days near the point of death.[67] His condition then changed for the better, and though he remained confined to his room he continued a slow improvement through succeeding weeks despite the fact that his doctor bled him repeatedly as much as he could stand without fainting.[68] He followed the compromise effort under Clay's skillful direction and learned that the House had rejected the report of the committee of thirteen, whereupon Clay arranged for a joint committee of thirty to try again. Lowndes expressed acute disappointment over his inability to lend assistance. It was, he said, "a little mortifying when one's interest in every public measure is so much heightened by having thought of it for two or three months to be excluded from Congress just at the time when it begins to act effectually."[69] When Clay secured the final compromise on February 26, Lowndes was relieved to learn that its terms in substance were the same as he and Eaton had offered in December. Missouri was admitted on condition of a promise from the state legislature never to construe the controversial clause so as to deprive any American citizen of rights guaranteed by the Constitution of the United States. Free blacks as a group, of course, did not hold citizenship status.

Secretary Adams made a misleading comment on Clay's achievement: "By a singular piece of good fortune for him, just at the moment of his arrival here Mr. Lowndes, in whose management it had been, was confined by severe illness to his chamber, and is so still."[70] Whatever personal sentiment might have colored Adams's opinion, his remark misconstrued the contributions of both Clay and Lowndes. Although the practical art of political management has rarely inspired the degree of public praise showered on Clay after the settlement, Lowndes had little claim to the plaudits his colleague received. After the best efforts of Lowndes failed, Clay succeeded. No two congressional performances during the Missouri Controversy better illustrated the contrast between the politics of the republican past and the politics of the democratic future.

XIV

Ave atque Vale

William Lowndes's truncated service in the second Missouri Compromise was to be his last contribution of any significance in Congress. After the session closed, he stayed with the Calhoun family until his health improved enough for him to make the journey home in March. During the summer of 1821 he devoted as much time as he could to improve production at the Horseshoe. His sister attributed the Horseshoe's declining yields to consistently bad luck, which unreliable overseers did little to improve.[1] Lowndes's latest orders for plowing and planting, however, indicate that the Horseshoe's "days of jubilee" were gone forever. He gave repeated instructions for deep "trench plowing," deep enough, he insisted, "to bring up the yellow dirt," in a losing effort to coax out of his fields nutriment no longer there. He tried alfalfa to replenish the soil—"Write me how the lucerne comes on"—and talked of making the Horseshoe a "grass farm," but the extent of depletion lay beyond his remedy.[2] After seventy years of continuous production, the plantation was suffering the irreversible effects of old age. Its "almost inexhaustible swamp muck" was finally exhausted.[3] The fate that loomed for the Horseshoe could be seen in the desolate district of old rice plantations west of Charleston abandoned since the turn of the century, their twenty thousand acres of wornout fields awaiting conversion to duck hunting preserves in the century to come.[4]

Routinely elected to the Seventeenth Congress, Lowndes felt well enough by the fall of 1821 to return to Washington, but he wanted no part of another election for House Speaker. Clay had given up his House seat at the close of the last session, so Lowndes waited until Congress had been in session for a week before he sailed from Charleston.[5] Thus he avoided the contest that saw a combination of Virginians and New York Bucktails, the disciplined New Yorkers guided by their new senator, Martin Van Buren, remand John Taylor to his House seat and put Philip

Barbour of Virginia in the chair.[6] When Lowndes finally arrived in Washington to claim his own seat on December 21, he probably did as he had done the previous year and took advantage of Calhoun's invitation to stay with them until he settled into his quarters at the mess.[7] If so, it was doubtless early in Lowndes's stay there that Calhoun confided his decision to run for president in the election of 1824.[8] Calhoun said he had already written to several friends explaining that circumstances left him no alternative.[9]

The circumstances that inspired Calhoun's decision concerned his fellow cabinet members Adams and Crawford, whom most observers including Lowndes considered the only two candidates in the race. The secretary of state, an uncertain heir apparent to the presidency, confronted an imposing barrier in the Treasury secretary, who was backed by his Virginia-led "Radicals" and commanded the inside track to the heretofore decisive nomination by congressional caucus. Adams drew support primarily from advocates of centralized power, opponents of slavery, and northern men of the Federalist tradition. Crawford was strongest among traditional republicans, proslavery men, and advocates of limited and frugal government. Excepting the slavery issue, the New Englander's nationalist views were more compatible with those of Calhoun, who had pursued a consistently nationalist course both as congressman and as head of the War Department, while Crawford had become the champion of state rights and limited government. The conflicting policies of Crawford and Calhoun had combined with the presidential ambitions of both to bring the War and Treasury secretaries into sharp disagreement since the spring of 1820, when Crawford and his Radical allies began a campaign of retrenchment that appeared to Calhoun and his partisans to be designed to emasculate the Department of War and discredit its secretary.[10] By the fall of 1821, this factional feuding had intruded into the politics of Georgia and South Carolina, the partisans of each secretary attempting to undermine the other in his home state. Rather than see Crawford elected president and doubtful that Adams alone could defeat the Georgian, Calhoun had decided to enter the race, not so much to win as to divide the southern vote and that of Pennsylvania, and possibly other Middle Atlantic states where he had substantial support, and thus hand defeat to his southern rival.[11] What determined Calhoun to enter the race at this time was a rumor that "improperly identified" him with Adams, an association which threatened the South Carolinian's southern support.[12]

Lowndes assured Calhoun that he "should greatly prefer his election to that of any of his Competitors for the office."[13] If Lowndes had a preference for either of Calhoun's rivals, it was probably Crawford, although Lowndes had spoken positively of both. He had acknowledged the New Englander's presidential potential as early as 1817 and had recently told Plumer that the next president should come from the North, where Lowndes considered Adams the only viable candidate.[14] That Lowndes did not share Calhoun's alarm over the prospect of Crawford's election was demonstrated in his recent defense of the Georgian's *"moral integrity"* against the severe criticism of congressional colleague and Calhoun partisan Eldred Simkins of Edgefield. He told Simkins, "[W]e have to hope and for myself I believe, that if Mr. Crawford should be President, he will not attempt to manage the Union as his friends are represented to have managed Georgia." Further, Lowndes said Crawford's critics had assailed him with "more violence than discernment" and were actually injuring their own cause in attacking the least vulnerable points of his character.[15] Simkins replied that Lowndes "had spread so wide a mantle of charity" over Crawford out of his "goodness of heart and unsuspecting disposition."[16]

But Lowndes, though nonpolitical by disposition, was hardly the political innocent Simkins implied. At that time, June 1821, he had no reason to believe Calhoun would soon enter the race, and if it were to be a choice between Crawford and Adams, he thought Crawford's "organized party" could secure his election and viewed the prospect with his usual calm.[17] As chairman of the Committee of Foreign Relations, he had had frequent opportunities to observe at close range the secretary of state's conduct of confidential business and came away with serious reservations about his character. Lowndes cited these to Elizabeth as one of his strongest reasons for refusing an appointment as minister to France a few months later. He was unwilling, he said, "to correspond as Minister with Mr Adams who is so imprudent (or rather so selfish for to avoid responsibility himself he exposes the character of his correspondents and the interests of the gov[ernmen]t to risk) that I should either suppress in my letters to him what I ought to communicate or be mortified by the publication of confidential communications."[18] Lowndes also disagreed with Adams on the legitimate exercise of federal power to restrict slavery expansion. That he should have defended Crawford against the partisans of Calhoun in full knowledge of the factional feud also suggests that he felt Calhoun had taken a narrow if not myopic view of his somewhat grandiose plans for military defense in an era of peace and economic depression.[19] But like most South Carolinians, Lowndes preferred someone else to either Adams or Crawford, and when Calhoun confided his plan to run, the assurance Lowndes gave him was doubtless sincere.

Unfortunately for Calhoun, the South Carolina legislature had already dealt his candidacy a crippling blow. While Lowndes was still on his way to Washington, and without his knowledge, lowcountry moderates in the South Carolina legislature made an unprecedented foray into presidential politics. Led by James Hamilton, Jr., an idealistic young Charleston lawyer and kinsman of the Pinckney clan, the Charleston delegation, along with others from the tidewater parishes and Middle District counties east of the Broad River, quietly organized behind a plan to nominate Lowndes for president in the election of 1824. They called a caucus of the legislature that met in the hall of representatives on December 18, with some two-thirds of both houses in attendance. Here Hamilton moved the expediency of nominating a candidate for the next presidential election and followed up with a speech that left no doubt of his choice.[20]

Opposition to the motion consisted primarily of upcountry partisans of Calhoun. Caught off guard, the Calhoun men argued for delay, declaring the proposal premature and condemning the very idea that a single small state should attempt to name a president for the whole nation as the essence of presumption.[21] With the caucus almost evenly divided between the partisans of Lowndes and Calhoun, debate on the motion of expediency evolved into a discussion of their relative merits as potential candidates. The friends of Lowndes readily conceded Calhoun's credentials but maintained that Lowndes was a figure of greater national prominence who would be more acceptable to citizens throughout the nation.[22] The crucial vote came on the expediency motion, which narrowly passed, 58 to 54. Then both sides joined together in a unanimous vote for the following resolutions:

> BE IT RESOLVED, that it is the sense of this Meeting . . . in reference to our next President, that no individual in the Union, unites more entirely the qualifications of this station . . . than our distinguished fellow-citizen, WILLIAM LOWNDES.
> . . . that . . . remote from all feelings of state partiality, if an individual more highly gifted, possessing stronger claims than himself, and more unanimously supported, should be produced as a candi-

date, this State ... would cheerfully acquiesce in the superior pretensions of such an individual; but, where such an individual is to be found, is a difficulty, not easily to be surmounted.

BE IT THEREFORE RESOLVED, That, WILLIAM LOWNDES, of South Carolina, is a person well qualified to fulfill the important duties of the President of the United States, and we do recommend him to the good people of the several States, at the ensuing Election.[23]

Among those who engineered Lowndes's nomination, the most active besides Hamilton appear to have been Lowndes's lifelong friend, Daniel Huger; another old friend, Judge William Drayton; and a highly promising Charleston lawyer, Robert Y. Hayne.[24] None of the presidential aspirants was involved, at least no further than to furnish separate reasons to nominate Lowndes. Certainly Calhoun had nothing to do with it, Adams remained aloof from such activity, Henry Clay was not yet an active candidate, and Andrew Jackson had recently disclaimed with apparent conviction any intention to run.[25] Crawford was too shrewd a politician to risk raising up Lowndes in order to put down Calhoun, because the entry of another southerner in the race would demonstrate to northern observers, as indeed it did,[26] Crawford's own weakness in a South more divided than he had led them to believe. Moreover, Crawford and Thomas Cobb, one of his chief lieutenants, saw the nomination as aimed at Crawford himself. On no stronger evidence than his own fertile imagination and a deep-seated suspicion of Clintonians, Cobb thought he saw the long arm of DeWitt Clinton reaching into South Carolina in order to injure Crawford and his Bucktail allies in New York.[27]

Observations such as Cobb's along with Lowndes's brief and reluctant candidacy have encouraged the view that the nomination was conceived rather as a means to prevent the election of Crawford than a serious effort to elect Lowndes.[28] It is true that Hamilton, Huger, Hayne, and their allies meant to defeat Crawford, preferring both Lowndes and Calhoun to either of the other candidates.[29] There is little if anything in their correspondence, however, to suggest that they thought it desirable to have both Lowndes and Calhoun in the field in order to draw more southern support away from Crawford, and a great deal to suggest that they thought otherwise.[30] It is clear that the amateur politicians promoting Lowndes considered his presidential "pretensions" equal if not superior to those of any other potential candidate including Calhoun. They were equally convinced that neither Lowndes nor anyone else in Washington would lift a hand to advance his prospects there. As Huger later told Lowndes, "You had no active friends in Washington and would do nothing for yourself.... I admit, it would have been better that the ball should have been commenced elsewhere; but that was not the question. It was to be commenced here or not at all."[31]

The friends of Lowndes, however, had no apparent strategy to accomplish their object. Huger and Hamilton's friend Joseph Cardozo, editor of the *Southern Patriot*, favored the customary nomination by congressional caucus rather than risk, as Huger said, "leaving it to the House of Representatives, where bribery in some shape or the other will be practiced."[32] Cardozo feared a "disastrous result" if the presidential election went into the House, where the northern majority could elect an antislavery protectionist to the presidency.[33] To forestall such a pass, Lowndes appeared to be the best candidate acceptable to South Carolina. His friends believed his prominence and prestige among House members easily surpassed that of Calhoun, giving Lowndes the better prospect of support in the congressional caucus and consequently in the general election as well. If, as they expected, the election should bring out a crowded field of contenders, they believed the statesmanlike Lowndes was certain to benefit from the inevitable collisions among his rivals, and once the election came into the House, the same advantages would apply as in a congressional caucus. On the whole, though, it seems his friends planned little more than to see their expectations realized in the normal course of events as they unfolded. The purpose of their action at Columbia was not so much to raise Lowndes up on the slender reed of South Carolina's recommendation, but to send a message to Washington calling attention to the superior credentials of a candidate otherwise likely to be overlooked in the congressional caucus and the presidential sweepstakes of 1824.

When Lowndes received Hamilton's brief note informing him of his nomination, he immediately "communicated its purport" to Calhoun, and the two friends had a full and frank discussion on the subject, although neither recorded its details. The only details Lowndes communicated in his reply to Hamilton were that Calhoun said he had already informed several friends that circumstances left him no choice but "to consent to be held up for the Presidency," and these friends, believing he had support in several states, considered it "impossible that he should [then] retract what he ha[d] done."[34] A group from the Pennsylvania delegation had recently called on Calhoun to offer their support in that pivotal state, and there can be little doubt that Lowndes encouraged Calhoun to enter the race in spite of his setback at Columbia.[35] Lowndes had no ambition for the presidency and doubtless said so in their discussion; even if he had had, the state of his health precluded any serious thought of actively seeking the office. Still suffering the effects of his recent illness, he had made no secret of his tentative plans for another recuperative voyage to Europe.[36]

If Calhoun's ambition and his rivalry with Crawford prevented him from considering withdrawal, neither could Lowndes readily decline his nomination, although he would attempt as gracefully as he could to persuade his friends to transfer their support to Calhoun. He may have agreed with Calhoun that the caucus at Columbia had committed a "rash and foolish" act,[37] but, genuinely moved by their extraordinary expression of confidence in himself and acutely sensible of the embarrassment a hasty rejection would surely cause his friends, he had no more of an alternative to entering the race, at least temporarily, than did his friend Calhoun. Then there was the matter of the duty of public service, which Lowndes took as seriously as any man in national politics. His commitment to republican principles could not condone withdrawal on the frivolous ground of personal preference. Of equal if not greater importance was the fact that the damage done to Calhoun's hopes could not be undone by anything Lowndes might do. The public knowledge that Calhoun was at best the second choice of his home state could not be eradicated, and for Lowndes to attempt a correction through withdrawal now could easily compound the problem by giving the fact greater notoriety.[38]

The solution they agreed on was that neither should alter his present course. Calhoun would enter the race as planned, and Lowndes would neither decline the nomination nor encourage an active campaign in his own behalf but follow the course dictated by his health. As this would most likely result in a voyage abroad, effectively removing Lowndes from further consideration, the difficulty presented by his nomination would be resolved and his friends could transfer their support to Calhoun. If Calhoun ever considered a temporary postponement of his own plans in deference to the declared preference of his fellow South Carolinians, his recent interview with members of the Pennsylvania delegation argued against it. Current speculation held that if Crawford could carry Pennsylvania he could win the election, and his support there was strong enough to persuade Calhoun that any postponement of his candidacy would jeopardize his support in Pennsylvania, thus delivering the state and with it the presidency to Crawford.[39] Preoccupied with such concerns, and with Lowndes's approval, Calhoun authorized the announcement of his candidacy without giving sufficient consideration to the likelihood of negative reaction to its timing. Coming so soon after the news from Columbia reached Washington, it created an indelible impression of overweening ambition, which immediately cost him the friendship of Secretary Adams and imposed on Calhoun partisans an awkward burden of unconvincing explanation.[40]

The sudden appearance of Lowndes and Calhoun as presidential contenders raised a fever of speculation in Washington. During the first week of the new year the Congress could talk of nothing else. As Lowndes told Elizabeth, "The House is in terrible confusion. I thought when I came here that the question was in fact confined to two persons Mr Crawford and Mr Adams. Now we have all the Secretaries and at least two who are not secretaries named. Indeed if the example of our own State were followed as there are 24 States there ought to be 48 candidates."[41] The last comment was not entirely in jest.

Much of the excitement in Washington concerned the ramifications of the way Lowndes had been nominated, because through their initiative the State Legislature of South Carolina liberated presidential politics from the dictatorship of the congressional caucus. This stunning political innovation carried the potential for an unprecedented proliferation of presidential candidates, each with as legitimate a claim to public consideration as the state legislature that nominated him could give. Congressman Micah Sterling of New York thought it "would set the whole continent to premature electioneering."[42] By wresting the nomination process away from the center of national power and bringing it down to the state level, South Carolina had brought the presidency that much closer to the people through a process better suited to the democratic tastes of the rising generation. Whether the practice of nomination by state legislature would ultimately fragment traditional party alignments into a plethora of regional, state, and individual loyalties remained to be seen. The current crop of candidates immediately saw its advantages. Except for Crawford, every presidential candidate in the election of 1824 would come forward by the South Carolina method, thrust into contention on the recommendation of a state legislature.[43] When this happened, the Republican reign of "King Caucus" was over, ironically toppled from his throne by a group of political amateurs whose candidate had no intention to run. And with equal irony, the blow that shook the foundations of Crawford's support came not from Calhoun but inadvertently from Lowndes.

Lowndes treated his nomination with all due respect. In his reply to Hamilton, he said it was the favor of one's own state "which comes most home to [one's] feelings," and expressed his gratitude "for the good opinion" that the state legislature had expressed of him. In response to Hamilton's query on the course he now intended to pursue, Lowndes answered with a classic statement of republican principle regarding the presidency. He said,

> I do not see that I can deviate from that which I have pursued hitherto. I have never taken a step, and never shall, to draw the public eye upon me as a Competitor for the high place of which you speak. I have no reason to think that there is any wish out of our own State to raise me to it, nor did I know until I received your letter that there was such a wish in the state, except on the part of two or three Personal Friends. However this may be, the Presidency of the United States is not in my opinion an office to be either solicited or declined.[44]

The remainder of his letter was a masterful exercise in tactful suggestion. He professed great anxiety on the effect the action at Columbia might have on the reputation of the state. South Carolina, he said, had an admirable reputation for disinterestedness, and while treating her public men always with a liberal confidence, she had "never overrated their claims to the honors of the general government nor been disposed to press them upon a reluctant or less partial community." He would feel a regret, he said, "more painful than any personal mortification if my name should be connected with any imputation upon the State to which I belong." The obvious inference was that this imputation might be removed through the withdrawal of his name, which he proceeded to justify by pointing out the merits of Calhoun, the advanced stage of his candidacy, and his reputed strength in several northern as well as the southern states. "For the interest of the Country and for the character of the State," Lowndes hoped "that means may be found to remove" the impression that South Carolina opposed the candidacy of Calhoun. He closed by stating his hope and belief that, if his own election should appear to be impossible and Calhoun's prospects continued to improve, his most partial friends would transfer their support to Calhoun.[45]

Hamilton, Huger, Hayne, and Drayton fired back a fusillade of argument, advice, and entreaties to stay in the race. He should abandon his plan for a voyage abroad. He should not believe the overly sanguine views of George McDuffie, his congressional colleague from Edgefield, and other Calhoun partisans. His own presidential pretensions were to be treated with respect and not yielded to any other candidate whomsoever. His friends concurred in his view of Calhoun's credentials and would willingly support him if the election of their choice should appear to be impossible; but if they had considered Calhoun's credentials superior to his own, they would have named Calhoun in the first place. It was not for them to say what course Calhoun should pursue, but they believed his entry into the race, notwithstanding Lowndes's nomination, was a mistake that could not but retard the future progress of his political career. And if Congressman Joel Roberts Poinsett of Charleston could not make up his mind between Lowndes and Calhoun, then his Charleston constituents would find a more decisive Representative in the next election.[46]

Lowndes remained in the race, but he never took his candidacy seriously. On first learning of his nomination, he had told Elizabeth, "I hope you have not set your mind too strongly upon being *President's lady*. While you wish only a larger fence for the poultry yard, or a pond for the ducks I may be able to gratify you but the business of making a President of oneself or of another, I have no cunning at."[47] The brief duration of his passive campaign hardly gave observers outside his state time to assess its significance before it was over, for his rapidly failing health soon removed him from consideration entirely. The Lowndes-for-president movement was from the beginning an impractical dream; and in the end, it was the last hurrah of lowcountry moderation and a parting salute to Lowndes.

When Lowndes developed the symptoms of tuberculosis in March, it was the beginning of the end.[48] In April he asked for a leave of absence and resigned his seat in May. His further decline through the terrible heat of June, "the burning atmosphere, [in which] The whole of animated nature suffers," prompted a decision to go north for the summer, and he booked passage to sail for New York with his wife and daughter on June 17.[49]

During his last ten days in Charleston, two unrelated events occurred whose portent for the future of his state neither Lowndes nor any other informed South Carolinian could have mistaken. On June 9, news came up from the Savannah River that George McDuffie lay dying on the riverbank with a pistol ball lodged against his spine, shot in a duel with Colonel William Cumming of Georgia, a Crawford man.[50] McDuffie was all black powder and short fuse, unrestrained in debate and fearless master of "vituperation witheringly pungent."[51] When John Randolph of Roanoke, for example, took exception to a rebuttal that the young South Carolina congressman delivered in a style the Virginian had made famous, McDuffie sent back a curt reply and went immediately to the Washington Naval Yards for target practice with his dueling pistols.[52] McDuffie's duel with Cumming, the first of three such interviews (for the South Carolina firebrand did indeed recover), had grown out of the recent election in Georgia where McDuffie had intruded with a series of anti-Crawford essays written in his own unique style.[53] To an unfortunate if not indeed a tragic degree, McDuffie, like Ruffin of Virginia, represented the wave of the future for the slaveholding South. In both states, slave insurrections put an emphatic period to the passing era and paved the way for the Ruffin-McDuffie style of southern belligerence.[54] Stunned Charlestonians discovered the first one on the eve of Lowndes's departure.

The night before Lowndes sailed from Charleston, he received a cryptic message from James Hamilton, Jr. Hamilton regretted his inability to pay his respects in person before Lowndes's departure as he had planned to do, but the press of business of an unusual nature, involving a "commotion" among a portion of the population, had occupied all his attention during the past twenty-four hours and must regrettably deprive him of the honor of bidding his esteemed friend a personal farewell. He assumed that his friend had been informed on the subject to which the note alluded and assured him that the proper measures had been taken and the danger had passed.[55] In this manner Lowndes received official notice of the alleged conspiracy of Denmark Vesey, whose very name was connected with if not taken from the family from whom Lowndes had purchased the Grove. Having dismissed several earlier hints of a planned insurrection, Charleston authorities during the past week had been persuaded by the testimony of one of those involved that Vesey, a former slave who had purchased his freedom with the proceeds from a winning lottery ticket, had organized an insurrection with the help of his principal accomplice, Gullah Jack. The conspiracy reputedly involved many of the most trusted servants in Charleston and possibly thousands of other lowcountry slaves.[56] Thoroughly alarmed, Hamilton and other authorities had begun to seize the alleged principals and conduct interrogations when he sent the cryptic note to Lowndes. As the interrogations continued, they expanded the plot to astonishing proportions. Eventually some three dozen persons were executed for involvement in the conspiracy and slightly more than that number sent into exile.[57]

The magnitude, indeed the very existence of the insurrection attributed to Denmark Vesey has been the subject of scholarly debate, but there can be little doubt of the impact the incident had on Charlestonians of Lowndes's generation. It made a profound impression on Lowndes's family, judging by the suggestions Elizabeth's father offered for public consideration later that year. General Pinckney reviewed the incident, assessed its ramifications, and concluded that Charlestonians could no longer live in safety in the midst of a black population. His solution was to make Charleston an all-white city. All blacks would be exiled. Domestic servants and other slaves would be sent into the country for employment on plantations, the practice of slaves' hiring out their skills with their masters' permission would be abolished, and free blacks would be legislated into exile anywhere so long as it was not Charleston. The services performed by each of these groups could be taken over by white immigrants from the Old World at no more cost, he figured, than it took to maintain the present black population in town. The only difficulty would come during the transition period between the departure of the blacks and the arrival of enough white immigrants to take their places.[58]

Pinckney published his proposal in hopes of public approval, but two factors doomed it from the start. His supporting argument contained a more devastating indictment of urban slavery than the most optimistic abolitionist could hope for from such a source or the thoroughly alarmed lowcountry was willing to hear.[59] And everybody knew that the very existence of slavery in the South deflected all but a trickle of European immigration into the free-state North.

That the old lowcountry aristocrat and revolutionary soldier should have proposed such a radical scheme reflected the magnitude of change the aborted insurrection had wrought. The domestic peace and social stability of the world the Pinckneys had always known had suddenly vanished, and a footfall in a darkened hallway or mansion staircase would never sound the same again. The fearfully altered perception of nightsounds, of a whispered confidence between house servants or a coachman's over-the-shoulder glance, signified the emotional power suddenly infused into the slavery issue by the aborted insurrection. In the aftershocks that reverberated through the lowcountry and beyond, emotion shouldered reason aside, the demagogue claimed a more prominent place in the public forum, and northern agitation of the slavery question took on a decidedly malevolent cast. This great awakening claimed as its first casualty a political tradition of long standing in lowcountry South Carolina, a commitment to nationalism as old as the Republic itself. As for the politics of moderation, the frail, tubercular Lowndes had suddenly become an all-too-fitting symbol, and his impending death an appropriate metaphor for the end of an era and the dying dream of a classically mixed and balanced constitutional republic.

On June 17, accompanied by his wife and daughter, Lowndes sailed from Charleston for the recuperative benefits of a New England summer. When his condition continued to deteriorate there, a voyage to Europe was decided upon as a last expedient. The party of three boarded the ship *Moss* and left Newcastle, Delaware on Monday morning, October 21, bound for London. The end came sooner than expected. Lowndes was very feeble, according to a fellow passenger, "but still able to sit up a part of the day until the succeeding Friday, when he became greatly exhausted. On Saturday night his symptoms became alarming, and early on Sunday morning it was evident that his dissolution was at hand; and about 9 o'clock on Sunday morning, the 27th Oct., 1822, his immortal spirit winged its way to the God who gave it."[60]

Through a mistaken kindness to Mrs. Lowndes and her daughter, owing to foul weather and violent seas, they were not informed of the hour of burial. On Monday afternoon, October 28, the Episcopal burial service was read. Then the "heavy-shotted shroud" struck the water and sank into the eternal cold of the ocean deep.[61]

Ave atque vale.

Epilogue

In writing this biography my intentions were to give Lowndes the liberty to tell his own story, insofar as scholarly standards and the necessity for periodic commentary would permit, and to grant him at its conclusion the dignity of dying without the intrusive distraction of an attempt to assess the meaning of his life. The purpose of this epilogue is, first, to tie up some loose ends concerning his family and, secondly, to address in a somewhat more personal way a few of the questions the story as told here has raised.

When news of Lowndes's death reached Washington in January 1823, the House resolved to wear mourning, an exceptional tribute to Lowndes considering the fact that he was not a member at the time of his death. The successor to his seat, James Hamilton, Jr., gave the House formal notice of Lowndes's death and followed the announcement with eulogistic remarks suitable to the occasion and typical of the era. Among others who followed Hamilton, the remarks of John W. Taylor of New York more precisely suited the character of his departed colleague, who had repeatedly confronted the New Yorker throughout the contest over Missouri. Taylor said,

> The highest and best hopes of this country looked to WILLIAM LOWNDES for their fulfillment. The most honorable office in the civilized world—the Chief Magistracy of this free people—would have been illustrated by his virtues and talents. . . . To manners the most unassuming, to patriotism the most disinterested, to morals the most pure, to attainments of the first rank in literature and science, he added the virtues of decision and prudence, so happily combined, so harmoniously united, that we know not which most to admire, the firmness with which he pursued his purpose, or the gentleness with which he disarmed opposition. His arguments were made not to enjoy the triumphs of victory, but to convince the judgment of his hearer; and when the success of his efforts were most signal, his humility was most conspicuous![1]

In South Carolina, as might have been expected, public reaction to the news of Lowndes's death and the eulogistic rhetoric that followed were even more pronounced.[2] Specialists in the study of iconography like my friend and colleague Barry Schwartz, whose splendid work on the eulogies to George Washington has delineated contemporary perceptions of the virtuous man in public life,[3] might regard my decision not to discuss the eulogistic reaction to the death of Lowndes as a lost opportunity. In response I could only say that the evidence in Lowndes's case is more limited than the needs of an instructive discussion would require and the discussion itself would tend to enshroud Lowndes in an aura of hagiography, which Lowndes himself would have found embarrassing and his biographer would prefer to avoid.

Elizabeth Lowndes and her daughter remained in Europe until the early summer of 1823. None of their correspondence during this period has survived, though there was probably not much to preserve. Although Elizabeth wrote to inform her father of the loss of her husband soon after the event, thereafter weeks went by with no word.[4] Mrs. Lowndes had always been a reluctant correspondent, a characteristic that her husband had tried to remedy through repeated coaxing to little avail. That this was no indication of the depth of her love for him is plainly evident in a letter she wrote to Elizabeth Cheves shortly after her return from Europe. This one, fleeting glimpse into the heart of the woman who shared the life of William Lowndes finds her in the desolation of grief:

> My Dear Friend—I have undergone so much distress of mind since my return to Charleston, that I have allowed a most unpardonable length of time to elapse since I received your kind letter of 18th ul[ti]mo but I know your goodness, so I know that your feeling heart will induce you to excuse me. This summer has indeed my dear friend been to me most trying. I have had several painful duties to perform but what I consider the severest trial is yet to come. I have not been to the grove—that *Home*, where for eighteen years it was my greatest happiness to be with my lamented Husband. It was his favorite residence—he delighted in it, and was always making some improvement both to the House and the grounds, to render it a more convenient and pleasant residence to me during his absences at Washington as well as with a view of our enjoying it together when he should have retired from public life—how I ever shall be able to return there, when every spot in and out of the house will so forcibly remind me, of my dreadful loss, I know not—but still I must en-

deavor to go there in the winter tho' it will be for a short time, for I never again can make it my residence—my heart sinks within me at the thoughts of my being there deprived of *him*.[5]

Considering how much this one letter reveals about the happiness of their life together, their mutual devotion, and their hopes and plans for the future, we can only regret the more her husband's decision to keep family matters private by routinely burning the letters she wrote him.

The years of self-reliance that her husband's periodic absences in Washington imposed on Elizabeth Lowndes had better prepared her to face the future without him than she realized at the time of his death. In time she returned to the Grove, but she never remarried. Lowndes left his entire estate in trust to Elizabeth with provisions to divide it into quarters as their children came of age. Debts that incumbered the estate delayed its settlement for another decade, and the absence of an inventory of what remained makes it difficult to determine the amount and specific disposition of his property.[6]

Elizabeth Lowndes lived out the thirty-five remaining years of her widowhood in what contemporaries were accustomed to call a useful life of Christian piety. The sons became planters. During the prowar enthusiasm of 1812, their father had expressed the hope that one would become a great general and the other a great admiral. Failing that, he hoped both would become good men.[7] Neither had the talent or temperament to realize their father's first hope, but by contemporary standards in the slaveholding South, both realized the second. Supplied with the dowry her father had left her, Rebecca Lowndes, when she came of age, married a Rutledge. The wedding symbolically closed the book on the old antagonisms that had alienated the two families in the revolutionary era.[8]

As the name of Lowndes faded from prominence in South Carolina, that of Calhoun ascended while the state under Calhoun's influence pursued an increasingly militant course. Observing these events, Nathan Sargent thought that Lowndes, had he lived, would have exerted a moderating influence on Calhoun and the state as well.[9] Whether Sargent was right or wrong, and I believe he was right, his observation illustrates perhaps the most important intellectual difference between South Carolina's two most gifted public men. That both men possessed genius was generally acknowledged, but Daniel Huger, who knew both well enough to judge, pointed out the difference: "Lowndes' *wisdom* keeps his *Genius* in check."[10] A plausible illustration of what Huger seems to have meant may be seen in their response to the slavery issue, where Lowndes elected the defensive strategy of state rights based on the Constitution and refused to discuss slavery, whereas Calhoun eventually defended slavery as a positive good.

One might question the wisdom of Lowndes's choice, I believe, without imposing on nineteenth-century behavior the standards of the twentieth. George Dangerfield judged Lowndes's performance in the Missouri Controversy "rather sad" and supported the judgment with references to the moral issue involved.[11] The problem with this kind of moral judgment has always been the difficulty of fitting it into the context of the times and finding support for it in contemporary standards of moral conduct. To do otherwise is to do an injustice to the person so judged. From the perspective of hindsight, there seems little doubt that Lowndes's choice of the strategic defense was unfortunate, however wise it might have appeared at the time. When one of the wisest men by all accounts that South Carolina sent to Congress in this era declined to discuss the greatest question his country had faced, one whose peaceful solution would require all the classical virtues, he revealed the all-too-human limitations of his wisdom. And it could be argued that his decision not to discuss it was the strongest indictment of slavery a slaveholder could make.

Having argued in the preceding chapters that Lowndes and his colleagues in the Sixteenth Congress witnessed a collision between antagonistic strains of traditional republicanism, the one more liberal and predominantly northern and the other more traditional and predominantly southern, I might add here a concluding comment on scholarly discussion of this value system and its implications for the decades of increasing intersectional controversy after Lowndes died. My debt to the growing community of scholars, who have located the classical origins of republicanism, defined its principles, traced its evolution, and enhanced our understanding of our nation's history through the perspective of their collective scholarship, is admittedly great, and I welcome this opportunity to acknowledge the debt. For the antebellum era, however, the sectional cleavage that resulted in civil war should be considered from a perspective broadened enough to include the Lockean view of what constituted full citizenship and the way it came to supplant the more elitist republican definition.[12]

The American nation underwent profound change between the Revolution and the Civil War. One of the most influential areas of change was in the concept of citizenship, then more commonly called republican liberty, which moved steadily away from its basis in property in the

Aristotelian sense toward the Lockean definition of the individual's person, his labor, and his liberty. This was all but inevitable in a republic of free men where an ever-increasing percentage of the population provided services and consequently measured their personal worth in terms of their labor. Moreover, as John Locke became "America's Philosopher" during the antebellum years, the nation's strong evangelical inclinations infused the Lockean concept of liberty with a distinctly moral character.[13] When universal white manhood suffrage became a reality before the Civil War, the American republic of 1789 had evolved into a Lockean democracy, and opposition to slavery had become for the northern majority a moral imperative.

This evolution and the way it changed the meaning of liberty and property brought increasing pressure to bear on the institution of slavery. The slaveholding South, where traditional republicanism persisted to a far greater degree than elsewhere, responded by insisting on state and constitutional rights and protested that the citizens of the free-state North intended to prevent the distribution of justice to southern citizens who held property in slaves. Northerners appealed to what we would call human rights and they called a higher law than the Constitution. In the process, each section constructed such a distorted image of the other that neither could compromise, and the war came. The Civil War brought changes in the Constitution that not only abolished slavery but altered the terms of debate over the concept of citizenship in ways that rendered obsolete the traditional republican view.[14]

William Lowndes and the traditional republicans of his era doubted the capacity of the numerical majority to govern without degenerating into a tyrannical and corrupt ochlocracy. The history of corruption both in and out of government from the Age of Jackson to the present day, along with the democratic despotism that women, blacks, and racial and ethnic minorities generally have endured, would tend to confirm their doubts.[15] But the democratic quest for the virtuous ideal has proved no less persistent than the republican. One has but to glance over the daily newspaper to see the vigilance of a free press constantly calling the political leadership to account, then take a random sample of grand jury presentments from almost anywhere in America to discover that ordinary citizens all across the nation are conscientiously striving to practice civic virtue and to realize the elusive republican ideal. I suspect William Lowndes might be surprised. I know he would be pleased.

Notes

Abbreviations

AA	Alabama Department of Archives and History
Annals	U.S. Congress. *Annals of Congress: The Debates and Proceedings in the Congress of the United States.* 42 vols. Washington: Gales and Seaton, 1834–56
ASPF	U.S. Congress. *Finance.* Vols. 9–13 of *American State Papers.* 38 vols. Washington: Gales and Seaton, 1832–61
CLS	Charleston Library Society
DU	Duke University Library
LC	Library of Congress
MHS	Massachusetts Historical Society
NYHS	New-York Historical Society
NYPL	New York Public Library
OMC	Office of Mesne Conveyance, Charleston County Courthouse
OPC	Office of Probate Court, Charleston County Courthouse
SCA	South Carolina Department of Archives and History
SCHS	South Carolina Historical Society
SCL	South Caroliniana Library
SHC	Southern Historical Collection

Introduction

1. Pope, *Impact of the Ante-bellum Tariff.*
2. Lebergott, *Americans, an Economic Record,* pp. 139–61.
3. Freehling, *Prelude to Civil War,* pp. 7–48, 361–64; Gray, *History of Agriculture,* 2:1030–31.
4. The discussion of Aristotelian thought as summarized here is derived from Pocock, *Machiavellian Moment,* pp. 67–76. Moreover, the brief outline of its evolution to the American Revolution has depended for the most part on Pocock's thesis, although the outline itself gives no hint of the complexity of a brilliant and immensely learned book in which custom, grace, and the polarity of fortune and virtue are the three components of its model (ibid., pp. 349–51).

5. Ibid., pp. 70–76.
6. Ibid., p. ix.
7. Ibid., pp. 162–82.
8. Banning, *Jeffersonian Persuasion*, pp. 25–31.
9. See Peter Laslett's introduction to Locke, *Two Treatises*, pp. 106–35.
10. Ibid., pp. 118–23.
11. Ibid., pp. 114–16.
12. Banning, *Jeffersonian Persuasion*, pp. 53–62. For an authoritative study of this era, see Kramnick, *Bolingbroke*.
13. Banning, *Jeffersonian Persuasion*, pp. 62–69.
14. Weir, " 'Harmony,' " pp. 473–501.

Chapter I

1. *Charleston Royal Gazette*, Feb. 2, 1782.
2. Ibid., Feb. 2, 6, 1782.
3. Wallace, *South Carolina, a Short History*, p. 316.
4. Ibid., p. 321.
5. *Charleston Royal Gazette*, Feb. 6, 1782; Mills, *Atlas of the State of South Carolina*, Colleton District. On Rawlins Lowndes and "protection," see Vipperman, *Rawlins Lowndes*, pp. 228–30.
6. Ravenel, *William Lowndes*, p. 2.
7. *Charleston Royal Gazette*, Mar. 27, 1782.
8. Weir, " 'Harmony,' " pp. 473–501. For the central position of this value system in Jeffersonian Republicanism and its importance to men of William Lowndes's generation, see Banning, *Jeffersonian Persuasion*, and McCoy, *Elusive Republic*.
9. Pocock, *Machiavellian Moment*, pp. 67–76, and passim.
10. See Vipperman, *Rawlins Lowndes*, passim, for information on his life not otherwise documented in this chapter.
11. Ibid.
12. Rebecca Lowndes Rutledge, "Notes . . . I have heard of my Father," William Lowndes Papers (LC).
13. Ibid.
14. Receipt dated Oct. 31, 1787, William Lowndes Papers (LC).
15. Vipperman, *Rawlins Lowndes*, p. 254.
16. Ravenel, *William Lowndes*, pp. 35–36.
17. Ibid.
18. John Savage to Rawlins Lowndes, Dec. 3, 1790, William Lowndes Papers (SHC).
19. Ibid.
20. Rutledge, "Notes," William Lowndes Papers (LC).

Notes to Pages 7–16 : 273

21. Ibid.
22. Ibid.
23. Receipts dated Aug. 1792 and Apr. 1794, signed Tho. Osborne, William Lowndes Papers (SCHS).
24. Rutledge, "Notes," William Lowndes Papers (LC).
25. Statement by James Deas, 1859, quoted in Ravenel, *William Lowndes*, p. 38.
26. Ibid., pp. 38–39.
27. Ibid.
28. Receipts dated Nov. 1793, Feb. and Apr. 1794, St. Julien Ravenel Childs Collection (SCHS).
29. *Charleston City Gazette*, Jan. 7, 1794.
30. Chase, *Lowndes*, p. 24; Thomas, *Reminiscences*, p. 103.
31. *Charleston City Gazette*, Dec. 29, 1796.
32. Ibid., Jan. 12, 1798, supplement.
33. Undated newspaper clipping, William Lowndes Papers (LC); Daniel Ravenel, "Memoranda," Oct. 8, 1860, Miscellaneous Papers (NYPL).
34. Cibber, *Apology*, pp. 230–36.
35. Daniel Ravenel, "Memoranda," Oct. 8, 1860, Miscellaneous Papers (NYPL); Davis, *Intellectual Life*, 3:1301–2.
36. Alfred Huger to Robert Gourdin, July 27, 1859, Alfred Huger Letterpress Book, pp. 470–73 (DU). Huger, in a comment typical of contemporary opinion on William Lowndes, said, "He is to this day the very highest authority in the all virtuous man." See also Watterson, *Letters*, p. 101.
37. *Charleston City Gazette*, Oct. 24, 1797.
38. Ibid., Feb. 10, 1798.
39. Chase, *Lowndes*, p. 24.
40. Rutledge, "Notes," William Lowndes Papers (LC).
41. Vipperman, *Rawlins Lowndes*, pp. 259–60.
42. Ibid., p. 250.
43. Ibid., p. 255n.
44. Rutledge, "Notes," William Lowndes Papers (LC).
45. Ibid.
46. Fraser, *Reminiscences*, p. 86.
47. Vipperman, *Rawlins Lowndes*, pp. 138–43.
48. Unsigned note in item no. 101, William Lowndes Papers (LC).
49. Rutledge, "Notes," William Lowndes Papers (LC); William Lowndes to James Lowndes, Oct. 16, 1818, Lowndes-Pinckney Papers (SCHS).
50. *Charleston City Gazette*, Aug. 27, 1800; Ravenel, *William Lowndes*, p. 50.
51. Rutledge, "Notes," William Lowndes Papers (LC); Alice Izard, in a

letter to Margaret Manigault, June 10, 1801, placed the accident about the first of May, 1801, Manigault Family Papers (SCL).

52. Martin, "Letters," pp. 20–21.

Chapter II

1. Ravenel, *William Lowndes*, p. 39; Mary Catherine Brisbane said that James and Ruth Lowndes, in addition to their brother William, were unusually tall, "Memoir of the Brisbane Family," typescript, pp. 7–11 (SCHS).

2. See portrait of William Lowndes in Chase, *Lowndes*, frontispiece.

3. Will of Rawlins Lowndes, Will Book D (1800–1807), pp. 26–36 (OPC). Provisions relating to William are on p. 31.

4. The records examined for this period contained no hint of William's ill health before the fall of 1808.

5. Thomas Lowndes to Robert Goodloe Harper, Mar. 27, 1787, Lowndes Papers (SCL). Thomas Lowndes mentioned studying with a local lawyer, whom he did not identify, to gain a "more easy admittance to the Bar."

6. *Charleston City Gazette*, Dec. 7, 1798; Oct. 4, 1800; *Charleston Courier*, Jan. 19, Feb. 9, 11, 19, Mar. 10, 1803.

7. *Charleston Courier*, Jan. 28, 30, 1804.

8. Ibid., Jan. 23, 1804.

9. Ibid., Mar. 15, 1804.

10. Ibid., Aug. 22, 1804.

11. See Chapter 4 for a detailed discussion of Charleston politics, 1806–8.

12. Rogers, *Smith*, pp. 289–95; Vipperman, *Rawlins Lowndes*, p. 256.

13. Rogers, *Smith*, pp. 289–95; cf. Broussard, *Southern Federalists*, pp. 26–27, 29–31, 33–35.

14. See below, Chapter 3.

15. Cardozo, *Reminiscences of Charleston*, p. 38; *Charleston City Gazette*, July 17, 26, Aug. 15, Sept. 24, 1800.

16. See numbers one and two in Lowndes's "Planter" essays, *Charleston Courier*, Apr. 23, 26, 1806, discussed in Chapter 3; Alfred Huger to Robert Gourdin, July 27, 1859, Albert Huger Letterpress Book, pp. 470–73 (DU); Bruce, *Randolph*, 1:369.

17. Henry W. DeSaussure and Timothy Ford, Cashbooks, volume dated 1797–99, unpaged, entries dated Jan. 9 and Oct. 1, 1800, DeSaussure Family Papers (SCHS).

18. William Lowndes copybook, unpaged, William Lowndes Papers (SHC); manuscript notebook of William Lowndes, Miscellaneous Papers (CLS).

19. See Henry W. DeSaussure to Edward Rutledge, Aug. 27, 1796, DeSaussure Family Papers (SCHS); DeSaussure to Jedidiah Morse, June 27, 1800, and to Robert Goodloe Harper, May 13, 1805, DeSaussure Family Papers (SCL); O'Neall, *Bench and Bar*, 1:243–52; 2:150–53; Stourzh, *Hamilton*, pp. 9–37.

20. DeSaussure and Ford Cashbook (1797–99), entries of Jan. 1799, Nov. 1800, and June 1801, DeSaussure Family Papers (SCHS).

21. Entries in William Lowndes's notebook (Miscellaneous Papers, CLS) conclude on Nov. 1, 1803.

22. DeSaussure and Ford Cashbook (1797–99), entry of Dec. 24, 1804, DeSaussure Family Papers (SCHS).

23. *Charleston City Gazette*, July 8, 1802; O'Neall, *Bench and Bar*, 1:209.

24. Ravenel, *William Lowndes*, p. 58.

25. Margaret Manigault to Alice Izard, Feb. 20, 1805, Izard Papers (LC); Zahniser, *Pinckney*, pp. 261–68.

26. Vipperman, *Rawlins Lowndes*, pp. 244–51.

27. Will of Rawlins Lowndes, Will Book D (1800–1807), pp. 26–36 (OPC).

28. *Charleston Courier*, Apr. 2, 1804.

29. The letters of Lowndes to his wife contain numerous references to his tastes in social activity, William Lowndes Papers (SHC).

30. Margaret Manigault to Alice Izard, Feb. 23, 1805, Izard Papers (LC).

31. Ravenel, *William Lowndes*, pp. 56–57.

32. Ibid., p. 58; Ravenel states that Major Pinckney objected on the additional ground that Lowndes was a Republican, a conclusion possibly drawn from a comment made by the major's son, Thomas Pinckney, Jr., long after Lowndes had died, that in 1808, he was "a decided Democrat," Rutledge, "Notes," William Lowndes Papers (LC). Lowndes was not decidedly democratic, but a traditional republican, in his politics.

33. *Charleston City Gazette*, Sept. 18, 1802.

34. Alice Izard to Margaret Manigault, Aug. 31, 1801, Manigault Family Papers (SCL).

35. Ibid., Sept. 10–Oct. 2, 1802.

36. Ibid., Sept. 24, 27, Oct. 2, 1802.

37. Ibid., Oct. 2, 1802.

38. M[ary] L[owndes] to William Lowndes, Dec. 6, 1801, William Lowndes Papers (SHC).

39. Smith, "Charleston Neck," p. 15; also map opposite p. 3.

40. *Charleston City Gazette*, Feb. 27, 1804; Deed Book L-7, p. 208 (OMC).

41. O'Neall, *Bench and Bar*, 2:217.

42. Ibid., 2:215–16.

43. Ibid., 2:216. Judge William Johnson became President Thomas Jefferson's first appointment to the United States Supreme Court.

44. See Common Pleas, Minutes, unpaged, entry of June 4, 1805 (SCA).

45. Bill no. 26, Chancery Court Records, 1804, Charleston, S.C., microfilm (SCA).

46. For procedure in common pleas, see Common Pleas, Minutes, Jan. 29, May 13–16, 1805 (SCA).

47. Huff, *Langdon Cheves*, p. 31.

48. Common Pleas, Minutes, June 6, 1805 (SCA); for a more complete view of Cheves's civil practice, see ibid., May and June, 1805, passim.

49. See ibid., especially June 7, 1805.

50. Lowndes knew Pringle well and spoke effectively in response to criticism of the attorney general in the legislative session of 1804. See S.C. House Journal (1804), p. 100 (SCA).

51. *Charleston City Gazette*, Oct. 13, 1804; *Charleston City Directory, 1809*, pp. 116–48.

52. S.C. House Journal (1804), pp. 63, 112–19 (SCA).

53. Common Pleas, Minutes after June 1805 contain no mention of William Lowndes.

54. Ravenel, *William Lowndes*, p. 63.

55. "James Moles v. Edward Johnson," Bill no. 26, Chancery Court Records, 1804, Charleston, S.C., microfilm (SCA).

56. Common Pleas, Minutes, Jan. 14, 1805 (SCA).

57. *Charleston Courier*, Sept. 10–20, Oct. 30, 1804.

58. Lesesne, *Constitution of 1790*, p. 2.

59. *Charleston City Gazette*, Oct. 2, 1804.

60. See *Charleston Courier*, *Charleston Times*, and *Charleston City Gazette*, Oct. 2–9, 1804.

61. Ibid.

62. *Charleston Courier*, Oct. 10, 1804.

63. Ibid.; *Charleston City Gazette*, Oct. 10, 1804; and South Carolina Election Returns, 1800–1806 (SCA), all list winners for 1804 in the order shown.

64. *Charleston City Gazette*, Sept. 28, 1804.

65. For use of the term "cousinry" to denote interconnecting kinship systems, see Thornton, *Politics and Power*, p. 8; for their importance, see Wyatt-Brown, *Southern Honor*, pp. 184–86; for the Pinckney Family connections, see Rogers, *Smith*, p. 406; for the Lowndes Family, see Chase, *Lowndes*, passim.

Notes to Pages 33–39 : 277

Chapter III

1. Meriwether, *Constitution of 1778*, pp. 3–4. The upcountry, as commonly defined in this era, began in the pine belt at the back of the tidewater parishes some forty miles inland and extended inward across the Fall Line and through the fertile piedmont some two hundred miles to the northwestern corner of the state.
2. U.S. Bureau of the Census, *Second Census* (1800), South Carolina.
3. Meriwether, *Constitution of 1778*, p. 4.
4. Schaper, "Sectionalism," pp. 408–19.
5. Ibid., p. 413.
6. In 1789, 1790, and 1791 the lowcountry paid £28,081 in taxes, the upcountry £8,390. Schaper, "Sectionalism," pp. 418–19.
7. For a recent attempt to explain South Carolina radicalism without this linkage see Kenneth Greenberg's *Masters and Statesmen*, which is focused primarily on antebellum South Carolina.
8. S.C. Senate Journal (1803), pp. 18–19 (SCA); Rogers, *Smith*, p. 208; S.C. Senate Journal (1803), pp. 18–19 (SCA).
9. S.C. House Journal (1803), pp. 147–51 (SCA).
10. *Charleston Courier*, Feb. 15, Mar. 3, 8, 10, 1804.
11. Ibid., Apr. 2, 5, 9, 1804.
12. The *Charleston City Gazette*, Oct. 24, 1804, reported 4,272 slaves imported since January 1; on specie drain, see the *Charleston Courier*, Dec. 2, 1805.
13. S.C. House Journal (1804), p. 15 (SCA).
14. A miscellaneous item dated 1805 describes the Speaker's robe, in Thomas Worth Glover Papers (SCL); see also S.C. House Journal (1804), p. 225, and (1806), pp. 111, 142 (SCA).
15. Lesesne, *Constitution of 1790*, pp. 4–5.
16. S.C. House Journal (1804), pp. 6, 63, 94–98, 112–24, 140, 161–64, 183 (SCA).
17. Ibid., pp. 9, 11, 13, 39, 48, 55, 66–67, 69, 77, 92, 101, 104, 227–29.
18. Ibid., pp. 109, 216–17, 219–20, 231–32.
19. Ibid. (1805), p. 112; the amount of tobacco brought down to Charleston was too small to pay the cost of inspection, ibid., p. 124.
20. Ibid. (1804), pp. 25, 91–92, 95; (1805), p. 24.
21. Ibid. (1804), pp. 192–96.
22. Ibid., pp. 172, 187–90.
23. Ibid., p. 43.
24. Ibid., pp. 169, 176–81. The quotation is on p. 204.
25. Ibid., p. 249.

26. Henry W. DeSaussure to Ezekiel Pickens, Sept. 10, 1805, DeSaussure Family Papers (SCL).
27. Thomas, *Reminiscences*, 2:35–36.
28. *Charleston Courier*, Jan. 1, 1808.
29. S.C. House Journal (1805), pp. 10–14, 25–26, 60, 64, 232–33 (SCA).
30. Ibid., pp. 25, 33–34, 38, 79, 91, 110–11. Mark Kaplanoff, "Making the South Solid," p. 403, ranked Lowndes fourteenth among House members in terms of committee appointments.
31. S.C. House Journal (1805), pp. 67–70, 72–73.
32. Ibid., pp. 143–52.
33. Ibid., p. 178.
34. *Charleston Courier*, Jan. 1, 1808.
35. U.S. Bureau of the Census, *Third Census* (1810), South Carolina, p. 79. Patrick S. Brady, "Slave Trade and Sectionalism," pp. 601–20, argues that South Carolina importation supplied slaves for the internal trade.
36. S.C. House Journal (1806), pp. 1–2, 5–7, 9–10, 13, 14, 20–21, 25, 28, 60, 81, 101 (SCA).
37. Ibid., pp. 29, 55–56, 65, 78; on transportation see ibid. (1807), p. 7, 35–36.
38. Ibid. (1806), pp. 11, 23–24, 37, 63, 95, 112, 125.
39. See *Charleston Courier*, July 3–31, 1807.
40. S.C. House Journal (1807), p. 119 (SCA).
41. Ibid., pp. 14–15, 20–21, 119.
42. Ibid., pp. 69–72.
43. Henry W. DeSaussure to Ezekiel Pickens, Sept. 12, 1808, DeSaussure Family Papers (SCL).
44. S.C. House Journal (June 1808), pp. 157–58 (SCA); *Charleston Courier*, June 25, 1808.
45. S.C. House Journal (June 1808), pp. 158–59 (SCA).
46. Ibid., pp. 166, 174, 178, 186–87.
47. Ibid., pp. 189, 195–96.
48. Harper, *Memoir*, p. 24.
49. Alfred Huger to Robert Gourdin, July 27, 1859, Alfred Huger Letterpress Book, pp. 470–73 (DU).
50. Ravenel, *William Lowndes*, p. 70.
51. Lowndes Papers (SHC).
52. Henry W. DeSaussure to Ezekiel Pickens, Sept. 12, 1808, DeSaussure Family Papers (SCL).
53. Lesesne, *Constitution of 1790*, p. 7.
54. Edgar, *Biographical Directory*, 1:227, Table 5.

55. Schaper, "Sectionalism," pp. 436–37; Barnwell, *Love of Order*, Chap. 2, suggests the linkage mentioned above.
56. U.S. Bureau of the Census, *Third Census* (1810), South Carolina, p. 79.
57. Edgar, *Biographical Directory*, 1:227, Table 5.

Chapter IV

1. For Lowndes see Kershaw and Lewis Account Book for William Lowndes (SCHS).
2. Perkins, *Prologue to War*, pp. 1–3.
3. Smelser, *Democratic Republic*, pp. 138–41.
4. *Charleston Courier*, Mar. 25, 1804.
5. S.C. House Journal (1805), p. 57; *Charleston Courier*, Dec. 14, 1804; Nov. 16, 1805.
6. *Charleston Courier*, Mar. 28, 1804.
7. Ibid., Apr. 10, 1804.
8. Ibid., June 7, 1805.
9. Ibid., July 15, 19, 1805.
10. Smelser, *Democratic Republic*, pp. 142–46.
11. The Phocion "letters," later collected and published in both England and America, are summarized in Wolfe, *Jeffersonian Democracy*, pp. 206–9.
12. See Lowndes's copies in copybook in William Lowndes Papers (SHC).
13. Perkins, *Prologue to War*, pp. 74–78.
14. *Charleston Courier*, Mar. 8, 18, 1806.
15. Brant, *James Madison*, who supplies the phrase, provides an excellent summary of Stephen's and Madison's opposing arguments, 4:293–301.
16. Ibid., 4:296–98.
17. *Charleston Courier*, Mar. 18, 20, 24, 26, 1806.
18. Ibid., Apr. 20, 1806; Wolfe, *Jeffersonian Democracy*, pp. 207–9.
19. *Charleston Courier*, Mar. 20, 1806.
20. Wolfe, *Jeffersonian Democracy*, pp. 208–9. Wolfe made no reference to Lowndes's "Planter" essays. For editorial comment on Phocion, see *Charleston Courier*, Mar. 20, 1806.
21. *Charleston Courier*, Apr. 23, 1806.
22. Ibid.
23. Ibid., Apr. 26, 1806.
24. Ibid., Apr. 29, 1806.
25. Ibid., Apr. 30, 1806.

26. Ibid. Lowndes was quite close to Madison's argument on this point. See Brant, *James Madison*, 4:294, 299.
27. *Charleston Courier*, May 9, 1806.
28. Ibid., May 10, 1806; see also May 13, 1806.
29. Ibid., May 14, 1806.
30. Ibid., May 31, 1806.
31. Ibid., May 15, 22, 26, 27, June 11, 14, 15, 18, 23, 25, July 2, 1806.
32. Ibid., July 9, 1806.
33. Ibid., May–July, 1806; Planter was mentioned favorably in ibid., June 6, 1806.
34. Lowndes copybook, William Lowndes Papers (SHC).
35. Wormser, *Story of the Law*, pp. 513–14.
36. Ibid., pp. 106, 504–9, 511–15.
37. Ibid., p. 504.
38. Thomas, *Reminiscences*, p. 105.
39. Wormser, *Story of the Law*, pp. 511–12.
40. Lowndes copybook, William Lowndes Papers (SHC).
41. *Charleston Courier*, Sept. 23, 1806.
42. *Charleston Times*, Sept. 17–Oct. 15, 1806.
43. *Charleston City Gazette*, Sept. 17–Oct. 15, 1806.
44. Election returns for St. Philip and St. Michael parishes, 1806, South Carolina Election Returns, 1800–1806 (SCA).
45. Ibid.
46. Ibid.
47. See correspondence of Margaret Manigault and Alice Izard, Jan. and Feb., 1805, Izard Papers (LC).
48. *Charleston Courier*, Oct. 9, 1806.
49. See *Charleston Courier*, *Charleston Times*, and *Charleston City Gazette*, Oct. 10–15, and published returns Oct. 16, 1806.
50. Smelser, *Democratic Republic*, pp. 146–50.
51. *Charleston Courier*, July 9, 1806.
52. *Annals*, 12th Cong., 1st sess., p. 1289.
53. *Charleston Courier*, July 3, 4, 9, 13, 1807.
54. Ibid., July 9, 10, 11, 13, 1807.
55. Ibid., July 21, 25, 28, 31, Aug. 12, 26, 1807.
56. Ibid., Sept. 5, 8, Oct. 2, 6, 23, 1807.
57. S.C. House Journal (1807), pp. 58–61 (SCA).
58. *Charleston Courier*, Feb. 5, 1808.
59. See, for example, correspondence of 1807–8 in Lewis Malone Ayer Papers (SCL); "Salwyn" to Mary M. Singleton, Feb. 5, 1808, Singleton Family Papers (SCL).
60. S.C. House Journal (June 1808), pp. 197–98.

61. William Lowndes to Elizabeth Lowndes, Feb. 13, 1821 [misdated 1820], William Lowndes Papers (SHC).
62. *Charleston Courier*, Oct. 10, 1808.
63. Ibid., Sept. 17, Oct. 8, 10, 11, 1808.
64. *Charleston City Gazette*, Oct. 4–11, 1808.
65. *Charleston Courier*, Sept. 17, 1808, in reference to the Republican party organ, the Philadelphia *Aurora*, edited by William Duane.
66. *Charleston Courier*, Oct. 14, 1808; *Charleston City Directory, 1809*. The other winning candidates, in addition to Cheves and Middleton, were O'Brien Smith (planter), John Johnson, Jr. (blacksmith), John Geddes (lawyer), Thomas Lehre (planter), William Clement (unlisted), John Horlbeck, Jr. (bricklayer), William Rouse (tanner), Peter Freneau (printer), James Pringle (planter), William Lee (lawyer), Philip Moser (druggist), Joseph Verree (storekeeper), and Thomas Bennett ("mechanick").
67. *Charleston City Gazette*, Oct. 14, 1808.
68. *Charleston Courier*, Oct. 13–15, 1808; *Charleston Times*, Oct. 13–15, 1808.
69. *Charleston Courier*, Feb. 20, 1809.
70. *Charleston Times*, Feb. 13, 20, 1809.
71. *Charleston Courier*, Feb. 23, 1809.
72. Latimer, "Protagonist," p. 921.
73. Wolfe, *Jeffersonian Democracy*, pp. 240–41.
74. On Taylor, see ibid., pp. 237–39; Kaplanoff, "Making the South Solid," Chap. 2; Barnwell, *Love of Order*, Chap. 2; Greenberg, *Masters and Statesmen*, Chap. 1.
75. *Charleston Courier*, Oct. 16, 18, 22, 30, 1810; *Charleston City Gazette*, Oct. 16, 18, 29, 1810. Taylor was compensated for his loss to Lowndes by the legislature which named him U.S. senator; see *Charleston Courier*, Dec. 22, 1810.

Chapter V

1. *Charleston Courier*, Oct. 4, 1811.
2. Ibid., Oct. 12, 1811.
3. Richardson, *Messages*, 1:476.
4. *Charleston Courier*, Mar. 9, 1809.
5. Perkins, *Prologue to War*, pp. 212–13; Richardson, *Messages*, 1:457.
6. *Charleston Courier*, Aug. 30, Sept. 6, Oct. 4, 1809.
7. William Lowndes to Elizabeth Lowndes, May 18, 1819, William Lowndes Papers (SHC).
8. Ibid., Oct. 23, 26, Nov. 2, 1811.

9. Ibid., Nov. 2, 1811.

10. Ibid.

11. Wiltse, *Calhoun, Nationalist*, p. 54, identified Bibb of the War Mess as Representative William Bibb of Georgia. Lowndes, however, wrote of attending an assembly with Mr. Bibb of Kentucky, "a senator of the mess." William Lowndes to Elizabeth Lowndes, Jan. 26, 1812 [misdated 1811], William Lowndes Papers (SHC).

12. William Lowndes to Elizabeth Lowndes, Nov. 7, 1811, William Lowndes Papers (SHC).

13. The term "chance" as used here refers to timing. For factors that influenced the choice of mess companions, see Young, *Washington Community*, pp. 97–108.

14. See Bailey, *Biographical Directory*, 3:114–16 for Butler, 3:779–81 for Winn, 4:176–77 for Earle, 4:411–12 for Moore. For Williams, see Cook, *Williams*, Chaps. 8–10.

15. Timothy Pickering to William Reed, Mar. 3, 1812, Timothy Pickering Papers (MHS); *Charleston Courier*, Jan. 29, 1813.

16. *Annals*, 12th Cong., 1st sess., pp. 330, 333, 343.

17. Richardson, *Messages*, 1:479.

18. *Annals*, 12th Cong., 1st sess., pp. 333, 343–44.

19. William Lowndes to Elizabeth Lowndes, Nov. 16, 1811, William Lowndes Papers (SHC).

20. Ibid., Dec. 1, 1811.

21. Brown, *Republic in Peril*, pp. 53–54.

22. Samuel Dana to Timothy Pickering, Jan. 30, 1812, Timothy Pickering Papers (MHS).

23. Risjord, *Old Republicans*, pp. 1–10; Dawidoff, *John Randolph*, pp. 11–19, 28–35.

24. William Lowndes to Elizabeth Lowndes, Nov. 2, 1811, William Lowndes Papers (SHC).

25. Ibid., Nov. 24, 1811, and Jan. 2, 1812 [misdated 1811].

26. Wiltse, *Calhoun, Nationalist*, pp. 55–56.

27. *Annals*, 12th Cong., 1st sess., pp. 373–76, 414–19.

28. Ibid., pp. 422–27.

29. Ibid., pp. 447, 455.

30. Ibid., pp. 476–77.

31. William Lowndes to Elizabeth Lowndes, Dec. 16, 1811, William Lowndes Papers (SHC).

32. *Annals*, 12th Cong., 1st sess., p. 546.

33. Ibid., pp. 546–48, 565.

34. William Lowndes to Elizabeth Lowndes, Dec. 25, 1811, William Lowndes Papers (SHC).

Notes to Pages 83–95 : 283

35. Ravenel, *William Lowndes*, p. 87; Daniel Ravenel, "Memoranda," Oct. 8, 1860, Miscellaneous Papers (NYPL).
36. William Lowndes to Elizabeth Lowndes, Dec. 1, 1811, William Lowndes Papers (SHC).
37. *Annals*, 12th Cong., 1st sess., pp. 623–25.
38. Ibid., pp. 633–34.
39. *Charleston Courier*, Jan. 16, 1812.
40. *Annals*, 12th Cong., 1st sess., p. 648.
41. Ibid., pp. 649–50.
42. Ibid., p. 650.
43. Ibid., pp. 651–52.
44. Quoted in *Charleston Courier*, Jan. 16, 1812.
45. Watterson, *Letters*, pp. 96–98.
46. William Lowndes to Elizabeth Lowndes, Jan. 28, 1821, William Lowndes Papers (SHC); Ravenel, *William Lowndes*, p. 96.
47. *Annals*, 12th Cong., 1st sess., pp. 717–18, 800.
48. Ibid., pp. 803–14.
49. Ibid., pp. 823–33, 878–85.
50. Ibid., pp. 885–88.
51. Ibid., p. 889.
52. Ibid., pp. 909, 938–39, 999, 1002, 1005.
53. Samuel Dana to Timothy Pickering, Jan. 30, 1812, Timothy Pickering Papers (MHS).
54. John Randolph to James N. Garnett, Feb. 5, 1812, in Randolph-Garnett Correspondence 1806–32, John Randolph of Roanoke Papers (LC).
55. Quoted in *Charleston City Gazette*, Feb. 18, 1812, from the *Richmond Enquirer*.
56. This statement excludes his rising briefly to comment on a tax measure on Mar. 4, 1812. See *Annals*, 12th Cong., 1st sess., p. 1152.
57. Ibid., pp. 1080–1199, passim.
58. William Lowndes to Elizabeth Lowndes, Feb. 2, 1812, William Lowndes Papers (SHC).
59. Ibid., Feb. 24, 1812.
60. *Annals*, 12th Cong., 1st sess., pp. 1622–23.
61. Ibid., pp. 1280–81.
62. Ibid., pp. 1281–90.
63. Ibid., pp. 1299–1300.
64. Ibid., p. 1325.
65. William Lowndes to Elizabeth Lowndes, Apr. 23, [1812], William Lowndes Papers (SHC).
66. Ibid., Dec. 25, 1811; Apr. 29, 1812.

284 : Notes to Pages 95–103

67. Ibid., [month torn] 4, 1812.
68. Ibid., Jan. 2, 1812.
69. Ibid., May 10, 1812.
70. Ibid.
71. Ibid., Mar. 28, May 27, 1812.
72. Ravenel, *William Lowndes*, pp. 106–7.
73. Benton, *Thirty Years' View*, 1:18–19.
74. Item 106, William Lowndes Papers (LC).
75. Brant, *James Madison*, 5:478–83.
76. William Lowndes, "Historical Anecdotes and Observations," manuscript notebook in William Lowndes Papers (LC).
77. Wiltse, *Calhoun, Nationalist*, p. 66.
78. William Lowndes to Elizabeth Lowndes, June 28, 1812, William Lowndes Papers (SHC).
79. Ibid.
80. Ibid.

Chapter VI

1. William Lowndes to Elizabeth Lowndes, Mar. 1, 15, 1812, William Lowndes Papers (SHC).
2. *Charleston Courier*, July 7, 1812; *Charleston City Gazette*, July 8, 1812.
3. *Charleston City Gazette*, Sept. 3, 1812.
4. Wolfe, *Jeffersonian Democracy*, p. 255.
5. *Charleston City Gazette*, Oct. 6, 1812.
6. The *Charleston Courier* had reported on Oct. 26, 1812 that Cheves and Lowndes had nearly drowned crossing a flooded stream in North Carolina, but the paper corrected the erroneous report the next day.
7. The total for the parishes of St. Paul's, St. John's (Colleton), St. Bartholomew's, St. Andrew's, and Beaufort gave Lowndes 839 votes to Elliot's 154. See the *Charleston Courier* and *Charleston City Gazette*, Oct. 14 through Oct. 24, 1812.
8. *Charleston Courier*, Oct. 26, 1812.
9. Ravenel, *William Lowndes*, pp. 130–31.
10. Adams, *History*, vol. 2, *First Administration of James Madison*, pp. 376–77.
11. Smilie was in declining health and died on Dec. 30, 1812, *Annals*, 12th Cong., 2d sess., p. 480.
12. Ibid., p. 300.
13. Ibid., p. 199.
14. Ibid., p. 218–35.

15. Ibid., pp. 235–40. The quotation is found on p. 240.
16. Ibid., pp. 241–56.
17. Ibid., p. 299.
18. Ibid., p. 319.
19. Ibid., p. 339.
20. Ibid., pp. 339–41.
21. Ibid., pp. 365, 450–51.
22. Ibid., p. 404; William Lowndes to "My Dear Sir" [Thomas Pinckney], Dec. 23, 1812, William Lowndes Papers (LC).
23. *Annals*, 12th Cong., 2d sess., p. 678.
24. William Lowndes to "My Dear Sir" [Thomas Pinckney], Jan. 16, 1813, William Lowndes Papers (LC).
25. *Annals*, 12th Cong., 2d sess., pp. 843–44.
26. William Lowndes to "My Dear Sir" [Thomas Pinckney], Jan. 16, 1813, William Lowndes Papers (LC).
27. *Annals*, 12th Cong., 2d sess., pp. 893–94, 919–20.
28. Ibid., pp. 1099–1100.
29. Ibid., pp. 1122, 1157, 1164, 1170. Calhoun's bill failed in the Senate.
30. Kershaw and Lewis Account Book, pp. 1–7 (SCHS).
31. Plantation Account Book, entries for 1813, 1816, 1817, 1821, William Lowndes Papers (LC).
32. Wolfe, *Jeffersonian Democracy*, pp. 268–71; *Charleston City Gazette*, Apr. 5–16, 1813; Huff, *Langdon Cheves*, p. 75.
33. William Lowndes to Elizabeth Lowndes, Jan. 7, 1813, William Lowndes Papers (SHC).
34. Adams, *History*, vol. 1, *Second Administration of James Madison*, pp. 54–55.
35. Ibid., 1:55–57; William Lowndes to "My Dear Sir" [Thomas Pinckney], Jul. 17, 1813, William Lowndes Papers (LC).
36. William Lowndes to Elizabeth Lowndes, June 27, 1813, William Lowndes Papers (SHC).
37. See Lowndes's correspondence of June and July, 1813, in William Lowndes Papers (SHC) and William Lowndes Papers (LC). On July 26, the *Charleston Courier* reported a British squadron headed for the Carolina coast and on Aug. 25 reported two British brigs at anchor in Port Royal Sound.
38. William Lowndes to Elizabeth Lowndes, June 23, 1813, William Lowndes Papers (SHC).
39. Ibid., July 6, 1813.
40. Ibid., June 23, 1813.
41. Ibid., July 10, Aug. 1, 1813.

42. Plantation Account Book, William Lowndes Papers (LC).
43. "Elick" [sic] to Dear Master, Apr. 27, 1817, and William Lowndes to Elizabeth Lowndes, Sept. 27, Oct. 9, 23, 1814, William Lowndes Papers (SHC).
44. Kershaw and Lewis Account Book (SCHS), pp. 14–19.
45. Ibid.
46. *Annals*, 13th Cong., 2d sess., pp. 781–86.
47. *House Journal*, 13th Cong., 2d sess., pp. 1–31.
48. *Annals*, 13th Cong., 2d sess., pp. 824ff.; *Charleston Courier*, Jan. 7, 13, 1814; Wiltse, *Calhoun, Nationalist*, pp. 84–85.
49. *Charleston Courier*, Mar. 18, 1814; *Charleston City Gazette*, Mar. 10, 1814. The loan bill passed 97 to 55 on Mar. 3, 1814 and became law later that month. *House Journal*, 13th Cong., 2d sess., pp. 472, 481.
50. Timothy Pickering to Samuel Putnam, Feb. 7, 1814, Timothy Pickering Papers (MHS).
51. *New York Evening Post*, Mar. 9, 1814.
52. *House Journal*, 13th Cong., 2d sess., pp. 345, 395–400, 436–38; *Annals*, 13th Cong., 2d sess., pp. 1799–1803.
53. Ibid., pp. 845–47.
54. William Lowndes to Elizabeth Lowndes, Oct. 23, Dec. 11, 1814, William Lowndes Papers (SHC).
55. Ibid., Dec. 4, 1814.
56. Ibid., Oct. 5, 1814.
57. See the *Charleston Courier* and *Charleston City Gazette*, Aug. and Sept., 1814.
58. *Charleston Courier*, Sept. 1, 6, 23, 1814.
59. William Lowndes to Elizabeth Lowndes, Sept. 25, 1814, William Lowndes Papers (SHC).
60. *Annals*, 13th Cong., 3d sess., pp. 403–6.
61. Ibid., p. 560ff. Calhoun's plan is outlined on pp. 587–89.
62. Ibid., pp. 618–22, 651–73, 685–86.
63. William Lowndes to Elizabeth Lowndes, Nov. 6, 1814, William Lowndes Papers (SHC).
64. *Annals*, 13th Cong., 3d sess., pp. 1025–26, 1031–44, 1167. The vote on the first postponement was 74 to 75, Lowndes voting for and Calhoun against.
65. William Lowndes to Elizabeth Lowndes, Feb. 17, 1815, William Lowndes Papers (SHC).
66. Ibid., Feb. 26, 1815.

Chapter VII

1. Huff, *Langdon Cheves*, p. 82.
2. Ibid., p. 86.
3. Ibid., pp. 88–95.
4. U.S. Congress, *Biographical Directory*, p. 1327.
5. Freehling, *Prelude to Civil War*, pp. 97–103.
6. William Lowndes to Elizabeth Lowndes, Jan. 22, 1815, William Lowndes Papers (SHC).
7. Kershaw and Lewis Account Book, pp. 22–26 (SCHS).
8. William Lowndes to Elizabeth Lowndes, Mar. 13, Nov. 6, 13, 30, 1812, William Lowndes Papers (SHC).
9. Ibid., Nov. 6, 13, 30, Dec. 4, 11, 1814.
10. Ibid., Nov. 30, 1814.
11. Kershaw and Lewis Account Book, pp. 22–26 (SCHS).
12. *Washington Daily National Intelligencer*, Oct. 26, 1815.
13. John Taylor to "My Dear Sir," Mar. 5, 1815, Taylor Papers (SCL).
14. *Annals*, 14th Cong., 1st sess., p. 1261.
15. Watterson, *Letters*, p. 96.
16. Ibid., pp. 96–98.
17. Ibid., p. 98.
18. Dangerfield, *American Nationalism*, p. 8; Hofstadter, *Idea of a Party System*, pp. 187–88.
19. Richardson, *Messages*, 1:552.
20. Stanwood, *Tariff Controversies*, 1:139; *Annals*, 14th Cong., 1st sess., p. 376.
21. For voting patterns of the committee members, see *Annals*, 14th Cong., 1st sess., pp. 680–82, 692–94, 738–39, 743–44, 746, 1313, 1315, 1352.
22. Ibid., p. 518.
23. Preyer, "Tariff of 1816," pp. 306–7; Freehling, *Prelude to Civil War*, p. 95; Stanwood, *Tariff Controversies*, 1:154–59.
24. *ASPF*, 3:85.
25. Walters, *Dallas*, p. 208. Lowndes considered the data adequate to establish evidence of need for specific duties.
26. *ASPF*, 3:85–95. Quotation is from p. 90.
27. *Annals*, 16th Cong., 1st sess., p. 2127.
28. *ASPF*, 3:90.
29. Ibid., 3:92–95.
30. Ibid., 3:32–35, 52–54 (cottons); 3:104–7 (woolens); quotation, p. 106.
31. *Niles' Weekly Register*, Mar. 23, 1816.

32. Walters, *Dallas*, p. 208.
33. *Washington Daily National Intelligencer*, Jan. 13, 1816.
34. *Annals*, 14th Cong., 1st sess., p. 517.
35. Ibid.
36. Ibid.
37. Ibid., pp. 517–18; *ASPF*, 3:90–91.
38. *Annals*, 14th Cong., 1st sess., pp. 520–22.
39. Ibid., p. 675.
40. Ibid., pp. 676–77.
41. Ibid., pp. 681, 684.
42. Ibid., pp. 685, 687–88.
43. Ravenel, *William Lowndes*, p. 153.
44. *Annals*, 14th Cong., 1st sess., pp. 694, 720–30, 733–43, 746, 1795–96.
45. Ibid., pp. 723, 776.
46. Ibid., pp. 720–23.
47. Ibid., pp. 723–28, 746–57.
48. Ibid., pp. 764, 767.
49. Ibid., pp. 791–92.
50. Ibid., pp. 792–802, 804–17.
51. Calhoun, *Papers*, 1:330n.
52. Calhoun's entire speech is found in *Annals*, 14th Cong., 1st sess., pp. 829–40.
53. *Washington Daily National Intelligencer*, Feb. 1, 1816.
54. *Annals*, 14th Cong., 1st sess., pp. 840–41, 845.
55. Ibid., p. 862.
56. Ibid., p. 939.
57. Ibid., p. 1234.
58. Ibid., p. 1237.
59. Ibid.
60. Ibid., pp. 1245–46.
61. Ibid.
62. Ibid., pp. 1247–48.
63. Ibid., p. 1270.
64. Ibid.
65. Ibid., pp. 1271–73.
66. Ibid., pp. 1288–89, 1312–13, 1315–16.
67. Ibid., pp. 1327–29.
68. Ibid., pp. 1268, 1270, 1275, 1283.
69. Ibid., p. 1329.
70. Stanwood, *Tariff Controversies*, 1:140–41; Taussig, *Tariff*, pp. 76–77.
71. *Annals*, 14th Cong., 1st sess., pp. 1327–28.

72. Ibid., pp. 1328–29, 1352.
73. Ibid., pp. 1262–63, 1313.
74. Ibid., p. 1352.
75. Preyer, "Tariff of 1816," pp. 306–7; Freehling, *Prelude to Civil War*, p. 95.
76. Preyer, "Tariff of 1816," pp. 306–22.
77. *Washington Daily National Intelligencer*, Apr. 30, 1816.
78. *Annals*, 14th Cong., 1st sess., pp. 234–35, 1060–1219, passim.
79. *Washington Daily National Intelligencer*, Mar. 12, 14, 18, 1816; *Charleston Courier*, Mar. 19, 21, 1816.
80. *Annals*, 14th Cong., 1st sess., p. 1188.

Chapter VIII

1. Kershaw and Lewis Account Book, pp. 22–34 (SCHS).
2. See Stommel and Stommel, *Year without a Summer*.
3. *Charleston Courier*, July 31, Aug. 1, Sept. 9, 1816.
4. Ibid., Sept. 9, 17, 19, 23, 26, 30, 1816.
5. Ibid., Sept. 10, 17, 1816.
6. Ibid., Sept. 9, 1816.
7. Ibid., Sept. 17–30, 1816.
8. Ibid., Sept. 5–10, 1816; Kershaw and Lewis Account Book, p. 37 (SCHS).
9. Freehling, *Prelude to Civil War*, p. 39.
10. Freehling based his analysis of lowcountry prosperity on rising prices without including statistical information on diminished production available in Gray, *History of Agriculture*, 2:1030–31. I have adopted Gray's method of considering October 1 the beginning of each crop year, September 30 the end.
11. *Charleston Courier*, Sept. 5–10, 1816; Kershaw and Lewis Account Book, p. 37 (SCHS).
12. Miscellaneous Records, MMMM, pp. 77, 96, 100, 109, 115, 123–25 (SCA).
13. Ibid., pp. 42, 44–45, 93.
14. *Annals*, 14th Cong., 2d sess., p. 235.
15. *Charleston Courier*, July 9, Aug. 29, 1816.
16. Ibid., Sept. 16, Oct. 28, 31, 1816; *Charleston City Gazette*, Oct. 28, 1816.
17. Adams, *History*, vol. 3, *Second Administration of James Madison*, p. 144.
18. *Annals*, 14th Cong., 2d sess., p. 235.
19. Ibid., p. 576.
20. Richardson, *Messages*, 1:563.

21. *Annals*, 14th Cong., 2d sess., pp. 478–81, 1323.
22. *Washington Daily National Intelligencer*, Feb. 15, 1817.
23. *Annals*, 14th Cong., 2d sess., p. 963.
24. Ibid., p. 970.
25. Ibid., pp. 986, 990, 995, 1015, 1020.
26. Richardson, *Messages*, 1:569.
27. *Annals*, 14th Cong., 1st sess., p. 934.
28. Ibid., 2d sess., p. 715.
29. Ibid., pp. 1308–10.
30. Ibid., p. 732.
31. Ibid., pp. 735, 747.
32. *Washington Daily National Intelligencer*, Mar. 5, 1817.
33. Ibid.
34. *Charleston Courier*, Aug. 2, 9, 1817.
35. See *Charleston Courier* and *Charleston City Gazette*, Aug.–Nov., 1817.
36. Mills, *Statistics of South Carolina*, pp. 450–51.
37. Gray, *History of Agriculture*, 2:1030–31.
38. Kershaw and Lewis Account Book, pp. 40, 42 (SCHS).
39. Ibid., pp. 22, 24, 26, 27, 29, 38.
40. William Lowndes, "Historical Anecdotes and Observations," manuscript notebook in William Lowndes Papers (LC).
41. Ibid.
42. James Madison to William Lowndes, Oct. 16, 1816, in Madison, *Letters and Other Writings*, 3:29–30; extract of Andrew R. Govan letter, July 19, 1816, William Lowndes Papers (SHC); *Washington Daily National Intelligencer*, Mar. 6, 1817.
43. Adams, *Memoirs*, 4:72, 77; 5:333–34; William Lowndes to Elizabeth Lowndes, Mar. 24, 1822, William Lowndes Papers (SHC).
44. Watterson, *Letters*, pp. 96–98.
45. Adams, *Memoirs*, 5:16–17.
46. Hofstadter, *Idea of a Party System*, pp. 188–200; Young, *Washington Community*, pp. 126–27, 137–42; Barnwell, *Love of Order*, pp. 25–30.
47. *Annals*, 15th Cong., 1st sess., pp. 417, 423–24.
48. Ibid., pp. 1116–28, 1151–64.
49. Ibid., pp. 1135–36, 1164–69.
50. Lowndes's speech is found in ibid., pp. 1235–49. See also ibid., pp. 1135–36.
51. Ibid., p. 1319.
52. Ibid., p. 1365.
53. Ibid., pp. 1380–89.
54. Ibid.

55. Kohn, *Internal Improvements*, pp. 97–98, 124, 141–42, 166, 229, 258, 261, 267, 276.
56. *Annals*, 15th Cong., 1st sess., p. 1403.
57. Ibid., p. 1407.
58. Ibid., p. 1412.
59. Ibid., pp. 1412–18, 1429.
60. The *Washington Daily National Intelligencer*, Mar. 26, 1818, noted that such a move from Clay had long been expected, but expressed surprise at the particular method chosen. Clay's speeches and incidental remarks throughout the debate on this question are reported in full with editorial comment in Clay, *Papers*, 2:512–62.
61. See speech of William Lowndes dated Mar. 18, 1818, William Lowndes Papers (SHC).
62. *Annals*, 15th Cong., 1st sess., pp. 1605–8.

Chapter IX

1. Calhoun, *Papers*, 2:39–40.
2. Richardson, *Messages*, 1:611–12.
3. Kershaw and Lewis Account Book, pp. 36–42 (SCHS).
4. *Charleston Courier*, July 30, Aug. 25, 1818; Gray, *History of Agriculture*, 2:1030–31.
5. Kershaw and Lewis Account Book, p. 46 (SCHS).
6. *Charleston Courier*, July 30, Aug. 25, 1818.
7. *Annals*, 15th Cong., 2d sess., p. 314.
8. Ibid., p. 583.
9. Ibid., p. 588.
10. Ibid., p. 655; Van Deusen, *Life of Henry Clay*, pp. 125–26.
11. *Annals*, 15th Cong., 2d sess., p. 703.
12. Ibid., pp. 913–21.
13. Ibid.
14. Ibid., pp. 1135–36.
15. Risjord, *Old Republicans*, pp. 188–91.
16. See below, Chapter 11, n. 3.
17. Timberlake, *Origins of Central Banking*, pp. 17–25.
18. Ibid.
19. Ibid.
20. *Annals*, 15th Cong., 2d sess., pp. 317–18, 328–29.
21. Risjord, *Old Republicans*, p. 205, maintains that Tyler, though anti-Bank in sentiment, was determined to be fair.
22. The committee report with accompanying documents is found in *ASPF*, 3:306–91.
23. Ibid., 3:306.

24. Catterall, *Second Bank*, pp. 59–60.
25. *Annals*, 15th Cong., 2d sess., pp. 572–73.
26. Catterall, *Second Bank*, pp. 58–59.
27. *Annals*, 15th Cong., 2d sess., p. 598.
28. Hammond, *Banks and Politics*, p. 263.
29. *Annals*, 15th Cong., 2d sess., pp. 1242–50.
30. Ibid., pp. 1253, 1271.
31. Munroe, *McLane*, pp. 85–90.
32. Watterson, *Letters*, pp. 100–101.
33. Lowndes's speech is taken from *Annals*, 15th Cong., 2d sess., pp. 1283–1309, delivered on Feb. 20, 1819.
34. Ibid.
35. Catterall, *Second Bank*, p. 60.
36. Adams, *Memoirs*, 4:346.
37. Risjord, *Old Republicans*, p. 207.
38. *ASPF*, 3:508.
39. Catterall, *Second Bank*, pp. 60–82.
40. William Lowndes to Langdon Cheves, Nov. 28, 1819, Langdon Cheves Papers (SCHS).
41. Hammond, *Banks and Politics*, p. 259.
42. Kershaw and Lewis Account Book, pp. 50–70 (SCHS).
43. For a discussion of deference in a much broader political context, see Formisano, "Deferential-Participant Politics," pp. 473–87. Throughout Lowndes's correspondence touching on his business affairs, the concerns he expressed were always about debt, never about credit. The availability of credit was assumed.
44. *Annals*, 15th Cong., 2d sess., p. 1170.
45. Moore, *Missouri Controversy*, p. 50.

Chapter X

1. William Lowndes to Elizabeth Lowndes, March 30, 1819, William Lowndes Papers (LC); "Journal and Notes of William Lowndes, 1819," unpaged notebook in ibid. Ravenel, *William Lowndes*, pp. 183–87, quotes extensively from this notebook in her detailed account of Lowndes's European tour. The St. Julien Ravenel Childs Collection (SCHS) contains several drawings and diagrams of machinery, bridges, etc., that Lowndes sketched while in Europe.
2. Wiecek, *Antislavery Constitutionalism*, pp. 106–10.
3. Ibid.; on the tendency to reason backward from result to cause, see Wood, "Conspiracy and the Paranoid Style," pp. 403–7, 429–41, and Davis, *Slave Power Conspiracy*, pp. 3–31.
4. Wiecek, *Antislavery Constitutionalism*, pp. 108–10.

5. Representatives of the free-state North and Delaware voted 88 to 10 for restriction and 81 to 18 for protection, *Annals*, 16th Cong., 1st sess., pp. 1572–73, 2155–56.

6. Pocock, *Machiavellian Moment*, p. ix, defines the crisis of republicanism in general terms, without reference to these circumstances.

7. The reelection of Lowndes without opposition had become routine.

8. *Annals*, 16th Cong., 1st sess., pp. 704, 707, 710.

9. Young, *Washington Community*, pp. 131–35.

10. James Tallmadge, Jr., to John W. Taylor, Jan. 11, Mar. 2, Dec. 4, 1820, John W. Taylor Papers (NYHS). George Dangerfield, *American Nationalism*, pp. 108–9, described Taylor as "a politician through and through, and who believed that a stand on slavery would increase his political influence."

11. John W. Taylor to Jane Taylor, Dec. 12, 1822, John W. Taylor Papers (NYHS).

12. William Lowndes to Elizabeth Lowndes, Nov. 17, 1820, William Lowndes Papers (LC).

13. *Annals*, 16th Cong., 1st sess., pp. 711, 732.

14. Ibid., pp. 732, 734–35.

15. Ibid., pp. 735–36.

16. Ibid., p. 1481; Moore, *Missouri Controversy*, pp. 86, 122–23.

17. *Annals*, 16th Cong., 1st sess., pp. 801–4.

18. Ibid., pp. 831–32.

19. John Walker to Charles Tait, Feb. 11, 1820, Charles Tait Papers (AA).

20. Moore, *Missouri Controversy*, pp. 87–89.

21. *Annals*, 16th Cong., 1st sess., pp. 937–38, 940.

22. Ibid., p. 947.

23. Brown, *Missouri Compromises*, p. 14 and note.

24. Wiecek, *Antislavery Constitutionalism*, pp. 112–22.

25. Ibid.

26. Moore, *Missouri Controversy*, p. 41.

27. *Annals*, 16th Cong., 1st sess., pp. 1170, 1405; *Niles' Weekly Register*, Aug. 26, 1820.

28. Brown, *Missouri Compromises*, p. 12.

29. *Annals*, 16th Cong., 1st sess., pp. 1415–16.

30. Ibid., p. 1470.

31. Ibid., pp. 1111, 1481.

32. Ibid., p. 1470.

33. Ibid., pp. 1526–28.

34. Ibid., pp. 1503–5.

35. "Congressional Portraits drawn by a Member of Congress," *Charleston City Gazette*, Mar. 10, 1820.

294 : Notes to Pages 194–205

36. Kaplanoff, "Charles Pinckney," pp. 85–90.
37. Ibid.; see *Annals*, 16th Cong., 1st sess., pp. 1310–29 for Pinckney's speech as quoted here.
38. Pinckney's reference to the South Carolina system of representation is found on p. 1315, ibid.
39. Ibid., pp. 1405–6.
40. Ibid., pp. 1405–9.
41. Ibid., pp. 1409–10, 1455–57.
42. Ibid., p. 1491.
43. Ibid., pp. 1539–40; Moore, *Missouri Controversy*, p. 92.
44. *Annals*, 16th Cong., 1st sess., pp. 1553–55.
45. Ibid., pp. 1572–73.
46. Moore, *Missouri Controversy*, p. 101.
47. *Annals*, 16th Cong., 1st sess., p. 1577.
48. Ibid.
49. Ibid., p. 1578.
50. Ibid., p. 1586.
51. Ammon, *Monroe*, pp. 457–58.
52. *Annals*, 16th Cong., 1st sess., pp. 1565–66.
53. Ibid.

Chapter XI

1. Bemis, *Adams*, pp. 315–40.
2. Richardson, *Messages*, 1:625.
3. *Annals*, 16th Cong., 1st sess., pp. 1618–20.
4. Adams, *Memoirs*, 5:16–17.
5. *Annals*, 16th Cong., 1st sess., p. 1688.
6. Ibid., pp. 1719–31.
7. Ibid., pp. 1731–38, 1743.
8. Ibid., p. 1756.
9. Preyer, "Tariff of 1816," pp. 306–7.
10. Pincus, *Antebellum Tariffs*, pp. 51–52.
11. Lebergott, *Americans, an Economic Record*, p. 130.
12. The market price of a yard of India cottons was usually "not more than ten cents," *Annals*, 16th Cong., 1st sess., p. 2006; Lebergott, *Americans, an Economic Record*, p. 157, gives the average price of comparable Lowell cottons also as ten cents a yard.
13. Lebergott, *Americans, an Economic Record*, table 12.3, p. 131; *Annals*, 16th Cong., 1st sess., p. 2131.
14. U.S. Bureau of the Census, *Historical Statistics*, p. 538. The figures stated above exclude reexports.

15. Pincus, *Antebellum Tariffs*, pp. 53–56.
16. *Annals*, 16th Cong., 1st sess., p. 2002.
17. Pincus, *Antebellum Tariffs*, pp. 56–62. Pincus found that industries well established by the War of 1812 such as textiles were "relatively well protected" by the Tariff of 1816, ibid., p. 39; *ASPF*, 3:440–44, 452–58, 460–63.
18. Ibid., 3:440–41.
19. Ibid., 3:443, 444, 453, 456, 458.
20. Pincus, *Antebellum Tariffs*, pp. 51–52.
21. *Annals*, 16th Cong., 1st sess., pp. 1663–69.
22. Richardson, *Messages*, 1:630.
23. *ASPF*, 3:426.
24. Ibid., 3:447–48, 463–68.
25. Ibid., 3:447–48.
26. Morris, *Free Men All*, pp. 18–22, 42. Cotton dominated southern exports, followed by tobacco and rice. Louisiana sugar, Kentucky hemp, and naval stores, all produced for the domestic market, enjoyed protective duties and thus provide exceptions to generalizations on traditional republicanism for the South as discussed here.
27. U.S. Bureau of the Census, *Historical Statistics*, p. 547. When the domestic supply of raw cotton exceeded domestic demand, forcing sale of the surplus on an unprotected world market, the price of cotton passed beyond the remedy of protective duties, for buyers would pay no more than the surplus could command. Lowndes maintained this point as "notorious fact" in 1820 (*Annals*, 16th Cong., 1st sess., pp. 2122–23), which Pincus (*Antebellum Tariffs*, p. 45) concedes thus: " 'protection' of raw cotton now [1820] was no longer significant."
28. Lebergott, *Americans, an Economic Record*, pp. 139–61, argues that the three-cent tariff on raw cotton, which never varied throughout the period discussed, had a significant impact on the cost of producing cotton cloth and thread in the United States. Unfortunately, the profuse documentation supporting his argument contains no demonstration or firm evidence on how this would be possible, given the massive cotton surplus.
29. *Annals*, 16th Cong., 1st sess., p. 2118.
30. For Baldwin's discussion of these advantages, see *Annals*, 16th Cong., 1st sess., pp. 1987–97.
31. *ASPF*, 3:463–68.
32. Ibid., 3:468–69.
33. William Lowndes to Langdon Cheves, Mar. 3, 1820, Langdon Cheves Papers (SCHS).
34. *Annals*, 16th Cong., 1st sess., pp. 1838–45.

35. Ibid., pp. 705–7.
36. Ibid., p. 1917.
37. Ibid., p. 1943.
38. Ibid., pp. 1921, 1922–23, 1929. Tables in ibid., pp. 1913–16 compare the 1816 rates with Baldwin's. For those of Dallas, see *ASPF*, 3:91–95.
39. *Annals*, 16th Cong., 1st sess., pp. 1914–46.
40. Ibid., p. 1921.
41. Ibid., pp. 1921, 1923, 1935.
42. Ibid., pp. 1917–18.
43. Ibid., pp. 1923–27.
44. Ibid., pp. 1933–34.
45. Ibid., pp. 1939–40.
46. Ibid., p. 1940.
47. Ibid., pp. 2155–56 and comment on vote distribution, Chapter 12, n. 35.
48. William Lowndes to Timothy Pickering, Apr. 14 and May 12, 1820, Timothy Pickering Papers (MHS); William Lowndes to Langdon Cheves, Apr. 19, 1820, Langdon Cheves Papers (SCHS).

Chapter XII

1. *Annals*, 16th Cong., 1st sess., p. 1846.
2. Ibid., pp. 1848–49.
3. Details of Lowndes's remarks were not reported here but have been reconstructed from selected parts of his later speech in ibid., pp. 2131–32. North, *Economic Growth*, pp. 185–86 has confirmed the greater decline of agricultural prices, especially for cotton.
4. *Annals*, 16th Cong., 1st sess., pp. 2127, 2131.
5. Ibid., p. 1917.
6. Ibid., p. 1933.
7. Ibid., p. 1953.
8. Ibid., pp. 1861–62.
9. Ibid., pp. 2126–27.
10. Ibid., p. 1943. On the correctness of Lowndes's position without specific reference to Lowndes, see Pincus, *Antebellum Tariffs*, p. 49.
11. *Annals*, 16th Cong., 1st sess., pp. 1861–62.
12. Ibid., p. 2126.
13. Ibid., p. 1946.
14. Ibid.
15. Ibid., pp. 1946–50.
16. Ibid., pp. 1952–63.

17. Ibid., pp. 1963–68, 2005.
18. See ibid., pp. 1663–69 for the tariff bill, pp. 1968–87 for the bill to abolish credits, and pp. 2173–74 for the bill on sales at auction.
19. Ibid., pp. 1987–97.
20. Ibid., pp. 1998–2008.
21. Ibid., pp. 2054–80.
22. Ibid., pp. 2034–51.
23. Ibid., pp. 2093–2115.
24. Stanwood, *Tariff Controversies*, 1:190–91, while paying this compliment to Lowndes, chose Tyler instead to represent the southern point of view, devoting four pages to Tyler's speech (pp. 185–88) and one paragraph to that of Lowndes (pp. 190–91).
25. *Annals*, 16th Cong., 1st sess., pp. 2115–16, 2125.
26. Ibid., pp. 2125–26.
27. Ibid., p. 2126.
28. Ibid., pp. 2131–32.
29. Ibid., pp. 2116–17.
30. Ibid., pp. 2117–18.
31. Ibid., pp. 2132–33.
32. Ibid., pp. 2122–23.
33. Ibid., p. 2118.
34. Ibid., p. 2128.
35. Ibid., pp. 2155–56. Representatives from the free-state North and Delaware voted 81 to 18 for passage; outside of New England, which voted 18 to 17 for passage, the only negative vote came from David Fullerton of Greencastle, Pennsylvania. Alabama, Mississippi, and the South Atlantic seaboard voted 51 to 5 against the bill as did the western South also, 9 to 4. The total number of votes for passage given here was compiled from the roll call, which lists one name less (90) than the reporter stated (91). This discrepancy does not appear to be related to another apparent error in which the reporter attributed votes probably cast by Francis Johnson of Kentucky in February and March to James Johnson of Virginia, who resigned his seat on February 1, 1820. See *Annals*, 16th Cong., 1st sess., pp. 1555–56, 1572–73, 1586–88, 2155–56; U.S. Congress, *Biographical Directory*, pp. 1126–27.
36. *Annals*, 16th Cong., 1st sess., pp. 2193–94.
37. Ibid., pp. 2171–72.
38. Ibid., pp. 2173–85, 2193–2202.
39. This trend may be attributed largely to William Freehling, *Prelude to Civil War*, whose interpretation has been reiterated in scholarly works ranging from Gavin Wright's specialized study of the southern economy, *The Cotton South*, pp. 130–31, to George Fredrickson's discussion of

the nullification crisis in a recently published college textbook, Divine et al., *America, Past and Present*, 1:285. In an even more recent essay, Kenneth Greenberg, *Masters and Statesmen*, ignores the tariff issue entirely in his preoccupation with the influence of slavery on this era of South Carolina history.

40. Howe, *Political Culture of the American Whigs*, pp. 1–8; Brown, *Politics and Statesmanship*, pp. 13–14, makes essentially the same argument.

41. Pocock, *Machiavellian Moment*, pp. 67–76; Weir, " 'Harmony,' " pp. 473–501; Brown, *Politics and Statesmanship*, pp. 3–5.

42. Pocock, *Machiavellian Moment*, p. 71; Wiebe, *Opening of American Society*, pp. 10–16, 22–24, 38–41; Publius [James Madison], No. 10, Cooke, *Federalist*, pp. 56–65. Two points of Madison's argument might be noted here. Although he referred to majority rule as "the republican principle," he added that "when a majority is included in a faction, the form of popular government [democracy] enables it to sacrifice to its ruling passion or interest both the public good and the rights of other citizens." Further: "[A] body of men are unfit to be both judges and parties at the same time; yet what are many of the most important acts of legislation but so many judicial determinations, not indeed concerning the rights of single persons, but concerning the rights of large bodies of citizens?" The illustration he selected was especially pertinent to the tariff issue:

> Shall domestic manufacturers be encouraged, and in what degree, by restrictions on foreign manufacturers? are questions which would be differently decided by the landed and the manufacturing classes, and probably by neither with a sole regard to justice and the public good. The apportionment of taxes on the various descriptions of property is an act which seems to require the most exact impartiality; yet there is, perhaps, no legislative act in which greater opportunity and temptation are given to a predominant party to trample on the rules of justice. Every shilling with which they overburden the inferior number is a shilling saved to their own pockets.

Ibid., pp. 59–61.

43. Wood, *Creation of the American Republic*, pp. 47–73, 97–103.

44. Publius [James Madison], No. 10, Cooke, *Federalist*, pp. 56–65.

45. For use of the term "democratic despotism" in discussing this era, see Wiebe, *Opening of American Society*, p. 12.

46. Ibid., pp. 113–16.

47. This was a persistent theme of Republican rhetoric throughout the first session of the Fourteenth Congress.

48. Hofstadter, *Idea of a Party System*, pp. 182–200; Young, *Washington Community*, pp. 107, 126–27.
49. Appleby, "Republicanism in Old and New Contexts," pp. 24–26.
50. Ibid.
51. Lowndes had defended the minimum principle when it came under attack in 1816, *Annals*, 14th Cong., 1st sess., p. 1237.
52. Ibid., 16th Cong., 1st sess., pp. 2250–51.
53. William Lowndes to Elizabeth Lowndes, Nov. 14, 1820, William Lowndes Papers (LC).

Chapter XIII

1. William Lowndes to "My Dear Sir" [Thomas Pinckney], Dec. 11, 1819, William Lowndes Papers (LC).
2. Kershaw and Lewis Account Book (SCHS), pp. 40–50.
3. Ibid., pp. 27, 29, 38, 43, 49–54.
4. William Lowndes to "My Dear Sir" [Thomas Pinckney], Dec. 11, 1819, William Lowndes Papers (LC).
5. Kershaw and Lewis Account Book, pp. 44, 50 (SCHS).
6. William Lowndes to Timothy Pickering, Apr. 14, May 12, 1820, Timothy Pickering Papers (MHS); Adams, *Memoirs*, 5:121–22.
7. Moore, *Missouri Controversy*, pp. 328–30.
8. *Niles' Weekly Register*, June 3, 10, 1820.
9. Ibid., June 3, 1820.
10. Moore, *Missouri Controversy*, pp. 328–31.
11. Wallace, *Rockdale*, pp. 422–24, explains how northern textile mill owners used southern opposition to tariff protection to promote better labor relations with mill employees, branding the slaveholding South the "scapegoat."
12. *ASPF*, 3:563–67.
13. Ibid., 3:577–78.
14. *Charleston City Gazette*, July 13, 1820. Hezekiah Niles said in April that the Missouri question "is settled, unless some fresh cause is started to revive it, with ten-fold animosities," *Niles' Weekly Register*, April 15, 1820.
15. *Charleston City Gazette*, Feb. 12, 1821. The editor concluded, "[W]e fully accord in opinion, with . . . Mr. Lowndes, who seems to us to have taken the same view from the commencement."
16. Adams, *Memoirs*, 5:201–2; John W. Taylor to Samuel DeForest, Dec. 27, 1820, John W. Taylor Papers (NYHS).
17. Extract of a letter to the editor of the *Baltimore Patriot*, quoted in *Charleston City Gazette*, Nov. 28, 1820; John C. Calhoun to William Lowndes, Oct. 12, 1820, William Lowndes Papers (SHC).

18. *Charleston City Gazette,* Nov. 28, 1820.
19. Ibid., Nov. 21, 1820.
20. Adams, *Memoirs,* 5:201–2.
21. *Charleston City Gazette,* Nov. 28, 1820.
22. Ibid.
23. William Lowndes to Elizabeth Lowndes, Nov. 14, 1820, William Lowndes Papers (LC).
24. *Charleston City Gazette,* Nov. 28, 1820.
25. William Lowndes to Elizabeth Lowndes, Nov. 17, 1820, William Lowndes Papers (SHC).
26. John W. Walker to Charles Tait, Dec. 20, 1819, Charles Tait Papers (AA). See also Adams, *Memoirs,* 4:528–29, and Ammon, *Monroe,* pp. 454–55.
27. William H. Crawford to Charles Tait, June 3, 1822, Charles Tait Papers (AA).
28. Salma Hale to John W. Taylor, Nov. 28, 1820, John W. Taylor Papers (NYHS). Hale added, "I trust it is now in the hands of those who will use it with equal moderation and equal wisdom, to those from whom they receive it."
29. William Lowndes to Elizabeth Lowndes, Nov. 27, 1820, William Lowndes Papers (LC).
30. Ammon, *Monroe,* pp. 454–55.
31. Ibid.; Moore, *Missouri Controversy,* pp. 16–18, 65–83.
32. Henry Meigs and Henry Storrs alone of the New York delegation voted against the Taylor amendment (*Annals,* 16th Cong., 1st sess., p. 1565), and they were among the Bucktails who voted against Taylor's election through twenty-one ballots, John W. Taylor to Samuel DeForest, Dec. 27, 1820, John W. Taylor Papers (NYHS).
33. Thomas Cobb to Charles Tait, Jan. 30, 1820, Charles Tait Papers (AA).
34. John W. Taylor to Samuel DeForest, Dec. 27, 1820, John W. Taylor Papers (NYHS). Taylor said his New York opponents included Henry Meigs, Caleb Tompkins, and Henry Storrs.
35. John W. Taylor to Jane Taylor, Nov. 8, 1820, John W. Taylor Papers (NYHS).
36. John W. Taylor to Samuel DeForest, Dec. 27, 1820, John W. Taylor Papers (NYHS).
37. Ibid.
38. Wallace, "Changing Concepts of Party," pp. 456–71, 475–79, 484–86; Remini, *Martin Van Buren,* pp. 7–11; McCormick, *Second American Party System,* pp. 3–17, 111–13.
39. Moore, *Missouri Controversy,* p. 141.
40. Adams, *Memoirs,* 5:203. Taylor's impartiality as Speaker was a

secondary factor in his loss of the speakership in 1821, John W. Taylor to Richard Taylor, Dec. 12, 1821, John W. Taylor Papers (NYHS).

41. Moore, *Missouri Controversy*, p. 146.
42. *Annals*, 16th Cong., 2d sess., pp. 453–55.
43. Ibid.
44. Ibid., p. 508. For the entire speech, see ibid., 508–16; Benton, *Thirty Years' View*, 1:18–19.
45. Brown, *Missouri Compromises*, p. 22.
46. *Annals*, 16th Cong., 2d sess., p. 41.
47. Ibid., pp. 518, 520, 531.
48. Brown, *Missouri Compromises*, pp. 22–23.
49. Ibid., pp. 23–24.
50. *Annals*, 16th Cong., 2d sess., p. 670.
51. Brown, *Missouri Compromises*, p. 24.
52. Ibid.
53. John W. Taylor to Jane Taylor, Dec. 29, 1820, John W. Taylor Papers (NYHS); William Lowndes to Elizabeth Lowndes, Jan. 14, 1821, William Lowndes Papers (LC).
54. William Lowndes to Elizabeth Lowndes, Dec. 7, 1818, William Lowndes Papers (SHC).
55. U.S. Congress, *Biographical Directory*, p. 93.
56. *ASPF*, 3:594–645. John Taylor of Caroline wrote a rebuttal to Baldwin's report, which Taylor titled "Tyranny Unmasked." Published in 1822, Taylor's essay elaborated on the traditional republican assumptions he had written on for decades. Shalhope, *Taylor*, pp. 204ff.
57. *ASPF*, 3:650–60, quotation on p. 660.
58. Brown, *Missouri Compromises*, pp. 24–27.
59. Nathaniel Macon to Charles Tait, Jan. 7, 1821, Charles Tait Papers (AA).
60. Brown, *Missouri Compromises*, pp. 30–31.
61. Eaton, *Clay and the Art of American Politics*, pp. 92–94.
62. In addition to those of Adams, Benton, and Watterson already cited, one of the more insightful comments came from "a Member of Congress from Pennsylvania," quoted in the *Charleston City Gazette*, Mar. 10, 1820: "Mr. Lowndes is undoubtedly the most influential member of the House of Representatives. His eloquence is neither showy nor graceful; but his mildness and candor, superadded to the useful information which he brings into the discussion of every important topic, win upon the confidence of the House, and give great weight to his opinions which can never be acquired by declamatory vehemence or pointed sarcasm." See also *Niles' Weekly Register*, Aug. 26, 1820.
63. *Charleston Southern Patriot and Commercial Advertiser*, Jan. 15, 16, Feb. 3, 1821.

64. *Annals*, 16th Cong., 2d sess., p. 983.

65. Other members were William Eustis of Massachusetts, William Ford of New York, John Campbell of Ohio, William Archer of Virginia, Samuel Moore of Pennsylvania, Thomas W. Cobb of Georgia, Gideon Tomlinson of Connecticut, Josiah Butler of New Hampshire, and Aaron Hackley of New York, ibid., p. 1027.

66. After the report was read and tabled, a member referred to Lowndes's absence, ibid., p. 1081.

67. William Lowndes to Elizabeth Lowndes, Feb. 13, 1821, Lowndes Papers (SHC); Adams, *Memoirs*, 5:307.

68. Adams, *Memoirs*, 5:307; William Lowndes to Elizabeth Lowndes, Feb. 15, 16, 19, 20, 22, 23, 24, 27, 29, 1821, William Lowndes Papers (SHC).

69. William Lowndes to Elizabeth Lowndes, Feb. 27, 1822, William Lowndes Papers (SHC).

70. Adams, *Memoirs*, 5:307.

Chapter XIV

1. R[uth] L[owndes] to "My Dear Brother," undated, William Lowndes Papers (SHC). Internal evidence places this letter in the spring of 1822.

2. William Lowndes to Elizabeth Lowndes, Nov. 24, 30, 1820, William Lowndes Papers (SHC); William Lowndes to Rawlins Lowndes, Dec. 1, 1820, ibid.

3. The quoted phrase is Freehling's, *Prelude to Civil War*, p. 28.

4. Kohn, *Internal Improvements*, pp. 376–77, 379.

5. *Charleston Southern Patriot and Commercial Advertiser*, Dec. 10, 1821.

6. John W. Taylor to Richard Taylor, Dec. 12, 1821, John W. Taylor Papers (NYHS); John W. Taylor to James Geddes, Jan. 22, 1822, ibid.; Remini, *Martin Van Buren*, pp. 16–17.

7. John C. Calhoun to William Lowndes, Oct. 12, 1820, William Lowndes Papers (SHC).

8. William Lowndes to James Hamilton, Jr., Dec. 29, 1821, William Lowndes Papers (SHC).

9. Ibid.

10. Wiltse, *Calhoun, Nationalist*, pp. 206–8, 225–27; Mooney, *Crawford*, pp. 155–58.

11. Wiltse, *Calhoun, Nationalist*, pp. 228, 237–38.

12. William Lowndes to James Hamilton, Jr., Dec. 29, 1821, William Lowndes Papers (SHC).

13. Ibid.

14. Brown, *Missouri Compromises*, pp. 51–52.

15. Eldred Simkins to William Lowndes, Aug. 13, Oct. 26, 1821, William Lowndes Papers (SHC).

16. Eldred Simkins to William Lowndes, Oct. 26, 1821, William Lowndes Papers (SHC).

17. Langdon Cheves to Henry Clay, Nov. 9, 1822, Clay, *Papers*, 3:313–17.

18. William Lowndes to Elizabeth Lowndes, Mar. 24, 1822, William Lowndes Papers (SHC).

19. On budgetary curtailments of 1820–21, see Mooney, *Crawford*, pp. 155–63.

20. James Hamilton, Jr., to William Lowndes, Jan. 9, 11, 1822, William Lowndes Papers (SHC). Lacy K. Ford suggests, in "Social Origins of a New South Carolina," p. 145, that Lowndes's lowcountry advocates received substantial support from the partisans of Senator William S. Smith of South Carolina because of their strong hostility toward Calhoun.

21. James Hamilton, Jr., to William Lowndes, Jan. 9, Feb. 22, 1822, William Lowndes Papers (SHC); Hugh Legare to William Lowndes, Jan. 26, 1822, ibid.

22. Daniel E. Huger to William Lowndes, Jan. 7, 1822, William Lowndes Papers (SHC); William Drayton to James Hamilton, Jr., Jan. 7, 1822, ibid.

23. Printed notice in William Lowndes Papers (SHC).

24. In addition to their correspondence cited above, see Robert Y. Hayne to William Lowndes, Jan. 21, 1822, William Lowndes Papers (SHC).

25. Other than Calhoun and mere notation of the fact in Adams, *Memoirs*, 5:466, 468, these presidential aspirants said almost nothing about Lowndes's nomination in their correspondence until after his health had removed him from contention. In June Crawford said, "[F]ew if any had ever thought of [Lowndes] for that office, the general impression being that he is not well qualified for executive duty." William H. Crawford to Charles Tait, June 3, 1822, Charles Tait Papers (AA). It was not until October that Clay mentioned Lowndes's candidacy, stating, "Lowndes is no longer pressed—pressed he never was—on the public notice." Henry Clay to Langdon Cheves, Oct. 5, 1822, Clay, *Papers*, 3:291–92. Jackson made no mention of Lowndes's nomination or candidacy, see Jackson, *Correspondence*, Vols. 3 and 4, covering this period.

26. Brown, *Missouri Compromises*, p. 69.

27. Thomas W. Cobb to Charles Tait, March 8, 1822, Charles Tait Papers (AA); William H. Crawford to Charles Tait, June 3, 1822, ibid.

28. Wiltse, *Calhoun, Nationalist*, pp. 242–43.

29. Daniel E. Huger to William Lowndes, Jan. 7, 1822, William Lowndes Papers (SHC); James Hamilton, Jr., to William Lowndes, Jan. 11, 1822, ibid.

30. Wiltse advanced this view, citing Robert Y. Hayne to William Lowndes, Jan. 21, 1822, from Jervey, *Hayne*, pp. 126–27. This letter, in William Lowndes Papers (SHC), contains no statement that would warrant the anti-Crawford inference Wiltse ascribed to it. For their strongest argument against Calhoun's entry into the contest following Lowndes's nomination, see William Drayton to James Hamilton, Jr., Jan. 7, 1822, William Lowndes Papers (SHC).

31. Daniel E. Huger to William Lowndes, Jan. 7, 1822, William Lowndes Papers (SHC).

32. Ibid.

33. *Charleston Southern Patriot and Commercial Advertiser*, Jan. 19, 1822.

34. William Lowndes to James Hamilton, Jr., Dec. 29, 1821, William Lowndes Papers (SHC).

35. Wiltse, *Calhoun, Nationalist*, p. 239; Brown, *Missouri Compromises*, pp. 70–71.

36. James Hamilton, Jr., to William Lowndes, Feb. 4, 1822, William Lowndes Papers (SHC).

37. John C. Calhoun to Virgil Maxcy, Dec. 31, 1821, Calhoun, *Papers*, 6:595.

38. William Drayton to James Hamilton, Jr., Jan. 7, 1822, William Lowndes Papers (SHC), argues this point at length.

39. Brown, *Missouri Compromises*, pp. 70–73.

40. Wiltse, *Calhoun, Nationalist*, p. 239, assumed that Lowndes first received word of his nomination on December 29, the morning after Calhoun authorized the Pennsylvania deputation to consider him a presidential candidate. Hamilton's first letter to Lowndes announcing his nomination has been lost, nor did Lowndes record its date in his answer. Adams wrote in his *Memoirs* (5:466) on December 29: "Frye told me that last evening a deputation from the Pennsylvania delegation had waited upon Mr. Calhoun and invited him to stand a candidate for the Presidency at the next election, to which he, after some hesitation, had assented. It is understood that a caucus of members of the South Carolina Legislature have recommended Lowndes." From Adams's phrasing it is not clear whether Frye informed Adams of Lowndes's nomination or whether Adams had already heard of it. If Frye communicated both facts, it is reasonable to assume that he had received both from the same source, most likely a member of the Pennsylvania deputation. If Lowndes did in fact receive first news of his nomination that morning, discussed it privately with Calhoun, then answered Hamilton that afternoon, it

seems unlikely that Adams would have learned of it in time to record the fact that evening or in the early hours of the next morning. Moreover, eleven days had passed since the nomination at Columbia, almost twice the length of time required for Columbia news to reach Washington. Consequently, I have assumed the more plausible sequence of events, that Calhoun knew of Lowndes's nomination before he announced his own candidacy.

41. Brown, *Missouri Compromises*, p. 71; William Lowndes to Elizabeth Lowndes, Jan. 8, 1822, William Lowndes Papers (SHC).

42. Adams, *Memoirs*, 5:470.

43. Dangerfield, *American Nationalism*, pp. 213–14.

44. William Lowndes to James Hamilton, Jr., Dec. 29, 1821, William Lowndes Papers (SHC).

45. Ibid.

46. Daniel E. Huger to William Lowndes, Jan. 7, 1822, William Lowndes Papers (SHC); James Hamilton, Jr., to William Lowndes, Jan. 9, 11, Feb. 4, 1822, ibid.; William Drayton to James Hamilton, Jr., Jan. 7, 1822, ibid.; Robert Y. Hayne to William Lowndes, Jan. 21, 1822, ibid.

47. William Lowndes to Elizabeth Lowndes, Jan. 8, 1822, William Lowndes Papers (SHC).

48. William Lowndes to Elizabeth Lowndes, Mar. 24, 1822, William Lowndes Papers (SHC).

49. *Charleston Courier*, June 11, 1822.

50. Ibid., June 12, 1822.

51. Edward Luther Green Manuscript, p. 16, George McDuffie Papers (SCL).

52. Memoranda of Thomas Hart Benton, including copies of John Randolph to George McDuffie, Feb. 25, Mar. 1, 1822, and McDuffie to Randolph, Feb. 28, 1822, George McDuffie Papers (SCL).

53. Mooney, *Crawford*, pp. 226–27; Eldred Simkins to William Lowndes, Oct. 26, 1821, William Lowndes Papers (SHC); Edward Luther Green Manuscript, pp. 16–21, George McDuffie Papers (SCL).

54. Aptheker, *American Negro Slave Revolts*, pp. 267–76, 293–324.

55. James Hamilton, Jr., to William Lowndes, June 16, 1822, William Lowndes Papers (SHC).

56. Freehling, *Prelude to Civil War*, pp. 53–59.

57. Ibid., pp. 59–60; *Charleston Courier*, June 29, July 3, 1822.

58. Pinckney, *Reflections*, pp. 6–7.

59. Ibid., pp. 8–14.

60. Copied letter from John Connell to W. C. Preston, copy dated Aug. 19, 1842, Papers of Thomas Lowndes and William Lowndes (DU).

61. Ibid.

Epilogue

1. *Annals*, 17th Cong., 2d sess., pp. 656–61.
2. See for example, *Charleston Courier*, Jan. 13, 1823; James Hamilton, Jr., to Langdon Cheves, Jan. 18, 1823 and Henry Clay to Langdon Cheves, Jan. 24, 1823, Langdon Cheves Papers (SCHS).
3. Schwartz, *Washington*.
4. Thomas Pinckney to "Dear Sir," Jan. 29, 1823, Langdon Cheves Papers, (SCHS).
5. Elizabeth Lowndes to "My Dear Friend," [Elizabeth Cheves] Aug. 25, 1823, Langdon Cheves Papers (SCHS).
6. Will of William Lowndes, Will Book, 1818–36, 36:910–11, (OMC).
7. William Lowndes to Elizabeth Lowndes, Jan. 12, 1812, [misdated 1811], William Lowndes Papers (SHC).
8. For the Lowndes family history see Chase, *Lowndes*, passim.
9. Sargent, *Public Men*, 1:31–33.
10. Alfred Huger to Robert Gourdin, July 27, 1859, Alfred Huger Letterpress Book (DU).
11. Dangerfield, *American Nationalism*, pp. 133–34, 138.
12. For a discussion of the changing concept of liberty and its implications in American history, one of such erudition and insight as to exert a pivotal influence on ideological discussion of the antebellum era, see Kammen, *Spheres of Liberty*.
13. Ibid., pp. 82–83.
14. Kettner, *American Citizenship*, pp. 287–351.
15. Mark Summers's *Plundering Generation* analyzes the spread of corruption in public life from the Jacksonian Era to the Civil War with the comprehensiveness of research, scholarly balance, and literary grace that should make it the standard for some time to come.

Select Bibliography

Manuscripts and Typescripts
Boston, Massachusetts
Massachusetts Historical Society
   Timothy Pickering Papers
Chapel Hill, North Carolina
Southern Historical Collection, University of North Carolina
   William Lowndes Papers
Charleston, South Carolina
Charleston Library Society
  DeSaussure Family Papers
  Miscellaneous Papers
South Carolina Historical Society
  Memoir of the Brisbane Family (Typescript)
  Langdon Cheves Papers
  St. Julien Ravenel Childs Collection
  DeSaussure Family Papers
  Kershaw and Lewis Account Book for William Lowndes
  Lowndes Papers
  Lowndes-Pinckney Papers
  Pinckney Papers
Columbia, South Carolina
South Carolina Department of Archives and History
   Miscellaneous Records
South Caroliniana Library, University of South Carolina
  Lewis Malone Ayer Papers
  DeSaussure Family Papers
  Thomas Worth Glover Papers
  Lowndes Papers
  George McDuffie Papers
  Manigault Family Papers
  Singleton Family Papers
  Taylor Papers
Durham, North Carolina
Duke University Library, Duke University

Alfred Huger Letterpress Book
Papers of Thomas Lowndes and William Lowndes
Montgomery, Alabama
Alabama Department of Archives and History
Charles Tait Papers
New York, New York
New-York Historical Society
John W. Taylor Papers
New York Public Library
Miscellaneous Papers
Washington, D.C.
Library of Congress
Izard Papers
William Lowndes Papers
John Randolph of Roanoke Papers

Published Papers and Memoirs

Adams, John Q. *Memoirs of John Quincy Adams, Comprising Portions of His Diary from 1795–1848.* Edited by Charles Francis Adams. 12 vols. Philadelphia: J. B. Lippincott and Company, 1875.

Benton, Thomas Hart. *Thirty Years' View.* 2 vols. New York: D. Appleton and Company, 1854.

Brown, Everett S. *The Missouri Compromises and Presidential Politics: 1820–1825.* St. Louis: Missouri Historical Society, 1926.

Calhoun, John C. *John C. Calhoun Papers, 1782–1850.* Edited by Robert Lee Meriwether, et al. 16 vols. to date. Columbia: University of South Carolina Press, 1959–.

Cardozo, Jacob N. *Reminiscences of Charleston.* Charleston: J. Walker, 1866.

Clay, Henry. *The Papers of Henry Clay.* Edited by James Hopkins and Mary Hargreaves. 8 vols. to date. Lexington: University of Kentucky Press, 1961–.

Cooke, Jacob E., ed. *The Federalist.* Middletown, Conn.: Wesleyan University Press, 1961.

Fraser, Charles. *Reminiscences of Charleston.* 1854. Reprint. Charleston: Garnier and Company, 1969.

Harper, William. *Memoir of the Life, Character, and Public Services of the Late Hon. Henry William DeSaussure.* Charleston: W. Riley, 1841.

Jackson, Andrew. *Correspondence of Andrew Jackson.* Edited by John Spencer Bassett. 7 vols. Washington: Carnegie Institution of Washington, 1926–35.

Kohn, David, ed. *Internal Improvements in South Carolina, 1817–1828*. Washington: Privately printed, 1938.
Locke, John. *Two Treatises of Government*. Edited by Peter Laslett. New York: Cambridge University Press, 1965.
Madison, James. *Letters and Other Writings of James Madison*. Congressional Edition. 4 vols. Philadelphia, 1865.
O'Neall, John B. *Biographical Sketches of the Bench and Bar of South Carolina*. 2 vols. Charleston: S. G. Courtenay and Company, 1859.
Richardson, James D. *A Compilation of the Messages and Papers of the Presidents*. 11 vols. Washington: Bureau of National Literature, 1897.
Sargent, Nathan. *Public Men and Events*. 2 vols. Philadelphia: J. B. Lippincott and Company, 1875.
Thomas, E. S. *Reminiscences of the Last Sixty-Five Years: Commencing with the Battle of Lexington*. 2 vols. Hartford, Conn.: Case, Tiffany, and Burnham, 1840.

Newspapers

Charleston City Gazette (Title varies)
Charleston Courier (Title varies)
Charleston Royal Gazette
Charleston Southern Patriot and Commercial Advertiser
Charleston Times
New York Evening Post
Niles' Weekly Register
Washington Daily National Intelligencer

U.S. Public Documents

U.S. Bureau of the Census. *Historical Statistics of the United States, Colonial Times to 1957*. Washington: U.S. Government Printing Office, 1960.
U.S. Bureau of the Census. *Second Census of the United States, 1800. Return of the Whole Number of Persons within the Several Districts of the United States*. Washington: William Duane, 1801.
U.S. Bureau of the Census. *Third Census of the United States, 1810. Aggregate Amount of Persons within the United States in the Year 1810*. Washington: 1811.
U.S. Congress. *Annals of Congress: The Debates and Proceedings in the Congress of the United States*. 42 vols. Washington: Gales and Seaton, 1834–56.
U.S. Congress. *Biographical Directory of the American Congress, 1774–1961*. Washington: U.S. Government Printing Office, 1961.

U.S. Congress. *Finance.* Vols. 9–13 of *American State Papers.* 38 vols. Washington: Gales and Seaton, 1832–61.
U.S. Congress. House. *House Journal.* 13th Cong., 2d sess.

South Carolina Public Records

Charleston County Courthouse
  Office of Mesne Conveyance, Deed Book L-7
  Office of Mesne Conveyance, Will Book 36, 1818–36
  Office of Probate Court, Will Book D, 1800–1807
South Carolina Department of Archives and History
  Chancery Court Records, 1804
  Court of Common Pleas, Minutes, 1804–6
  Election Returns, St. Philip and St. Michael Parishes, 1800–1806
  House of Representatives Journal, 1802–8
  Senate Journal, 1803, 1808

Books and Articles

Adams, Henry. *History of the United States of America.* 9 vols. New York: Charles Scribner's Sons, 1921.
Ammon, Harry. *James Monroe: The Quest for National Identity.* New York: McGraw Hill, 1971.
Appleby, Joyce O. "Republicanism in Old and New Contexts." *William and Mary Quarterly* 43(January 1986): 20–34.
Aptheker, Herbert. *American Negro Slave Revolts.* New 40th Anniversary Edition. New York: International Publishers, 1983.
Bailey, N. Louise, ed. *Biographical Directory of the South Carolina House of Representatives.* Vols. 2–4. Columbia: University of South Carolina Press, 1977–84.
Banning, Lance. *The Jeffersonian Persuasion: Evolution of a Party Ideology.* Ithaca, N.Y.: Cornell University Press, 1978.
Barnwell, John. *Love of Order, South Carolina's First Secession Crisis.* Chapel Hill: University of North Carolina Press, 1982.
Bemis, Samuel Flagg. *John Quincy Adams and the Foundations of American Foreign Policy.* New York: Alfred A. Knopf, 1949.
Brady, Patrick S. "The Slave Trade and Sectionalism in South Carolina, 1787–1808." *Journal of Southern History* 38(November 1972): 601–20.
Brant, Irving. *James Madison.* Vol. 4, *Secretary of State, 1800–1809.* Vol. 5, *The President, 1809–1812.* New York: Bobbs-Merrill Company, 1953, 1956.

Broussard, James H. *The Southern Federalists, 1800–1816.* Baton Rouge: Louisiana State University Press, 1978.
Brown, Roger H. *The Republic in Peril: 1812.* New York: W. W. Norton and Company, 1971.
Brown, Thomas. *Politics and Statesmanship: Essays on the American Whig Party.* New York: Columbia University Press, 1985.
Bruce, William C. *John Randolph of Roanoke.* 2 vols. New York: Octagon Books, 1970.
Catterall, Ralph Charles Henry. *The Second Bank of the United States.* Chicago: University of Chicago Press, 1960.
Charleston City Directory. [Charleston, S.C., 1809].
Chase, George B. *Lowndes of South Carolina, an Historical and Genealogical Memoir.* Boston: A. Williams and Company, 1876.
Cibber, Colley. *An Apology for His Life.* London: J. M. Dent and Sons, 1914.
Cook, Harvey Toliver. *The Life and Legacy of David Rogerson Williams.* Garden City, N.Y.: Country Life Press, 1916.
Dangerfield, George. *The Awakening of American Nationalism: 1815–1828.* New York, Evanston, and London: Harper and Row, 1965.
Davis, David B. *The Slave Power Conspiracy and the Paranoid Style.* Baton Rouge: Louisiana State University Press, 1970.
Davis, Richard Beale. *Intellectual Life in the Colonial South, 1585–1763.* 3 vols. Knoxville: University of Tennessee Press, 1978.
Dawidoff, Robert. *The Education of John Randolph.* New York: W. W. Norton and Company, 1979.
Divine, Robert A., et al. *America: Past and Present.* 2d ed. 2 vols. Glenview, Ill. and London: Scott, Foresman and Company, 1987.
Eaton, Clement. *Henry Clay and the Art of American Politics.* Boston: Little, Brown and Company, 1957.
Edgar, Walter B., ed. *Biographical Directory of South Carolina House of Representatives. Session Lists, 1692–1973.* Vol. 1. Columbia: University of South Carolina Press, 1974.
Ervin, Eliza Cowan, and Horace Rudisill Fraser. *Darlingtoniana: A History of People, Places, and Events in Darlington County South Carolina.* Spartanburg, S.C.: Reprint Company, 1976.
Ford, Lacy K. "Social Origins of a New South Carolina: The Upcountry in the Nineteenth Century." Ph.D. dissertation, University of South Carolina, 1983.
Formisano, Ronald P. "Deferential-Participant Politics: The Early Republic's Political Culture, 1789–1840." *American Political Science Review* 68(June 1974): 473–87.

Freehling, William W. *Prelude to Civil War*. New York and Evanston: Harper Torchbooks, 1968.
Gray, Lewis Cecil. *History of Agriculture in the Southern United States to 1860*. 2 vols. Washington: Carnegie Institution of Washington, 1933.
Greenberg, Kenneth. *Masters and Statesmen*. Baltimore and London: Johns Hopkins University Press, 1985.
Hammond, Bray. *Banks and Politics in America, from the Revolution to the Civil War*. Princeton: Princeton University Press, 1957.
Hofstadter, Richard. *The Idea of a Party System: The Rise of Legitimate Opposition in the United States, 1780–1840*. Berkeley: University of California Press, 1972.
Howe, Daniel Walker. *The Political Culture of the American Whigs*. Chicago and London: University of Chicago Press, 1979.
Huff, Archie V., Jr. *Langdon Cheves of South Carolina*. Columbia: University of South Carolina Press, 1977.
Jervey, Theodore D. *Robert Y. Hayne and His Times*. New York: Macmillan Company, 1909.
Kammen, Michael. *Spheres of Liberty: Changing Perceptions of Liberty in American Culture*. Madison: University of Wisconsin Press, 1986.
Kaplanoff, Mark D. "Making the South Solid: Politics and the Structure of Society in South Carolina, 1790–1815." Ph.D. dissertation, University of Cambridge, 1979.
———. "Charles Pinckney and the American Republican Tradition." In *Intellectual Life in Antebellum Charleston*, edited by Michael O'Brien and David Moltke-Hansen, pp. 85–122, Knoxville: University of Tennessee Press, 1986.
Kettner, James H. *The Development of American Citizenship, 1608–1870*. Chapel Hill: University of North Carolina Press, 1978.
Kramnick, Isaac. *Bolingbroke and His Circle*. Cambridge, Mass.: Harvard University Press, 1968.
Latimer, Margaret Kinard. "South Carolina: A Protagonist in the War of 1812." *American Historical Review* 61(July 1956): 914–29.
Lebergott, Stanley. *The Americans, an Economic Record*. New York and London: W. W. Norton and Company, 1984.
Lesesne, J. M., ed. *Basic Documents of South Carolina History: The Constitution of 1790*. Columbia: Historical Commission of South Carolina, 1952.
McCormick, Richard P. *The Second American Party System*. Chapel Hill: University of North Carolina Press, 1966.
McCoy, Drew R. *The Elusive Republic: Political Economy in Jeffersonian America*. New York and London: W. W. Norton and Company, 1980.

Martin, Julien Dwight. "The Letters of Charles Caleb Cotton, 1798–1802." *The South Carolina Historical and Genealogical Magazine* 52(October 1951): 17–25.
Meriwether, Robert L., ed. *Basic Documents of South Carolina History: The Constitution of 1778.* Columbia: Historical Commission of South Carolina, 1953.
Mills, Robert. *Atlas of the State of South Carolina.* 1825. Reprint. Columbia: Lucy Hampton Bostick and Fant H. Thornley, 1938.
———. *Statistics of South Carolina.* Spartanburg, S.C.: Reprint Company, 1972.
Mooney, Chase C. *William H. Crawford, 1772–1834.* Lexington: University Press of Kentucky, 1974.
Moore, Glover. *The Missouri Controversy, 1819–1821.* Gloucester, Mass.: Peter Smith, 1967.
Morris, Thomas D. *Free Men All.* Baltimore and London: Johns Hopkins University Press, 1974.
Munroe, John A. *Louis McLane: Federalist and Jacksonian.* New Brunswick, N.J.: Rutgers University Press, 1973.
North, Douglass C. *The Economic Growth of the United States, 1790–1860.* New York: W. W. Norton and Company, 1966.
Perkins, Bradford. *Prologue to War: England and the United States, 1805–1812.* Berkeley: University of California Press, 1961.
Pinckney, Thomas [Achates, pseud.]. *Reflections Occasioned by the Late Disturbances in Charleston.* Charleston: A. E. Miller, 1922.
Pincus, Jonathan J. *Pressure Groups and Politics in Antebellum Tariffs.* New York: Columbia University Press, 1977.
Pocock, J. G. A. *The Machiavellian Moment.* Princeton: Princeton University Press, 1975.
Pope, Clayne L. *The Impact of the Ante-bellum Tariff on Income Distribution.* New York: Arno Press, 1975.
Preyer, Norris W. "Southern Support for the Tariff of 1816: A Reappraisal." *Journal of Southern History* 25(August 1959): 306–22.
Ravenel, Mrs. St. Julien. *Life and Times of William Lowndes of South Carolina, 1782–1822.* Boston and New York: Houghton, Mifflin and Company, 1901.
Remini, Robert V. *Martin Van Buren and the Making of the Democratic Party.* New York: Columbia University Press, 1959.
Risjord, Norman K. *The Old Republicans: Southern Conservatism in the Age of Jefferson.* New York: Columbia University Press, 1965.
Rogers, George C., Jr. *Evolution of a Federalist: William Loughton Smith of Charleston, 1758–1812.* Columbia: University of South Carolina Press, 1962.
Schaper, William A. "Sectionalism and Representation in South Caro-

lina." *Annual Report of the American Historical Association for the Year 1900*, 1:237–463. Washington: U.S. Government Printing Office, 1901.

Schwartz, Barry. *George Washington: The Making of an American Symbol.* New York: Free Press; London: Collier McMillan, 1987.

Shalhope, Robert E. *John Taylor of Caroline: Pastoral Republican.* Columbia: University of South Carolina Press, 1980.

Smelser, Marshall. *The Democratic Republic, 1801–1815.* New York: Harper and Row, 1968.

Smith, Henry A. M. "Charleston and Charleston Neck." *The South Carolina Historical and Genealogical Magazine* 19(January 1918): 3–76.

Stanwood, Edward. *American Tariff Controversies in the Nineteenth Century.* 2 vols. New York: Russell and Russell, 1903.

Stommel, Henry, and Elizabeth Stommel. *The Story of 1816, the Year without a Summer.* Newport, R.I.: Seven Seas Press, 1983.

Stourzh, Gerald. *Alexander Hamilton and the Idea of Republican Government.* Stanford: Stanford University Press, 1970.

Summers, Mark W. *The Plundering Generation: Corruption and the Crisis of the Union, 1849–1861.* New York: Oxford University Press, 1987.

Taussig, Frank William. *The Tariff History of the United States.* New York: Putnam, 1931. Reprint. New York: Johnson Reprint Corp., 1966.

Thornton, J. Mills, III. *Politics and Power in a Slave Society.* Baton Rouge and London: Louisiana State University Press, 1978.

Timberlake, Richard H. *The Origins of Central Banking in the United States.* Cambridge, Mass., and London: Harvard University Press, 1978.

Van Deusen, Glyndon Garlock. *The Life of Henry Clay.* Boston: Little, Brown, and Company, 1937.

Vipperman, Carl J. *The Rise of Rawlins Lowndes, 1721–1800.* Columbia: University of South Carolina Press, 1978.

Wallace, Anthony F. C. *Rockdale: The Growth of an American Village in the Early Industrial Revolution.* New York and London: W. W. Norton and Company, 1980.

Wallace, David D. *South Carolina, a Short History.* Columbia: University of South Carolina Press, 1961.

Wallace, Michael. "Changing Concepts of Party in the United States: New York, 1815–1828." *American Historical Review* 74(December 1968): 453–91.

Walters, Raymond, Jr. *Alexander James Dallas.* New York: DaCapo Press, 1969.

Watterson, George. *Letters from Washington.* Washington, 1818.
Weir, Robert M. "'The Harmony We Were Famous For': An Interpretation of Pre-Revolutionary South Carolina Politics." *William and Mary Quarterly* 26(October 1969): 473–501.
Wiebe, Robert H. *The Opening of American Society.* New York: Vintage Books, 1985.
Wiecek, William M. *The Sources of Antislavery Constitutionalism in America, 1760–1848.* Ithaca, N.Y., and London: Cornell University Press, 1977.
Wiltse, Charles M. *John C. Calhoun, Nationalist, 1782–1828.* Indianapolis and New York: Bobbs-Merrill Company, 1944.
Wolfe, John H. *Jeffersonian Democracy in South Carolina.* Chapel Hill: University of North Carolina Press, 1940.
Wood, Gordon S. "Conspiracy and the Paranoid Style: Causality and Deceit in the Eighteenth Century." *William and Mary Quarterly* 39(July 1982): 401–41.
———. *The Creation of the American Republic, 1776–1789.* New York and London: W. W. Norton and Company, 1972.
Wormser, Rene A. *The Story of the Law.* New York: Simon and Schuster, 1962.
Wright, Gavin. *The Political Economy of the Cotton South: Households, Markets, and Wealth in the Nineteenth Century.* New York: W. W. Norton and Company, 1978.
Wyatt-Brown, Bertram. *Southern Honor.* New York: Oxford University Press, 1982.
Young, James Sterling. *The Washington Community, 1800–1828.* New York: Columbia University Press, 1966.
Zahniser, Marvin R. *Charles Cotesworth Pinckney, Founding Father.* Chapel Hill: University of North Carolina Press, 1967.

Index

Abraham, 38
Adams, John, 23
Adams, John Quincy, 153, 154, 163, 165, 169–70, 178, 200, 201, 202, 234, 239, 251, 253, 254–55, 259, 301, 303, 304–5
Adams, Samuel, 20
Adams-Onís Treaty, 201–4
Addison, Joseph, xviii
Albany Regency, 242
Alien and Sedition Acts, 19, 147, 228–29
Alston, Joseph, 41, 44, 45, 48, 108
Alston, Lemuel J., 71
Ambrister, Robert, 166, 169
American Revolution, xii, xvii, xviii, 3, 23, 84, 86, 150, 209, 268, 271
Amiens, Peace of, 52
Appleby, Joyce, 229–30
Appleton, Nathan, 204
Arbuthnot, Alexander, 166, 169
Archer, William, of Va., 302
Aristotle, xiv–xvi, 137, 228, 231, 269
Armstrong, John, 109

Bacon, Ezekiel, of Mass., 78
Bacot, Henry H., 28, 63
Bacot, Thomas, 36
Bailey, Henry, 28, 63
Bainbridge, William, 102
Baker, Thomas, 63, 64
Baldwin, Henry, of Pa., 204, 206–7, 209, 214–16, 218, 219, 220, 224, 226, 227–28, 234–35, 236, 248–49, 296, 297; Baldwin tariff bill of 1820, 204–27
Bank of the United States, Second, 115, 123, 143–44, 150, 170–80, 182
Barbour, Philip, of Va., 155, 157, 185, 186, 188, 217, 221–22, 247, 252–53
Beecher, Philemon, of Ohio, 199
Bellinger, Joseph, 47
Bennett, Thomas, Jr., 31, 63, 281
Benoit, Peter, 10–11
Benton, Thomas Hart, of Mo., 96, 301
Bibb, George M., of Ky., 76
Bibb, William, of Ga., 104, 282
Blackstone, William, 22
Blanding, Abraham, 44, 46–48, 160
Bonaparte, Napoleon, 53
Bonus Bill, 144, 150–51, 155
Brant, Irving, 96
Briggs, Isaac, 128
"Broken voyage," 54, 56, 57
Bryan, Joseph H., of N.C., 171
Bucktails, 241–42, 256
Buist, Arthur, 9
Burr, Aaron, 20, 37
Burril, James, Jr., of R.I., 248
Burwell, James, of Va., 125
Butler, Josiah, of N.H., 302
Butler, Pierce, 19
Butler, William, of S.C., 77, 90

Calhoun, John C., of S.C., xi, 22, 51,

71–72, 76–77, 78, 80, 82, 87, 88,
90, 91, 92, 94, 96, 97, 98, 100,
102–4, 105, 106, 107, 108, 111,
112, 113, 115, 116, 117, 119–20,
121, 134, 135–37, 139–40, 143–
44, 147–48, 150–51, 153, 154,
164–65, 197, 229, 230–31, 236,
237, 238, 240, 252–53, 254–55,
256, 257, 258, 259, 260, 261, 267–
68, 303, 304–5
Calhoun, Joseph, 71
Campbell, John, of Ohio, 302
Cardozo, Jacob, 20
Cardozo, Joseph, 257
Carey, Mathew, 205, 206–7, 214
Case, Walter, of N.Y., 199
Charleston, S.C., xi, 1, 2, 18, 20, 21,
24, 25, 27–32, 34, 35–36, 37, 38,
40, 41, 43, 44, 45, 48, 51, 52, 53,
54, 55, 59, 62, 65, 66, 67, 68, 71,
74, 110, 111, 114, 115, 120, 121,
152, 235, 236, 252, 255, 256, 261–
63, 266, 277
Charleston Theatre, 24
Chesapeake-Leopard outrage, 45, 67,
73
Cheves, Elizabeth, 101, 266
Cheves, Langdon, 20, 21, 27–29, 44,
47, 51, 63, 64, 68, 69–70, 72, 74,
75, 76–77, 82, 88, 90, 91, 94, 96,
100, 102, 103, 104, 105, 106–7,
108, 111, 112, 113, 116, 117, 119,
120, 123, 178, 179, 281, 284, 295
Citizenship, xiv–xix, 27, 268–69
Civic virtue, xiv–xix, 34, 210, 229,
231, 242, 269
Civil War, 48, 51, 268, 269
Clay, Henry, of Ky., xi, 76, 77–78, 80,
83, 90, 92, 97, 102, 103–4, 106,
108, 111, 113, 122, 123–24, 132,
133–34, 137, 138, 139, 148, 153,
154, 155–56, 159, 160, 163, 166–
67, 180, 183, 185–86, 188, 190,
203, 213–14, 217, 219–20, 221,
222, 226, 230, 231–32, 233, 234,
237–38, 240, 249, 250–51, 256,
291, 303
Clements, William, 63, 281
Clinton, DeWitt, 241, 242, 256
Clinton, George, 36, 94
Cobb, Thomas W., of Ga., 166, 167,
180, 241, 249, 256, 302
Cochran, Charles B., 31
Cogdell, John, 26–30, 36, 40
College of Charleston, 8–9, 26
Commonwealth of Oceana, xvi
Compromise of 1808, xii, 46–51, 195
Concurrent majority, 50
Constitution, U.S., 18, 19, 23–24,
39–40, 84, 101, 137, 148, 155,
156–59, 160, 162, 168, 181–82,
184–85, 189–90, 191, 192, 194,
195, 213, 228, 229, 251, 268, 269
Constitutional Convention of 1787,
19, 194
Cook, Daniel, of Ill., 191
Coram, Thomas, 8
Cornwallis, Earl of, 1
Cotton gin, 35, 37, 210–11
Country ideology, xviii, 9
Court party, xvii–xviii
Cox, Thomas Campbell, 63
Crawford, William H., 144, 153, 171,
178, 208, 213, 240, 253, 254–55,
256, 258, 259, 260, 303
Croft, Edward, 28
Cross, George W., 22
Culbreth, Thomas, of Md., 185
Cumming, William, 262

Dallas, Alexander J., 115–18, 125,
126–29, 130, 138, 141, 143, 153,
214, 215, 218–19
Dana, Samuel, of Mass., 79, 90

Dangerfield, George, 268
Dawson, John, Jr., 29, 31–32, 63, 64, 68
Dean, William, 78
Dearborn, Henry, 101
Deas, Henry, 29, 31–32, 38, 42, 63, 64, 70–71
Decatur, Stephen, 102
Declaration of Independence, 34, 189
Democracy, xiv–xvii, 31, 34–35, 44–45, 50, 64, 227–31, 268–69
DeSaussure, Henry William, 21–22, 28, 36, 40, 48–49
Dickinson, Francis, 29, 31–32
D'Oyley, Daniel, 31
Drayton, John, 31, 70
Drayton, William, 28, 63, 64, 68, 256, 261
Duality principle, 34, 47, 195, 294
Dunlap, Samuel, 47

Earle, Elias, of S.C., 71, 77, 90, 108
Eaton, John, of Tenn., 246–47, 251
Edwards, Henry, of Conn., 199
Edwards, Thomas, 45
Election: of 1796, 20; of 1800, 18, 19; of 1803, 18; of 1804, 20, 30–32, 36, 62; of 1806, 62–65; of 1808, 68–70, 71; of 1809, 70–71; of 1810, 71–72; of 1812, 100–101; of 1814, 122; of 1816, 147–48; of 1824 (presidential), 253–61
Ellick (Lowndes's slave), 108, 110, 114
Elliott, Stephen, 100
Embargo: of 1807, 46, 67–68, 73–74, 75, 147; of 1812, 92, 93, 94; of 1813, 111, 112, 113
Emmot, James, of N.Y., 76
Eppes, John W., of Va., 108, 111, 123
Erskine, David, 74
Essex case, 54

Eustis, William, 97–98, 109, 302

Falconer, William, 38–39, 41
Farr, John, 147
Federalist, The, 155, 158, 228
Federalist party, 12, 18–20, 23, 31–32, 59, 62, 63, 64–65, 69–70, 76, 77, 79, 92, 93, 100, 101, 106, 109–10, 111, 112, 114, 116, 120, 124, 131, 132, 133, 134–35, 194, 228, 229, 230, 238, 241, 253. *See also* Election
Ferdinand VII, King of Spain, 202
Flander (Lowndes's slave), 147
Florida, annexation of, 201–4
Ford, Timothy, 21–22, 28
Ford, William, of N.Y., 302
Forrest, Thomas, of Pa., 248
Forsyth, John, of Ga., 140, 141–42, 151, 153, 161–62
Fraser, Charles, 20, 29
Fredericksburg petition, 208–11, 221, 227, 228, 235, 237
Free blacks, 237, 247, 251, 263
Freehling, William, xiii–xiv, 126, 142, 289
Freneau, Peter, 63, 64, 74, 281
Fugitive Slave Act of 1793, 210–11
Fuller, Timothy, of Mass., 185, 190–91, 192, 218
Fullerton, David, of Pa., 297
Fullerton, Eliza, 6

Gaillard, John, of S.C., 28, 98, 100, 119
Gaillard, Theodore, 45, 47
Gaines, Edmund P., 164
Gallagher, Simon Felix, 8–9, 11, 20, 83
Gallatin, Albert, 97, 103, 108
Gaston, William, of N.C., 125
Geddes, John, 63, 281

320 : Index

Gentilis, Albericus, 61
Ghent, Treaty of, 118, 119, 122, 147
Gibbes, John, 26
Gilchrist, Adam, 63
Gist, Joseph, 42, 45, 47, 48
Glorious Revolution, xvi, xvii
Glover, Moses, 63
Gordon, Thomas, xviii
Gray, Lewis, xiv, 289
Greene, Nathanael, 1–2
Gross, Ezra, of N.Y., 197, 227
Grosvenor, Thomas P., of N.Y., 112, 140
Grotius, Hugo, 57, 61
Grove. *See* Lowndes' Grove
Grundy, Felix, of Tenn., 76, 81, 82, 96
Gullah Jack, 262

Hackley, Aaron, of N.Y., 302
Hale, Salma, 240
Hamilton, Alexander, 19, 37, 115, 129–30
Hamilton, James, Jr., 255, 256, 257, 260, 261, 262, 265, 304
Hamilton, Paul, 36
Hammond, Bray, 179
Hanson, Alexander C., of Md., 116
Hardin, Benjamin, of Ky., 133, 140, 185, 186
Harper, William, 48
Harrington, James, Jr., xvi
Harrison, William Henry, 111
Hartford Convention, 114, 117, 118, 229
Hayne, Robert Y., 256, 261
Hill, Mark, of Mass., 198
Hill, William, 39, 41
Hinds, Thomas, 29, 31, 63, 64
Holmes, John, of Mass., 183, 186, 197, 198, 199, 200
Hopkinson, Joseph, of Pa., 134–35, 141
Horlbeck, John, Jr., 63, 64, 281

Horseshoe plantation, 2, 22, 24, 25, 30, 43, 99, 107–8, 110, 122, 145–47, 152, 233, 234, 252
Howe, Daniel Walker, xix, 227
Huger, Alfred, 48
Huger, Benjamin, of S.C., 68, 131
Huger, Daniel E., 22, 47, 48, 256, 257, 261, 267
Hulbert, John, of Mass., 139, 141
Hull, Isaac, 102
Hull, William, 101

Impressment, 75
Ingham, Samuel D., of Pa., 125, 138–39, 141
Insurrection, 35–36, 38, 40, 262–64
Internal improvements, 124, 125, 134, 136, 142, 150, 155–60
Izard, Alice, 25

Jackson, Andrew, 111, 118, 119, 164–65, 166–70, 256, 269, 303
Jacksonborough, S.C., 1–2, 115
Jay, John, and Treaty of London, 19–20, 52, 59
Jefferson, Thomas, 12, 18–20, 36, 45, 52–53, 54–56, 59, 63–65, 66, 68–70, 73–74, 77, 129, 132, 136
Johnson, Edward, 29–30
Johnson, Francis, of Ky., 297
Johnson, James, of Va., 149, 173–74, 178, 221, 297
Johnson, John, Jr., 281
Johnson, Richard, of Ky., 38, 43, 45, 47, 88–89, 90, 97, 103, 108, 116, 144, 148, 167
Johnson, William, 26, 276
Jones, Jacob, 102
Jones, William, 170, 172, 173, 178
Jones family, of Ga., 2

Kennedy, James, 70–71
Kershaw and Lewis, factors, xii, 95,

99, 107, 114, 122, 145, 147, 233
King, Cyrus, of Mass., 134–35
King, Rufus, of N.Y., 182, 241
"King Caucus," 259–60
Kinsey, Charles, of N.J., 198, 200

Lebergott, Stanley, xiii, 295
Lee, William, 29, 31–32, 63, 64, 68, 281
Lehre, Thomas, 31–32, 63, 281
Leopard-Chesapeake outrage, 45, 67, 73
Little, Peter, of Md., 218
Livermore, Arthur, of N.H., 185, 197, 217
Lobbying, organized, 182, 204–7, 214, 215
Locke, John, xvi–xvii, 228, 268–69
Lowell, Francis C., 141, 204–5
Lowndes, Amarinthia Elliott, 4
Lowndes, Charles (grandfather of W. L.), 3–4
Lowndes, Elizabeth Pinckney (wife of W. L.), xi, xii, 22–25, 40, 76, 79, 83, 91, 94, 95, 96, 97, 99, 101, 107, 109, 110, 114, 117, 118, 121, 122, 152, 166, 232, 233–34, 239, 240, 254, 259, 261, 263, 264, 266–67
Lowndes, James (brother of W. L.), 15, 18–19, 31–32, 63, 64, 65, 68, 274
Lowndes, Mary Cartwright, 4
Lowndes, Pinckney (son of W. L.), 79, 266
Lowndes, Rawlins (father of W. L.), 2–6, 11–16, 23–24, 26, 272
Lowndes, Rawlins (son of W. L.), 79, 106, 267
Lowndes, Rebecca "Becky" (daughter of W. L.), 79–80, 264, 266, 267
Lowndes, Ruth (sister of W. L.), 274
Lowndes, Sarah Jones (mother of W. L.), 2, 5–7, 15–16, 24
Lowndes, Thomas (brother of W. L.), 15, 18–19, 25, 31–32, 69–70, 274
Lowndes, William: characteristics of, xi–xii, 20–21, 25, 78–79, 83, 85, 95–96, 98, 124, 143, 154–55, 274; republicanism of, xiv, 51, 87, 94, 153–54, 202, 229–31, 242, 249–50, 251, 258, 260, 264, 268–69, 272, 273, 275; slaves of, xix, 73, 75, 95, 99, 107, 108, 110, 114, 118, 146–47, 241; birth and childhood of, 2–11; education of, 6–15; health of, 7–8, 17, 75–76, 79, 149, 165–66, 174, 180–81, 251, 261, 274, 292, 302; debating style of, 11–15, 21, 83, 87; study and practice of law, 21–22, 26–30, 40; militia service of, 22–23, 32, 67, 68, 73, 100; inheritance of, 24; social tastes of, 24, 36, 275; courtship and marriage of, 24–25; politics of, 30–32, 62–64, 66–67, 68–72; election contests of, 30–32, 62–65, 69–72, 100–101, 122, 147–48, 253–61, 281, 293; and representation controversy, 33, 35, 36–38, 41, 46–51, 72; state legislature, service of, 33–51, 68–69; and committee service in state legislature, 37, 41–42, 44, 46–48, 278; and foreign slave trade issue, 38, 42–43, 72; and neutral rights and national honor, 54–56, 73–75, 85–86; Planter essays of, 56–62, 66–67, 85, 279, 280; election to Congress of, 71–72; friendship with and impressions of Cheves and Calhoun, 75–76; and the War of 1812, 76–80, 82, 85–87, 91, 92, 97–98, 99–115, 118; and service on Commerce and Manufactures committee, 78, 92–94, 102; and naval power, 88, 89–90,

105–6; and issue of Merchants' Bonds, 92–94, 102–5; and the caucus principle, 94, 96–97; and attitude toward congressional service, 95–96, 97–98; plantation overseers of, 99, 107–8, 110, 252; business affairs of, 107–8, 110–11, 114, 117, 121, 145–47, 152, 165, 233, 234, 292; and chairmanship of Naval Affairs committee, 111, 112–13, 119; and national bank issue, 115–18; cabinet offers to, 119–20, 153–54; contemplated retirement of, 121–22; and chairmanship of Ways and Means, 123–44, 148–50, 154–55, 163, 166; and tariff protection, 124–32, 137–43, 204, 213, 214, 215, 216, 217–18, 221, 222–26, 227, 229, 233, 234, 235, 236, 287, 295, 296, 297; and Bank of the United States, 144, 170–80; and Bonus Bill, 150–51; and neutrality issue, 151, 160–63; and internal improvements, 156–60; and invasion of Florida, 165, 167–70; and Missouri Controversy, 183–86, 188, 190–92, 198–200, 243–51; and annexation of Florida, 201–4; and House Speaker election of 1820, 232, 238–40; and presidential election of 1824, 253–61, 303, 304–5; final illness and death of, 261, 264; and eulogies to, 265–66. *See also* Lowndes' Grove; Horseshoe plantation

Lowndes' Grove, 26, 40, 95, 107, 110, 146, 152, 262, 266, 267

McDonough, Thomas, 116
McDuffie, George, of S.C., 197, 261–62
Machiavelli, Niccolò, xv–xvi
"Machiavellian moment," xv, 183

McKee, Samuel, of Ky., 88, 89
McKibben, James, 68
McLane, Louis, of Del., 171, 172, 174, 197, 222
Macon, Nathaniel, of N.C., 249
Madison, Dolley, 80
Madison, James, 55, 56, 61, 69, 72, 73–75, 78, 80, 92, 96–97, 102, 107, 108–9, 111, 113, 115, 117–18, 119, 124–25, 132, 143, 150, 151, 153, 155, 159, 228, 279, 280, 298
Maine Bill, 186, 187, 188, 197, 198, 199
Manigault, Peter, 14
Manufactures. *See* Baldwin, Henry, of Pa.; Protectionism; Tariff of 1816
Marion, Robert, 18, 31–32, 63, 65, 69–70
Mayrant, William, of S.C., 148
Mays, Samuel, 42
Meigs, Henry, 300
Middleton, Henry, 31–32, 42, 63, 64, 69, 121, 147, 281
Milnor, William, of Pa., 140, 141
Minimum principle, 141, 142, 204–5, 211–12, 231, 299
Missouri Controversy, xii–xiii, xiv, 123, 180, 181–200, 201, 226, 230, 231, 232, 237, 238, 240, 242, 243–51, 252, 268, 299
Mitchell, Samuel, of N.Y., 103
Moles, James, 29–30
Monroe, James, 101, 144, 151–53, 155, 160, 161, 163, 164, 165, 166, 168, 170, 200, 201, 202–3, 208, 294
Moody, Mr., 26
Moore, Glover, 190, 235
Moore, Samuel, of Pa., 302
Moore, Thomas, of S.C., 77, 90, 108
Morse, Samuel F. B., xi
Moseley, Jonathan, of Conn., 125

Moser, Philip, 63, 70, 281

Napoleonic Wars, 52–54, 65–66, 73–74, 86
National debt, 122, 125, 129, 133, 134
National honor, 84, 85, 93
Nelson, Hugh, of Va., 238
Neutrality, 151, 160–63
Neutral rights, 52–62, 65–69, 72, 194, 230
New Orleans, Battle of, 118, 119
Newton, Thomas, of Va., 78, 92, 214
Niles, Hezekiah, 205, 234–35, 299
Non-Importation Act (1811), 78, 92–94, 102–5
Non-Intercourse Act (1809), 74–75

Old Republicans, 79, 83, 86, 92, 230
Orders in Council, 65, 74–75, 84, 85, 86, 102–4
Ordinance of 1787, 182, 189
Osborne, Henry, 7, 8

Panic of 1819, 170, 179, 181, 182, 206–7, 208, 218, 224
Parker, James, of Mass., 198
Peace, Joseph, 27–28
Peek, Hermanus, of N.Y., 199
Perry, Oliver Hazard, 111, 112–13
Pfufendorf, Samuel, 57, 61
Philomathean Society, 20–21, 33, 61
Phocion essays, 54–55, 62, 65
Physick, Dr., 75–76
Pickens, Ezekiel, 48–49
Pickens, Israel, of N.C., 85
Pickering, Timothy, of Mass., 79, 112, 140–41, 234
Pinckney, Charles, 19, 44, 45, 47, 74, 77, 194–97, 294
Pinckney, Charles Cotesworth, 11–12, 23–24, 36, 67, 69–70, 194
Pinckney, Thomas, 11–12, 18, 20, 23–25, 99, 106, 109, 194, 233, 263, 275
Pinckney, Thomas, Jr., 22, 275
Pinckney, William C., 36, 38, 39, 41
Pinckney family, 24, 32, 255
Pincus, Jonathan J., 295
Pindall, James, of Va., 174
Pitkin, Timothy, of Conn., 139, 141
Platonic virtues, xiv–xv
Pleasants, James, of Va., 93
Plumer, William, Jr., of N.H., 190, 246–48, 249, 254
Pocock, John G. A., xv
Poindexter, George, of Miss., 167
Poinsett, Joel R., 22, 261
Polly case, 54
Pope, Clayne, xiii
Porter, Peter B., of N.Y., 78, 80, 92, 97, 102, 108
Preyer, Norris, 126, 142–43
Pringle, John Julius, 29, 276, 281
Prioleau, John, 36
Protectionism, xii–xiv, 51, 97, 118, 123, 124–43, 182–83, 204–31, 234, 235–36, 237, 240, 248–49, 293, 295, 296, 299. *See also* Baldwin, Henry, of Pa.; Tariff of 1816
Purcell, Henry, 9

Quincy, Josiah, of Mass., 76, 106

Raguet, Condy, 207
Ramsay, David, 21
Randolph, John, of Va., 79, 81, 82, 83, 86, 90–91, 97, 106, 108, 131–32, 133–34, 135, 137, 141, 142, 151, 198, 230, 250, 262
Representation controversy, in S.C., 21, 32, 33–35, 38–39, 41, 44, 45, 46–51. *See also* Compromise of 1808
Republicanism, xiv–xix, 3, 12, 22, 34–35, 39, 48, 50–51, 71, 87, 100,

117, 122, 129, 131, 132, 133, 135, 136, 137, 143, 147, 148, 153, 179, 183, 189, 191, 194, 200, 209–10, 211, 216, 222, 227–31, 242, 250, 253, 258, 264, 268–69, 274, 293, 295, 298, 301

Republican party, 10–12, 17–20, 22–23, 30–34, 36, 51, 62–72, 79, 90, 96–97, 100–101, 119–20, 120–21, 124, 129, 131, 132, 144, 147–48, 152–53, 166–67, 170, 184, 194–95, 227–34, 238–42, 249–51, 252–61. *See also* Jefferson, Thomas

Rhea, John, of Tenn., 85, 92, 93, 94, 165

Richardson, James, 35

Risjord, Norman, 178

Robertson, Thomas B., of La., 123, 125, 161

Roper, Thomas, 70

Ross, John, of Pa., 139–40

Rouse, William, 63, 64, 281

Ruffin, Edmund, 237, 262

Ruggles, Nathaniel, of Mass., 141

Rule of 1756, 54, 56, 57–59, 60

Russell, Jonathan, 104

Rutledge, Edward, 11–12, 20, 23, 31

Rutledge, John, 11–12, 20, 23, 31

Rutledge, John (nephew of J. R.), 63

St. Cecilia Society, 24

St. John, Henry (Viscount Bolingbroke), xviii

Salem, Mass., petition of, 208–9, 211–13, 227, 235

Santo Domingo, 35

Sargent, Nathan, 267

Schaper, William A., 49–50

Schwartz, Barry, 266

Scott, John, of Missouri Territory, 185, 188, 192–93, 198, 200

Scott, Sir William, 54

Sectionalism and slavery. *See* Baldwin, Henry, of Pa.; Compromise of 1808; Missouri Controversy; Representation controversy, in S.C.

Seminole War, 164–65

Sergeant, John, of Pa., 218, 238, 243, 246–47, 250

Seybert, Adam, of Pa., 88

Sheffey, Daniel, of Va., 83–84, 85, 86

Shelby, Isaac, 153

Silsbee, Nathaniel, of Mass., 221

Simkins, Eldred, of S.C., 254

Simons, Keating L., 28, 29, 31–32, 37, 42, 47, 63, 64, 68, 74

Sinking fund, 129, 148–50, 177

"Slave power conspiracy," 235

Slavery, xii–xiii, xiv, 2, 3, 12, 20, 25, 34, 35, 42–43, 46, 50, 51, 99, 110, 120, 123, 146–47, 180–200, 201, 210–11, 227, 234, 235, 238, 239, 240–41, 253, 254, 267, 268, 269, 278, 293, 298; and foreign slave trade, 18, 19, 35, 36, 38, 40, 41, 42–43, 46, 68, 72, 189; and insurrection, 35, 36, 38, 40, 262–64. *See also* Missouri Controversy

Smilie, John, of Pa., 102

Smith, Adam, 179

Smith, O'Brien, 281

Smith, Peter, 10

Smith, Samuel, of Md., 139–40, 213, 219, 238, 239, 243, 250

Smith, Thomas Rhett, 31–32

Smith, William Loughton, 28, 54–56, 59–60, 62, 63, 64–65, 69, 74

Smith, William S., of Charleston, 29, 31–32, 42

Smith, William S., of Yorkville, 121, 303

Smyth, Alexander, of Va., 101, 167

Somarsall, Thomas, 31

Southard, Henry, of N.J., 140

Spencer, John C., of N.Y., 171, 172

Stanford, Richard, of N.C., 81–82

Stanwood, Edward, xiii, 126, 222
Starke, Alexander, 47
Stearns, Isahel, of Mass., 141
Stephen, James, 55, 56, 279
Sterling, Micah, of N.Y., 259
Storrs, Henry, of N.Y., 188, 197, 221, 246–47, 300
Strong, James, of N.Y., 183, 185
Strong, Solomon, of Mass., 138
Strother, William, 47
Sumter, Thomas, 36

Tallmadge, James, Jr., of N.Y., 167, 180, 182, 184, 241
Tariff, xii–xiv, 51, 97, 118, 123, 182–83, 204–31, 234, 235–36, 237, 240, 248–49, 293, 299. *See also* Baldwin, Henry, of Pa.
Tariff of 1816, 123, 124–43, 204, 205, 206, 208, 211, 212, 214–15, 217, 218–19, 229, 230, 231, 293, 295, 296, 299
Taxes, internal, 127, 130, 133–37, 147, 148–50, 155, 208, 213
Taylor, John, of Abbeville, 41
Taylor, John, of Columbia, 71–72, 100, 281
Taylor, John W., of N.Y., 125, 180, 183, 184–85, 186, 188, 197, 198, 199, 200, 238, 239, 240, 241, 242, 243, 250, 252, 265, 281, 293, 300
Thomas (Lowndes's slave), 73, 75, 118
Thomas, Ebenezer, 40
Thomas, Jesse B., of Ill., 187–88
Tomlinson, Gideon, of Conn., 302
Tompkins, Caleb, of N.Y., 199, 300
Tompkins, Daniel, 184
Tragedy of Cato, The, 9
Trenchard, John, xviii
Trimble, David, of Ky., 173, 178, 203, 204, 221
Troup, George, of Ga., 111

Index : 325

Tucker, George, of Va., 155, 159, 192–93
Tucker, Starling, 42, 43
Turnbull, Robert, 28
Turpin, William, 70–71
Tyler, John, of Va., 171, 178, 218, 220, 221, 291, 297

Van Buren, Martin, of N.Y., 241, 242, 252
VanderHorst, Richard, 47
Van Rensselaer, Stephen, 101
Vattel, Emmerick de, 61
Veree, Joseph, 281
Vesey, Denmark, 262–63
Vesey, Mary C., 26

Walker, Felix, of N.C., 198
Walker, John, of Ala., 187, 240
Walpole, Robert, xvii, 131
Ward, Artemus, of Mass., 139, 141
Ward, James M., 28, 63, 64, 68
War Hawks, 72, 75, 78, 79, 80, 84, 87, 88–89, 92, 93, 96–97, 108, 122, 134–35
War in Disguise: or, The Frauds of the Neutral Flags, 55, 58
War Mess, 76, 77, 80, 82, 97
War of 1812, xii, 97, 98, 99, 101–18, 119, 122, 126, 134, 147, 194, 295
Washington, George, 23, 59, 68, 86, 266
Watterson, George, 153–54, 301
Webster, Daniel, of N.H., xi, 108, 111–12, 117, 139, 140, 141, 144
Weir, Robert M., xviii
Whitman, Ezekiel, of Mass., 197, 206, 221
Whitney, Eli, 37
Williams, David R., of S.C., 71, 77, 78, 82, 90, 91, 96, 97, 102, 108, 119, 120
Williams, Lewis, of N.C., 149–50

Williamson, John, 63
Wiltse, Charles, 304
Winn, Richard, of S.C., 77, 90
Witherspoon, Robert, 71
Wright, Robert, of Md., 92

XYZ Affair, 23

Yellow fever, 152